ECONOMICS AND CONTEMPORARY LAND USE POLICY

Development and Conservation at the Rural-Urban Fringe

EDITED BY

ROBERT J. JOHNSTON AND STEPHEN K. SWALLOW

RESOURCES FOR THE FUTURE

WASHINGTON, DC, USA

An RFF Press book
Published by Resources for the Future
1616 P Street NW
Washington, DC 20036–1400
USA
www.rffpress.org

Library of Congress Cataloging-in-Publication Data

Economics and contemporary land use policy: development and conservation at the rural-urban fringe / edited by Robert J. Johnston and Stephen K. Swallow.
     p. cm.
  Includes bibliographical references.
  ISBN 1-933115-21-1 (hardcover : alk. paper) — ISBN 1-933115-22-X (pbk. : alk. paper)
    1. Land use—Economic aspects.   2. Economics.   I. Johnston, Robert J., PhD. II. Swallow, Stephen K.
HD156.E225   2006
333.73′13—dc22

                                               2005026956

The paper in this book meets the guidelines for permanence and durability of the Committee on Production Guidelines for Book Longevity of the Council on Library Resources. This book was typeset by TechBooks. It was copyedited by Joyce Bond. The cover was designed by Rosenbohm Graphic Design.

ISBN 1-933115-21-1 (cloth)   ISBN 1-933115-22-X (paper)

About Resources for the Future *and* RFF Press

Resources for the Future (RFF) improves environmental and natural resource policymaking worldwide through independent social science research of the highest caliber. Founded in 1952, RFF pioneered the application of economics as a tool for developing more effective policy about the use and conservation of natural resources. Its scholars continue to employ social science methods to analyze critical issues concerning pollution control, energy policy, land and water use, hazardous waste, climate change, biodiversity, and the environmental challenges of developing countries.

RFF Press supports the mission of RFF by publishing book-length works that present a broad range of approaches to the study of natural resources and the environment. Its authors and editors include RFF staff, researchers from the larger academic and policy communities, and journalists. Audiences for publications by RFF Press include all of the participants in the policymaking process—scholars, the media, advocacy groups, NGOs, professionals in business and government, and the public.

Contents

PART I
Economic Approaches to Land Use Policy

PART V
Conclusion

Foreword

The reemergence of the economics of land use as a compelling field of inquiry reflects the many dimensions in which land contributes to social well-being and the many policy arenas in which land plays an important role. Once viewed only as an input in the production of food and fiber, land now stands as a key element in the definition of households' quality of life. As a factor of production, land is clearly important, but for households, land possesses the critical attribute of location. People make important decisions on where they live and work based at least in part on the amenities of location, broadly defined. And in purchasing location, they make the largest expenditures of their lifetimes. What is immediately around them matters, as does accessibility to income-earning opportunities and amenities they enjoy. Because distances map into time costs (admittedly at varying "prices" depending on where one is in the landscape), location links to the most fundamental of scarce resources, time.

Some economists still challenge the notion that land use poses relevant economic problems that need addressing. Why does the market not work perfectly well in achieving a good allocation of land across uses? A simple answer is externalities. Externalities exist when economic agents affect one another, but their interdependencies are not captured in the market, preventing these agents from taking into account the full positive or negative effects of their actions. Examples of industry imposing negative externalities on neighboring households are too obvious to bother mentioning. But spatial interactions are complex and more pervasive. Neighboring woodlands, especially ones that are shrinking as a result of increasing development in a region, can impose costs on farming by increasing damage from wildlife; residential uses can impose costs on neighboring residences through increased congestion and aesthetic disamenities; farmland may impose costs on households because of heavy chemical or manure use but provide positive externalities through open space and pleasing vistas.[1]

All of these externalities are inherently spatial. What matters is not just the aggregate amount of activity of different sorts, but also the spatial location of emitters of externalities relative to receivers and the ecological, physical, and social pathways that connect them. This spatial dimension complicates economic analysis. Economics has always been about micro-level behavior adding up to markets, which further aggregate up in an interdependent way to macro-level outcomes. But now different individual land use decisions aggregate up not only to different market effects for such goods as agricultural and forest products and housing, but also to different spatial outcomes—different spatial patterns of land use associated with different patterns of spatial externalities. Exactly how spatially heterogeneous micro-level decisions—which are interrelated through both markets and spatial interactions—play out is an interacting agent problem whose systems' implications are difficult to deduce.

The spatial pattern of land use evolves over time as a result of these interrelated micro-level decisions. Because changes in land use states (even between agriculture and forest, but most notably between undeveloped and developed uses) require investment, there is a time lag between signals and outcomes. In addition, some states, notably development and sometimes preservation, may be virtually irreversible. These attributes of the problem combined with spatial externalities of all sorts create a landscape that evolves through a complex, path-dependent process. Spatially related agents interact, and changes can be irreversible, so outcomes in one period circumscribe the set of potential future evolutionary paths. The path-dependent nature of the evolutionary process that alters the landscape means that tomorrow's possibilities depend on yesterday's and today's decisions and the public policies that affect those decisions. In this context, public policy takes on immense importance, and mistakes are difficult to correct.

Because of the pervasive importance of land in so many arenas, policies never aimed at affecting land use pattern—such as gas taxes that affect the cost of travel—can conceivably do so. Certainly many policies outside the scope of land use management affect the relative returns and therefore likely emergence or survival of different land uses. Diverse examples include transportation policies that alter the road network, environmental policies that raise development costs such as those governing stormwater control, and commodity programs that support agricultural prices. Other policies are adopted explicitly to redirect the spatial location of land use change, such as zoning or purchase of development rights. Whatever the motivation, policies that alter the costs or returns from alternative land uses can alter the path of land use change, often in quite unintended and irreversible ways.

Another consequence of path dependence is that different areas, with different initial conditions, evolve differently, producing quite different patterns of land use in different parts of the country. Because land use policy in the United States is made largely at the local level, public policy may actually have exacerbated these regional differences. This is especially true if the composition of constituents affects local land use policy. For example, growth control is unlikely to be a priority until residential lot owners outvote the owners of undeveloped land.

Heterogeneity of initial conditions and the resulting differences in evolutionary paths pose problems for researchers. It is often difficult to formulate a sensible research question at the national level, but research at the local level can be hard to generalize beyond the study area. Comparison of research results across regions is further compromised by the lack of consistent spatial data. The advent of geographical information systems (GIS) has certainly been a catalyst for land use research, but spatially explicit economic data are still unevenly provided and costly to obtain. They tend to be available in areas that view themselves as already in crisis, but not in those that are earlier in their evolutionary growth process. Also, better data seem to be available for residential than for agricultural activity, largely because of the confidentiality and privacy restrictions that allow the dissemination of only very aggregate agricultural data. Data that are comparable over time are even more difficult to acquire. GIS data are increasingly available because of rapidly changing technology, but they are extremely costly if not impossible to retrieve from the past.

Research on land use and other fundamentally spatial problems is further complicated by the fact that elements in space tend to be highly correlated. It is easy in the spatial context to confuse correlation for causation. For one example, as a result of finding lower-valued residential land in less developed areas, one might easily reject the hypothesis that households value undeveloped land as a neighbor. But areas with large amounts of undeveloped lands are, for possibly unobservable reasons, less valuable in a developed use. As a consequence, residences with more undeveloped neighbors are in less valued locations, irrespective of the nature of neighboring land uses. Hypothesis tests of the effects of spatially differentiated policies may be hampered by a similar phenomenon. If policies are imposed differentially depending on existing land use patterns, then the effects of differing policies cannot be separated from those related to the stage of the development process. In some cases, policies aimed at achieving some goal are applied differentially based on location attributes that wind up contributing to the policies' success or failure. Although selection problems and correlated omitted variable problems plague much economics research, they seem either more prevalent or more obvious in the spatial context of land use change.

The convergence of land use and policy therefore represents a critical area of ongoing research, yet one that is fraught with special challenges. The authors of this book seem especially cognizant of both the importance and the challenges of land use research. They deal with the externalities generated by certain land uses, the path, or evolutionary process, of land use change, and the effects of regulations or externalities on that process.

Chapters in the first section of this book adopt a broad perspective, among other things reviewing the past and potential contributions of economics to land use policy. Following this introduction, chapters in the second section elucidate the multiple ways in which open space in general, and farmland in particular, affects society, highlighting spatial heterogeneity in the importance of open space both within and across regions of the country. They also consider the process of land use change—especially from farmland to developed uses—including interactions among neighboring land uses and the array of policies that can exacerbate, delay, or permanently prevent land use conversion. The land use policies of greatest interest here include direct growth controls, such as zoning regulations; direct conservation activities, such as the purchase of undeveloped lands or development rights to these lands; and indirect policies, such as those that influence property taxation or impact fees on new development.

A third set of chapters considers relationships between such factors as land use pattern, land value and taxation, and incentives to either preserve undeveloped land or convert land to developed use. As in the analyses of land use change discussed above, researchers in this area are increasingly recognizing challenges related to spatial correlation, path dependence, and other complexities associated with human uses of land. Following this is a set of chapters with an especially important message: in the land use arena, economic and ecological systems are inextricably merged. Natural features of the landscape affect land use decisions, which are central in determining the nature of human impacts on ecosystems. Few areas of research present a more compelling argument for cooperation between ecologists and economists. The final chapter draws together prior sections of the book, emphasizing the contributions of current research towards our understanding of critical issues in land use policy, and important questions for which answers remain elusive.

One goal of this book is to offer relevant, understandable contributions to the policy debate. As the authors show, such a goal does not mean that analysis needs to be less than high quality. Rigorous work about an important problem will always be accessible to policymakers deeply involved in that problem as long as the analysis is relevant and well explained. The classic papers in the applied economics literature, the ones that have survived the test of time, have insightful and compelling messages even today.

The authors also recognize that contributing to the policy debate does not require allowing "political realities" to affect the questions one asks. Resource and environmental economics has a long history of framing and answering questions that, over the long haul, have changed the way society manages resources and the laws that protect them. Just as the landscape is evolving over time, so are the ways in which humans interact with and govern this multidimensional resource.

NANCY E. BOCKSTAEL
University of Maryland

---

[1] In many respects, farming may be viewed as a good neighbor for what it is not. If neighboring land is not in one use, it will most assuredly be in another, and farming may be preferred to what would happen to the land otherwise.

Acknowledgments

Chapters in this book were developed from material originally conceived as part of the 2002 Northeastern Agricultural and Resource Economics Association (NAREA) Land Use Policy Workshop. This book would not have been possible without generous workshop support from the Northeastern Regional Center for Rural Development (through the U.S. Department of Agriculture) and the assistance of its director, Stephan J. Goetz. We thank Peter J. Parks, editor of the *Agricultural and Resource Economics Review,* for assistance with earlier academic presentations of workshop material reflected in book chapters. We also thank the Board of Directors of NAREA (copyright holder for *Agricultural and Resource Economics Review*) for allowing this research to be published. Finally, we recognize the efforts of the planning committee of the NAREA workshop that provided the motivation for this book. The committee included the editors of this book (Robert J. Johnston and Stephen K. Swallow), along with Joshua M. Duke, Lori Lynch, Elizabeth Marshall, and James Shortle. All opinions are those of the authors and do not reflect endorsements by any of the agencies funding or otherwise supporting this work.

We thank our families—Christy, June, Erin, and Jessica—for their love, support, and patience.

Contributors

SANDRA S. BATIE is the Elton R. Smith Professor of Food and Agricultural Policy in the Department of Agricultural Economics at Michigan State University. She has been president of the Southern Agricultural Economics Association and the American Agricultural Economics Association (AAEA), and is a Fellow of AAEA. She is a member of the Blue Ribbon Panel advising the USDA Conservation Effects Assessment Project. She has recently edited a two-volume set, *Agri-environmental Policy*, part of the International Library of Economics and Policy.

DANA MARIE BAUER is a Ph.D. candidate in Environmental and Natural Resource Economics at the University of Rhode Island. Her current research, for which she received an EPA STAR fellowship, examines the economic and ecological tradeoffs between development and preservation in rural fringe communities. She has co-authored publications in *Conservation Biology, Land Economics*, and the *American Journal of Agricultural Economics*.

KATHLEEN P. BELL is an assistant professor in the Department of Resource Economics and Policy at the University of Maine. Her recent research has focused on the spatial aspects of economic behavior and rural land use change. She is a co-editor of a forthcoming book, *Economics of Rural Land-Use Change*. She has published in journals including the *Review of Economics and Statistics, Land Economics, Journal of Regional Science*, and *Estuaries*.

NANCY E. BOCKSTAEL is a professor at the University of Maryland. Her research areas include applied welfare economics with a focus on non-marketed goods and the spatial modeling of land use change. She has been president of the Association of Environmental and Resource Economists, and is a fellow of the American Agricultural Economics Association. Dr. Bockstael is co-author of *Environmental Valuation with Revealed Preference: A Theoretical Guide to the Empirical Literature.*

DANIEL W. BROMLEY is Anderson-Bascom Professor of applied economics at the University of Wisconsin-Madison. He publishes on the institutional foundations of the economy; legal and philosophical dimensions of property rights; economics of natural resources and the environment; and economic development. He is editor of the journal *Land Economics* and a fellow of the American Agricultural Economics Association.

SHAWN J. BUCHOLTZ is a GIS specialist with the Economic Research Service of the U.S Department of Agriculture. His most recent research has focused on the impacts of agricultural conservation programs on housing values and rural communities. His latest journal publication is "Slippage in the Conservation Reserve Program or Spurious Correlation? A Comment" in the *American Journal of Agricultural Economics.*

EMERY N. CASTLE is professor emeritus at Oregon State University and former president and senior fellow emeritus at Resources for the Future. He is a fellow of the American Academy of Arts and Sciences, the American Academy for the Advancement of Science, and the American Agricultural Economics Association. His most recent books include *The Changing American Countryside: Rural People and Places* (editor), and *U.S. Interests and Global Natural Resources-Energy, Minerals and Food* (co-editor).

RICHARD W. ENGLAND is a professor of economics and natural resources at the University of New Hampshire and a research fellow at the Lincoln Institute of Land Policy. He is editor of and contributor to *Evolutionary Concepts in Contemporary Economics.* His research focuses on the use of property tax reform and state gasoline taxation to moderate land use change in the United States.

PAUL J. FERRARO is an assistant professor in the Andrew Young School of Policy Studies at Georgia State University. His research focuses on the design of cost-effective environmental policies and institutions, and the use of behavioral economics to explore human decisionmaking. He is a collaborating author on the *2005 Millennium Ecosystem Assessment*, and his research appears in journals such as the *American Journal of Agricultural Economics, Conservation Biology, Land Economics,* and *Science.*

JACQUELINE GEOGHEGAN is an associate professor in the Department of Economics and an adjunct associate professor in the Graduate School of Geography at Clark University. Her research focuses on developing spatially explicit models of land use change. Her book publications include a volume edited with B.L. Turner II and D. F. Foster: *Integrated Land-Change Science and Tropical Deforestation in the Southern Yucatán: Final Frontiers,* and a book co-edited with Wayne B. Gray: *Spatial Environmental Policy.*

DANIEL M. HELLERSTEIN is an economist at the USDA Economic Research Service. His recent research has focused on farmland preservation issues, the impacts of federal land retirement programs on recreation and rural economic well-being, and the development of applied econometric tools for use in valuation research. His book publications include chapters in *Valuing Recreation and the Environment: Revealed Preference Methods in Theory and Practice,* and *Contingent Valuation Handbook.*

DIANE HITE is an associate professor in the Department of Agricultural Economics and Rural Sociology at Auburn University. Her recent research is in the areas of nonmarket valuation, economic impacts of amenities and disamenities, local public goods, land use, and agricultural competitiveness. Her book publications include a chapter, "Capitalization of Environmental Amenities at the Urban Rural Fringe," in *Environmental Valuation: Intraregional and Interregional Perspectives.*

ELENA G. IRWIN is an associate professor in the Department of Agricultural, Environmental, and Development Economics at Ohio State University. Her research interests include spatial models of urbanization and dynamic models of human-environment interactions. Her recent work has been published in *Journal of Economic Geography, Regional Science and Urban Economics, American Journal of Agricultural Economics, Land Economics,* and *Applied Economic Letters.*

ROBERT J. JOHNSTON is associate director of the Connecticut Sea Grant College Program and an assistant professor of agricultural and resource economics at the University of Connecticut. His areas of expertise include non-market valuation, the economics of land use, and economic evaluation of coastal and marine policy. His research has appeared in journals including the *American Journal of Agricultural Economics,* the *Journal of Environmental Economics and Management, Land Economics,* and *Water Resources Research.*

JEFFREY D. KLINE is a research forester with the USDA Forest Service's Pacific Northwest Research Station in Corvallis, Oregon. He has worked on forestry and land use issues for 20 years with nonprofit, state, and federal agencies and organizations. His current research examines the effects of population growth and land use change on forests and their management, as well as related changes in how the public uses and values forests.

JOHN LOOMIS is a professor in the Department of Agricultural and Resource Economics at Colorado State University, and Distinguished Scholar of the Western Agricultural Economics Association. He has served as Vice-President of the Association of Environmental and Resource Economics. Dr. Loomis has published more than 100 articles on valuation of non-market resources and benefit-cost analysis. His books include *Integrated Public Lands Management, Environmental Policy Analysis for Decision Making*, and *Recreation Economic Decisions*.

LORI LYNCH is an associate professor in agricultural and resource economics at the University of Maryland. Her recent research has focused on land use issues, in particular farmland preservation and conservation practices. Her published articles address landowners' participation in conservation programs, easement restrictions and farmland prices, the relative efficiency of farmland preservation programs, landowners' participation in farmland preservation programs, and value of characteristics in easement payments.

ROBERT D. MOHR is an assistant professor of economics at the University of New Hampshire. His research focuses on environmental policy, with an emphasis on innovation and technology adoption. His scholarly publications include contributions to the *Journal of Environmental Economics and Management, Contributions to Economic Analysis and Policy*, and the *Agricultural and Resource Economics Review*.

CYNTHIA J. NICKERSON is an economist in the USDA's Economic Research Service. Her recent research has focused on the design and effectiveness of conservation policies, farmland preservation, and land use change in urbanizing areas. She serves as a member of the Board of Directors of the Northeast Agricultural and Resource Economics Association. Recent publications include articles in *Agricultural and Resource Economics Review, American Journal of Agricultural Economics*, and *Choices*.

LISA D. PHILO is a research associate and communications specialist with the University of Rhode Island's Cooperative Extension Water Quality Program. Her recent research has spanned the economics of water resources, economic evaluation of land use, and the communication of environmental issues, including climate change, land use, storm water pollution, and source water protection.

VICKI RAMEKER holds a master's of science degree in agricultural and resource economics from Colorado State University. Her thesis research was based on an alternative valuation strategy for public open space in Colorado. The results from her thesis were published in the *Journal of Environmental Planning and Management.* Vicki has taught resource economics at the secondary school level and is currently fulfilling research requirements for her Ph.D.

KERRI L. ROLLINS is the fund development and outreach specialist for the Larimer County Open Lands Program. Over the past six years, she has worked extensively with local government open space programs in Colorado and is chair of the Steering Committee for a statewide organization of publicly funded open space programs known as the Colorado Open Space Alliance (COSA). Rollins has also coauthored an article for the *Journal of Agricultural and Resource Economics.*

ANDREW F. SEIDL is an associate professor and public policy extension specialist in the Department of Agricultural and Resource Economics at Colorado State University. He is also a professor at the Central American Institute for Business Administration (INCAE), Latin American Center for Competitiveness and Sustainable Development (CLACDS), in Costa Rica. His research involves the community implications of natural resource-driven economic development, particularly in areas highly endowed in scenic and recreational natural amenities.

BRENT SOHNGEN is an associate professor in the Department of Agricultural, Environmental, and Development Economics at Ohio State University. His recent research has focused on modeling land use change within the U.S. globally, and developing instruments for nonpoint source pollution control. His book publications include *Climate Change: The International Library of Environmental Economics and Policy.*

STEPHEN K. SWALLOW is a professor of environmental and natural resource economics at the University of Rhode Island. He has served as president of the Northeastern Agricultural and Resource Economics Association. He is currently serving as an editor of the *American Journal of Agricultural Economics* and was formerly an associate editor for the *Journal of Environmental Economics and Management.* He has published in those journals as well as *Land Economics, Southern Economic Journal,* and elsewhere.

JOSHUA TEMPLETON is a National Research Council postdoctoral research associate at the U.S. Environmental Protection Agency. His recent research involves the design of market incentives for controlling of stormwater runoff.

ECONOMICS AND CONTEMPORARY LAND USE POLICY

Development and Conservation at the Rural-Urban Fringe

Introduction

Economics and Contemporary Land Use Policy

ROBERT J. JOHNSTON AND STEPHEN K. SWALLOW

This book highlights areas in which economists can make—and are making—positive contributions to policy that guides land conservation and development. It is intended for policymakers, students, academics, and others interested in the practical application of economics to land use policy. It emphasizes contemporary research solutions to land use questions and issues, but research that is also directly applicable to the often pressing questions and issues facing land use policymakers.

Recent decades have experienced a growing societal interest in issues related to land use, development, and conservation. Discussions of contemporary land use are often accompanied by a growing sense of urgency, associated with the perceived irreversibility of development and increasing evidence of suburban sprawl (Abdalla 2001). Matching this growing interest in land use is an explosion of research into the forces driving land use conversion, the impacts of land use change, and the design of land use policy. Researchers are increasingly questioning traditional economic and social science approaches to land and exploring ones better suited to contemporary land use patterns (Irwin and Bockstael 2002).

Alongside methodological advances, researchers have placed increasing emphasis on policy alternatives rarely applied until recent decades—ones beyond the zoning and fee-simple purchase mechanisms common in many areas. These include impact fees, the purchase or transfer of development rights, and smart-growth approaches to land use policy (American Farmland Trust 1997; Arendt et al. 1994; Bills et al. 2004; Calthorpe 1993; Nelson and Duncan 1995; Nickerson 2001). Simultaneously, a burgeoning literature has developed addressing

1

nonmarket values and public motivations associated with farm, forest, and open-space conservation (e.g., Beasley et al. 1986; Bergstrom et al. 1985; Duke and Hyde 2002; Gardner 1977; Garrod and Willis 1992; Johnston et al. 2001, 2003; Kline and Wichelns 1994, 1998; Ready et al. 1997; Rosenberger and Walsh 1997).

This research is timely. As external forces increase the demand for land conversion, rural and urban-fringe communities are increasingly willing to support policies that encourage conservation of productive forest and agricultural lands. Frequently cited evidence of public interest in land conservation includes voter support of open space ballot measures; increased federal, state, and local funding for farm and forest conservation; greater public support of alternative land use policy mechanisms; and the emergence of more than 1,000 state- and local-level land trusts nationwide (Albers and Ando 2003; American Planning Association 2002; Land Trust Alliance 2003; Roe et al. 2004). Simultaneous to this upswell in public support, federal and state policy analysts are evaluating alternative roles in land use and conservation policy (Feather et al. 1999), while local, state, and federal government agencies are calling on the academic community to provide research of greater relevance to local issues (e.g., Owens 2004).

Many have argued that the recent upsurge in public support for land conservation and smart growth is a reaction to contemporary patterns of land conversion, characterized by an increase in dispersed, low-density rural and urban-fringe development (e.g., Irwin and Bockstael 2002; Nickerson 2001). Although this expansion of low-density development does not threaten the nation's overall ability to produce food and fiber—and, in fact, affects only a small percentage of the total land area in the continental United States (Heimlich and Anderson 2001)—economists generally recognize it as a symptom of the market's failure to internalize the full range of nonmarket benefits associated with farm, forest, and open space. Among other impacts, associated landscape changes may impose often unforeseen service costs on communities, reduce local production of high-value or specialty crops, disrupt social or community structure, and cause a loss of ecosystem services and other rural amenity benefits that would otherwise be realized by the public (Heimlich and Anderson 2001).

Such patterns have left many urban-fringe communities struggling to adapt, limited by zoning-based land use controls never meant to control contemporary suburban sprawl (Nickerson 2001). Local governments often are slow to develop adequate capacity to influence development and hence unable to channel land use to more desirable uses (Heimlich and Anderson 2001). Many would argue that, exacerbating the challenge facing local communities, the most common local suburban growth controls, such as zoning, are largely responsible for the excessive conversion of farm- and forestlands on the urban fringe (Pasha 1996; University of Connecticut Cooperative Extension 1999). Others, in contrast, argue that recent development patterns are due to other factors, including government spending policies, land speculation, home-buyer preferences, or local property tax policies (Fischel 1985; Gordon and Richardson 1998).

The disagreement over causes of current development patterns is emblematic of a broader uncertainty facing land use policymakers. That is, despite the widespread public and academic interest in land conservation and management, specific consequences of land use policies and drivers of land conversions are often unclear (Abdalla 2001; Lynch and Duke 2003). This lack of information may hinder otherwise beneficial policy changes and in some cases contribute to misdirected or ineffectual conservation programs. One might expect that the surge of research into land use, development, and conservation would allay some of this uncertainty. At least two factors constrain the ability of researchers to influence policy, however. Issues of contemporary land use are inherently complex, and research findings accordingly are subject to considerable uncertainty or limited applicability. Perhaps more vexing, findings from academic researchers often fail to reach—or are not used by—those directly responsible for land use policy (Johnston 2002; Prendergast et al. 1999).

This situation represents a critical challenge to academic and other researchers seeking to inform land use policy: contemporary land use issues require increasingly complex modeling approaches, yet published descriptions of such models and their implications are often poorly suited for public consumption. Without appropriate communication by social scientists, even the most appropriate and relevant models may fail to effect positive change. This book represents a response to this challenge, inspired by the 2002 Northeastern Agricultural and Resource Economics Association (NAREA) Land Use Policy Workshop.[1]

Outline and Purpose of This Book

Together, the chapters in this book illustrate an interaction of conceptual, theoretical, and empirical approaches to land use policy—advances in policy-oriented economics associated with the conservation and development of rural and urban-fringe land. Chapters are also meant to be of practical relevance to issues surrounding land use policy at the local, state, and federal levels. With this goal in mind, each chapter draws on at least one of four fundamental questions that have arisen as a focus of contemporary land use policy and economics: What is the appropriate role of social science in guiding land conservation and development policy? Why, where, and when does land conversion occur? What are the implications of land conversion and conservation for property values and taxes, and vice versa? And what are the practical relationships among rural amenities, rural character, and the policies designed to protect them?

Economic Approaches to Land Use Policy

Economists differ from other professionals, such as planners, sociologists, and ecologists, in their fundamental approaches to land. For example, more so than the others, economists consider land use policy as influencing the allocation of scarce resources. This allocation problem is viewed through the lens of choices, trade-offs, and incentives—that which is gained and lost as a result of individual or group choices under various policy contexts, and their implications for human behavior. An economic perspective might, for example, consider the influence of endogenous or exogenous factors on landowners' decisions to convert farm and forest to alternative uses, as well as the implications of such choices for landscape pattern, social well-being, and the economic viability of particular activities (e.g., regional farming).

Economic perspectives also tend to incorporate fundamental concepts related to efficiency, social welfare, and the benefits and costs of resource policies. Such concepts are considered relevant in terms of both forecasting human behavior and evaluating policy. They relate to the economic concern with social well-being in a quantifiable or utilitarian sense, the idea that policies should be designed to increase human welfare (Freeman 2003, 6–9), and the assumption that individuals behave so as to maximize expected utility or net benefits. Although such notions are so common in economic inquiry as to remain frequently unstated, they nonetheless represent one of the more fundamental distinctions between economic and noneconomic approaches to land. As a result, unless appropriately placed in perspective, they can create a barrier to the incorporation of economic insight into policy dialogues (see Portney 2004).

Economics offers a unique set of tools and insights to those studying land. Yet what is the appropriate role of economics in guiding land conservation and development policy? Economists and other social scientists have played an increasing role in questioning whether land use policies have had the desired or expected impacts over time, identifying changes that may improve policy performance, and designing innovative means to obtain desired policy outcomes (e.g., Kramer and Shabman 1993; Nickerson 2001; Parks and Schorr 1997; Plantinga 1996; van Kooten 1993). Recent work has shown an encouraging willingness among researchers to incorporate methods from other disciplines to improve analysis of complex land use issues and extend research beyond assessments of benefits and costs to incorporate elements such as equity, financing, and political feasibility. Researchers are increasingly recognizing incentives and institutional structures that influence the actions of program managers and administrators, and assessing whether these actions are in the best interest of the public. Economists are also beginning to address complexities related to spatial and ecological linkages that have been widely disregarded in past work.

These encouraging signs notwithstanding, those seeking to inform land use policy face complex problems and research challenges, including the challenge of adapting research approaches to rapidly evolving issues associated with contemporary land use. The first two chapters of this book emphasize ongoing changes in land use and policy and means through which economists and other social scientists can increase the practical relevance of their work. Despite differing perspectives, these chapters share a common theme—that the work of social scientists should be driven by current and pressing problems in land use, and should reflect a more "common sense" view of the policy process and the role of research within that process. Together these chapters offer a broad perspective on the most appropriate, pragmatic, and useful roles of social science within land use policy.

In Chapter 1, Emery Castle explores the motivations of researchers who seek to understand land use issues in different geographic and social contexts. Based on a historical perspective of land use issues and associated modes of social science inquiry, Castle argues that one cannot assess the appropriateness of particular research perspectives outside of the historical and policy contexts in which they originate. He presents a role for the land economist consistent with Caldwell's (1982) pluralistic approach and contrasts this to prevailing patterns in economic inquiry dominated by the neoclassical paradigm. Castle's central message is that the driving force behind a research agenda should not be an unswerving dedication to a single methodological approach, but rather the practical circumstances and social dynamics surrounding contemporary land use issues.

Chapter 2 offers a more critical perspective of economics within the policy process, along with advice on how researchers may seek to improve the relevance of their work among policymakers. Daniel Bromley argues that a disconnect often exists between the theories of applied economists—typically based on the concepts of welfarism (Sen 1993) and benefit–cost analysis—and the way policy decisions are made. He suggests that economists recognize the increasing need to adjust to new priorities through a changing concept of the meaning of property rights. According to Bromley, economists' approaches to land use issues should reflect the common sense of the policy process, without overriding constraints imposed by theoretical or empirical constructs that may be at odds with ways in which noneconomists view land. Bromley's is a thought-provoking critique of common economic approaches to policy guidance.

Both Castle and Bromley address a fundamental challenge faced by economists seeking to inform land use policy. That is, although economic models (and their associated theories and analytical frameworks) provide a unique source of insight into land use issues, unyielding adherence to such models can hinder the acceptance of these insights by policymakers. These arguments are akin to those made more broadly by Portney, who counsels economists to "be clear about what economics can and cannot tell us, and clear as well about the premises upon which it is based" (2004, *159*).

Explaining Land Use Conversion: Spatial Perspectives

A second critical question facing land use policymakers concerns the timing and location of land conversions: Where and why does land development occur? Notwithstanding some who have argued that the "processes of land use change are well understood" (Heimlich and Anderson 2001, *vi*), there is increasing recognition of limitations in economists' understanding of the spatial dynamics and underlying causes of land use change (Bockstael 1996). The chapters in this section describe empirical and theoretical research that seeks to better understand the land conversion process, with particular emphases on spatial patterns and dynamics. These often complex analyses face the challenge of ensuring that the results are accessible to land use managers, many of whom may lack extensive training in technical aspects of economic and land use modeling (Johnston 2002; Prendergast et al. 1999).

This section looks at different approaches to the problem of forecasting land conversions, each best suited to a particular policy circumstance. In Chapter 3, Elena Irwin, Kathleen Bell, and Jacqueline Geoghegan describe a parcel-level, spatially disaggregated model, which estimates the temporal probability that a parcel will be developed for residential purposes, based on an underlying hazard model. Joshua Templeton, Diane Hite, and Brent Sohngen illustrate a similar survival-time approach in Chapter 4, as applied to the conversion of rural lands for residential, commercial, and industrial use. The format and writing style communicate a complex model in terms easily understandable by a nonacademic policy audience.

Despite similarities in the approaches of Chapters 3 and 4, the policy implications of the two models differ. For example, whereas Templeton, Hite, and Sohngen stress the importance of tax policies and zoning for parcel-level land conversion, Irwin, Bell, and Geoghegan emphasize implications for the coordinated use of policies that both target development and preserve open space lands. This distinction highlights one of the more significant challenges facing those who conduct research of this type: how to reconcile diverse findings from different geographic regions or policy contexts in order to generate a more universal understanding of the dynamics of land use change suitable for dissemination to policymakers.

In contrast to these essentially binary, parcel-level approaches to development (i.e., a parcel is either developed or not developed), Chapter 5 illustrates a density-oriented, gravity-model approach. Jeffrey Kline models change in observed building density in relatively undeveloped forestlands, based on data from the Pacific Northwest Research Station's Forest Inventory and Analysis Program. The alternative focus of Kline is a direct result of differences in study context. Whereas the models in Chapters 3 and 4 are designed to inform local planning, with an emphasis on where and when individual parcels will be converted to a developed use, Kline's work is designed to assist in ecological and timber management, a policy context in which building density is more critical than the designation of individual parcels as developed or undeveloped. Such distinctions, and the methodological shifts that accompany them, add verisimilitude to Castle's contention in Chapter 1 that the primary driving force behind a research agenda should not be an unswerving dedication to a single methodological approach, but the practical circumstances surrounding particular policy issues.

Chapter 6 provides yet a third perspective on the question of land conversion. Rather than seeking to forecast the spatial location and extent of development, Lori Lynch uses empirical data to address a critical question: How many acres are enough to sustain local agriculture? Her work springs from observed patterns suggesting that the difficulty of retaining remaining farmland may increase when the total amount of farmland in an area drops to a certain level. That the decline in rural lands may hasten once a certain critical threshold is reached is an important recognition, often absent in work regarding land conversion.

Chapters 3 through 6 illustrate the richness of approaches that may be employed to answer questions regarding the timing, causes, and location of land use conversions. Beyond this divergence in topic areas and methodological perspectives, however, the chapters in this section share an emphasis on spatial aspects of land use. Although economists long have been accused of affording too little attention to spatial attributes of land use and other data (Bockstael 1996), these chapters exemplify recent attempts to incorporate spatial influences within economic analysis of land use change. All include data from either geographical information systems (GIS) or other sources that capture explicit spatial attributes, and incorporate attributes that vary across space. The formal link to spatial databases and attributes can facilitate coordination with land use managers and other noneconomists, who are increasingly familiar with GIS and similar data but may have limited exposure to economic models. Although such individuals may have little interest in reading tables of model statistics, map-based illustrations of model results are often more easily digested and incorporated into policy dialogues.

The increasing relevance of spatial models notwithstanding, attempts to incorporate certain types of spatial factors into economic models have produced mixed results, a pattern also in evidence here. For example, of particular interest in the literature has been the potential impact of spatial autocorrelation in land use data (Anselin 1988; Anselin et al. 2004; Bockstael 1996). Simply put, land use patterns of neighboring parcels, or behaviors of households, may be statistically correlated in ways solely related to their proximity in space. Such effects have been clearly demonstrated by Irwin and Bockstael (2002, 2004) and Case (1991, 1992), among others. Other attempts to isolate the effects of such correlation have found little practical impact, however, even when spatial effects remain statistically significant (e.g., Geoghegan et al. 2003). Kline's results (Chapter 5) are similar: his models incorporating such patterns show little divergence from simpler models that do not include spatial correlation. This illustrates a continuing challenge of spatial data complexity to land use research: identifying relevant spatial patterns as well as spatial factors that may be of less influence and may be safely suppressed in both models and policy.

Together, the chapters in this section make a strong case that land use conversions can be predicted through models that address both the incentives facing those with existing or potential property rights to land and the explicit spatial aspects of land use. Results from this section, however, also clearly indicate the complexity of the many interrelated factors that influence land conversions and the difficulty of modeling them over space and time. Each chapter finds at least some results or patterns that do not conform to prior expectations. Moreover, given the diversity of approaches evident in these four chapters, it is clear that no single "best" way exists (as yet) to model land use change. In contrast, these chapters illustrate the types of insights that may be obtained through diverse perspectives.

Land Conservation: Implications for Value and Taxation

Land development and conservation occur in a dynamic environment in which the land use, conversions, and policies can have substantial and interrelated impacts on property values and tax revenues (e.g., Anderson and King 2004). Improved understanding of these relationships may help managers forecast political and fiscal implications of their decisions and influence the extent to which communities can afford land preservation initiatives. Researchers in this area are challenged with having to estimate results from limited data in the face of complex spatial and behavioral interactions that may determine land values. To be useful to land managers, however, implications of these often intricate models must be communicated in an accessible manner. Chapters 7 through 9 present various responses to this challenge.

It is well known that farm, forest, and open-space preservation can have a positive effect on nearby land values because of the desirability of attributes associated with rural landscapes. If preservation programs increase nearby land values, can this effect generate sufficient increases in property tax revenues to finance these programs? Jacqueline Geoghegan, Lori Lynch, and Shawn Bucholtz address this question in Chapter 7. Using a spatially explicit database, they explore ways in which economists predict increases in property values and associated changes in property tax revenues. This information is used to determine whether the preservation of farmland can pay for itself.

Chapter 8 deals with the tax question, not as a result of conservation activity, but as a potential cause. Richard England and Robert Mohr model landowners' decisions to develop parcels that are enrolled in current use value assessment programs. Their results highlight different factors that influence the effectiveness of these programs in delaying development. Unlike other analyses in this book, this is a purely theoretical approach to land use and taxation, meant to complement empirical works in providing guidance to land use policy. The analysis builds on a long history of research addressing the implications of taxation for land conversion (Anderson 1986, 1993; Bentick 1979, 1997). It is distinguished, however, by a focus on practical improvements in differential taxation policies, including potential implications of land conversion penalties.

In Chapter 9, John Loomis, Andy Seidl, Kerri Rollins, and Vicki Rameker consider valuation aspects of land conservation, exploring different ways in which economists seek to establish the public value of farm, forest, and open space. Specifically, they examine evidence for open-space values implicit in prices paid for open-space lands, compared with that derived from public surveys. A unique feature of this analysis is the ability to contrast implicit preferences of public agencies that preserve land—revealed through their purchase behavior—with the preferences of the public, revealed using stated preference methods. This chapter emphasizes implications for the underlying value of open space and associated land use policies, including whether ongoing conservation sustains the attributes of greatest value to the public.

Rural Amenities and Landscape Conservation

The neoclassical economics literature often devotes little space to the policy process or institutions through which land is managed, viewing them as "black boxes" through which certain desired land use outcomes are achieved. This lack of attention notwithstanding, a wide array of policy tools and institutions may be applied to land use issues. The choice of management tools often has significant implications for the conservation of rural amenities and may indeed influence the public benefits of conservation and development.

Beyond implications of policy for land management, the process itself, as applied in different regions, may offer important insights regarding rural amenities and their values to society. Chapters 10 through 13 emphasize the critical link between rural amenities and the policy process—a link often ignored by economic researchers (Johnston 2002). These chapters address several questions: How can research and policy adjust to the increasing importance of multifunctional attributes of farm and forest, which frequently are unrelated to food or fiber production? What can the policy process itself reveal concerning underlying rural amenity values? Are preferences for land use outcomes correlated with matching support for the underlying policy process? Finally, do simple methods exist to improve the cost-effectiveness of rural amenity conservation?

Sandra Batie, in Chapter 10, offers a broad perspective on the recent and increasing focus on the multifunctional attributes of agricultural land. These include environmental, recreational, and other services unrelated to the consumption of traditional agricultural products (Josling 2002), often referred to more broadly as rural amenities. Batie gives specific advice for a research and policy agenda that recognizes multifunctional attributes of agriculture, particularly in the northeastern United States. She emphasizes the unmet public demand for multifunctional attributes and suggests research that economists might conduct to encourage more appropriate policy toward, and conservation of, these valued rural amenities. She also places the current situation in the Northeast within a larger perspective, discussing parallels between concepts and assessments of multifunctional agriculture common in the region and those prevalent elsewhere.

Whereas Batie emphasizes potential changes in policy to address public preferences for rural amenities, Cynthia Nickerson and Daniel Hellerstein approach rural amenity preservation from a contrasting viewpoint in Chapter 11. Theirs is an empirical study of public choice, based on the ideas that public preferences influence government program design and that analysis of public programs themselves may provide insights regarding underlying preferences. Their model studies enabling legislation for farmland preservation programs in the Lower 48 states, in an effort to discern that which official program objectives reveal about underlying public preferences. It also examines how differences in alternative land protection programs and socioeconomic characteristics influence the design of farmland preservation policies. Results shed light on the particular attributes of farmland that are most valued in different regions of the United States and how public programs seek to protect these attributes. Like Chapter 9, this chapter emphasizes public preferences revealed through government activities—an approach often overlooked by economists studying land use issues.

In contrast to the public-choice approach of Nickerson and Hellerstein, Robert Johnston, Stephen Swallow, Dana Marie Bauer, and Lisa Philo address the policy process from the perspective of public preferences in Chapter 12. They start from the premise that the public may not always support land use policies that are consistent with its preferences for land use outcomes. Although economists typically assume that the public's policy support and land use preferences are consistent, they may not be, particularly if residents have incomplete information regarding particular policy tools. For example, some individuals may reveal strong preferences for land use outcomes while being unwilling to accept the policy processes required to generate those outcomes. This chapter examines relationships between the rural public's support for the policy process and preferences for land management outcomes. Findings confirm the suspicion that policy support and land use preference are not always related, calling into question a relationship often taken for granted by economists.

In Chapter 13, Paul Ferraro takes still another perspective to land use policy and rural amenities. A key issue in the design of land use policy is the integration of information concerning ecological and economic factors into cost-effective conservation and development plans. The associated work of natural and social scientists, however, is often too technical to be of practical use to policymakers (Prendergast et al. 1999). In such cases, policy decisions may be made without the benefit of either social or natural science input. This chapter demonstrates ways in which conservation agencies can integrate information regarding the economic and ecological benefits of conservation on specific parcels, without the need for sophisticated biophysical modeling. Using common scoring methods in combination with economic data and simple optimization methods, it illustrates how one can identify a set of priority land parcels for cost-effective conservation. Ferraro compares conservation contract portfolios selected with and without the benefit of such input and finds that failure to incorporate even simplified economic and ecological information can have a dramatic influence on cost-effectiveness. He illustrates simple means through which coordinated economic and ecological information may be provided to the policy process and points out the potential benefits of doing so.

The Role of Economics in Land Use Policy: Challenges and Opportunities

Despite their various approaches to land use policy, the chapters of this book converge on at least one fundamental issue: improving the role of economic and social science research in land use policy. Each provides a different perspective on how economists and social scientists may better inform land use policy. The book does not generate a list of formal recommendations for research and outreach; these are provided elsewhere (e.g., Abdalla 2001, 2004; Johnston 2002; Lynch and Duke 2003; Northeast Regional Center for Rural Development 2002). Rather, the primary goals are to highlight contemporary and practical contributions of economics to land use policy, illuminate challenges facing economists who seek to inform the policy process, and call attention to unresolved questions with key implications for policy development and implementation.

Arguably one of the most significant policy contributions that may be made by economists is an increased recognition and elucidation of the role of incentives facing individual decisionmakers, landowners, and land users. The emphasis on quantifiable incentives sets economics largely apart from other disciplines and allows insights unavailable through other perspectives toward human land use. Nonetheless, the ability of economists to contribute to policy dialogues can be lost if economics cannot be integrated with the many other disciplines that seek to inform policymakers—all of which offer valid information that may be used to guide land policy. The remainder of this introduction highlights the role of incentives in land use policy, particularly as related to subsequent chapters in this book. It also discusses the ongoing challenge of broadening the horizon of economic inquiry, such that the insights of economists might be more successfully integrated into land use policymaking.

The Role of Incentives in Land Use Policy

Land use is determined by choices made by individuals and groups; these decisions are influenced by a variety of factors. One of the primary contributions of economics to the land use policy debate is a recognition of the critical importance of incentives, or the motivations provided by self-interest. In the land use arena, for example, economic models may seek out the incentives created by policies or institutions, then assess the implications of these incentives for the choices of individuals and resulting land use outcomes. Although this is not often made explicit in economic analyses, the importance of incentives to human behavior pervades much of economic inquiry, including most of the cases considered in this book.

The concern with incentives may manifest in different ways, both implicit and explicit. Chapter 12 (Johnston et al.) considers preferences for development and conservation outcomes among New England residents—information that may provide incentives to elected political representatives as they develop or implement land use policy. Incentives of another type are at the core of Chapter 6 (Lynch). Underlying this analysis is a clear sense of the incentives facing agricultural landowners as local agricultural infrastructure (e.g., farm supply businesses) diminishes with the loss of a critical mass of nearby farms. Similar arguments may be made for the analyses of Chapters 3 and 4 (Irwin et al.; Templeton et al.), which both address drivers of land conversion. Intended or unintended incentives of preferential tax policy on landowner decisions are at the heart of Chapter 8 (England and Mohr). The public-choice approach of Chapter 11 (Nickerson and Hellerstein) incorporates incentives in still another way, through the (perhaps arguable) assumption that the democratic election of government officials creates incentives for government actions to reflect the preferences and values of the public. Similar arguments may be made for virtually every other chapter in this book.

The critical role of incentives is at the core of much of economists' contributions to land use policy. Many would argue, however, that we have a long way to go in incorporating appropriate incentives into U.S. land use policy. For example, the perverse incentives presented by ad valorem property taxes—typically assessed on the value of land in its "highest and best" developed use—with regard to the conservation of farm and forest are well known (American Farmland Trust 1997). Similar tax- and policy-based incentives that encourage the conversion (or development) of farm, forest, and open space are well documented (e.g., Fischel 1985). The successful promotion of more appropriate land use incentive structures represents a significant challenge facing policy-oriented economists.

Chapters 1 and 2 (Castle; Bromley) also remind us that incentives are contingent upon the current state of the world—including legal institutions and income distribution. The incentives reflected by benefits and costs, measured using tools of neoclassical economics, are similarly dependent on the existing allocation of property rights. A greater recognition of such issues among economists may ameliorate some of the concerns of noneconomists and policymakers with the policy prescriptions of economists, and enable resulting land use policies to better reflect exogenous incentives facing individuals and households, as well as incentives created by (or endogenous to) policy.

Broadening the Horizon of Economic Inquiry

Although economics contributes unique approaches to land use policy, such contributions are often most useful (and better accepted) when integrated with the insights and approaches of other disciplines. The trend toward increasing involvement of researchers with those in management roles and with practical policy challenges represents an important strength of much ongoing land use research. As this hopeful trend continues, applied economists and social scientists have increasingly discovered the benefits of nontraditional research methods and cooperative work with those from outside their own disciplines. This willingness to explore alternative methods that might offer practical solutions and insights for policy, both inside and outside of traditional economics, is revealed by many of the chapters in this book. The challenge is maintaining the rigor, formal consistency, and validity of economic research while at the same time integrating elements from other disciplines and approaches to land use policy.

Economics, and social science more broadly, can play a greater positive role in land use policy. The increased use of social science in the land use policy process presents numerous challenges, however; some of these are highlighted in Chapters 1, 2, and 10. Although simple solutions rarely exist, explicit recognition of these challenges may help economists and social scientists provide more effective policy support. It is hoped that future research may address potential solutions.

One of the primary challenges facing both researchers and policymakers is the lack of effective avenues through which research advances can benefit policymakers and stakeholders. Applied economists are increasingly working alongside policymakers to address land use and policy issues of immediate practical concern. Research has improved our ability to address pressing land use issues, and extension activities have communicated these results to appropriate policy audiences. Nonetheless, although many individual researchers have provided significant outreach and extension to government and stakeholder groups, a divergence remains between research findings that are most useful to policymakers and the type of research typically encouraged by academic institutions and professional journals. This pattern is exacerbated by an incentive system that provides greater reward for highly technical or methodological work, as typically published in academic journals, that may be less accessible to those on the front lines of management.

Beyond issues of complexity, economists' perspectives of land use, driven by such concepts as social welfare, equilibrium, and efficiency, may differ markedly from those of policymakers and stakeholders. As highlighted by Bromley in Chapter 2, this can lead to conceptual disagreements among economists, policymakers, and stakeholders. This issue is broader than a simple misunderstanding of economic concepts among noneconomists. It reflects the reality that many in the policy arena are equally, if not more, concerned with alternative issues such as equity, fairness, political feasibility, and the operation of policy institutions—issues sometimes suppressed by economists (see Portney 2004). Policymakers also may face institutional constraints and incentive systems that encourage meeting the agencies' requirements above the search for more optimal land use policy—a variant of the classic principal-agent problem. Hence, even when research identifies clear areas in which policy may be improved, recommendations may not be incorporated into the policy process.

Economists' perspectives on land use issues also tend to differ from those held by other disciplines, including ecology, forestry, and planning (Simpson 1998). Differences are common even within the social sciences. As a result, policy guidance may vary, leading policymakers or program administrators to discount findings from one or more disciplines. For instance, whereas economic models traditionally have relied on the concept of a stable equilibrium, other disciplines tend to emphasize movement between states and the lack of stable equilibria—a fundamental difference in perspective. A second common example relates to fundamentally differing concepts of value associated with natural resources, including land, with economists espousing a utilitarian perspective sometimes rejected by noneconomists (Turner 1999). Finally, the role of spatial dynamics and relationships—often critical in ecological and natural inquiry—only recently has become a more primary emphasis in economic analyses (Bockstael 1996).

The above exemplify some of the challenges to truly interdisciplinary work addressing land use and policy; despite the significant benefits of joint research with ecologists and others, such work is often hindered by limitations in data and existing knowledge, as well as fundamental differences in disciplinary perspectives and core models. Such difficulties notwithstanding, the ability to conduct effective cross-disciplinary policy analysis may have an important influence on the continuing role of economics in land use policy. Chapters 5 and 13 illustrate some of the challenges faced when working in multidisciplinary settings, but also the potential benefits.

Future Work: The Promise and Challenge

Despite the wealth of economic and social science research addressing issues relevant to land management, there is much to gain from future work. The acceleration of recent land conversions, particularly to residential uses in urban-fringe areas, renders this work all the more pressing. Market failures related to land use continue largely unabated in many areas. Considerable uncertainty remains regarding many aspects of land conservation, development, social value, and policy. Research often generates conflicting, unexpected, or otherwise uncertain results. Empirical work is often beset by data limitations, the complexity of spatial effects, and the influence of human behavior on land use. Despite these challenges, policymakers are increasingly recognizing the benefits of economic research for land use policy. It is the goal of this book to illustrate practical contributions that economics can make to our understanding of land use issues and the development of appropriate policy responses.

Endnotes

1. Papers from this workshop, reflecting some of the same topics and authors as are reflected in this volume (albeit written for an audience of professional economists), may be found in the *Agricultural and Resource Economics Review*, 32(1), 2003.

References

Abdalla, C. W. (2001). Protecting Farmland at the Fringe: Do Regulations Work? Strengthening the Research Agenda. Northeast Regional Center for Rural Development Paper no. 7. University Park, PA: The Pennsylvania State University.

———. (2004). What the Public Values about Farm and Ranch Land: Workshop Summary. Regional Rural Development Paper no. 23. Northeast Regional Center for Rural Development. University Park, PA: The Pennsylvania State University.

Albers, H. J., and A. W. Ando. (2003). Could State-Level Variation in the Number of Land Trusts Make Sense? *Land Economics* 79(3): 311–327.

American Farmland Trust. (1997). *Saving American Farmland: What Works.* Northampton, MA: American Farmland Trust Publications Division.

American Planning Association. (2002). Planning for Smart Growth: 2002 State of the States. Chicago: American Planning Association.

Anderson, C. M., and J. R. King. (2004). Equilibrium Behavior in the Conservation Easement Game. *Land Economics* 80(3): 355–374.

Anderson, J. E. (1986). Property Taxes and the Timing of Urban Land Development. *Regional Science and Urban Economics* 16(4): 483–492.

————. (1993). Use Value Property Tax Assessment: Effects on Land Development. *Land Economics* 69(3): 263–269.

Anselin, L. (1988). *Spatial Econometrics: Methods and Models*. Dordrecht, The Netherlands: Kluwer Academic Publishers.

Anselin, L., R. Florax, and S. Rey (eds.). (2004). *Advances in Spatial Econometrics. Methodology, Tools and Applications*. Berlin: Springer-Verlag.

Arendt, R., E. Brabec, H. Dodson, C. Reid, and R. Yaro. (1994). *Rural by Design: Maintaining Small Town Character*. Chicago: American Planning Association.

Beasley, S. D., W. G. Workman, and N. A. Williams. (1986). Estimating Amenity Values of Urban Fringe Farmland: A Contingent Valuation Approach. *Growth and Change* 17(1): 70–78.

Bentick, B. L. (1979). The Impact of Taxation and Valuation Practices on the Timing and Efficiency of Land Use. *Journal of Political Economy* 87(4): 859–868.

————. (1997). The Economic Effects (Neutrality) of Taxes on Land. *American Journal of Economics and Sociology* 56(3): 369–371.

Bergstrom, J. C., B. L. Dillman, and J. R. Stoll. (1985). Public Environmental Amenity Benefits of Private Land: The Case of Prime Agricultural Land. *Southern Journal of Agricultural Economics* 17: 139–149.

Bills, N., C. Geisler, and A. Sokolow. (2004). Conservation Easements as Encumbered Ownership: Issues at Hand. Rural Development Paper no. 25. Northeast Regional Center for Rural Development. University Park, PA: The Pennsylvania State University.

Bockstael, N. E. (1996). Modeling Economics and Ecology: The Importance of a Spatial Perspective. *American Journal of Agricultural Economics* 78: 1168–1180.

Caldwell, Bruce J. (1982). *Beyond Positivism: Economic Methodology in the Twentieth Century*. Boston: George Allen and Unwin.

Calthorpe, P. (1993). *The Next American Metropolis: Ecology, Community, and the American Dream*. New York: Princeton Architectural Press.

Case, A. (1991). Spatial Patterns in Household Demand. *Econometrica* 59(4): 953–965.

————. (1992). Neighborhood Influence and Technological Change. *Regional Science and Urban Economics* 22(3): 491–508.

Duke, J. M., and R. A. Hyde. (2002). Identifying Public Preferences for Land Preservation Using the Analytic Hierarchy Process. *Ecological Economics* 42(1-2): 131–145.

Feather, P., D. Hellerstein, and L. Hansen. (1999). Economic Valuation of Environmental Benefits and the Targeting of Conservation Programs: The Case of the CRP. Agricultural Economic Report no. 778. Resource Economics Division, Economic Research Service, U.S. Department of Agriculture.

Fischel, W. A. (1985). *The Economics of Zoning Laws: A Property Rights Approach to American Land Use Controls*. Baltimore, MD: Johns Hopkins University Press.

Freeman, A. M., III. (2003). *The Measurement of Environmental and Resource Values: Theory and Methods*. Washington, DC: Resources for the Future.

Gardner, B. D. (1977). The Economics of Agricultural Land Preservation. *American Journal of Agricultural Economics* 59(5): 1027–1036.

Garrod, G., and K. Willis. (1992). The Environmental Economic Impact of a Woodland: A Two-Stage Hedonic Price Model of the Amenity Value of Forestry in Britain. *Applied Economics* 24: 715–728.

Geoghegan, J., L. Lynch, and S. Bucholtz. (2003). Capitalization of Open Spaces into Housing Values and the Residential Property Tax Revenue Impacts of Agricultural Easement Programs. *Agricultural and Resource Economics Review* 32(1): 33–45.

Gordon, P., and H. W. Richardson. (1998). Prove It: The Costs and Benefits of Sprawl. *Brookings Review* 16(4): 23.

Heimlich, R. E., and W. D. Anderson. (2001). *Development at the Urban Fringe and Beyond: Impacts on Agriculture and Rural Land.* Agricultural Economic Report no. 803. Economic Research Service, U.S. Department of Agriculture.

Irwin, E. G., and N. E. Bockstael. (2002). Interacting Agents, Spatial Externalities, and the Evolution of Residential Land Use Patterns. *Journal of Economic Geography* 2(1): 31–54.

———. (2004). Endogenous Spatial Externalities: Empirical Evidence and Implications for Exurban Residential Land Use Patterns. In *Advances in Spatial Econometrics*, edited by L. Anselin, R. Florax, and S. Rey. Berlin: Springer-Verlag.

Johnston, R. J. (2002). Conserving Farm and Forest in a Changing Rural Landscape: Current and Potential Contributions of Economic Research. Regional Rural Development Paper no. 11. Northeast Regional Center for Rural Development. University Park, PA: The Pennsylvania State University.

Johnston, R. J., J. J. Opaluch, T. A. Grigalunas, and M. J. Mazzotta. (2001). Estimating Amenity Benefits of Coastal Farmland. *Growth and Change* 32(Summer): 305–325.

Johnston, R. J., S. K. Swallow, T. J. Tyrrell, and D. M. Bauer. (2003). Rural Amenity Values and Length of Residency. *American Journal of Agricultural Economics* 85(4): 1000–1015.

Josling, T. (2002). Competing Paradigms in the OECD and Their Impact on the WTO Agriculture Talks. In *Agricultural Policy for the 21st Century* edited by L. Tweeten and S. R. Thompson. Ames: Iowa State University Press, 245–264.

Kline, J., and D. Wichelns. (1994). Using Referendum Data to Characterize Public Support for Purchasing Development Rights to Farmland. *Land Economics* 70(2): 223–233.

———. (1998). Measuring Heterogeneous Preferences for Preserving Farmland and Open Space. *Ecological Economics* 26(2): 211–224.

Kramer, R. A., and L. Shabman. (1993). The Effects of Agricultural and Tax Policy Reform on the Economic Return to Wetland Drainage in the Mississippi Delta Region. *Land Economics* 69(3): 249–262.

Land Trust Alliance. (2003). *Americans Invest in Parks and Open Space: LandVote 2003.* Washington, DC: Land Trust Alliance.

Lynch, L., and J. M. Duke. (2003). Linkages between Agricultural and Conservation Policies: Workshop Proceedings. Regional Rural Development Paper no. 21. Northeast Regional Center for Rural Development. University Park, PA: The Pennsylvania State University.

Nelson, A. C., and J. B. Duncan. (1995). *Growth Management Principles and Practices.* Chicago: American Planning Association.

Nickerson, C. (2001). Smart Growth: Implications for Agriculture in Urban Fringe Areas. *Agricultural Outlook.* April. Economic Research Service, U.S. Department of Agriculture.

Northeast Regional Center for Rural Development. (2002). Land Use Problems and Conflicts in the U.S.: A Comprehensive Research Agenda for the 21st Century. Rural Development Paper no. 10. University Park, PA.

Owens, N. (2004). Economic Analysis at EPA: Requirements and Research Needs. Paper presented at the annual meeting of the American Agricultural Economics Association. August 1–4, Denver, CO.

Parks, P. J., and J. P. Schorr. (1997). Sustaining Open Space Benefits in the Northeast: An Evaluation of the Conservation Reserve Program. *Journal of Environmental Economics and Management* 32(1): 85–94.

Pasha, H. A. (1996). Suburban Minimum Lot Zoning and Spatial Equilibrium. *Journal of Urban Economics* 40(1): 1–12.

Plantinga, A. (1996). The Effect of Agricultural Policies on Land Use and Environmental Quality. *American Journal of Agricultural Economics* 78(4): 1082–1091.

Portney, P. R. (2004). The Obligations of a Policy Economist. *Agricultural and Resource Economics Review* 33(2): 159–161.

Prendergast, J. R., R. M. Quinn, and J. H. Lawton. (1999). The Gaps between Theory and Practice in Selecting Nature Reserves. *Conservation Biology* 13(3): 484–492.

Ready, R. C., M. C. Berger, and G. C. Blomquist. (1997). Measuring Amenity Benefits from Farmland: Hedonic Pricing vs. Contingent Valuation. *Growth and Change* 28(Fall): 438–458.

Roe, B., E. G. Irwin, and H. A. Morrow-Jones. (2004). The Effects of Farmland, Farmland Preservation, and Other Neighborhood Amenities on Housing Values and Residential Growth. *Land Economics* 80(1): 55–74.

Rosenberger, R. S., and R. G. Walsh. (1997). Nonmarket Value of Western Valley Ranchland Using Contingent Valuation. *Journal of Agricultural and Resource Economics* 22(2): 296–309.

Sen, A. (1993). Markets and Freedoms: Achievements and Limitations of the Market Mechanism in Promoting Individual Freedoms. *Oxford Economic Papers* 45: 519–541.

Simpson, R. D. (1998). Economic Analysis and Ecosystems: Some Concepts and Issues. *Ecological Applications* 8(2): 342–349.

Turner, R. K. (1999). The Place of Economic Values in Environmental Valuation. In *Valuing Environmental Preferences: Theory and Practice of the Contingent Valuation Method in the US, EU, and Developing Countries*, edited by I. J. Bateman and K. G. Willis. Oxford: Oxford University Press.

University of Connecticut Cooperative Extension, Nonpoint Education for Municipal Officials (NEMO) Project. (1999). Conservation Subdivisions: A Better Way to Protect Water Quality, Retain Wildlife, and Preserve Rural Character. NEMO Project Fact Sheet. Storrs: University of Connecticut College of Agriculture.

van Kooten, C. G. (1993). Bioeconomic Evaluation of Government Agricultural Programs on Wetlands Conversion. *Land Economics* 69(1): 27–38.

PART I

Economic Approaches to Land Use Policy

1

Land, Economic Change, and Economic Doctrine

EMERY N. CASTLE

L and plays numerous roles in economic doctrine. Economies, always in a state of change, move on unique trajectories through time. Those who make use of economic models may have different motivations for doing do. If the treatment of land in economics is to be understood, one must account not only for economic change, but also for the motivation of economists who study land.

Three distinct situations are considered in this chapter. One pertains to agricultural land use in an industry connected to the rest of the economy through commodity and input markets. A different situation is encountered if, in the presence of unregulated markets, land use has "externality" effects on the remainder of the economy. A third arises when alternative land use policies affect the rate, direction, or impact of economic activity. Within each of these situations, this chapter emphasizes the main points that land plays different roles in economic affairs, and that more than one valid analytic approach to land exists. This view is consistent with a pluralistic economic research methodology described by Caldwell (1982) and stands in contrast to the contrary view asserting a single basic paradigm (i.e., the neoclassical paradigm) for contemporary economic inquiry into land use policy.

The reader's attention is directed to two issues at the outset. First, the term *land* has both narrow and broad definitions. Used narrowly, it refers to a particular geographic space on the surface of this planet. This usage is consistent with the common understanding, although economists distinguish between land in its natural state and land that has been modified, either positively or negatively, by humans. The broad definition includes land as defined narrowly, along with such things as the atmosphere, oceans, and natural plant and animal species, to the extent that they have beneficial powers. In this chapter, the context makes clear whether the broad or narrow view is taken.

The second issue is subtle and less obvious. Most of what we believe about reality has been filtered through conceptual constructs, or frames of reference. These include preconceptions of our own and of those who have processed the information coming to our attention. If we are to evaluate whether information constitutes knowledge, we need to understand the information itself, as well as the framework through which it is processed and organized.

The primary objective of this chapter is to trace the changing role of land as viewed by Western-world economists, particularly as affected by economic development and institutional change. A secondary objective is to assist readers in evaluating the various conceptual constructs that have been used to process land-related information relevant to public policy formation and individual decisionmaking. It is hoped that the historical approach espoused in this chapter will assist readers in appreciating both the power and the limitations of the conceptual frameworks used by economists.

Land and Agriculture

Land in Classical Economics

David Ricardo lived from 1772 to 1823, and Thomas Malthus from 1766 to 1834. Adam Smith's *Wealth of Nations* was published in 1776. Food production was a principal economic activity when Smith, Ricardo, and Malthus contributed to economic doctrine; they might well be considered the first agricultural economists. Land, labor, and capital were thought to be the principal factors of production; the returns to these factors were labeled rent, wages, and profits (or interest), respectively. The determination of the returns to the various factors was a subject of great interest, with an apparent consensus that land rent was in the nature of a residual claimant. In other words, the rent to land was the residual benefit that remained for the landowner after wages for labor and profit (or interest) for capital were paid, as determined in the marketplace. Smith clearly stated that land rent was determined by commodity prices, not the other way around.

As classical economics matured, a more general treatment was given to some subjects. Although economists continued to show interest in the adequacy of agricultural land for food production, a broader concept of land emerged. The end of the classical era saw apparent consensus that land should include all beneficial powers of nature (Senior 1836). This consensus, occurring early in the history of economic thought, legitimized environmental economics when it later emerged as a potential field of study within economics.

The Perspectives of Early Neoclassical Economics

The publication of Alfred Marshall's *Principles of Economics* in 1890 is often used to date the transition from classical to neoclassical economics. Marshall integrated many strands of economic thought into a coherent system. He employed marginal analysis in the systematic development of both demand and supply. He dealt with price determination, as well as the behavior of firms within an industry. He further demonstrated the power of partial equilibrium analysis by applications to numerous and varied economic situations.

Food production technology changed greatly after the classical economics era. It is not surprising that twentieth-century economists revisited classical economic doctrine about land and food production. Two important milestones can be identified. One, of a conceptual nature, was the work of Frank Knight (1921), who concluded that it was not necessary to distinguish land from other forms of capital in terms of his treatment of risk and uncertainty. The second was empirical, occurring when the economics profession came to recognize that food–land relationships had changed in a fundamental way from those prevalent during the time of Smith, Ricardo, and Malthus. Consider the 1951 T.W. Schultz article, "Declining Importance of Agricultural Land." Schultz was careful to confine his attention to agricultural land. His empirical work led to the conclusion that technology had made it possible to substitute management and capital for agricultural land in U.S. food production. The clear implication was that an inadequacy of agricultural land was unlikely to threaten the nation's food supply. The major thesis of this article, as reflected in its title, has been confirmed by experience and numerous empirical investigations (see Crosson 1982, especially). Nonetheless, even now, policymakers sometimes contend with a common perspective that the loss of agricultural land threatens domestic food supplies.

After World War II, Earl Heady's *Economics of Agricultural Production and Resource Use* (1952) was responsible for yet another significant shift in the view of land among agricultural economists. Following Knight, Heady did not give special treatment to land and believed that only labor (including management) and capital needed to be considered as factors of production. He placed great emphasis on the farm firm within the agricultural industry. The underlying theoretical base of much of Heady's empirical work assumed constant returns to scale, atomistic competition, and homogenous products. Technical change typically was considered an exogenous variable and assigned responsibility for declining agricultural output costs. This work reflected a growing trend among agricultural economists at the time toward quantitative and empirical analysis, and away from more fundamental issues of theoretical development.

The policy conclusions resulting from such models emphasized the production of marketable commodities and usually either explicitly stated or implied that government price supports were inefficient. It was assumed that supply–demand imbalances would disappear if the industry could just "get through" whatever short-term crises existed at the time. This traditional approach did not anticipate the industrialization of agriculture, even though economic theory had long recognized the importance (suggested by empirical findings) of decreasing as well as constant costs. Even now, much remains to be discovered about the welfare of those in decreasing-cost industries under conditions of secular economic growth.

The methodology that production economists used after World War II was based largely on partial equilibrium models pioneered by Marshall (1920). Theoretical advances of John R. Hicks (1939) and others permitted ordinal utility to be substituted for the cardinal utility formulations of Marshall. Yet the partial equilibrium approach of the early production economists and the assumption of "all other things remain the same" generally were not modified.

Computable general equilibrium models and data-processing technology have improved on these early partial equilibrium approaches. Yet even the most elaborate computable general equilibrium model neglects a great deal of economic reality. Still, such equilibrium models often reveal significant and policy-relevant important information unavailable through simpler partial equilibrium models. For example, a recent general equilibrium study demonstrates that even modest increasing returns (decreasing costs) in an industry can have a significant effect on demand for factors of production (Antweiler and Trefler 2002).

There are many interests in rural land, beyond its contributions to agricultural production. Nonetheless, agricultural economists have a special responsibility to understand the role that land plays in agricultural production. A full understanding of that role requires a better understanding than we currently have of the relationship of technical change to economies of scale in agricultural production. The frequently employed assumption of constant returns to scale is convenient in both econometric and programming work, although the empirical base for such an assumption in agricultural production is not well established. Could T.W. Schultz (1951) have concluded that agricultural land was declining in importance if constant returns to scale actually prevailed in farming? Removal of the ambiguity surrounding this important relationship requires the following:

- Clarity as to whether reference is being made to agriculture or farming. With the passage of time, farms have purchased more inputs, and much processing and marketing have moved off the farm. The economic role of farms in the industry has not been constant.
- Recognition that the quality and quantity of inputs used in farming have varied with time. Traditional economic theory has treated technical change as exogenous to the industry, causing shifts in the long-run supply function. Yet technical changes occur in many ways. If the productivity of an input varies as a result of technical change, it may be difficult to measure the

quantitative change in the input over time. To clarify this point, consider that the least-cost way of providing inputs from one time period to the next may be in the form of heterogeneous rather than homogeneous goods. For example, in one period, fertilizer from an organic source, such as manure, may be applied to provide nitrogen and lesser amounts of other nutrients, as well as contribute to soil structure. Yet in the next time period, greater productivity may result from increased use of nitrogen obtained at least cost from inorganic ammonium sulfate. In subsequent time periods, a more balanced fertilizer may be more profitable than ammonium sulfate. Clearly it would make little sense to compare the various forms of fertilizer over time in terms of a common denominator, such as pounds per acre. Yet it would also be difficult to disaggregate the different forms of fertilizer used over time in terms of the nutrients and soil benefit contributed by each.

- An understanding that much technical change has been associated with the shift of traditional farming activity to nonfarm firms. This shift has occurred in both input supply and output processing and marketing. The consequence is that the per-unit cost of farm output over time does not pertain to a homogenous product. On what basis can it be maintained that costs are constant over time if the nature of the output changes and the firms producing that output also have changed?

Despite substantial progress in economists' conceptualization of land from the turn of the century through the postwar years, the view that land was not distinct from other forms of capital reinforced the assumption that agriculture was connected to the rest of the economy only through input and commodity markets. The emphasis during this period was on the productive aspects of farming with regard to marketable products. Possible positive or negative nonmarket (or external) effects of agricultural output or activity typically were neglected. Nevertheless, even prior to the growth of resource and environmental economics as a discipline in the late 1960s and 1970s, some economists devoted considerable attention to the potential nonmarket implications of land use (Castle et al. 1981). Yet it was not until relatively recently that externalities associated with agricultural and other land uses became a significant concern of economists.

Land, "Rules of the Game," and Environmental Economics

As economic growth occurs, the face of the earth almost unavoidably is modified, and human perceptions and expectations also are affected. Some human interventions in nature may be benign, but not all are, and uncertainty surrounds others. As incomes rise and the location and concentration of people change, perceptions of various facets of the natural environment may be altered as well. Such patterns are reflected in economic inquiry.

By the time Earth Day was first observed in April 1970, resource economics had become a recognized specialty in both economics and agricultural economics. It had arisen from a concern that unregulated markets could not internalize all of their consequences and represented a fundamental shift from the purely production-oriented approaches of earlier agricultural economics. Early on, this was manifested by government investment in the conservation and development of natural resources. Benefit–cost analysis was created to evaluate economic consequences that were not internalized by markets and was well established on theoretical grounds by 1970. The resource economics specialization shifted emphasis from agricultural land, narrowly defined, to the encompassing, broad definition of land formulated by the classical economists: "all beneficial powers of nature."

Economists have taken two general approaches to nonmarket phenomena. One is to estimate, simulate, or deduce how the economy would operate if certain conditions were present. Benefit–cost analysis is one such method. A different perspective, known as the "rules of the game" approach, is reflected in studies of nonmarket institutions that establish relationships among individuals and groups in management of the natural environment. Land as broadly defined has been studied from both perspectives, and a brief sketch of each approach follows.

Institutional Economics and "Rules of the Game"

Institutional economics serves as an example of the "rules of the game" approach. Societies long have had special institutional devices to deal with the unique characteristics of land. Its durability, indivisibility in certain circumstances, capacity to absorb human-created capital across generations, and ability to serve multiple ends often have resulted in special "rules of the game." The late Maurice Kelso provided a brief, competent account of the origin and content of institutional economics and how land economics arose from it (in Castle et al. 1981, 394–406).

Institutional land economics once occupied a respectable, but never dominant, place in agricultural economics. Three considerations led to its decline after World War II. First, institutional economics was basically incompatible with logical positivism, the dominant philosophy of science in the second quarter of the twentieth century. It did not have a formal theoretical structure to guide empirical work, although it was, and is, empirically oriented. Second, especially since the war, developments in neoclassical economic theory and quantitative techniques stimulated research on farm and marketing firm problems, demand analysis, and industry adjustments. Economic theory, used to guide data collection and analysis, seemed to be more "scientific" than the writings of institutional land economists. Third, shortly after the war's end, natural resource economists arrived on the scene in both economics and agricultural economics, and made considerable use of neoclassical theory and quantitative techniques. Since that time, land economics as a specialization within agricultural economics has declined significantly. A major contribution of the land economists was to document that resource-using industries such as agriculture long have had many institutional connections with the remainder of the economy and society in addition to commodity and factor markets. When resource economics was in its infancy, this accumulated knowledge about economic institutions permitted greater realism in resource economics investigations.

The economics of institutions, in contrast to the subfield of institutional land economics, flourishes. Douglas North (1990) has become a Nobel laureate stemming from his work in institutional economics. Rutherford (1994) draws a distinction between the "old" and "new" institutional economics, in part because the "new" institutional economists often come to more conservative policy positions than do the "older" ones. That probably is the case, but a sharp methodological distinction also exists between the two. The "new" institutional economists are more inclined to make use of the market paradigm in their research, often as a standard for judging the adequacy of other institutions.

Arguably, neoclassical economics is becoming more institutional in its orientation and emphasis. It is generally recognized that markets themselves are institutional devices dependent on other institutions, such as property rights and efficient government. And institutional economics increasingly makes use of the economic theory of markets to explain as well as evaluate economic development and change. If each approach makes use of the knowledge base of the other, much good potentially can come from such interaction. A less desirable outcome is likely if one or the other approach becomes dominant.

Environmental and Natural Resource Economics

Environmental and resource economics depends heavily on markets and market-type institutions for statements of the "rules of the game." It employs market-type incentives and outcomes to judge the success or failure of environmental nonmarket institutions, policies, and programs. The norms assumed typically are derived from welfare economics. Environmental and resource economics considers its scope to encompass "all of the beneficial properties of nature." This specialization now has its own association and journals, and it has attracted considerable talent from other fields in economics and agricultural economics, as well as from outside the discipline.

The growth, development, refinement, and use of benefit–cost analysis are correlated with the emergence of resource and environmental economics as a field of specialization. Benefit–cost analysis was invented in response to a congressional mandate that both costs and benefits, regardless of their origin or incidence, be considered in the evaluation of public flood-control expenditures. This mandate was issued before World War II, but major development of the technique occurred in the postwar years. Those responsible for developing principles and procedures of benefit–cost analysis turned to economists for guidance.

A "new" welfare economics literature was emerging, with a theoretical framework based largely on a vision of welfare maximization. The maximization of net national income (or net social benefits) became a goal. Pareto optimality, the capacity of those who gain from an economic reorganization to compensate those who lose, served as a criterion for judging the desirability of government intervention. Benefit–cost analysis became the tool for providing an empirical evaluation of theoretical possibilities. The emerging field of benefit–cost analysis incorporated a number of fundamental assumptions, including the following:

- It is possible to estimate the economic worth of nonmarket goods and services. Resource and environmental economists have been in the forefront of developing and applying such estimation techniques as contingent valuation, hedonic pricing, and the travel cost method.
- The maximization of net benefits is an explicit and appropriate goal when benefit–cost analysis is used in the allocation of public expenditures or formulation of public policies. This requires a benefit–cost ratio greater than one (or net present value greater than zero) and is consistent with the requirement that gainers be able to compensate losers.
- Prices and market conditions are estimated for a competitive economy in equilibrium, and the current distribution of income and wealth is an acceptable baseline for estimation of benefits and costs.

None of these assumptions is without controversy. With regard to the first assumption, each of the techniques for estimating the value of nonmarket goods has been subject to criticism, as has the need to value nonmarket goods. As for the second assumption, the requirement that gainers be able to compensate losers without the requirement that they do so is subject to criticism on ethical grounds (Samuelson 2004, *144*). Finally, even the use of market prices to value goods traded in markets does not escape criticism. Markets are not equally competitive and rarely reach equilibrium at the same time. Some prices are more influenced by government programs than others. Moreover, the truism that all prices are derived from the existing distribution of income and wealth in the economy gives rise to the argument that such distributions may be far from optimal (see Bromley 1990, 1997; Gowdy 2004; Vanberg 2004 for critical discussions of the use of economic optimality concepts in the establishment of public policy).

Land and Economic Growth

Economic growth and change have influenced the role of location and space in economic inquiry and models. Land is no longer viewed only as an item entering individual production and consumption functions, even with allowance for externalities. A single conceptual framework has not been discovered that is appropriate for an understanding of the multiple roles of land under conditions of growth and change.

The theory of the firm provides one framework for the analysis of agricultural land, if it is assumed that the agricultural industry is connected to the remainder of the economy through input and commodity markets. Welfare economics and benefit–cost analysis provide a comparable framework for the consideration of environmental externalities. The role of land in economic growth and development is even more complex. Public and private land use and competing private land uses all are involved. Decisions intermediate between the micro and macro levels envisioned in typical economic analysis become increasingly important.

Central Place Theory

Central place theory provides the principal conceptual lens economists use to understand the geographic implications of private-sector activity. Such understanding is of great importance in public land use policy, even though "optimal" private-sector activity is not necessarily an appropriate normative standard for collective decisions. With this orientation, the central city is the beginning point from which all other economic activity stems and has become the principal orientation within the field of urban economics. In its original formulation, central place theory did not make the hinterlands interesting places, although Hite (1997, 1999) believes it implies a spatial aspect of asset fixity, which, he argues, is likely to increase with remoteness from centers of economic activity. Krugman modified traditional central place theory with concepts that have become a part of "new growth theory" (1991, 1995). These include differentiated products and scale economies. The theoretical and empirical work of Kilkenny (1998a,b) draws on this "new economic geography." She concludes that one of the best alternatives for many rural places wishing to stimulate economic activity is improvement in the quality of rural life.

In recent research, Wu (2001) further modified the assumptions typically associated with central place theory. Rather than assuming a featureless plane, he permitted amenity values to enter location decisions. Based on such an approach, Wu and Plantinga (2002) examined the impacts of open-space designation on the urban landscape in a spatial city model with two empirically relevant characteristics: that residents prefer to live close to open space, and that open-space amenities attract migrants to the city. This model indicates that open-space policies should be viewed as neither independent of or necessarily compatible with growth-management goals. Different reasons may exist for urban sprawl than traditional central place theory suggests.

Economists and lawyers long have recognized that use and development rights in land could be separated and have devised policies for permitting this to happen, thereby accommodating individual and collective objectives. In the opinion of this author, we have done less well with zoning and similar land use policies. So-called smart-growth policies have emerged in response to the type of sprawl development discussed by Wu and Plantinga (2002) and many others, but they have not yet spawned a literature with significant standing in economic doctrine. A concept of "metropolitanism" has also been advanced, but it appears to be at odds factually with descriptive literature about "edge" and "galactic" cities (Garreau 1998; Katz and Bradley 1999; Lewis 1995).

Natural Resources and Local Places

Starting in the early twentieth century, the federal establishment assumed increasing responsibility for the development and conservation of natural resources. More recently, especially since the first Earth Day, the federal government has passed environmental legislation pertaining to water, air, and species preservation. Use rights have remained largely under state jurisdiction. Integration at the local level, other than by specific legislation, stems in part from the role state agencies play in the administration of federal programs and from local initiative within the framework of state law. Federal and state programs frequently are manifested in an inconsistent and uncoordinated fashion at the local level. Local government effectiveness is affected greatly by whether local groups have sufficient common interests and shared norms to advance a collective cause.

In standard economic theory, a decentralized market system arises from individual decisionmaking at the micro level, and the maximization of net national income guides benefit–cost analysis at the macro level. No provision exists for intermediate, or local, group decisionmaking in systemwide economic analysis. Central place theory is a theory of individual decisionmaking when space and distance become explicit. Articles by Bromley and Rausser (Dinar 2000) demonstrate that interdependence in natural resource use requires cooperation at the local level if individual aspirations are to be met, a result not obtained by a decentralized market system. Rausser (2000) shows that collective choice approaches are useful in the analysis of individual situations at the local level but yield results that are not suitable for integration into economy-wide formulations.

Agricultural land illustrates the difficulty of integrating choice indicators among the individual, local, and national levels. The work of T.W. Schultz

(1951) on the declining importance of agricultural land reflects individual decisions in response to macro trends. Crosson's (1982) work on agricultural cropland deals with the adequacy of this land from a national standpoint. Yet the concerns of local groups about agricultural land are not often reflected in either national or individual objectives. Local places may view agricultural land as a source of open space, as having potential to accommodate residential or industrial growth, or as creating positive externalities for urban living. Macroanalysis obscures this variation and fails to reflect the extent and intensity of local preferences.

This is a serious deficiency when viewed from the standpoint of local natural resource management. Federal and state public policies typically are applied at the local level, where local groups are intermediaries between central government and local firms and individuals. Land use planning, water resource development, water pollution, and species preservation all involve local groups in the application of public policies (see Braunworth et al. 2002 for one example). Neither decentralized market prices nor national benefit–cost indicators afford realistic choice guides for local decisionmaking. Rather, institutional, economic, and environmental forces provide boundaries, or constraints, within which local decisionmaking occurs. And every locality has unique resources. These have been classified elsewhere as human, human-created, natural, and social capital (Castle 2002).

Social Capital and Local Places

The local capital concept recognizes distinctions among the various forms of capital but requires that no one form be emphasized to the exclusion of the others. The interdisciplinary concept of social capital, as formulated by Coleman (1990), may be of value in meshing individual aspirations with group activity. Does social capital qualify as capital as economists define the term? As Coleman advanced the concept, social capital arises when individuals can better achieve their aspirations through group action than if they act independently. Social capital is in the form of a public good, as is true for certain types of natural capital. The demand for social capital is a derived demand, and because it does not have an explicit price, it acquires an implicit value from within the economic system. Clearly, social capital creation requires sacrifice and investment (Sobel 2002).

Specific, as well as general, types of social capital need to be considered. Coleman (1990) believed that family and community were the primary forms of social capital; he maintained that incentives for social capital formation were weak, and that it arose primarily as a by-product of other activities. Early empirical work on social capital by Putnam (1995) emphasized civic or social organizations that did "good works" in addition to providing socializing functions. Woolcock (1997) generalized the concept and discussed social capital formation both across and within groups. Across-group, or intergroup, social capital relations tend to be more formal and impersonal. Viewed in this way, institutional economics covers some of the same subjects as social capital. Consistent with this view, social capital arrangements would include partnerships, cooperatives, and community-based economic development groups.

The social capital concept holds the promise of permitting intermediate decisionmaking to become endogenous in economic analysis. "Local place" typically is a vague concept. Yet if local intermediate decisionmaking is to become an integral part of economic analysis, precise treatment is required. Local place is envisioned here as an integration of a particular geographic space (geography), local community (sociology), and jurisdictional unit (political science). Additional discussion of this concept may be found elsewhere (see Castle and Weber 2002).

Distinctions between rural and urban, metropolitan and nonmetropolitan, and city and countryside locations are becoming increasingly blurred, despite popular discussions of the rural-urban divide. Population density, space, and distance are of fundamental importance even as the identification of local places has become necessary. The Federal Office of Management and Budget (OMB) has developed a core-based statistical area (CBSA) classification system to improve traditional definitions and categories. The system is based on metropolitan statistical areas (MSAs), representing counties with urbanized areas of 50,000 or more in population plus outlying counties with close economic or social ties. Also included is a new statistical area classification, micropolitan statistical areas (MiSAs), counties with one urban cluster having 10,000 to 49,999 in population plus outlying counties with strong economic and social ties. Noncore counties are those that do not have an urban cluster of 10,000 or more in population or strong economic and social ties to a core based statistical area.

This classification system is based on considerations of population density, space, and distance, which are fundamental to the local management of natural resources (land) located within each of the three classifications. In the United States, considerable land use control often is delegated to local governments; such control has become a significant public policy tool for many places. In the core counties, land is often a tool of growth management, with space and distance as attributes of importance. Enterprises making extensive use of space, such as farming or forestry, need to be integrated with activities that make intensive use of space. In Virginia, the Carolinas, and Georgia, a combination of urban sprawl, retirement development, and the demand for second homes has driven land prices to such levels that the production of traditional agricultural commodities is feasible only in small, remote enclaves (Hite et al. 1998). Noncore places (remote hinterlands) need to discover ways of integrating their activities with those in more densely populated areas. For example, either the attraction of economic activity or outmigration will be important locally, with each having different land use implications.

In the intermediate decision model described earlier, it was postulated that three boundary conditions—institutional, environmental, and economic in nature—would constrain much local intermediate decisionmaking (Castle and Weber 2002). Differences among places may result in comparative advantages for some and may arise from any of the capital sources identified earlier. The degree of comparative advantage, if any, will affect the possible scope of decisionmaking, as will the boundary conditions.

Conclusions

Economic change affects the role of land in economic and political affairs, as well as the perspective of economists who study land. Clearly, the role of land in human affairs varies with economic change. It is also clear that economists have provided useful information about land to their contemporaries. This author is especially impressed with the classical economists, who had to develop much of their analytical framework as they proceeded. They related land to other factors of production, and much of their contribution to rent theory has endured. Even though agricultural land was of great importance, their broad definition of land legitimizes contemporary environmental economics.

Economic change accelerated rapidly as neoclassical economic emerged late in the nineteenth century, and the role of agricultural land in economic affairs changed as well. This was noted formally, although perhaps somewhat belatedly, near the middle of the twentieth century. As this occurred, other economists emerged and took advantage of a broader definition of land that permitted natural resources and the environment to become focal points of economic investigation. That this occurred prior to Earth Day (1969) is noteworthy. Economic events since that time have changed the role of land in human affairs even more. Land use policy now has become intertwined with other public policy issues, and this complicates economic analysis immensely. The performance of conceptual models under varying circumstances reveals much about the power and the applicability limits of those models. How have economic conceptual models of land performed over the past two centuries? The classical economists could have avoided some problems if they had access to present-day tools; nevertheless, they were aware of many unsolved conceptual issues and laid the groundwork for improvement. It does not appear that they neglected significant bodies of knowledge available at that time. Neoclassical economic analysis of land in the mid-twentieth century in agricultural economics often focused on the farm firm and the farming industry. This was not a sufficiently broad perspective to accommodate emerging natural resource and environmental issues. A broader perspective was provided by the institutional land economists, however, and subsequently by resource economists coming both from agricultural economics and economics. Many resource and environmental economists embraced welfare economics as a source of conceptual models, resulting in the use of economic optimality models for public policy purposes.

It cannot be denied that such models can provide useful information. All economic models, however, must be viewed in the context of the assumptions on which they are based. For example, when intergenerational issues are involved, the selection of a discount rate for benefit–cost analysis depends on ethical judgments (Lind 1999; Nordhaus 1999; Page 1988). Nor can benefit–cost analysis substitute for ethical or political decisions (e.g., Vatn and Bromley 1994). This point has been made in the literature for some time, but those in the mainstream of optimality studies have been slow to accept it. Moreover, welfare maximization will not necessarily result in sustainable outcomes (Arrow et al. 2004).

The examination of economic models in this chapter brings a fundamental issue into the open. Conceptual models, constructs, or frameworks are, by their very nature, abstractions of reality. They seek to capture the essence, even if not the totality, of reality for certain circumstances or problems. If they are to be useful, they will permit us to understand some part of reality better than we can without them. All such models are incomplete or inexact, or both, and their applicability always has limitations.

The other chapters in this book report on a wide range of investigations concerning land-related problems. These studies are admirably varied and diverse. A doctrinaire view of land in our society is not warranted. The applied economist does not have the luxury of using a single conceptual lens to view reality.

As we look to the future, applied economists concerned with land will need to give special attention to the particular circumstances and social problems driving their inquiry. This may limit the scope of economic models, as implied by the theoretical core of economics, and may require the participation of noneconomists as well. Economists should not necessarily resist such tendencies. Land has long been a complicating factor in economic analysis, but it is important that its role be understood in the context of actual situations and the social problems of concern at the time. When viewed in this way, it can become a source of breadth and depth for both economists and economic doctrine.

References

Antweiler, Werner, and D. Trefler. (2002). Increasing Returns and All That: A View from Trade. *American Economic Review* 92(1): 93–119.

Arrow, Kenneth J., et al. (2004). Are We Consuming Too Much? *Journal of Economic Perspectives.*

Braunworth, William S. Jr., T. Welch, and R. Hathaway. (2002). *Water Allocations in the Klamath Reclamation Project, 2001: An Assessment of Natural Resource, Economic, Social and Institutional Issues With a Focus On the Upper Klamath Basin.* Oregon State University Extension Service, Special Report 1037. December.

Bromley, Daniel W. (1990). The Ideology of Efficiency: Searching for a Theory of Policy Analysis. *Journal of Environmental Economics and Management* 19(1): 86–107.

Bromley, Daniel W. (1997). Rethinking Markets. *American Journal of Agricultural Economics* 79(5): 1383–1393.

Bromley, Daniel W. (2000). Property Regimes and Pricing Regimes Water Resource Management. In *The Political Economy of Water Pricing Reforms,* edited by A. Dinar. New York: Oxford University Press, Chapter 2.

Caldwell, B. J. (1982). *Beyond Positivism: Economic Methodology in the Twentieth Century.* Boston: George Allen and Unwin.

Castle, E. N. (2002). Social Capital: An Interdisciplinary Concept. *Rural Sociology* 67(3): 331–349.

Castle, E., M. Kelso, J. Stevens, and H. Stoevener. (1981). Part III. Natural Resource Economics, 1946–75 in *A Survey of Agricultural Economics Literature,* edited by L. Martin. Minneapolis: University of Minnesota Press, Volume III, pp. 394–406.

Castle, E. and B. A. Weber. (2002). *Policy and Place: Requirements of a Successful Place-Based Policy.* Rural Public Policy Research Institute, Institute Symposium. Rural Matters: Making Place and Culture Count. October 16–18, 2002, Nebraska City, NE.

Coleman, J. S. (1990). *Foundations of Social Theory.* Cambridge, MA: Harvard University Press.

Crosson, P. R. (1982). *The Cropland Crisis: Myth or Reality?* Baltimore, MD: Johns Hopkins Press for Resources for the Future, Inc.

Dinar, A. (2000). *The Political Economy of Water Pricing Reforms.* New York: Oxford University Press.

Garreau, J. (1998). Edge Cities. *Landscape Architecture* 78(8): 51–52.

Gowdy, John M. (2004). The Revolution in Welfare Economics and Its Implications for Environmental Valuation and Policy. *Land Economics* 80(2): 239–257.

Heady, E. O. (1952). *The Economics of Agricultural Production and Resource Use.* Englewood Cliffs, NJ: Prentice-Hall.

Hicks, J. R. (1939). *Value and Capital.* Oxford: Clarendon Press.

Hite, J. C. (1997). The Thunen Model and the New Economic Geography as a Paradigm for Rural Development Policy. *Review of Agricultural Economics* 19(2): 230–240.

Hite, J. C. (1999). Rural Development, the Thunen Paradigm and the Death of Distance: Does Space Still Matter? Page 11 in *Conceptual Foundations of Economic Research in Rural Studies: A Proceedings.* National Rural Studies Committee Western Rural Development Center. Corvallis, Oregon State University.

Hite, J. C., Emily J. Terrill, and Kang Shou Lu. (1998). Land Prices and the Changing Geography of Southern Agriculture. Southern Rural Development Center, Mississippi State, Mississippi.

Katz, B. and J. Bradley. (1999). Divided We Sprawl. *Atlantic Monthly* (December): 28–37.

Kilkenny, M. (1998a). Transport Costs and Rural Development. *Journal of Regional Science* 38(2): 293–312.

Kilkenny, M. (1998b). Transport Costs, the New Economic Geography, and Rural Development. *Growth and Change* 29(3): 259–280.

Knight F. (1921). *Risk, Uncertainty, and Profit.* Boston: Houston Mifflin.

Krugman, Paul. (1991). *Geography and Trade.* Cambridge, MA: MIT Press.

Krugman, Paul. (1995). *Development, Geography, and Economic Theory.* Cambridge, MA: MIT Press.

Lewis, P. (1995). The Urban Invasion of Rural America: The Emergence of the Galactic City. In *The Changing American Countryside: Rural People and Places,* edited by E. N. Castle. Lawrence, KS: University Press of Kansas, 39–62.

Lind, R. C. (1999). Analysis for Intergenerational Decision-Making. In *Discounting and Intergenerational Equity,* edited by P. R. Portney and J. P. Weyant. Washington, DC: Resources for the Future, 173–180.

Marshall, A. (1920). *Principles of Economics: An Introductory Volume.* 8th edition. London: Macmillan.

Nordhaus, W. D. (1999). Discounting and Public Policies that Affect the Distant Future. In *Discounting and Intergenerational Equity,* edited by P. R. Portney and J. P. Weyant. Washington, DC: Resources for the Future, 145–162.

North, D. (1990). *Institutions, Institutional Change, and Economic Performance.* Cambridge UK: Cambridge University Press.

Page, T. (1988). Intergenerational Equity and the Social Discount Rate. In *Environmental Resources and Applied Welfare Economics,* edited by V. K. Smith. Washington, DC: Resources for the Future, 71–89.

Putnam, R. (1995). Bowling Alone: The Strange Disappearance of Civic America. *Journal of Democracy* 6: 65–78.

Rausser, Gordon C. (2000). Collective Choice in Water Resource Systems. In *The Political Economy of Water Pricing Reforms,* edited by A. Dinar. New York: Oxford University Press, Chapter 3.

Rutherford, M. (1994). *Institutions in Economics: the Old and the New Institutionalism.* New York: Cambridge University Press.

Samuelson, Paul A. (2004). Where Ricardo and Mill Rebut and Confirm Arguments of Mainstream Economists Supporting Globalization. *Journal of Economic Perspectives* 18(3): 135–146.

Schultz, T. (1951). Declining Importance of Agricultural Land. *Economic Journal* 61(December): 725–40.

Senior, N. W. (1836) (reprinted 1965). *An Outline of the Science of Political Economy.* New York: Kelly Reprints.

Smith, A. (1776) (reprinted 1937). *An Inquiry into the Nature and Causes of the Wealth of Nations,* edited by E. Cannon. New York: The Modern Library.

Sobel, J. (2002). Can We Trust Social Capital? *Journal of Economic Literature* 40(1): 139–154.

Vanberg, V. J. (2004). The Rationality Postulate In Economics: Its Ambiguity, Its Deficiency, and Its Evolutionary Alternatives. *Journal of Economic Methodology* 11(1): 1–29.

Vatn, A., and D. Bromley. (1994). Choices without Prices without Apologies. *Journal of Environmental Economics and Management* 26(2): 129–148.

Woolcock, M. (1997). Social Capital and Economic Development: Toward a Theoretical Synthesis and Policy Framework. *Theory and Society* 27(2): 151–208.

Wu, J.-J. (2001). Environmental Amenities and the Spatial Pattern of Urban Sprawl. *American Journal of Agricultural Economics* 83(5): 691–697.

Wu, J.-J., and A. J. Plantinga. (2002). The Influence of Public Open Space on Urban Spatial Structure. *Journal of Environmental Economics and Management* 46(2): 288–309.

2

Property Rights and Land Use Conflicts

Reconciling Myth and Reality

Daniel W. Bromley

A number of economists have recently become interested in the legal issues that attend land use matters, with particular reference to the Fifth Amendment's "takings clause" and financial compensation to landowners for regulatory actions that redefine their choice sets, or fields of action. Examples of this work include Fischel (1995), Innes (1997), Knetsch (1983), and Miceli and Segerson (1996). In much of the writing on land use matters, economists have focused on the incentive effects—the efficiency properties—that attend land use conflicts. It is common in this work to see reference not to legal scholars, but to other economists who, in their tendentious treatment of property rights, betray their own confusion about the core ideas of rights, property, and property rights (Barzel 1989; Coase 1960; Demsetz 1967). That is, the concepts and accounts invoked in this literature are usually at odds with the law as it plays out in the legislature and courts (Samuels 1989). As a result of this conceptual confusion, several legal scholars recently admonished economists to take greater care to incorporate well-established legal scholarship into their work and use concepts and terminology in a way that is consistent with existing legal traditions (Cole and Grossman 2002). In other words, if economists are going to incorporate the law into their work, they would be well advised to draw on legal scholarship, not on other economists who have it wrong.

One example of conceptual confusion is found in two reliable yet false presumptions: that property rights in land are clear and unchanging, and that if currently permissible land use activities are suddenly altered by government regulations, then compensation for the aggrieved owners must be forthcoming. These two presumptions do not flow from a careful reading of legal history—or of the case law on property disputes (Becker 1977; Bromley 1991, 1993, 1997a; Christman 1994). Instead, they are brought into the analysis by the demands of economic theory: if economic agents are to be able to maximize income (or utility), they must have clear and secure property rights over all valuable objects deployed in that activity. In addition, if the plans of economic agents are foiled by government "interference"—zoning, new restrictions on draining wetlands, restrictions on timber harvesting under the Endangered Species Act—then compensation is said to be necessary to mitigate the whims of government getting in the way of "the market." In other words, economists appear to want property rights to be clear and durable because those are precisely the conditions that conduce efficiency as they reckon that idea. And they want regulatory interventions to be compensated because such unforeseen changes in economic circumstances hold both efficiency and equity implications. Such conditions often bear little relation to the reality of property law out on the ground. It is here that many economists will denounce the inefficiency of new rules pertaining to land use. These new rules, it is often said, interfere with some vague yet certain thing called property rights.

Curiously, these denunciations of collective action in the legislatures and courts overlook the crippling fact that efficiency judgments of alternative institutional arrangements are inherently self-referential and thus circular (Bromley 1990; Chipman and Moore 1978; Field 1979, 1981; Graaff 1957; Little 1950; Mishan 1969, 1980). Institutions—the legal rules of an economy—determine what is (must be) recorded as a cost (expense) or a benefit (profit). If polluters are free to discharge their wastes into the air or a nearby river, then they have no need to enter waste disposal costs on their books. As long as it is legal to shift those costs to others, it appears to be efficient for firms to ignore such costs, termed externalities. These constitute a major, though contested, tradition within economics (Dahlman 1979; Vatn and Bromley 1997). Any calculation of, and judgment concerning, efficiency is necessarily predicated upon the institutional structure that indicates which costs must be accounted for—and by whom. Moreover, any explanation of institutions and efficiency must be grounded upon the two fundamental theorems of welfare economics.

The first theorem, the "direct" theorem, tells us that in the absence of external effects, every competitive market equilibrium is Pareto optimal; that is, it would be impossible to make one person better off without, at the same time, making at least one other person worse off. The second theorem, the "indirect" theorem, holds that starting from any particular institutional setup (the working rules) and wealth endowments, every Pareto optimal state is a competitive equilibrium. The first theorem is a ratification of the idea of competitive markets that economists find particularly endearing. The second is more encompassing: it tells us that any initial wealth endowment and rule structure will result in a Pareto optimal state as long as competitive markets are the means whereby trades are negotiated. Indeed, as Sen (1993) has remarked, the second welfare theorem might well comprise the essence of the "Revolutionary's Handbook." That is, for any particular structure of institutions (property rights) and endowments, competitive markets will yield a Pareto optimal outcome. And because each of the infinitely many institutional arrangements can produce optimal outcomes, the decision on which particular structure to adopt cannot be decided on economic grounds. It is here that confusion exists in the economics literature between efficiency and productivity (Saraydar 1989).

It is common to see economists suggest that new property rights arrangements with respect to land are, or ought to be, the outcome of consensual bargaining among political and economic agents (Buchanan 1972; Coase 1960). According to this line of argument, those institutions (rules) emerge that will yield the greatest benefit stream in the future (Demsetz 1967; North 1990). Demsetz insists that property rights emerge to internalize externalities—as if polluters and victims of pollution actually ought to sit down and negotiate who gets to harm whom. Although such stories make charming examples in undergraduate textbooks, it is silly to suppose that this is how property rights evolve in the real world. And it is naïve, not to mention a strong moral assertion, to insist that this is how institutional change ought to emerge. The competition model regards institutional change—new legal rules over acceptable and unacceptable land uses—as the inevitable outcome of a bargaining process among the potential gainers and losers of that institutional change. Those who gained had more "power," and those who lost had less. In addition to the circularity, the collective authority—the state—is absent in this model, appearing only at the end to ratify the outcome resulting from the interaction of differentially powerful bargaining entities.

To pursue this approach is not to offer a theory, but is instead a mere rationalization or apologia for the use of marketlike processes in the realm of legal relations. In fact, the state is necessarily at the center of new institutional arrangements. Power is the capacity of one party in a dispute to put another party in an unfavorable and unwanted legal situation (Bromley 1989). There is only one way to do that: one party is able to enlist the collective authority of the state to force an unwanted institutional arrangement upon an unwilling party. Just as changes in ownership of future benefit streams in a market require the presence of the state to ratify those new arrangements, changes in legal standing among contending parties in land use conflicts require the presence of the state to formulate, implement, and then agree to enforce those new legal relations. The state is a necessary party to every legal transaction for the simple reason that it is the collective authority that is called upon to enforce new legal arrangements. And it is the state that necessarily enters—via the courts and legislature—into any dispute between citizens.

The central issue here concerns how economists choose to approach the analysis of new legal arrangements. That approach invariably entails an appeal to the market as the guiding metaphor, and it uses marketlike outcomes as the truth rule by which institutional change is to be judged efficient or otherwise (Bromley 1997b). Unfortunately, these are mere stories wishing to become theories (Bromley 1990). They cannot because they seek to explain institutional change by appeal to rational choice models whose raison d'être is to understand and explain individual behavior undertaken within specific rule structures (institutions). If one seeks to explain collective action from the perspective of methodological individualism, then failure is the only possible outcome. Institutions, because they are the product of collective action in the legislature and courts to liberate and restrain individual action, cannot possibly emerge from marketlike competition or bargaining.

The next section considers an alternative account of how property rights emerge, evolve, and undergo change when new settings and circumstances arise. It requires abandoning the flawed heuristic of modern welfare economics and embracing instead a new way of producing plausible belief.

Property Rights in America: The Durable Myth

John Locke plays a central role in the American idea of property rights. Locke's story starts from a mythical state of nature in which a beneficent God directs man to take dominion over land by mixing his labor with it (Krueckeberg 1999). Once this has been done, it is then necessary to bestow permanence of control over the thing labored on. It is here that the idea of ownership emerges. Locke and his followers insist that the essential purpose of the state is to protect those who have labored as God commanded, and thereby bestow on others the beneficial effects arising from this class of hardworking citizens. The state is thus obligated to protect those who now hold property. If one acquires land in the Lockean way, then one says it has been justly acquired, and its continued holding is justified on moral grounds. Equally important, it is justified on prudential grounds, as the effect of individuals holding land is the production of benefits to the community at large.

But history reveals that there must always be a balance between the interests of the individual owner and what serves the community at large. To quote the British historian R.H. Tawney (1981):

> Property was to be an aid to creative work, not an alternative to it. . . . The law of the village bound the peasant to use his land, not as he himself might find most profitable, but to grow the corn the village needed. . . . Property reposed in short, not merely upon convenience, or the appetite for gain, but on a moral principle. It was protected not only for the sake of those who owned, but for the sake of those who worked and of those for whom their work provided. It was protected, because, without security for property, wealth could not be produced or the business of society carried on. (*139*)

Locke recognized that as people filled the earth, and as less and less of God's Commons was available for free expropriation, a certain inconvenience would arise. As Locke put the matter, his theory of justified acquisition and subsequent justified holding worked only so long as there was "enough and as good" for others. This Lockean proviso brings us to Immanuel Kant, who noted that rights are not tangible empirical realities; rather, they are noumena, things that cannot be apprehended by the senses but are knowable only by reason.

The essence of property rights is the necessarily correlated idea of inclusion and exclusion. To be an owner is to have the capacity—backed up by the coercive authority of the state—to exclude others. That is, the state stands ready to enforce the exclusion of nonowners. This idea of inclusion and exclusion is found in the ability of an individual—the owner—to make conceptually and legally internal that which is physically external. Kant asked what conditions were necessary in order that an individual might be able to make internal something that is, by its very nature, external (Williams 1977). The key idea here is one of belonging to; something external to an individual is made internal by understanding this concept. How is it decided that something physically external suddenly belongs to an individual? What mental processes are required to make something internal to an individual that is physically external?

In the Lockean sense, an individual may quite easily declare that some particular object belongs to him or her. This is a claim against all others to whom the object or situation might otherwise belong. It is a declaration of exclusivity against all others; by dint of unilateral proclamation, an object now becomes internal to the speaker. Kant recognized that such claims represent negations of the interests of others within the same community—indeed, of all others in the world. He suggested that although one individual may announce and display physical possession of something external, this was not the same as having the socially sanctioned authority to make that declaration binding on others who might wish to make internal that same thing. That is, unless others to whom the possessor directs his or her assertion are predisposed to respect those claims, the situation is unstable and therefore cannot settle the matter once and for all. Kant insisted that it is only from the consent of others that one can make internal that which is clearly external. For if that external thing can belong to anyone within the community, what mental work is required that will allow it to become internal, or belong, to any particular member of that community? Why should others willingly accept binding duties on nothing more compelling than the self-serving assertions of those already in possession of something of value to others?

Kant's position is that such assertions are nothing but the affirmation of empirical possession. And by being based on mere possession, they confuse physical control with something much more profound: what Kant called intelligible possession. We see this at work when a community of sentient beings reaches agreement that indeed it is both right (moral) and good (prudential) that someone among them should be able to make internal something that has hitherto been external. On this account, what is mine depends not on what I say about its being mine, but on the assertions of all others who, by their declaration, acquiesce in their own disenfranchisement from the benefits associated with that object or circumstance. Others grant me *possessio noumenon*—I cannot take it for myself.

Locke gave us a basis for justified acquisition and holding of land as long as there is "enough and as good" for others. But he stopped short of a complete theory of what is to be done when there is *not* enough and as good for others. That is, Locke developed a theory of acquisition and holding that works best when it is needed least. It is here that Kant insisted that the continued holding of land in the face of scarcity requires something very special. For scarcity raises the specter of deprivation and exclusion if Lockean acquisition and holding works against the interests of others in the community who, by virtue of coming late, find that all of God's Commons has already been justly acquired. How can we justify holding of land once there is no more of it to be justly acquired?

Lockeans have an answer to this question: let the latecomers buy it from those who have justly acquired it or previously purchased it. Once the initial acquisition has been transferred to another for a price, the logic seems compelling and without end: all future acquisitions must be mediated by due consideration to the existing holder of land. And what is transferred in this way is, and must be, precisely what earlier acquirers obtained. Just acquisition and holding continues in perpetuity.

This seeming escape from the grips of scarcity leaves one fundamental issue still to be addressed: What if the current holding results in land use practices that, in time, are found to be neither moral nor prudential? Given this possibility, on what grounds can payment then be justified in order to induce the current holders to stop using their land in an antisocial manner? What is to preclude holders of land from engaging in social extortion? Land justly acquired may evolve into land unjustly held, where its current use is no longer moral or prudential. Here Locke joins Kant in admitting that under certain circumstances, the presumed beneficial link between acquisition and holding might be severed.

Locke presumed that land justly acquired would be used in a manner that redounded to the benefit of the entire community, and that was part of the justification for its acquisition and continued holding. Indeed, that has been the one durable idea behind the social grant of exclusive control over something as scarce and as essential to human survival as land. But what if this is not the case? Kant answered with the proposition that the community itself must determine whether land justly acquired remains justly held. How is this done? It is accomplished through reason emerging from a *burgerliche gesellschaft*—a civil society. In other words, it is the community itself that sets the standards by which continued holding of justly acquired land, or property, remains justified. If this is the case, then the security and timeless stability of the idea of property rights are suddenly undermined. How is it possible that something as foundational as property rights can rest on nothing more solid than the whims of an entire community?

We are, it would seem, in need of a new theory of holding that takes into consideration difficult decisions about just and prudential holdings into the future. In more practical terms, this alternative theory must address the issue of what to do when extant holdings are found to warrant just attenuation—and then under what circumstances, if any, compensation for that attenuation must be forthcoming from the public purse. Must payment using public funds always be forthcoming for this attenuation? This is the "takings" question. Can the government, acting as an agent for those whose interests are contravened by the actions of a landowner, prevent those actions? And if so, must the owner be compensated from the public treasury for this new inability?

It is here that economists will show an interest in discerning whether regulations are efficient, seek to discover the optimal regulation of land use practices, or assess the efficiency properties of various approaches to the "takings" question. These are the wrong questions to ask, however, if one is seeking clarity about property rights and land use conflicts. Something more profound is required.

Escaping Welfarism: Entertaining Volitional Pragmatism

"Outcomes of *available* actions are not ascertained but created. We are not speaking . . . of the objective recorded outcomes of actions which have been performed. Those actions are not 'available.' An action which can still be chosen or rejected *has no objective outcome.* The only kind of outcome which it can have exists in the imagination of the decision-maker." (Shackle 1961, *143*)

If economists are to develop a plausible theory of property rights in American legal practice, they first must abandon deduction and the flawed prescriptions of Paretian welfarism. Deduction is faulty because it starts from incorrigible presumptions about human behavior (the familiar axioms of neoclassical economics) and anchors all explanation on those durable, though contested, "truths." The alternative epistemological program is abduction, a class of inference that yields explanatory hypotheses for, or explanations of, observed phenomena. In contrast to deduction, abduction is not the result of the application of axioms, assumptions, and applicability postulates to produce a theory. Instead, abduction starts with specific empirical circumstances and then deploys particular axioms, assumptions, and applicability postulates to produce explanatory propositions (testable hypotheses) about the observed phenomena. These propositions might then come to constitute a theory of the nature and content of the thing under scrutiny. Abduction is the method of explanation deployed by natural scientists as they search for explanations of observed phenomena (Peirce 1934). Some philosophers prefer to call it diagnosis, and it is indeed the diagnostic process that those engage in whose task it is to explain known empirical phenomena, be they physicians, automobile mechanics contemplating an engine that will not start, or pathologists who perform autopsies (Bromley 2006).

In the realm of land use conflicts, the deductivist would start with some axiomatic idea of property rights and then be inclined to ask whether this particular court protects or fails to protect property rights. The deductivist next would invoke particular hypotheses that will render a tentative answer to that question, or the deductivist may ask a somewhat subtler question: What is the position of this particular court with respect to property rights? Both of these questions start with a prior idea of the nature of property rights, and in each case the investigator seeks to answer the question by reading carefully and analyzing particular legal decisions concerning land use conflicts.

The abductivist would find these questions seriously flawed, because they presume the prior nature and scope of something (property rights) that is the very idea requiring explanation. That is, they presume some tangible and knowable thing (property rights) that is immediately and unmistakably identifiable—and for which a clear answer is possible concerning whether they are protected by particular courts. It is akin to asking a three-year-old if she is telling the truth.

The epistemology of the abductivist is more promising. For instance, the abductivist could observe that a number of Supreme Court decisions over the past 60 to 80 years seem to hold quite different implications for the a priori idea of property rights. These cases—the empirical phenomena requiring explanation—might include a few classic ones of recent memory: *Euclid v. Ambler Realty, Teleprompter Co. v. Loretto, Hadachek v. Sebastian, Mugler v. Kansas, Penn Central Transportation Co. v. New York City, Agins v. City of Tiburon, Lucas v. South Carolina Coastal Council, Keystone Bituminous Coal Association v. deBenedictis, Nollan v. California Coastal Commission, Pennsylvania Coal Co. v. Mahon, Palazzolo v. State of Rhode Island,* and *Tahoe-Sierra Preservation Council v. Tahoe Regional Planning Agency.* To the deductivist, the findings in these cases appear idiosyncratic and without logical coherence. Indeed, these cases provide the grist for a number of exegetical law review articles in search of some unifying explanatory thread. The deductivist feels certain that the Supreme Court must have some guiding principles by which it resolves property rights disputes, that there must be durable legal doctrines that inform decisions in such important cases. From the empirical record of the above cases, it would be quite impossible for the deductivist to advance a plausible theory of property rights in America. The only conclusion possible from this empirical account is that no conclusion can be drawn as to whether property rights are more or less protected than previously. The deductivist has reached a dead end because the inquiry began in the wrong place.

The abductivist, on the other hand, would not be deterred by the confounding reality of these cases, but would use this richness as the starting point for working out a theory of property rights (Bromley 2006). That is, these cases and their findings are the very reality that requires an explanation. And a plausible one exists for these disparate decisions by the Supreme Court.

The only way to come to grips with the idea of property rights in the American experience is to understand that this term is merely the benediction applied to those settings and circumstances that, when the dust of consideration by various levels of jurisprudence has finally settled, are found worthy of protection by the state. The concept of property rights is not something known axiomatically, something whose essence is clear by intuition or introspection before a particular legal struggle is joined. Rather, the idea of property rights is arrived at—created—in the process of resolving mutually exclusive rights claims before the court. Property rights are not a priori "essences" that exist and await mere discovery in a particular legal scuffle. Rather, they are constructed in the process of resolving disputes originating in conflicting claims brought before the courts. This means that the American judicial system does not seek to discover where the a priori property right lies. It means, instead, that courts offer a necessary forum before which conflicting and mutually exclusive rights claims will be brought. When the more compelling claim has been determined, the courts will issue a decree to that effect. Efficiency calculations so familiar to the economist are sometimes informative in this construction project, but never decisive. The courts seek to avoid absurdly costly solutions to land use problems, and this concern is simply a reflection of the necessary common-sense balancing that goes on in daily life. It is the application of mature reason to difficult choices, but it is most assuredly not an exercise in Paretian welfare economics.

Property rights are made (created), not found (discovered). Richard Posner (2003), the distinguished legal scholar and judge of the U.S. Court of Appeals for the Seventh Circuit, argues that when disputes come to the courts, judges first seek to formulate rules that will guide similar conflicts in the future. Once those rules for the future have been worked out, they are applied to the contested situation currently before the courts. This is an exercise in volitional pragmatism—judges and juries looking to the future and figuring out how it should unfold (Bromley 2006).

This follows necessarily from the meaning of "right." To have a right signifies that one has been granted the ability to compel the coercive power of the state to come to one's assistance against the contrary claims of others. Rights enable an individual to enlist the wondrous powers of the state as a special ally. The granting of a right by the state (and the courts are but the final arbiters of state action) does not imply passive support. Rather, it bestows active assistance for those granted the status of a right. That is, the state stands ready to be enlisted in the cause of those to whom it has granted rights. Rights expand the capacities of the individual by indicating what one can do with the aid of the collective power (Bromley 2006).

Property is not an object, but a value. When one buys a piece of land (in the vernacular, a piece of property), one acquires not merely some physical object, but rather control over a benefit stream arising from that setting and circumstance that runs into the future. That is why one spends money—one benefit stream—in order to acquire a different benefit stream, a new one arising from the fact of ownership. The magnitude of that new benefit stream is a function of the legal parameters associated with it: Can one build a tall office tower on it or a mere bungalow? Is it now covered by water six months out of the year, and if so, will local ordinances allow it to be drained for some "higher," more remunerative use? The price paid to acquire that new benefit stream is none other than the expected discounted present value of all future net income appropriable from owning the thing. This is why property is the value, not the object. And we put together two concepts—property and right—to arrive at the understanding that this pertains to the grant of authority by the state to a person now called an owner. That authority promises that the state is a willing participant in the imposition of binding duties on all those in the class of individuals called nonowner.

I insisted above that the courts create property rights out of the disputes that come before them. This act of creation stands in contrast to the idea that the courts discover property rights as they confront conflicting rights claims. And it assuredly contradicts the notion among many economists that property rights are some known and fixed a priori essence that simply awaits discovery. But perhaps clarification is called for when I assert that courts create property rights. Here I draw on Louis Menand's book *The Metaphysical Club* (2001). Menand's subject concerns the origins of pragmatic philosophy in America. Central players in this story include William James, John Dewey, Oliver Wendell Holmes, and Charles Sanders Peirce. Holmes turned out to be one of the most celebrated of American legal theorists. Menand writes, "It was Holmes's genius as a philosopher to see that the law has no essential aspect."

Menand notes that Holmes's famous book *The Common Law* (1881) was intended to trace and explain the evolution of legal doctrine. More important, the book is an attempt to elaborate and expound on the remark that Holmes had made in his first law review article in 1870 that "it is the merit of the common law that it decides the case first, and determines the principle afterwards." This is a paradox. If legal principles do not decide cases, what does? Holmes's answer, which Menand conveys as follows, provides the basis of all his subsequent jurisprudence:

A case comes to court as a unique fact situation. It immediately enters a kind of vortex of discursive imperatives. There is the imperative to find the just result in this particular case. There is the imperative to find the result that will be consistent with the results reached in analogous cases in the past. There is the imperative to find the result that, generalized across many similar cases, will be most beneficial to society as a whole—the result that will send the most useful behavioral message. There are also, though less explicitly acknowledged, the desire to secure the outcome most congenial to the judge's own political politics; the desire to use the case to bend legal doctrine so that it will conform better with changes in social standards and conditions; and the desire to punish the wicked and excuse the good, and to redistribute costs from parties who can't afford them (like accident victims) to parties who can (like manufacturers and insurance companies).

Hovering over this whole unpredictable weather pattern—all of which is already in motion, as it were, before the particular case at hand ever arises—is a single metaimperative: not to let it appear as though any one of these lesser imperatives has decided the case at the blatant expense of the others. A result that seems just intuitively but is admittedly incompatible with legal precedent is taboo; so is a result that is formally consistent with precedent but appears unjust on its face (Menand 2001, *340*).

Volitional pragmatism is the core idea of American jurisprudence, and it offers a theory that is not only of general jurisprudence, but also particularly apt to land use conflicts charged with figuring out where the most compelling (not necessarily correct or efficient) property interests lie. The problem here is to blend moral and prudential arguments in search of the best thing to do. That best thing will constitute the "truth" in that particular setting. In fact, we may say that truth is merely that which it is better, at the moment, to believe. Or, as William James would put the matter, truth happens to an idea. Specifically, truth is the compliment we pay to our settled deliberations concerning a specific matter (Bromley 2006).

Conclusions

The land use conflicts of interest to applied economists can be several. Perhaps a community wishes to establish a policy on teardowns and the spread of so-called McMansions. Maybe it wants to stop the spread of suburbs into green space now occupied by agriculture or open–space, halt the destruction of trees on private property, or control the kinds of landscaping acceptable for houses and commercial buildings. Perhaps a jurisdiction, say a state, wishes to regulate the draining of wetlands no longer protected under federal law by the Clean Water Act.

Each of these actions assuredly will alert those who somehow imagine that landowners are the final judges of what uses may be made of private land, and with that myth in mind, these same individuals will demand financial compensation for landowners faced with newly restricted land use options. The reality of American jurisprudence is quite clear: the courts will sanction such actions if the proposed restriction will enhance the general well-being of the community as articulated in some process by that community. Notice here the connection between democratic processes and community articulation of a particular vision for the future. This is not an exercise in benefit–cost analysis as applied economists understand that idea. It is, instead, recognition of the need and desire for the nation–state or local communities to adjust accepted land use practices to new priorities, tastes and preferences, and threats to desired futures.

These desired futures are created out of a process of the human will in action, looking to the future and deciding how we wish that future to unfold for us (Bromley 2006). Landowners viewing this process may regard themselves as victimized by the shifting whims of public sentiment about the purposes of nature. Aren't wetlands for draining so that crops might be planted or some commercial development undertaken? Aren't forests for the production of harvestable timber? Aren't rivers for damming to control floods and generate electricity? They are not—not anymore—and it is increasingly unlikely that landowners will be able to manufacture plausible claims for compensation ("takings") in the future when their plans and schemes are disallowed by local planning bodies or state legislatures.

Public policy is simply collective action in liberation, restraint, and expansion of individual action. That collective action in America occurs in the legislature and courts. And as collective ideas about what seems better to do with land and related assets continues to evolve, the courts will be less and less likely to order the expenditure of tax receipts to compensate private landowners who appear to be slow learners. John R. Commons (1931, 1968) would call this reasonable valuing. Pragmatists would call it new settled belief. The general public, whose taxes stand exposed to the predations of those who still wish to defy evolving social norms about land use practices, would call it good old common sense. And truth is just common sense clarified.

References

Barzel, Y. (1989). *Economic Analysis of Property Rights.* Cambridge: Cambridge University Press.

Becker, L. C. (1977). *Property Rights.* London: Routledge and Kegan Paul.

Bromley, D. W. (1989). *Economic Interests and Institutions: The Conceptual Foundations of Public Policy.* Oxford: Blackwell.

———. (1990). The Ideology of Efficiency: Searching for a Theory of Policy Analysis. *Journal of Environmental Economics and Management* 19(1): 86–107.

————. (1991). *Environment and Economy: Property Rights and Public Policy.* Oxford: Blackwell.

————. (1993). Regulatory Takings: Coherent Concept or Logical Contradiction? *Vermont Law Review* 17(3): 647–82.

————. (1997a). Constitutional Political Economy: Property Claims in a Dynamic World. *Contemporary Economic Policy* 15(4): 43–54.

————. (1997b). Rethinking Markets. *American Journal of Agricultural Economics* 79(5): 1383–93.

————. (2006). *Sufficient Reason: Volitional Pragmatism and the Meaning of Economic Institutions.* Princeton: Princeton University Press.

Buchanan, J. M. (1972). Politics, Property, and the Law: An Alternative Interpretation of *Miller et al. v. Schoene. Journal of Law and Economics* 15(October): 439–52.

Chipman, J. S., and J. C. Moore. (1978). The New Welfare Economics: 1939–1974. *International Economic Review* 19(3): 547–84.

Christman, J. (1994). *The Myth of Property.* Oxford: Oxford University Press.

Coase, R. (1960). The Problem of Social Cost. *Journal of Law and Economics* 3: 1–44.

Cole, D., and P. Grossman. (2002). The Meaning of Property Rights: Law vs. Economics. *Land Economics* 78(3): 317–30.

Commons, J. R. (1931). Institutional Economics. *American Economic Review* 21(December): 648–57.

————. (1968). *Legal Foundations of Capitalism.* Madison: University of Wisconsin Press.

Dahlman, C. J. (1979). The Problem of Externality. *Journal of Law and Economics* 22(April): 141–162.

Demsetz, H. (1967). Toward a Theory of Property Rights. *American Economic Review* 57(2): 347–59.

Field, A. J. (1979). On the Explanation of Rules Using Rational Choice Models. *Journal of Economic Issues* 13(March): 49–72.

————. (1981). The Problem with Neoclassical Institutional Economics: A Critique with Special Reference to the North/Thomas Model of Pre-1500 Europe. *Explorations in Economic History* 18: 174–98.

Fischel, W. A. (1995). *Regulatory Takings: Law, Economics, and Politics.* Cambridge, MA: Harvard University Press.

Graaff, J. de V. (1957). *Theoretical Welfare Economics.* Cambridge: Cambridge University Press.

Innes, R. (1997). Takings, Compensation and Equal Treatment for Owners of Developed and Undeveloped Property. *Journal of Law and Economics* 40(October): 403–432.

Knetsch, J. L. (1983). *Property Rights and Compensation.* Toronto: Butterworths.

Krueckeberg, D. A. (1999). Private Property in Africa: Creation Stories of Economy, State, and Culture. *Journal of Planning Education and Research* 19(Winter): 176–182.

Little, I. M. D. (1950). *A Critique of Welfare Economics.* London: Oxford University Press.

Menand, L. (2001). *The Metaphysical Club.* New York: Farrar, Strauss, and Giroux.

Miceli, T. J., and K. Segerson. (1996). *Compensation for Regulatory Takings: An Economic Analysis.* Greenwich, CT: JAI Press.

Mishan, E. J. (1969). *Welfare Economics: An Assessment.* Amsterdam: North-Holland.

———. (1980). How Valid Are Economic Evaluations of Allocative Changes? *Journal of Economic Issues* 14(March): 143–161.

North, D. C. (1990). *Institutions, Institutional Change and Economic Performance.* Cambridge: Cambridge University Press.

Peirce, C. S. (1934). *Collected Papers* (Volume 5). Cambridge, MA: Harvard University Press.

Posner, R. A. (2003). *Law, Pragmatism, and Democracy.* Cambridge: Harvard University Press.

Samuels, W. J. (1989). The Legal-Economic Nexus. *George Washington Law Review* 57(6): 1556–78.

Saraydar, E. (1989). The Conflation of Productivity and Efficiency in Economics and Economic History. *Economics and Philosophy* 5(1): 55–67.

Sen, A. (1993). Markets and Freedoms: Achievements and Limitations of the Market Mechanism in Promoting Individual Freedoms. *Oxford Economic Papers* 45: 519–41.

Shackle, G. L. S. (1961). *Decision, Order, and Time in Human Affairs.* Cambridge: Cambridge University Press.

Tawney, R. H. (1981). Property and Creative Work. In *Property: Mainstream and Critical Positions*, edited by C. B. Macpherson. Toronto: University of Toronto Press, 135–51.

Vatn, A., and D. W. Bromley. (1997). Externalities: A Market Model Failure. *Environmental and Resource Economics* 9: 135–51.

Williams, H. (1977). Kant's Concept of Property. *Philosophical Quarterly* 27: 32–40.

PART II

Explaining Land Use Conversion: Spatial Perspectives

3

Forecasting Residential Land Use Change

Elena G. Irwin, Kathleen P. Bell, and
Jacqueline Geoghegan

O ver the last decade, growth management has gained increased prominence as a policy issue. Coverage of growth-management issues by the popular press (e.g., Lacayo 1999; Mitchell 2001) has risen substantially, and terms such as "sprawl" and "smart growth" have become household phrases. Citizen polls (e.g., Pew Center for Civic Journalism 2000) demonstrate concern over urban sprawl, and organizations representing the full spectrum of political beliefs have published reports commenting on growth management (e.g., Shaw and Utt 2000; Sierra Club 2000). In addition, this issue has surfaced at the ballot box. From 1997 to 2003, some 800 initiatives dealing with growth management and the preservation of open space appeared on local and state ballots across the nation, and about three-quarters of them passed. Together these initiatives committed approximately $24 billion to public land acquisition (Land Trust Alliance 2003).

Numerous state and local governments have recently advanced legislation to manage growth or reform land use planning. More than 2,000 land use bills were introduced into state legislatures between 1999 and 2001, with about 20 percent enacted into law (American Planning Association 2002; Frank 2000). Notable examples include the growth management and planning legislation adopted in Minnesota, New Jersey, Maryland, Pennsylvania, and Tennessee (Hirschhorn 2000).

Despite this rise in prominence, the public dialogue on growth management is rife with ambiguity and controversy. Framing it as a public policy issue has proven difficult for several reasons. First, growth pressures are difficult to measure rigorously, and measures appropriate for one region may not be suitable for others. Definitions of sprawl are typically vague and evasive. Some quantitative definitions, such as *USA Today*'s sprawl index, use population or housing density measures to describe this form of development, in which lower densities of development are interpreted as indicative of sprawl.

Similarly, growth-management policy tools are often complex and cumbersome. For example, "smart growth" (Benfield et al. 2001), which calls for targeting infrastructure projects in select growth areas, encouraging transit-oriented development, and preserving more green spaces via compact development, is not widely understood or easily defined. In addition, many communities and regions simply lack the data resources required to track growth and understand changes in development patterns. Although remotely sensed and geographical information system (GIS) land use and land cover data are becoming more common, few communities have established historical data resources that permit the documenting of changing land use patterns and assessment of growth-management strategies. Furthermore, understanding of the benefits and costs of alternative development patterns and the effectiveness of different growth-management tools is limited. As a result, public discussions of growth management are often one dimensional, with some groups focusing on costs and others on benefits.

Studies have addressed the public finance (e.g., cost of providing public services) and ecological impacts of alternative development patterns, emphasizing the divergence between private and social costs of individual development decisions. Several works have demonstrated that the costs are higher to service a more dispersed population than one that is more clustered because of the increased capital outlays necessary to reach a population that is more spread out (see Burchell et al. 1998). These studies have come under criticism, however (see Gordon and Richardson 1997; Shaw and Utt 2000) because of the range of costs considered and the assumptions made regarding behavioral differences across development types. Studies on the environmental impacts of alternative patterns of development also have produced mixed conclusions. For instance, changes in habitat under different patterns of development will favor some species and harm others. As better data resources become available, it is likely that our understanding of the linkages among development patterns and changes in the quality and quantity of habitat, as well as air and water pollution, will improve.

Finally, public discussions of growth management are affected by issues of governance. Because growth management is often a local government responsibility, discussions easily can become segmented and may overlook regional trends as well as interdependencies across jurisdictions. Numerous studies have called for greater consideration of the linkages among urban, suburban, and rural areas (Downs 1999; Katz and Bradley 1999; Orfield 1997; Rusk 1999).

As many local and state governments in the United States grapple with increasing growth pressures, the need to understand the economic and institutional factors that underlie these events has taken on added urgency. From an economic perspective, individual land use decisions play a central role in the manifestation of growth pressures. Changes in land use patterns are the cumulative result of numerous individual decisions regarding the use of lands. Accordingly, the study of land use change at the individual decision-maker scale provides a good opportunity to understand how policy decisions influence individual choices regarding land use and the cumulative impacts of these decisions on environmental, public finance, and growth-management outcomes.

In this chapter, we develop a spatially disaggregated, microeconomic model that examines how various growth-management policies have influenced individual land conversion decisions. We then consider how the baseline versus alternative policy scenarios influence changes in the aggregate pattern of urban land conversion. We believe that models such as the one described here offer great potential to contribute to the broader public discourse on growth management, because they consider how growth-management policies influence individual choices, and how these choices in turn determine land use patterns.

This spatially explicit model addresses the conversion of rural lands to residential use (residential land use change) at the rural-urban fringe, which begins where suburbs end and extends into rural areas. Here, changes in land use often coincide with transitions from traditional, rural communities to more developed, urban communities. Urban and suburban growth at the rural-urban fringe is of unique concern to citizens and policymakers alike, as these areas have outpaced urban and suburban areas in population growth for the last several decades (Daniels 1999; Nelson 1992).

We estimate the model using data on land conversion in Calvert County, Maryland. The pattern of land use change in what is one of the fastest-growing counties in Maryland is typical of urban growth occurring elsewhere in the United States at the rural-urban fringe. Such growth often involves the conversion of agricultural lands to residential use and features large-lot developments that comprise scattered single-family homes on parcels greater than 10 acres in size. Between 1980 and 2000, population approximately doubled in Calvert County, reaching almost 75,000. Associated with this population growth was an almost 200 percent increase in the number of acres in low-density residential use (see Figure 3-1).

This chapter takes a spatially disaggregated approach to modeling residential land use change that accounts for the spatial heterogeneity of policies (e.g., zoning) and landscape features (e.g., slope, soil type, locational amenities) influencing individual land use decisions. Our ability to address the spatial heterogeneity of the landscape over time is the direct result of having access

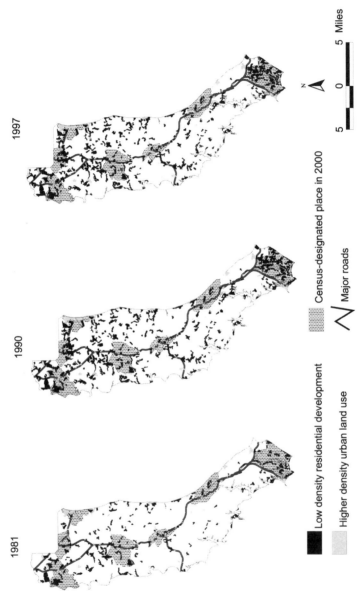

Figure 3-1. Changes in Urban Land Use Pattern, 1981–1997, Calvert County, MD

to parcel-level land use data. A duration modeling framework allows us to better capture how the cumulative effects of changes in variables over time influence future land use decisions and the timing of land conversion. The model developed here builds on other spatially explicit and disaggregate models of urban land use change, including work in California by Landis (1995) and Landis and Zhang (1998a, 1998b); and work in the central Maryland region by Bockstael and Bell (1998), Geoghegan and Bockstael (2000, 2002), and Irwin and Bockstael (2002, 2004).

Following the estimation of the empirical model of residential land use change, the parameter estimates are used to simulate future growth patterns under alternative policy scenarios. The objective of this predictive exercise is to assess the effectiveness of various strategies in reaching stated growth-management objectives. We do not address the economic efficiency of these alternative growth patterns. Rather, we assume that an important goal of growth management is to concentrate development in targeted growth areas and deflect it from rural areas. Taking this as the stated goal of local and state efforts, we then consider the actual effectiveness of policies that were designed to accomplish this goal in Calvert County, Maryland.

Next, we give a brief description of the economic model of individual land conversion decisions. (The full details and in-depth exposition of both the theoretical and empirical models used in this chapter can be found in Irwin and Bockstael 2002). A detailed discussion of the dependent and explanatory variables used in the statistical model follows. After providing a summary of the results of the statistical model, we examine the implications of these results for managing development patterns and look at the simulated impacts of several alternative policy scenarios.

The Economic Model

Consider the viewpoint of a profit-maximizing landowner who owns an undeveloped land parcel—which is either used for agriculture or another resource-producing activity, such as commercial forestry, or is in a natural state—and makes a discrete choice in every period regarding the parcel's subdivision for residential use. At the beginning of each time period, the individual landowner decides whether to convert the parcel to residential use, by subdividing it into multiple lots, or keep it in its current undeveloped state. Assuming that the landowner wants to maximize profits, he or she will choose to convert the parcel to residential use when the expected present discounted value of the parcel in residential use net of conversion costs and opportunity costs is greatest.

Given several simplifying assumptions regarding the future evolution of growth pressures and conversion costs, the optimal time for a parcel to be developed is when two conditions are met. The first is the intuitive decision rule that the net value of conversion should be positive: the one-time return from selling residential lots developed from the parcel, net of conversion costs, exceeds the present value of returns from the current nondeveloped use. The second considers that although the net returns could be positive in a particular time period, there may still be benefits to waiting because of the potential for even higher benefits at some future date. Therefore, the second decision rule for the optimal timing of development requires that there will be no further increases in the net present value of converting land if development is postponed.

These net returns to parcel conversion are hypothesized to be a function of a variety of parcel-level features, including physical variables that influence the parcel's expected returns in an agricultural use as well as the costs of conversion (e.g., soil type and slope), infrastructure variables that influence a parcel's value in residential use (e.g., public sewer access), locational features that are expected to influence the parcel's residential value (e.g., proximity to an urban center), and interdependencies among neighboring land use decisions (e.g., in the form of land use externalities).

Not all elements of the conversion decision are captured in these variables, however. Variation over parcels in the timing of development can be due to heterogeneity, not just among the parcels, but also among the landowners. This may affect individuals' willingness to sell land for development. For example, a farmer who is particularly good at what he or she does will be able to extract more profit from the land, all else equal. Another farmer nearer retirement may be more interested in liquidating his or her farming assets. An owner of undeveloped forestland may value it for recreational or aesthetic reasons. All these individual idiosyncrasies will induce a distribution of unobservable errors in the development decision. These factors may be very important, but they rarely are observed by researchers or the public sector, unless individual household survey data are accessible (as in Lynch and Lovell 2003), and therefore usually are included in the empirical model as a stochastic error term.

A variety of statistical methods can be used to empirically estimate this land use conversion decision rule, depending on the assumptions made about the behavior of certain variables as well as the structure of the error term. We opt to employ a duration model (also called a survival time or hazard model) because it is capable of describing both the temporal and spatial aspects of land conversion decisions. Duration models explicitly account for the timing of a qualitative change from one state to another and therefore are an appropriate way to capture the cumulative effects of explanatory variables on the probability of land conversion to residential use. Given the nature of land use changes in growing areas at the urban-rural fringe, in which the timing of the conversion is often of great interest, duration models offer an intuitively appealing approach.

These models typically estimate the conditional probability of exiting a state given that the state has been occupied for some length of time. The dependent variable, the duration, is the length of time that elapses from the beginning of the state until its end or until measurement is taken and therefore truncates the observation. Here we are interested in the change in state of land use, specifically, the timing of land conversion from an undeveloped to a residential state. We use the proportional hazards model (or Cox regression model) to estimate the land use conversion model (Allison 1995; Greene 2000). Intuitively, this specification estimates the effects of explanatory variables on the underlying survival time or "hazard" of conversion from undeveloped to residential use.

In Chapter 4, Templeton et al. examine the effects of taxation and zoning policies on the timing of land development using the same overall method to estimate the land conversion model. The models presented here and in Chapter 4 differ in their statistical assumptions and other details, however. Our proportional hazards model is a semiparametric model that makes no explicit assumption about the distribution of the error terms but does impose a relative restrictive assumption about the separability of the "baseline" hazard function. In comparison, the model estimated in Chapter 4 imposes a specific distributional assumption (the so-called Gumbel, or extreme value, distribution) but makes less restrictive assumptions concerning the functional form. The models are also somewhat different in their application: whereas Templeton et al. consider all types of urban conversion and focus on the effects of taxation and zoning, we look at the effects of a comprehensive set of growth management policies on residential land conversion specifically. Hence, the two chapters illustrate alternative ways that an otherwise similar methodology may be applied to forecast development under different policy scenarios.

Description of Data

The model is estimated using parcel-level land use change data from Calvert County, an urban-rural fringe area of southern Maryland about 50 miles from Washington, D.C., and Baltimore. Bounded by the Chesapeake Bay on the east and the Patuxent River on the west, Calvert County historically had been a rural and agricultural region. The county is approximately 219 square miles in area and has two incorporated towns—North Beach and Chesapeake Beach—and seven "town centers": Dunkirk, Owings, Huntingtown, Prince Frederick, St. Leonard, Lusby, and Solomons.

In 2000, county population was estimated to be 74,563. Calvert County had experienced a doubling in population between 1980 and 2000 and an even greater growth in low-density residential land use. The pace of growth and the type (large-lot subdivisions) are typical of urban-rural fringe areas in Maryland and other parts of the United States (Heimlich and Anderson 2001). Accordingly, this county is a logical area in which to examine urban growth at the urban-rural fringe. Although some attributes of the county's physical and political geography are specific to the case study, the goal of this chapter is to demonstrate the methods involved in the analysis. Given appropriate data, one easily can modify this modeling approach for other geographic regions.

Before giving the details of the explanatory variables and data resources employed in the empirical model, we need to describe the growth-management and land use planning policies that apply to land use decisions in Calvert County. The county-level scale of these policies is notable and distinguishes land use and growth management in this region from those in areas where subcounty units make such decisions.

The state of Maryland has responded to the sustained growth that it has experienced over the past several decades by passing a host of smart-growth policies. In 1992, the state passed the Maryland Economic Growth, Resource Protection, and Planning Act, which brought attention to the linkages between land use pattern and economic and ecological health. In 1997, it passed smart-growth legislation in the form of Senate Bill 389, which further documented these linkages and established a framework for the development of specific policies. A synopsis of the bill is as follows:

> ... establishing priority funding areas in the State so as to preserve exist-ing neighborhoods and agricultural, natural, and rural resources; pro-hibiting State agencies from approving specified projects that are not in priority funding areas; providing for specified exceptions; establishing a certification process for the designation of eligible priority funding ar-eas; requiring municipal corporations to adopt specified development standards and assist counties in the collection of fees to finance specified school construction; etc. (Maryland General Assembly, Senate 1997)

Because these policy initiatives have been in place for several years now, Maryland is an advantageous place to study the effects of such policies on land conversion patterns. We incorporate the impact of this legislation on residential land use change in Calvert County by explicitly considering the location of priority funding areas (PFAs), which are growth areas designated by each county to which the state directs support for infrastructure devel-opment. Further, we also consider the state objective of preserving agricul-tural, natural, and rural areas by explicitly considering lands designated as protected or critical areas or enrolled in agricultural preservation or rural legacy programs.

In addition to state-sponsored policies, land use decisions in Calvert County are also influenced by a host of county-level policies. In 1997, the county approved a revised comprehensive plan whose goals include "directing growth to suitable locations, promoting economic growth, and practicing stewardship of the Chesapeake Bay and the land" (Calvert County 1997, 2). To meet these goals, the comprehensive plan specifically notes the need to reduce the rate of residential growth and preserve prime farm, forest, and sensitive lands. The county controls the provision of public sewer and water, which is expected to influence land use decisions. The empirical model developed here includes multiple variables describing Calvert County's zoning and public service policies.

To estimate the land use conversion model, we used spatially defined, micro-level data on land parcels from the Maryland Department of Planning (2002) statewide property map and parcel database files. The construction of this data set required merging data from several tax assessment sources, some of which are not spatially explicit, in order to compile an eight-year history of convertible parcels within Calvert County. The data comprise all parcels that, as of January 1993, were large enough to accommodate a major subdivision of at least five houses, given current zoning, and could have been converted to residential use. The year is also included for those that were converted between 1993 and 2000. This yields a total of 1,962 observations.

The data contain variables that pertain to each individual parcel, including lot size and land use. Because the data associated with each parcel includes information on its location, a GIS was used to generate a variety of additional associated spatial attributes, including zoning, distance measures, and public sewer access.

The model estimates the conditional probability that an event occurs in a particular time period, given that the event has not yet occurred up until that time period. An event is defined here as the subdivision of an undeveloped parcel into residential lots in preparation for house construction. For this study, any parcel that was not converted by the year 2000 is censored. Based on this definition, the data set contains 163 events and 1,799 censored observations, where events are parcels that were converted to residential use, and censored observations are parcels that remained in undeveloped use from 1993 through 2000.

Variables included in the model are those hypothesized to help explain the costs of conversion from undeveloped to residential use and returns in both residential and undeveloped use. The final set of explanatory variables describes the costs of developing the parcel; the location of the parcel; the availability of public services; and growth-management policies. Table 3-1 displays descriptive statistics for the final set of explanatory variables.

The costs of converting the parcel from undeveloped to residential use are measured using biophysical indicators of lands that are less suitable for development, including those that are serviced by septic and have poorly draining soils (BADSEPTIC) or have steeply sloped terrain (HILLY). Specifically, these

Table 3-1. Descriptive Statistics of Explanatory Variables:
Hazard Model of Residential Land Conversion, Calvert County, Maryland

Variable	Description	Mean	Standard deviation	Min.	Max.
AGPRES	Enrolled in agricultural preservation program (dummy variable)	0.0815	0.2846	0.0000	1.0000
AGPRIME	Proportion of parcel land area in prime farmland	0.3036	0.3553	0.0000	1.0000
BADSEPTIC	Poorly draining soils and serviced by septic (dummy variable)	0.1555	0.2429	0.0000	1.0000
CRITAREA	Proportion of parcel within critical area	0.1304	0.3174	0.0000	1.0000
HDURB200	Proportion of neighborhood within 200 meters that is in high-density urban use	0.0568	0.0904	0.0000	0.6701
HDURB2-400	Proportion of neighborhood between 200 and 400 meters that is in high-density urban use	0.0585	0.1644	0.0000	1.0000
HDURB4-800	Proportion of neighborhood between 400 and 800 meters that is in high-density urban use	0.0588	0.1473	0.0000	0.9636
HDURB8-1600	Proportion of neighborhood between 800 and 1,600 meters that is in high-density urban use	0.0672	0.1312	0.0000	0.9003
HILLY	Steeply sloped terrain (dummy variable)	0.4072	0.3800	0.0000	1.0000
LN_DCDIST	Natural log of distance to Washington, D.C. (meters)	4.1745	0.2308	3.6990	4.6249
LN_TWNDIST	Natural log of distance to nearest town (meters)	7.1857	1.4311	−1.655	9.0289
MDPROT	Proportion of parcel classified as protected land	0.0055	0.0491	0.0000	0.8991
MINLOT	Minimum lot size allowed by zoning (acres)	2.4958	2.1138	0.2500	5.0000
NUMLOTS	Maximum number of lots allowed by zoning	16.5411	56.6213	0.7200	1483.36
OPENCLS200	Proportion of neighborhood within 200 meters that is clustered open space	0.0242	0.0353	0.0000	0.2954
OPENCLS2-400	Proportion of neighborhood between 200 and 400 meters that is clustered open space	0.0354	0.1106	0.0000	1.0000

Table 3-1. (*Continued*)

Variable	Description	Mean	Standard deviation	Min.	Max.
OPENCLS4-800	Proportion of neighborhood between 400 and 800 meters that is clustered open space	0.0253	0.0745	0.0000	0.8384
OPENCLS8-1600	Proportion of neighborhood between 800 and 1,600 meters that is clustered open space	0.0257	0.0537	0.0000	0.8045
OPENPUB200	Proportion of neighborhood within 200 meters that is public open space	0.0396	0.1042	0.0000	0.8404
OPENPUB2-400	Proportion of neighborhood between 200 and 400 meters that is public open space	0.0046	0.0513	0.0000	1.0000
OPENPUB4-800	Proportion of neighborhood between 400 and 800 meters that is public open space	0.0125	0.0806	0.0000	0.8848
OPENPUB8-1600	Proportion of neighborhood between 800 and 1,600 meters that is public open space	0.0260	0.0913	0.0000	0.8337
PFA	Proportion of parcel within a priority funding area	0.2129	0.3955	0.0000	1.0000
PTAX	Local property tax rate	2.2730	0.1535	2.2300	3.3800
REQOPEN	Amount of parcel land that must be preserved as clustered open space (acres)	2.0172	9.8357	0.0000	203.985
RURLEG	Proportion of parcel within a rural legacy area	0.0390	0.1833	0.0000	1.0000
SCHOOLQ	Proportion of graduating high school students who go on to four-year universities	30.913	4.9540	27.5000	38.1000
SEWER	Access to public sewer (dummy variable)	0.1773	0.3820	0.0000	1.0000
TC	Located in town center (dummy variable)	0.1304	0.3368	0.0000	1.0000
WFACCESS	Inverse distance to Chesapeake Bay (meters; = 0 if parcel is located beyond 2 miles)	0.003	0.0289	0.0000	1.1040
WFBOAT	Within two miles of Chesapeake Bay or lower Patuxent River (dummy variable)	0.4600	0.4985	0.0000	1.0000

conversion cost variables are equal to one for parcels on septic systems that have poorly drained soils and those with steep slopes (more than 15 percent), and zero otherwise. Both of these measures indicate higher costs and, as a result, are expected to have a negative influence on the hazard rate and reduce the probability of conversion, all else being equal.

The proportion of parcel land that the Soil Conservation Service characterizes as prime farmland (AGPRIME) is used as a measure of the value of land in agricultural use or profitability. Because this variable reflects the opportunity cost of converting from agricultural to residential use, it is expected to have a negative influence on the hazard rate and reduce the probability of conversion, all else being equal.

The location of the parcel is characterized using a suite of explanatory variables. Although location affects the return to parcels in a variety of uses, the majority of these variables are expected to influence the return to the parcel in residential use. A parcel's value in residential use is expected to be a function of its accessibility to major metropolitan areas, in this case Washington, D.C. Distance to Washington is measured via the road network and is included in logarithmic form (LN_DCDIST) to allow for potential nonlinearities in this effect. All else equal, parcels that are located within closer proximity to this urban area are expected to have a higher hazard rate of conversion, implying that the expected sign of this coefficient is negative.

Accessibility to a town also generally influences a parcel's value in residential use. Distance as the crow flies to the nearest town (LN_TWNDIST) is included in logarithmic form to capture proximity. A binary dummy variable identifies parcels located in the town centers (TC) identified in Calvert County's comprehensive plan. This variable is equal to one if the parcel is located in a town center, and zero otherwise.

A parcel's value in residential use is expected to be a function of its proximity to the waterfront, which includes access to the Chesapeake Bay to the east and the Patuxent River to the west. A measure of accessibility (WFACCESS) is equal to the inverse of the parcel's distance to the water if the parcel is within two miles of the Chesapeake Bay, and zero otherwise. Parcels located nearer to the bay are hypothesized to have a higher hazard rate, implying that the expected sign of the estimated coefficient is positive. In addition, another variable (WFBOAT) is included to indicate if the parcel is within two miles of either the Chesapeake Bay or the lower portion of the Patuxent River, as these waters are navigable but the middle and upper portions of the Patuxent are not.

The final set of explanatory variables used to describe location measure the surrounding land use pattern. Spillover effects from neighboring land uses can create an interdependence among neighboring landowner decisions regarding conversion (Irwin and Bockstael 2002) and as such are likely to influence the value of a parcel in a residential use (Geoghegan et al. 1997). Such interdependencies are likely to be in effect over time and therefore can be captured by measures of existing land uses within a parcel's neighborhood. The spillover effects of surrounding high-density urban development and open space are featured here.

We measured land use surrounding the parcel using four concentric circular buffers, with the buffers extending from the center of each individual land parcel in the data set. The ranges of these buffers were specified as follows: 0 to 200 meters, 200 to 400 meters, 400 to 800 meters, and 800 to 1,600 meters. After characterizing all of the land use types surrounding the parcel, we estimated the proportion of high-density urban development, public open space, and clustered open space within these four buffers. High-density urban development includes commercial, industrial, and multifamily residential land uses (denoted by the variables HDURB200, HDURB2-400, HDURB4-800, and HDURB8-1600).

Calvert County has two different residential zoning categories requiring development to be clustered so that a certain percentage of the parcel remains in open space. We measured the amount of surrounding land that is in a preserved open-space use as a result of this clustering policy (OPENCLS200, OPENCLS2-400, OPENCLS4-800, OPENCLS8-1600). Public open space includes federal, state, and local government lands (OPENPUB200, OPENPUB2-400, OPENPUB4-800, OPENPUB8-1600). The influence of these surrounding land use measures is an empirical question. As Irwin and Bockstael (2002, 2004) discuss, both positive and negative spillovers can be expected. Typically, one might expect high-density urban development to lower and open space to increase the return in residential use of nearby parcels.

The availability, quality, and cost of public services influence the value of a parcel in residential use. Three different explanatory variables capture these effects. School quality is approximated using a measure of college attendance. Specifically, the percentage of students who graduate from high school and go on to four-year colleges is used as a proxy for school quality (SCHOOLQ). Higher school quality is expected to increase the return in residential use, and therefore the likelihood of conversion. A binary variable identifies parcels that have access to public sewer services (SEWER). This variable equals one if sewer access is available, and zero otherwise. Because public sewer is also likely to increase the return in residential use, a positive estimated coefficient is expected. The local property tax rate (PTAX) is used to capture the costs of public services. Higher rates, all else being equal, may lower the likelihood of conversion to residential use.

The last set of explanatory variables reflects the diverse set of growth-management policies in place in Calvert County. These policies are expected to influence a parcel's value in residential use because they establish the intensity at which a developer can build and define the costs and terms of development. For example, the number of lots allowed by zoning (NUMLOTS), amount of land that must be held in open space (REQOPEN), and minimum lot size allowed (MINLOT) are expected to affect the return to conversion. As the number of lots allowed increases, the return is expected to increase. Higher requirements for open space may reduce the likelihood of conversion as they increase the cost. As the minimum lot size increases, the number of lots per parcel decreases, likely reducing returns to developing the parcel.

In a dynamic setting in which returns to development increase over time, the optimal density of development does so as well (Arnott and Lewis 1979; Capozza and Helsley 1989). As a result, an increase in the minimum lot size would be expected to accelerate the timing of development (i.e., increase the hazard rate) if developers build out to the mandated minimum lot size. This is because developing at a higher density in the future would not be possible, and therefore postponing development would result in reduced gains. On the other hand, if it actually is optimal to develop at a lower density than what is mandated, then this variable would not be expected to have any discernible effect on the returns to development.

Other types of growth-management policies expected to influence the conversion to residential use include those that designate "special" lands. These include priority funding areas (PFAs), which encourage development by directing state support for infrastructure to these growth areas, and agricultural and ecological preservation areas, which discourage development. The PFAs, established as part of Maryland's smart-growth legislation, are growth areas identified by each county to which the state directs support for infrastructure development in an attempt to direct new urban growth.

In contrast, the state has several programs in place to prevent urban growth in select areas. Maryland's Rural Legacy Program reallocates state funds to purchase conservation easements for large contiguous tracts of agricultural, forest, and natural areas subject to development pressure. A similar program administered by the Maryland Department of Agriculture places easements on agricultural lands. Maryland protected lands are those that are considered ecologically sensitive by the Maryland Department of Natural Resources, and development is not allowed on them. The state's 1984 Critical Area Act designated all lands within 1,000 feet of tidal waters or adjacent tidal wetlands of the Chesapeake Bay as critical areas, and development is restricted there as well.

Related to these designations, explanatory variables used in the empirical model include the proportions of the parcels that fall within the state's priority funding areas (PFA), critical areas (CRITAREA), rural legacy areas (RURLEG), and protected lands (MDPROT). Also included is an indicator variable that equals one if the parcel is enrolled in an agricultural preservation program

(AGPRES), and zero otherwise. The PFA variable reflects Maryland's smart-growth policy and is expected to have a positive influence on the hazard rate. Conversely, the other four special land designations are expected to have a negative influence.

Empirical Results

The results from the proportional hazards model of residential land conversion are presented in Table 3-2. The statistical significance of the parameter estimates is indicated by a chi-square test of the null hypothesis that the estimates are not significantly different from zero. The parameter estimates show the direction of the effect of a variable on the hazard rate, which is the probability that the parcel, given that it has survived to this event time, will be converted to residential use at this time. That is, a positive (negative) and statistically significant parameter estimate is interpreted as increasing (decreasing) the likelihood of conversion, holding all else constant.

A more intuitive interpretation of the estimated coefficients of a Cox proportional hazard model is to calculate the hazard ratio, which conveys the magnitude of the effect of each individual variable on the hazard rate. For binary indicator variables, this is the ratio of the hazard rate for a parcel with the binary indicator variable equal to one to the hazard rate for a parcel with the same binary indicator variable equal to zero, holding all other variables constant. For continuous variables, the hazard ratio can be transformed into an elasticity measure by subtracting 1 and multiplying by 100 to give the estimated percent change in the hazard rate for each one-unit increase in the continuous variable, again holding all other variables constant.

Two of the three development cost variables are statistically significant, although the sign on the measure of prime agricultural land (AGPRIME) is unexpected. This measure, which was included as a proxy for the opportunity costs of converting a parcel from an agricultural use, has a positive and statistically significant effect on the hazard rate. Rather than capturing the opportunity cost of developing as originally hypothesized, this result likely reflects the fact that prime agricultural land is also prime residential land in many cases. Poorly draining soils where septic fields are required (BADSEPTIC) are found to lower the likelihood of a parcel's development significantly. Specifically, the hazard ratio of 0.357 implies that the hazard rate of parcels with poorly draining soils that require septic is only 35.7 percent of those that have adequately draining soils. Steeply sloped parcels (HILLY) are not found to have a statistically significant effect on a parcel's hazard rate of conversion.

Table 3-2. Results from a Hazard Model of Residential Land Conversion, Calvert County, Maryland

	Variable	Parameter estimate	Standard error	Pr > chi square	Hazard ratio
Proxies for development costs	BADSEPTIC	−1.02987	0.50104	0.0398	0.357
	HILLY	−0.45859	0.33938	0.1766	0.632
	AGPRIME	0.63213	0.32853	0.0543	1.882
Locational features	LN_DCDIST	−0.24304	0.73287	0.7402	0.784
	LN_TWNDIST	−0.25278	0.07577	0.0008	0.777
	WFACCESS	3.88677	1.97792	0.0494	48.753
	WFBOAT	0.23736	0.20723	0.2521	1.268
	TC	−0.80989	0.42857	0.0588	0.445
Neighborhood land use variables	HDURB200	−2.70372	0.92627	0.0035	0.067
	HDURB2-400	−2.14518	0.93145	0.0213	0.117
	HDURB4-800	−0.19877	0.76848	0.7959	0.82
	HDURB8-1600	0.30199	1.04941	0.7735	1.353
	OPENCLS200	−0.02384	0.71658	0.9735	0.976
	OPENCLS2-400	1.50419	0.8276	0.0691	4.501
	OPENCLS4-800	2.17433	1.24819	0.0815	8.796
	OPENCLS8-1600	2.72436	2.12789	0.2004	15.247
	OPENPUB200	1.62277	1.77596	0.3609	5.067
	OPENPUB2-400	−0.5438	1.68631	0.7471	0.581
	OPENPUB4-800	−1.67156	1.4303	0.2425	0.188
	OPENPUB8-1600	−0.24646	0.90275	0.7848	0.782
Public services	SCHOOLQ	0.01809	0.02762	0.5125	0.120
	SEWER	1.28926	0.43221	0.0029	3.63
	PTAX	−4.21655	1.16946	0.0003	0.015
Zoning regulations	MINLOT	0.44248	0.05902	<0.0001	1.557
	NUMLOTS	0.00216	0.000676	0.0014	1.002
	REQOPEN	0.00511	0.00766	0.5041	1.005
Smart-growth policies	PFA	1.40315	0.39809	0.0004	4.068
	CRITAREA	−1.99796	0.51093	<0.0001	0.136
	RURLEG	−0.11873	0.50817	0.8153	0.888
	AGPRES	−0.85016	0.37278	0.0226	0.427
	MDPROT	−6.20935	5.883	0.2912	0.002

Notes: Dependent variable: indicator variable = 1 if parcel was developed in a given year between 1993 and 2000; otherwise = 0. Number of observations = 1,962, events = 163. Time period: 1993–2000.

Model fit statistics	Without covariates	With covariates
−2*(log likelihood)	2,457.79	2,276.38
AIC	2,457.79	2,338.38

Several of the locational attributes of parcels are found to influence the hazard rate. Surprisingly, distance to Washington, D.C. (LN_DCDIST) is not statistically significant. This suggests that the most recent growth in Calvert County has been driven by households that are either very tolerant of long commutes or not tied to Washington for employment or other reasons (e.g., retirees attracted by recreational opportunities). Results showing the influence of other locational variables support this explanation. Distance to the nearest small town (LN_TWNDIST) is found to be negative and statistically significant, confirming the importance of access to local shopping and other services. Access to the waterfront (WFACCESS) is found to be positive and statistically significant, indicating that a premium is associated with parcels with high recreational potential or scenic views located nearest to either the Chesapeake Bay or Patuxent River. A statistically significant difference was not found, however, between those parcels located near the navigable portions of the water (WFBOAT)—the Chesapeake Bay and the lower portion of the Patuxent River—and those that are not. Location within one of the town centers (TC), holding constant the level of services and other variation captured in this model, is found to reduce the hazard rate. Specifically, the hazard rate of a parcel that is located within a town center is estimated to be only 44.5 percent of the hazard rate of an identical parcel that is not.

Several of the surrounding land use measures are found to be statistically significant in the expected directions. Neighboring high-density urban development within 400 meters of a parcel conveys a negative and statistically significant effect on the hazard rate of conversion: a 1 percent increase (0.3 acre) in the amount of high-density urban development within 200 meters (HDURB200) reduces the hazard rate by 93.7 percent, whereas a 1 percent increase (0.93 acre) in the amount of high-density urban development between 200 and 400 meters (HDURB2-400) reduces the hazard rate by 88.3 percent. Neighboring open space created by the clustering of neighboring development conveys a highly positive and statistically significant effect when located within 200 to 800 meters of a parcel. A 1 percent increase (0.93 acre) in the amount of clustered open space between 200 and 400 meters (OPENCLS2-400) increases the hazard rate by 350 percent, and a 1 percent increase (3.7 acres) in the amount of clustered open space between 400 and 800 meters (OPENCLS4-800) increases the hazard rate by 779 percent. These results are not directly comparable, however, as a 1 percent increase in land in the smaller neighborhood is much less in absolute terms than a 1 percent increase in the larger neighborhood. Putting these in comparable terms, a 1-acre increase in the amount of clustered open space within 200 to 400 meters increases the hazard rate of conversion by 376 percent, whereas the same change within 400 to 800 meters increases the hazard rate of conversion by 211 percent. Therefore, a distance-decay effect is associated with neighboring clustered open space, but this effect decreases at a slow rate as distance from the parcel increases.

Our proxy for school quality, the percentage of students graduating from high school and going to college within the school district (SCHOOLQ), is not statistically significant. It is possible that this is a poor proxy for school quality, or quality may be relatively homogeneous across the county. The other public service variable that is included in the model, however, the presence of public sewer on a developable land parcel (SEWER), has a statistically significant and very positive effect on the hazard rate of conversion. Based on the estimated hazard ratio, the mean hazard rate of those parcels with public sewer, holding all other variables constant, is 363 percent greater than those without. Thus just the provision of public sewer to a parcel would increase the hazard rate of conversion by almost fourfold. Household expenditures on public services are captured by the property tax rate variable (PTAX), which is statistically significant and negative: a 1 percent increase in the property tax rate applied to a parcel of land is found to lower the hazard rate of conversion by 1.5 percent.

Zoning regulations have a highly significant effect on the hazard rate of conversion. The minimum lot size restriction on a parcel (MINLOT) has a positive and statistically significant effect on the hazard rate. This result is consistent with the theory of optimal timing and residential density: assuming that returns to development are increasing over time, an increase in the minimum lot size, which lowers the allowable density of development, will accelerate the optimal timing of development if this constraint is binding, and assuming that any countervailing premium that may be attached to large-lot restrictions by consumers is sufficiently small. Empirically, this effect is found to be substantial. An increase in the minimum lot size of a parcel by 1 acre is found to increase its hazard rate by 55 percent. The maximum number of allowable lots that can be developed on a parcel (NUMLOTS) significantly influences the hazard rate of conversion in a positive direction. This is consistent with expectations, as an increase in the number of developable lots on a parcel will increase the returns to developing. The magnitude of this effect is quite small, however: an additional lot increases the hazard rate by only 0.2 percent. The amount of open space required by the clustering of development regulation (REQOPEN) is not found to have a statistically significant effect on the hazard rate.

Finally, several of the growth-management and open-space preservation policies implemented within Calvert County have had a significant effect on conversion rates. Parcels that fall within the areas designated as priority funding areas (PFA) have a much higher hazard rate of conversion. Compared with parcels outside these designated areas, the hazard rate of parcels located within a PFA is about four times larger. In addition, the location of a parcel within a designated critical area (CRITAREA) and the enrollment of a parcel in an agricultural preservation program (AGPRES) both significantly reduce the parcel's hazard rate of conversion, although the magnitude is less than the effect of the PFA designation. The hazard rate of parcels within critical areas is just 14 percent of the rate of those located outside these areas, whereas the hazard rate of parcels within an agricultural preservation area is 43 percent. In contrast, the hazard rate of a parcel located within either a rural legacy area (RURLEG) or a protected area (MDPROT) is found to be unaffected by these designations. The former likely reflects the limited budgets that the state has allocated for this program since its inception in the mid-1990s.

Implications for Growth Management at the Rural-Urban Fringe

The findings of this analysis suggest a number of interesting relationships among parcel-level characteristics, growth-management policies, and the resulting pattern of residential development in our study area. First, spatial heterogeneity among on-site parcel characteristics, including soil type, access to public sewer, and size of the parcel, clearly has an effect on the parcel's hazard rate of conversion. To the extent that these variables are positively spatially correlated—that is, neighboring parcels have similar values—these sources of spatial heterogeneity would tend to encourage clustered development.

Other such sources that have a similar effect include access measures. For example, if proximity to urban or town centers is desirable, then clustering of development will occur near these centers. Interestingly, distance to the region's large urban center, Washington, D.C., is not found to be significantly different from zero. The absence of this effect may be explained by the particular geography of Calvert County. The southern area of the county is surrounded by the Chesapeake Bay, an amenity that could exert an offsetting effect on residential location decisions. The most plausible explanation is that households located in the county are heterogeneous; in other words, a portion of the population may be concerned with access to Washington, but these households are not the majority. The population is composed of other types of households, including retirees and those who may be tied to the local economy within Calvert County. As a result, development is more dispersed than it otherwise would be if access to Washington were a dominant concern. In contrast, access to small towns exerts a relatively substantial effect, suggesting that development patterns may tend to cluster on a lesser scale around the smaller towns dispersed throughout the county.

The influence of the neighboring land use variables is of interest, but the estimates must be interpreted with caution. As argued by Irwin and Bockstael (2002), externalities generated by land uses that are the result of past decisions by neighboring landowners are in some sense codetermined with the development process. In this case, although the effects are lagged over time and therefore not a simultaneously determined variable, the process by which neighbors were converted in the past clearly is very much related to the process that influences a parcel's conversion potential today. To the extent that any of the underlying influencing factors are time-invariant and unobserved, problems of consistency will arise, and the parameter estimates associated with the neighboring land uses from the statistical analysis will be biased. Generally, this would tend to be in a positive direction because of the likely positive spatial autocorrelation of unobserved factors not included in the statistical model. Therefore, the positive estimates of the neighboring clustered open-space parameters do not necessarily convey a positive relationship, as they likely are biased in a positive direction. But the negative spillovers associated with neighboring high-density urban development are identified as clearly having a negative influence on the hazard rate of conversion. This result, coupled with the negative influence of a parcel being located within an area designated as a town center, shows a clear repelling effect associated with higher-density urban areas. Such effects will tend to offset the ones that encourage clustering and therefore increase the pattern of scattered development within the county.

Of primary interest is the potential effect of the growth-management policies on the spatial pattern of residential development in our study area. The results suggest several spatial trends. First, minimum lot zoning, if used as a growth control measure by itself, could result in a rush of development in areas for which lot size is restricted. This finding is consistent with theoretical models of optimal timing of development, which demonstrate that the optimal density of development increases when development is postponed into the future (see Arnott and Lewis 1979; Capozza and Helsley 1989). By restricting the density at which development can occur in the future, a minimum lot size policy limits the returns to developing at some future period when the constraint becomes binding. Thus as soon as the constraint becomes binding, it will be optimal for development to occur. This result also is supported by other empirical results from the literature on land conversion (Geoghegan and Bockstael 2000, 2002; Irwin and Bockstael 2002, 2004).

Second, policies aimed at altering the spatial distribution of the costs and returns to development may be an effective restraint on scattered development. Specifically, the state's PFA program, in which financial support for new infrastructure is channeled to designated growth areas, is an effective policy tool for encouraging more concentrated development. Parcels within PFAs are much more likely to be converted, all else equal, than those located outside these areas. In addition, some of the policies designed to discourage development in rural areas appear to be having an effect. Both the critical area designation and enrollment in an agricultural preservation program have statistically significant effects on the timing of development, which tends to be deflected from these protected areas.

Although these results suggest how growth-management policies may impact future development patterns, they are limited because they convey only the marginal effect of each variable in isolation from all others. In reality, the conversion of a parcel is determined by a combination of many factors, and knowing their relative magnitudes is critical to understanding the extent to which policies will have a perceptible effect on altering development patterns.

To further evaluate the potential effect of policies on development patterns, we simulate predicted patterns within Calvert County under a baseline and several alternative policy scenarios:

- Baseline. This scenario assumes no change in the current mix of policies.
- Increased enrollment in an agricultural preservation program. This scenario posits an increase in the enrollment of parcels in an agricultural preservation program, based on the location of prime agricultural soils. All those parcels that have a very high proportion of prime agricultural soils (90 percent or greater) and are not yet enrolled are assumed to be. This yields a total of 104 additional parcels in such a program.
- Expansion of priority funding areas (PFAs). This scenario posits an expansion of the existing PFA boundaries by an additional mile. The hypothetical expansion of these targeted growth areas results in an additional 348 parcels being within a PFA.
- Combination of policies. This scenario assumes both increased enrollment in an agricultural preservation program and expansion of PFAs.

We generate the predicted patterns of development under each of these scenarios by using the estimated parameters from the statistical model to calculate the survival probabilities for each parcel still deemed developable as of the year 2000. Those parcels with the lowest survival probabilities are assumed to be converted. The predictions are based on the conversion of a constant number of parcels in each scenario, as the focus here is on the spatial distribution of conversion, and not some prediction of the total amount. Specifically, we assume that an additional 200 parcels (about 11 percent of the remaining parcels that are still developable as of 2000) are converted to residential use in each case. This is somewhat more than the 162 parcels converted between 1993 and 2000, and therefore would correspond roughly to the predicted amount of development over the following 8 to 10 years.

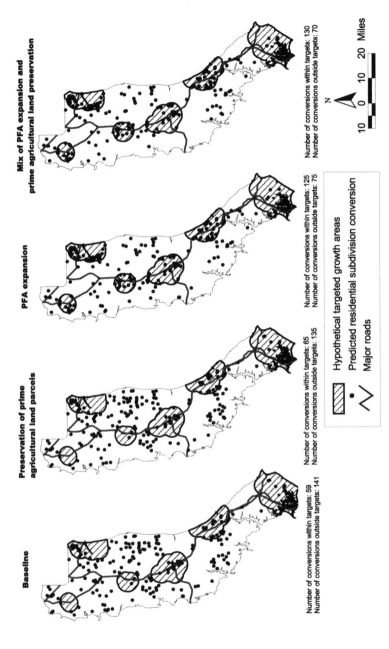

Figure 3-2. Predicted Effects of Alternative Growth Management Scenarios on Development Patterns (assuming a constant number of developed parcels across all scenarios)

Figure 3-2 illustrates the results of the simulations for each of the four policy scenarios. The hypothetical targeted growth areas—those encompassed by the expanded PFAs—are shown as the shaded areas in each image. The number of parcels that are predicted to be developed and fall within one of these areas under each scenario is reported below each figure.

Under the baseline scenario, which assumes no change in policies, 29 percent of the parcels that are converted (59 parcels) occur within the targeted growth areas. Under the second scenario, the increase in the number of parcels enrolled in an agricultural preservation program is successful at deflecting a moderate amount of development. The percentage of parcels predicted to be converted that fall within the targeted growth areas increases slightly, to 32.5 percent of the total number of parcels converted (65 parcels), thereby decreasing the total number of parcels developed outside the targeted growth areas from 141 to 135, or by 5 percent of the total.

Under the third scenario, which includes an expansion in the PFAs to target development within the shaded areas on the map, the concentration of development within these targeted growth areas is likely to increase dramatically. Relative to the baseline, expansion of the PFAs is predicted to increase the total number of parcels converted within these targeted areas from 59 to 125, or 112 percent. The final image illustrates the predicted pattern of development under the fourth scenario, in which both an increase in enrollment in an agricultural preservation program and expansion of the PFAs are implemented. The result is a minor improvement over the third scenario: 130 parcels (65 percent of the total) are predicted to be converted within the targeted growth areas, an increase of 4 percent relative to the third scenario and 120 percent relative to the baseline scenario.

The predictions from the simulation exercise are limited in an important respect, however, which is likely to result in an overestimate of the concentration of development that is achievable through the PFA policy. In performing the simulation, we assume a static world in which the spillover effect of predicted additional development is not incorporated into neighboring parcels' survival probabilities. In other words, the predicted pattern of development is generated as if all parcels were simultaneously developed. In reality, these conversions will occur over time and, to the extent that development generates land use externalities, will alter the survival probabilities of neighboring undeveloped parcels.

The empirical results from the hazard model of conversion suggest that these externalities can be significant. Specifically, higher-density urban development is found to convey negative externalities and depress the hazard rate of conversion of neighboring parcels. For this reason, our simulation results are likely to overstate the effectiveness of any policy that concentrates development, such as PFAs. As the density of development increases in the targeted growth areas, congestion effects are likely to set in, moderating the attractiveness of these areas as residential locations and reducing the overall amount of development that actually occurs there.

Conclusions

The results from the empirical hazard model of residential land use conversion and the simulation of predicted development patterns under alternative policy regimes suggest several further implications for effective growth-management policy. First, it is clear that several of the smart-growth policies that were put in place by the state of Maryland in the mid-1990s, as well as agricultural preservation programs that have operated at both county and state levels, have had significant effects on the pattern of residential growth in Calvert County. In particular, the empirical results show that the designation of priority funding areas (PFAs) has a significant influence on accelerating the time at which a parcel is developed. The magnitude of the empirical finding is borne out by the simulation of an alternative scenario in which the PFAs are hypothetically extended beyond their existing boundaries (scenario 3). Patterns of development are predicted to change in substantial ways under this alternative policy scenario.

Second, our simulation suggests that a growth-management approach based solely on open-space preservation programs is not as effective as one in which these are combined with policies designed to cluster development in targeted growth areas. In isolation, open-space preservation programs (such as the agricultural preservation program considered in scenario 2) are not effective means of achieving more clustered growth patterns concentrated in existing urban areas. This finding is made especially clear in comparing the second and third scenarios. Only moderate improvements in concentrating development in targeted growth areas are predicted under scenario 2. Relative to the baseline prediction, an increase in enrollment in an agricultural preservation program is predicted to increase development within targeted growth areas by 5 percent. In comparison, the expanded PFA scenario is predicted to cause a 112 percent increase, and the combined policy scenario a 120 percent increase. Minimum lot size restrictions and designation of PFAs generally have had a greater influence on the spatial distribution of residential land conversion decisions in Calvert County than the suite of policies designed to protect critical ecological, agricultural, and rural lands.

We can provide several explanations for the patterns manifested in our simulation exercise. First, our hazard model estimates suggest that parcels located in PFAs are significantly more likely to be converted, all else equal, than those located outside these areas. This marginal effect is further supported in the simulation exercises, where the increase in the expected return from conversion induced by the PFA extension lowers the survival probabilities of parcels in these areas enough to alter significantly the predicted development patterns. In short, the PFA extension dissuades developers from subdividing lands in outlying areas and encourages development within the boundaries of the PFAs.

Second, the PFA program has explicit spatial objectives. Hence, it is not surprising that this policy can effectively manipulate the spatial distribution of residential development. In contrast, the agricultural land preservation programs target individual parcels, and therefore face greater challenges in trying to achieve spatial policy objectives, such as protecting contiguous tracts of agricultural land. Our definition of scenario 2 posits that all parcels meeting an established standard for prime agricultural soils enroll in an agricultural preservation program. Admittedly, this scenario may underestimate the effectiveness of such a program to protect contiguous tracts, because the program ignores such objectives. In practice, the state and county agricultural land preservation programs have attempted to address such issues by giving favor to parcels located near others under easements.

Finally, in many instances, the private return from residential development far exceeds that from an undeveloped use. In such a situation, programs aimed at manipulating the spatial heterogeneity of returns to residential development may be expected to have a greater influence, all else equal, than policies that maintain the returns of undeveloped lands. In turn, given budget constraints, programs aimed at preserving lands in undeveloped or open-space uses through the purchase of development rights or agricultural easements are at a disadvantage when the difference in expected net returns of residential and undeveloped lands is greater. For these reasons, we have confidence in our finding that open-space preservation programs alone are unlikely to achieve smart-growth objectives.

At the outset of this chapter, we noted our focus on growth-management policies that concentrate development in targeted growth areas and deflect it from rural areas. The dual objectives of such policies are worthy of reflection. In short, emphasis must be given to factors that pull development into specific areas and push it from other areas. Our conclusions regarding smart-growth land use policies are consistent with the conclusions of researchers focusing on other policy areas related to smart growth and regional planning. In particular, studies that call for greater and comprehensive consideration of the linkages among urban, suburban, and rural areas have given much emphasis to the dynamics of addressing push and pull factors when dealing with land use, housing, public infrastructure, and regional economic issues (Downs 1999; Katz and Bradley 1999; Orfield 1997; Rusk 1999). Policymakers at the urban-rural fringe have a variety of growth-management policies at their disposal. Smart-growth objectives are inherently spatial, concentrating development in targeted growth or urban areas and intensifying open-space preservation in rural areas.

Based on the findings of this study, the efficacy of policies to meet such objectives may depend largely on the degree to which the policy instrument incorporates spatial influences. This has important implications for many rural-urban areas in the United States currently struggling with growth issues. For example, many localities and states have avoided what are perceived to be more aggressive policies, such as Maryland's PFAs, and instead have instituted open-space preservation programs with the hope that they will be sufficient to control development. This approach is not surprising, as open-space preservation is a goal that attracts the support of a diverse constituency, from farmers to homeowners to environmentalists. On the other hand, policies attempting to guide development through directed provision of infrastructure are perceived as being more interventionist and are more likely to be shot down on the basis of individual property rights, as they create a clearer picture of the potential loss in land values and therefore raise the prospect of a challenge to the policy via the "takings" clause of the Constitution.

For these reasons, we expect to observe considerable variation in future development patterns and growth-management strategies at the urban-rural fringe.

References

Allison, P. (1995). *Survival Analysis Using the SAS System: A Practical Guide*. Cary, NC: SAS Institute.

American Planning Association. (2002). Planning for Smart Growth: 2002 State of the States. Chicago: American Planning Association.

Arnott, R., and F. Lewis. (1979). The Transition of Land to Urban Use. *Journal of Political Economy* 87(11): 161–69.

Benfield, F. K., T. Jutka, N. Vorsanger, and P. Glendening. (2001). *Solving Sprawl: Models of Smart Growth in Communities across America*. Washington, DC: Natural Resource Defense Council.

Bockstael, N. E., and K. P. Bell. (1998). Land Use Patterns and Water Quality: The Effect of Differential Land Management Controls. In *International Water and Resource Economics Consortium, Conflict and Cooperation on Trans-Boundary Water Resources*, edited by R. Just and S. Netanyahu. Norwell, MA: Kluwer Publishers, 169–191.

Burchell, R., N. Shad, D. Listokin, H. Phillips., A. Downs, S. Seskin, J. Davis, T. Moore, D. Helton, and M. Gall. (1998). *The Costs of Sprawl—Revisited*. Transportation Cooperative Research Program Report 39. Washington, DC: National Academy Press.

Calvert County. (1997). *1997 Comprehensive Plan*. Calvert County, Maryland Planning Commission.

Capozza, D., and R. Helsley. (1989). The Fundamentals of Land Prices and Urban Growth. *Journal of Urban Economics* 26(3): 295–306.

Daniels, T. (1999). *When City and County Collide*. Washington, DC: Island Press.

Downs, A. (1999). Some Realities about Sprawl and Urban Decline. *Housing Policy Debate* 10(4): 955–974.

Frank. N. (2000). Exploring Sprawl: Findings of a Comprehensive Review of the Literature Related to Sprawl or What Do We Really Know? Paper presented at the Association of Collegiate Schools of Planning. November 2000, Atlanta.

Geoghegan, J., and N. E. Bockstael. (2000). Smart Growth and the Supply of Sprawl. Paper presented at the Association of Environmental and Resource Economists Workshop. June 2000, La Jolla, CA.

———. (2002). Testing for the Effect of Growth Control Measures Using Quasi-Experimental Design. Paper presented at the Association of Environmental and Resource Economists Workshop. June 2003, Madison, WI.

Geoghegan, J., L. Wainger, and N. E. Bockstael. (1997). Spatial Landscape Indices in a Hedonic Framework: An Ecological Economics Analysis Using GIS. *Ecological Economics* 23(3).

Gordon, P., and H. W. Richardson. (1997). Are Compact Cities a Desirable Planning Goal? *Journal of the American Planning Association* 63(1): 95–106.

Greene, W. (2000). *Econometric Analysis.* 4th ed. Upper Saddle River, NJ: Prentice Hall.

Hirschhorn, J. (2000). *Growing Pains: Quality of Life in the New Economy.* Washington, DC: National Governor's Association.

Irwin, E. G., and N. E. Bockstael. (2002). Interacting Agents, Spatial Externalities, and the Endogenous Evolution of Residential Land Use Pattern. *Journal of Economic Geography* 2: 31–54.

———. (2004). Land Use Externalities, Growth Management Policies, and Urban Sprawl. *Regional Science and Urban Economics* 34(6): 705–25.

Katz, B., and J. Bradley. (1999). Divided We Sprawl. *Atlantic Monthly* 284(6): 26–34.

Lacayo, R. (1999). The Brawl over Sprawl. *Time* March 22.

Land Trust Alliance. (2003). *Americans Invest in Parks and Open Space: LandVote 2003.* Washington, DC: Land Trust Alliance.

Landis, J. (1995). Imagining Land Use Futures: Applying the California Urban Futures Model. *Journal of the American Planning Association* 61: 438–457.

Landis, J., and M. Zhang. (1998a). The Second Generation of the California Urban Futures Model. Part 1: Model Logic and Theory. *Environment and Planning A* 30: 657–666.

———. (1998b). The Second Generation of the California Urban Futures Model. Part 2: Specification and Calibration Results of the Landuse Change Submodel. *Environment and Planning B.* 25: 795–824.

Maryland Department of Planning. (2002). *MdProperty View.* Statewide Property Map and Parcel Database. Baltimore, MD. http://www.mdp.state.md.ud/data.mdview.htm.

Maryland General Assembly, Senate. (1997). Smart Growth Priority Areas Funding Act of 1997. Regular Session, 1997. Senate Bill 389.

Mitchell, J. G. (2001). Urban Sprawl. *National Geographic* 200(1): 48–65.

Nelson, A. (1992). Characterizing Exurbia. *Journal of Planning Literature* 6(4): 350–368.

Orfield, M. (1997). *Metropolitics.* Washington, DC: Brookings Institution and Lincoln Institute of Land Policy.

Pew Center for Civic Journalism. (2000). Straight Talk from Americans–2000. A Na-
    tional Survey for the Pew Center for Civic Journalism conducted by Princeton Survey
    Research Associates. Washington, DC: Pew Center for Civic Journalism.
Rusk, D. (1999). *Inside Game, Outside Game.* Washington, DC: Brookings Institution.
Shaw, J. S., and R. D. Utt. (2000). *A Guide to Smart Growth: Shattering Myths, Providing
    Solutions.* Washington, DC: Heritage Foundation.
Sierra Club. (2000). *Smart Choices or Sprawling Growth.* Washington, DC: Sierra Club.

4

Forecasting Development at the Suburban Fringe

JOSHUA TEMPLETON, DIANE HITE, AND
BRENT SOHNGEN

In recent years, large areas of agricultural land have been converted to sub-urban use. A number of authors have expressed concern that such rapid suburbanization may contribute to congestion, diminish environmental qual-ity, and cause an inefficient use of land (e.g., Brueckner 2000; Hamilton and Roell 1982; Kahn 2000; Plantinga and Miller 2001). Offering an alternate view-point, Gordon and Richardson (2000) argue that rapid suburbanization is an efficient outcome of market forces, supplying desired housing and community attributes to home buyers.

Policymakers possess a wide array of tools that can influence how and when agricultural land converts to developed uses. Some policies, such as regional smart-growth planning and growth boundaries, are purposely designed to guide land use change (Gordon and Richardson 2000). Others, such as property taxation policies, are imposed for reasons that may be unrelated to land use planning, but nonetheless influence preservation and development (Anderson 1986; Turnbull 1988). Still other policies, such as zoning restrictions and impact fees, are imposed with fiscal as well as land use planning objectives (Fischel 1985; Gyourko 1991; Henderson 1985; Templeton 2004).

This chapter illustrates a means to forecast the timing of residential, in-dustrial, and commercial development at the suburban fringe. This has been accomplished by modeling the observed development of individual agricultural land parcels in Delaware County, Ohio, over a period of 10 years, as a function of parcel, community, and other attributes. The model is similar to that used in the previous chapter by Irwin, Bell, and Geoghegan, in their assessment of growth management policies in Calvert County, Maryland. In contrast to the situation there, however, the county addressed here is not covered by a comprehensive growth management plan of the type found in Maryland. Also, whereas the previous chapter examined the effects of policies explicitly targeted at growth management, this study looks at the effects of taxation and zoning policies for which growth management is only a secondary consideration. Hence the two chapters, although similar from a methodological perspective, offer very different policy conclusions.

Research Methods and Data

Using statistical models developed to predict the survival times of terminally ill patients, it is possible to predict the survival times of agricultural parcels at risk of conversion to developed suburban uses (residential, commercial, or industrial)—or the length of time that the parcels remain undeveloped. Just as one might predict a cancer patient's survival time based on personal characteristics (such as age and health) and the treatment regime, one may predict an agricultural parcel's survival time based on the desirability of its attributes to developers (such as distance to highways and local schools) and the public policies pursued by local government. More information regarding the statistical method used in this study can be found in Hite et al. (2003) and is summarized in the Appendix to this chapter. For an introduction to survival models in general, refer to Kleinbaum (1996) or Lawless (1982).

The empirical analysis was conducted in Delaware County, Ohio, one of the most rapidly growing counties in the Midwest. Located just north of the large urban center of Columbus, the county has its own smaller population center, the city of Delaware, which also influences growth. Two major interstate highways and two large rivers run north to south through the county. In addition, four large water reserves serve as regional recreational attractions and supply water to the entire Columbus area.

Table 4-1 provides statistics regarding land use change in Delaware County from 1988 to 1998. In 1988, approximately 167,878 acres were agricultural land primarily dedicated to row crops such as corn and soybeans. Of this undeveloped land, 20,171 acres had been converted to other uses by 1998, most of it for residential purposes. From a development timing perspective, however, the average conversion for industrial uses occurred nearly a year earlier than for residential uses (2,434.87 versus 2,759.67 days). These findings suggest that development timing and quantity are not always related.

Table 4-1. Agricultural Land Conversion in Delaware County, 1988–1998

Status	_N_	Mean days to conversion	Standard error (days)	Total acres	Mean lot size (acres)
To industrial	93	2,434.87	1,044.91	841	9.04
To commercial	209	2,690.67	1,303.96	1,324	6.33
To residential	8,843	2,759.67	979.42	18,006	2.03
No change	5,843	—	—	167,876	28.76

Model Variables

Table 4-2 provides a list of attributes of the parcels included in the survival time model, along with their definitions. Given the wide range of factors with potential influence on development patterns, we include a large number of control (independent) variables in the analysis. These characterize such features as proximity of the parcel to roads, highways, exit ramps, sewer lines, and transmission lines. Distances from each parcel to environmental, neighborhood, and infrastructure characteristics are measured using geographical information system (GIS) data.

Among factors with potential impact on parcel development are property taxes, which have been divided into two categories: rates for schools (SchoolTax) and for infrastructure (InfraTax). School property taxes are the primary revenue source for public schools, although state and federal sources provide some funding as well. In addition to infrastructure property taxes, a number of different sources fund police, firefighters, streets, and other infrastructure. Local income taxes from industrial and commercial enterprises often are an important revenue source for municipalities, funding a variety of local services. Many tax districts receive additional revenue from inheritance taxes, liquor licenses, and so on. As a result, the reliance on property taxes as a percentage of total revenue varies, ranging from 8 percent for Dublin, a relatively wealthy city with numerous corporate office parks, to more than 80 percent in some less prosperous rural townships.

To incorporate the potential effects of initial community land uses and zoning on development timing, we define control variables based on the calculated percentage of land per tax district in residential, commercial, and industrial uses in 1988 (%Res88, %Com88, and %Ind88). Moreover, to control for decisions made throughout the analysis period, annual agricultural land converted to residential, commercial, and industrial acres is calculated as a percentage of available land in the district (%CnvRes, %CnvCom, and %CnvInd). Table 4-2 provides definitions for other control variables, such as school quality (SchoolQ) and capital intensity (CapInt).

Table 4-2. Variables Used in Conversion Time Analysis

Name	Variable description	Mean (N = 14,988)	Standard error
SouthBnd_M	Log miles distance to Delaware County southern boundary	1.139	0.904
Delaware_M	Log miles distance to Delaware city center	2.090	0.616
Road_M	Log miles distance to nearest road	−3.005	1.101
Highway_M	Log miles distance to nearest major highway	0.815	0.974
TransLine_M	Log miles distance to nearest transmission line	−0.254	1.253
Water_M	Log miles distance to nearest water body	−1.883	1.305
Stream_M	Log miles distance to nearest stream	−0.808	1.042
School_M	Log miles distance to nearest school	0.471	0.884
Comm_M	Log miles distance to nearest commercial plot	−1.104	1.165
Industry_M	Log miles distance to nearest industrial plot	−0.002	1.005
Sewer_M	Log miles distance to nearest sewer line	0.257	1.825
RingMuni	Within one mile of city limits	0.303	0.460
SchoolQ	School quality as measured by test scores	75.318	6.273
Slope	Slope length of property	3.501	4.713
SchoolTax	All school taxes within a tax district, lagged one year	38.506	9.661
InfraTax	All taxes within a tax district except school, lagged one year	16.665	4.030
STaxXSlp	Lagged school taxes interacted with slope	134.918	198.158
AgLeftK	Acres of agricultural land left per year, lagged one year	88.498	83.498
CapInt	Per-district total structure size divided by lot size, lagged one year	0.072	0.091
%CnvRes	Per-district annual % agricultural land converted to residential, lagged one year	0.892	0.218
%CnvCom	Per-district annual % agricultural land converted to commercial, lagged one year	0.072	0.170
%CnvInd	Per-district annual % agricultural land converted to industrial, lagged one year	0.031	0.130
%Ind88	Percentage of industrial land per district in 1988	0.027	0.041
%Com88	Percentage of commercial land per district in 1988	0.045	0.044
%Res88	Percentage of residential land per district in 1988	0.175	0.134

Model Results

Statistical results of the study are presented in Table 4-3. The three columns show how parcel characteristics affect the timing of conversion to each of the three possible nonfarm land uses—residential, commercial, and industrial—relative to the alternative of remaining in agricultural use. Positive coefficients imply that a control variable tends to cause the associated parcel to remain in agricultural use for a longer period of time, increasing the average time of conversion to nonagricultural use. Negative coefficients imply the converse, with the control variable decreasing the average time to conversion.

Table 4-3. Residential, Commercial, and Industrial Change Models, Weighted by Acres

Variable	Residential change		Commercial change		Industrial change	
	Coefficient	Std. error	Coefficient	Std. error	Coefficient	Std. error
Intercept	4.957***	0.189	3.635***	0.473	8.288***	0.691
Stream_M	0.081***	0.005	—		—	
Delaware_M	0.521***	0.017	0.104**		0.233***	0.037
Road_M	0.267***	0.005	—	—	—	—
Highway_M	—	—	0.342***	0.016	0.150***	0.017
SouthBnd_M	—	—	0.251***	0.031	−0.030	0.064
TransLine_M	−0.037***	0.005	0.070***	0.013	0.031*	0.016
Water_M	0.154**	0.005	0.017	0.018	0.058***	0.018
School_M	−0.075***	0.010	−0.135***	0.036	—	—
Comm_M	0.107***	0.006	0.527***	0.017	−0.155***	0.018
Industry_M	−0.251***	0.010	0.278***	0.018	0.458***	0.026
Sewer_M	0.156***	0.006	0.077***	0.016	0.137***	0.023
RingMuni	0.041***	0.014	0.339***	0.047	0.235***	0.047
InfraTax	0.369***	0.004	0.080***	0.005	0.044***	0.005
SchoolTax	0.040***	0.001	0.107***	0.004	0.076***	0.005
SchoolQ	−0.018***	0.002	0.032***	0.006	0.249	0.012
Slope	−0.028***	0.005	0.072***	0.028	0.045	0.031
STaxXSlp	0.000***	0.000	−0.002***	0.001	−0.000	0.001
AgLeftK	−0.003***	0.000	−0.003***	0.000	0.000	0.000
CapInt	−3.414***	0.059	−2.524***	0.267	−2.993***	0.204
%Ind88	−9.428***	0.375	−3.403***	0.785	−6.808***	1.436
%Com88	22.992***	0.441	−1.761*	0.980	−3.792***	1.622
%Res88	−6.679***	0.085	−2.805***	0.245	0.991*	0.510
%CnvRes	−0.802***	0.112	0.816***	0.131	−1.098***	0.190
%CnvCom	0.140	0.121	−0.363***	0.138	—	—
%CnvInd	−0.655***	0.129	1.786***	0.208	−0.760***	0.199
Scale	0.689***	0.005	0.536***	0.013	0.249***	0.012
Weibull Shape	1.451***	0.010	2.120***	0.131	4.991***	0.704
	LnL $= -55,415$, $\chi^2 = 42,385$		LnL $= -3,502$, $\chi^2 = 11,411$		LnL $= -633$, $\chi^2 = 11,088$	

Note: * = Statistically Significant at 0.10; ** = Statistically significant at 0.05; *** = Statistically significant at 0.01.

For example, the coefficient in the residential change column for SchoolQ shows the effect of school quality on the probability that an agricultural parcel will convert to residential use. A negative sign indicates that higher school quality increases the probability and speed of potential conversion from agricultural to residential use. This is an expected result, because high-quality schools make parcels more desirable for residential development.

In order to examine the impact of public policies on the timing of development, it is important that the data incorporate a variety of public policy regimes. As is typical in Ohio, Delaware County is divided into many local governments, including townships, villages, and cities. It also has multiple school districts, whose boundaries do not coincide with the local governments'. Each of these local governments and school districts has its own tax regime and authority. Moreover, each local government has a sovereign right to impose zoning regulations within the vague guidelines implied by court decisions over the years. This diversity in local government and associated policies provides the variation in data necessary for a robust statistical study on the effects of policies on land use conversion. The following sections describe model predictions for the effects of industry, commerce, zoning, and property taxes on development timing.

Property Taxes

Property taxes may influence farmland conversion in a number of ways. They represent a financial burden to landowners and may encourage farmers to sell land (e.g., to developers) sooner rather than later. A parcel's property tax bill also increases, however, when structures are built on it. This may render some development projects unprofitable and discourage the conversion of certain parcels of agricultural land. Property taxes may be designed to favor agricultural use over residential, commercial, or other developed uses, providing an incentive to retain land for farming (American Farmland Trust 1997). The focus of this study is the effect of property tax levels on the timing of development, but the effect of Ohio's preferential taxation of agriculture will also be considered at the end of this section.

Before examining how tax policies affect the timing of development, the capitalization of property taxes must be carefully considered. Property tax capitalization implies that land prices adjust to account for property taxes. Imagine a farmer concerned with paying the future property tax on his farmland. He conceivably could open a bank account with sufficient funds so that the interest would pay the property tax. The amount he would need for such a bank account is the capitalized value of future property tax payment.

When farmers buy land, it is reasonable to assume that they consider the cost of future property taxes. If a farmer were to compare two identical farms, one subject to a property tax and the other not, we would expect the farmer to value the taxed farm less than the tax-free farm. The amount the farmer would be willing to pay for the farm subject to the property tax should be reduced by the capitalized value of future property taxes (i.e., the value of the hypothetical bank account). If all buyers of farmland react in a similar manner, and we have every reason to expect that they do, the capitalized value of future property taxes will be incorporated into market prices. If we accept this reasoning, it follows that buyers of land are compensated for the property tax burden through lower prices. Hence, changes in tax burden should not influence, at least in theory, the relative desirability of purchasing land for farming or development.

Property taxes *may*, however, affect farmers' decisions regarding the sale of land. For example, Bentick (1980) shows theoretically that, assuming full capitalization of taxes, higher property taxes will have no effect on the timing of conversion when only one potential nonfarm use exists. Bentick also shows, however, that higher property taxes may increase the rate of farmland conversion when there are two potential and mutually exclusive nonfarm uses. Based on such findings, with only one potential nonfarm use, the farmer's decision is simple (at least in theory): switch to the nonfarm use as soon as the rental rate for that use exceeds the rental rate for agricultural land. When there is only one potential nonfarm use, the farmer has no reason to hold out for a future higher-value use.

To examine the case where higher property taxes may increase the rate of farmland conversion, assume two potential mutually exclusive nonfarm uses, such as small-town residential housing and high-income suburban housing or commercial structures. The opportunity to convert to small-town housing arises before the higher-income suburbanites move to town. Should the farmer convert as soon as small-town housing is profitable or wait for the better opportunity?

The answer depends on the discount rate. This may be thought of as the minimum gross rate of annual return the owner requires to hold the land. This is equal to the property tax rate plus whatever net rate of return the owner requires to hold the land, which probably approximates the interest rate the owner can receive on the proceeds from a land sale. The lower the discount rate, the more attractive holding out for the second, higher-value land use appears to the landowner. Thus in this case, lower property taxes may encourage farmers to retain property for future sale, whereas higher property taxes prompt them to convert sooner.

The above analysis ignores one important point: developers, in general, always plan to build on the land they buy. Property taxes should not influence the attractiveness of land purchased at market prices, as market prices will capitalize future tax burdens on land. "On land," however, is an important caveat to this sentence. Property taxes are levied on structures as well as on land. As a result, the development of a parcel of land increases its property tax burden, because the developed parcel includes taxable structures. The higher the property tax rate, the higher the tax burden on these structures. And this tax burden may not be capitalized into raw land prices, because it is realized only if a parcel is developed. Farmers can always sell their land to other farmers if developers demand too large of a discount. Developers are aware of such property tax impacts and hence may avoid purchasing parcels in high-tax districts. This may result in higher tax rates *slowing* residential development—a result contrary to that discussed above.

One also could argue that tax rates bear some relationship to the services provided by local governments, and that quality public services help counteract the disincentive to develop high-tax parcels. But the relationship between tax rates and public service levels is tenuous. Any given tax rate can generate a wide variety of tax revenues, depending on the size of the tax base. Cities with expensive homes can generate more revenue with lower tax rates than can cities with less expensive homes. Income taxes are also an important source of revenue that can replace high property tax rates in cities with quality public services. This suggests that the quality of public services may do little to counteract a property tax's "disincentive to development" effect.

The above arguments point out two opposing impacts of property taxes: a "disincentive to development" effect and a "disincentive to hold land" effect. Given these potentially opposing impacts, the effect of property taxes on the timing of development is an empirical question—there are too many confounding factors to make an unambiguous theoretical prediction. Although theoretical results are ambiguous, empirical results from the survival time model (Table 4-3) show that property tax rate increases slow development. When a local government raises school property tax rates, it increases the probability that any given parcel in that tax district will remain in agriculture at any point in time. Infrastructure taxes are even more effective at slowing development. As the table shows, property taxes have similar effects on the conversion of agricultural parcels to commercial, industrial, or residential use.

These results suggest that increases in property taxes slow residential development—a significant empirical result. The extent to which this occurs may be illustrated using a policy simulation to predict the effect of changes in tax rates on farmland conversion. Because our statistical results cover the period 1988 to 1998, we only can make in-sample predictions for hypothetical changes in policy during that period. Assuming, however, that policy changes today are likely to have similar results, the policy simulation suggests that a 20 percent increase in school taxes for all districts in the county would result in the median agricultural parcel remaining undeveloped for an additional 17 months before converting to residential use. A 20 percent increase in infrastructure taxes would have an even more dramatic effect, slowing the conversion of the median agricultural parcel by 5.7 years.

The most obvious way in which property taxes may affect the timing of development is when governments offer preferential taxation to agricultural parcels. Under such programs, landowners receive a tax incentive to keep their land in agriculture. Ohio allows owners of farmland to pay property tax based on the value of their land in agricultural use (use value taxation), rather than on market value. This policy magnifies the increase in property taxes imposed on a newly developed parcel and makes incentives greater to slow development. Empirically, Templeton (2004) shows that Ohio's preferential taxation program has been effective at slowing farmland conversion in a rural Delaware County township, but ineffective in a suburban one.

Initial Land Use

Local governments can regulate the amount of commercial and industrial property development through zoning. Some communities may zone to prevent industrial and commercial development, in an attempt to preserve the environment and character of the community. Others may want to attract such development, believing that commercial and industrial development will generate increased tax revenues. Either way, communities have an intrinsic interest in the secondary effects of commercial and industrial development. Each type of development—commercial, industrial, or residential—may attract or repel other types.

From an aggregate perspective, commercial and industrial development has a fairly straightforward effect on regional growth. Such development attracts workers and thus tends to increase the urbanization of a region. At the tax district or suburban level of analysis, however, the effect of initial industrial and commercial property on development timing is more complex. Tax districts are small, so workers are not required to live within the one in which they work. Home buyers and developers may be attracted to communities with large amounts of industrial or commercial tax revenue (Templeton 2004) or, in contrast, to those with higher levels of rural amenities associated with the lack of such development.

The idea that industry-generated tax revenues might attract home buyers may require additional explanation. Ohio municipalities receive a large percentage of their tax revenue from local income taxes. Industry and commerce bring many employees to a suburb and thus generate tax revenue for that suburb. Because these employees do not necessarily live within the boundaries of the suburb in which they work, the tax revenues generated by industry are not balanced by significant increases in public expenditures. This allows local governments in commercial and industrial districts to offer lower property taxes and better services than local governments without industrial resources.

As a result, commercial and industrial property—as influenced by local zoning ordinances—has both positive and negative impacts on a location's desirability to homeowners. The net effect will depend on the nuisance caused by these land uses and the associated lack of rural amenities, balanced against potential gain tax revenues and associated gain in community services. Assuming this reasoning is correct, it is likely that land within the industrial tax district, but beyond the earshot of commercial or industrial nuisance, will be highly desired by homeowners. The associated hypothesis to be tested here is that homeowners are repelled by the physical attributes of industry, yet desire the fiscal benefits of living within the boundaries of a tax district with ample industrial property. If this is true, parcels within industrial tax districts, but as far as possible from industrial development, will tend to be developed first.

In order to test this hypothesis, we include two separate variables in the model. The first is the initial percentage of land devoted to industrial uses (%Ind88) within the parcel's tax district. The coefficient of this variable is expected to be positive, reflecting the attraction of tax districts flush with industrial tax revenue. The second variable of interest is the distance from each parcel to the nearest industrial parcel (Industry_M). The coefficient of this variable is expected to be negative, reflecting the nuisance associated with industrial property. By including both variables (%Ind88 and Industry_M), we can observe the effect of each while controlling for the other. If only one of the two were included, the hypothesized fiscal and nuisance effects would tend to cancel each other out.

Statistical results (Table 4-3) are consistent with our hypothesis. They show that higher initial percentages of land devoted to industrial uses (%Ind88) in a tax district cause more rapid conversion to residential use, holding all else constant. In fact, the absolute value of the effect of %Ind88 is larger than for %Res88. This suggests that industrial property may be a greater magnet for residential development than is existing residential development. As expected, the coefficient on distance to industry (Industry_M) is negative, showing that parcels more distant from industrial property convert sooner. Hence, empirical results bear out the expectations provided by theory and common sense.

Unlike industry, however, commercial property is not unequivocally a nuisance. Both industrial and commercial property can create noise and traffic, but commercial property may provide other services to homeowners, including shopping and entertainment opportunities. Thus one might expect tax districts with abundant commercial property to be a magnet for residential development. But the coefficient on existing commercial property is positive; the more commercial property a tax district has, the slower land converts to residential use.

In some instances, such patterns might be explained by considering the institutional incentives faced by local governments that enjoy significant income tax revenue from commercial property. Such governments typically are able to provide high-quality services to their residents without imposing high property tax rates—a popular outcome with residents. New entrants to such communities will demand additional services and hence may reduce the average quality of those available to existing residents for a given tax rate. As a result, elected local governments in cities with abundant commercial property may enact strict zoning restrictions to discourage new residential housing and the consequent strain on community services.

Assuming the above argument holds, it nonetheless remains uncertain why tax districts with a large amount of taxpaying industrial property are less vigilant about protecting the fiscal interests of residents than are tax districts with much commercial property. We only can speculate as to the answer. One possibility is that residential property attracts commercial property. Perhaps cities with industrial property hope that the dilution of their income tax revenue by new residents will be balanced by additional income tax revenue from new commercial property. Model results, however, contradict this hypothesis. Whereas commercial property is attracted to districts with a high level of existing residential property, it is not attracted to areas where residential property is growing rapidly. This can be seen from the positive coefficient on change in residential property (%CnvRes) in the commercial change regression. In the end, the tendency of commercial development to slow residential conversion is a pattern that escapes simple, unequivocal explanation—a finding that indicates the need for additional research in this area, perhaps investigating the precise nature of commercial entities. Although some authors have argued that the "processes of land use change are well understood" (Heimlich and Anderson 2001, *vi*), empirical results in the present case suggest that we do not yet have adequate explanations for a variety of processes and findings.

Conclusions

This chapter attempts to forecast the effects of tax and zoning policies on development at the suburban fringe. Theory suggests that changes in property tax rates and zoning policies can have either positive or negative effects on the timing of land conversion, with effects also differing according to the type of conversion (i.e., to residential, commercial, or industrial use). The net effect of these forces—and whether actual development timing coincides with theoretical expectations—is an empirical question. To address these issues, a survival time model is developed and estimated to investigate the effect of a number of variables on the development timing of residential, commercial, and industrial land.

Model results indicate that higher property tax rates slow development, as one might expect. Although residential development is repelled by industrial development in the immediate vicinity, it is attracted to industrial tax districts. This is likely due to the fiscal benefits of sharing the local tax burden with industry. Commercial property offers similar fiscal benefits with less environmental problems, but tax districts with abundant commercial property develop relatively slowly. Whereas most model results conform to expectations based on theory and intuition, some results are unexpected, including the development-slowing impacts of commercial development.

Appendix: The Survival Time Model

The material in this section is largely quoted from Hite et al. (2003) and provides the empirical details of the survival time model. In this chapter, we employ a survival model to estimate impacts of a number of factors on land use change. Survival models provide a standard approach to modeling the distribution of survival times until a particular event occurs (Lawless 1982). The method we use here recognizes that once a given event takes place because of one set of circumstances, the change will preclude other events from taking place as a result of other circumstances; this property of the model makes it particularly attractive for examining suburban development. In our analysis, once a change has occurred from agricultural to, say, industrial use, the particular piece of land can no longer change from agricultural to commercial use. Thus the analysis requires a specific type of censoring model.

Starting at time zero, we are interested in the length of time that a parcel remains in agriculture. This depends on a number of factors. In this analysis, we focus on zoning, capital intensity, and local tax changes while controlling for other factors such as infrastructure and local public goods. We employ both a nonparametric model and a parametric accelerated failure time (AFT) survival model to investigate the timing of this decision. AFT is applicable when it is thought that the covariates accelerate or slow survival time. Such would be the case in a model of land use conversion, where the presence of certain characteristics might increase the probability of conversion over time.

In survival analysis, the time at which an event occurs is a random variable, denoted by T, and estimating the distribution of T is the goal of the statistical modeling. The cumulative distribution function (CDF) of the random variable is denoted by $F(t) = \Pr(T \leq t)$. That is, $F(t)$ is the probability that an event T

occurs on or before some specified time t. The survivor function, a more intuitive measure derived from $F(t)$, is more commonly used in describing events, however. The survivor function is given by $S(t) = \Pr(T > t) = 1 - F(t)$ and is interpreted as being the unconditional probability of survival beyond t. In our analysis, $S(t)$ is interpreted as the probability that agricultural land can survive forces that cause its change to other uses.

Nonparametric analysis of the data can be informative. Of particular interest in our analysis is the hazard function, $\lambda(t)$, which quantifies the instantaneous probability that an event takes place at time t, conditioned on the probability of survival through time t. The hazard function is defined by $\lambda(t) = \lim_{\Delta t \to 0} \frac{\Pr(t \leq T < t + \Delta t)}{\Delta t}$ or $\frac{F'(t)}{S(t)}$. The importance of the hazard function in our analysis is that it recognizes the risk of change only for those properties that have not changed at a given point in time.

One drawback of nonparametric analysis, however, is that it is impossible to draw inferences about the impact that various risk factors have on the survival outcome. Thus the analysis presented in this chapter is drawn from a parametric survival model that controls for a large number of factors and allows us to focus on policy simulations and sensitivity analyses based on changes in various factors. For instance, we can predict differences in rates of change from agricultural to residential land as influenced by changes in timing or types of zoning. By such manipulation of the model, we investigate the way development patterns might form in reaction to changing taxes, land uses, or capital-to-land ratios.

The econometric model used to estimate conversion time is the multivariate Weibull AFT model. The Weibull distribution is a variant of the exponential distribution in which $T_i = \exp(\mathbf{Z}_i' \boldsymbol{\beta}) \cdot \sigma \varepsilon_i$. When the above model is linearized by taking logarithms, it is written as $\ln(T_i) = \mathbf{Z}_i' \boldsymbol{\beta} + \eta_i$, where $\eta_i = \ln(\sigma \varepsilon_i)$ and follows a Gumbel or extreme value distribution. That is, $\eta_i \sim G(0, \sigma)$ with $f(\eta_i) = \exp[\eta_i - \exp(\eta_i)]$ and survivor function $S(\eta_i) = \exp[-\exp(\eta_i)]$. The corresponding expressions for η_i as a function of failure time, T_i, the covariates, $\mathbf{Z}_i$, and the parameters, $\boldsymbol{\beta}$, are therefore written as

$$f(\ln(T_i),\, \boldsymbol{\beta},\, \mathbf{Z}_i) = \exp\left[\left(\frac{\ln(T_i) - \mathbf{Z}_i' \boldsymbol{\beta}}{\sigma}\right) - \exp\left(\frac{\ln(T_i) - \mathbf{Z}_i' \boldsymbol{\beta}}{\sigma}\right)\right]$$

and

$$S(\ln(T_i),\, \boldsymbol{\beta},\, \mathbf{Z}_i) = \exp\left[-\exp\left(\frac{\ln(T_i) - \mathbf{Z}_i' \boldsymbol{\beta}}{\sigma}\right)\right].$$

One model is estimated for each category of land conversion, while accounting for censored observations. For example, the residential model estimates time to residential use conversion, while accounting for censored observations from land that converts to commercial and industrial use during the observation period, as well as for those from land that remains in agriculture throughout. Thus for the residential conversion category, a log-likelihood function of the following form is estimated:

$$\ln L(\beta) = \sum_{i \in D} \ln[f(\ln(T_i), \boldsymbol{\beta}, \mathbf{Z}_i)] + \sum_{i \in C} \ln[S(\ln(T_i), \boldsymbol{\beta}, \mathbf{Z}_i)],$$

where D denotes the set of properties that convert to residential use during the time, and C represents the set of properties that remain in agriculture or convert to industrial and commercial use during the observation period. Analogous likelihood functions are estimated for the industrial and commercial conversion categories.

References

American Farmland Trust. (1997). *Saving American Farmland: What Works.* Northampton, MA: American Farmland Trust Publications Division.

Anderson, J. (1986). Property Taxes and the Timing of Urban Land Development. *Regional Science and Urban Economics* 16(4): 483–492.

Bentick, B. (1980). Capitalized Property Taxes and the Viability of Rural Enterprise Subject to Urban Pressure. *Land Economics* 56(4): 451–456.

Brueckner, J. (2000). Urban Sprawl: Diagnosis and Remedies. *International Regional Science Review* 23(2): 160–171.

Fischel, W. (1985). *The Economics of Zoning Laws.* Baltimore, MD: Johns Hopkins University Press.

Gordon P., and R. W. Richardson. (2000). Critiquing Sprawl's Critics. Policy Analysis no. 385. DC: Washington, Cato Institute. http://www.cato.org/pubs/pas/pa-365es.html.

Gyourko, J. (1991). Impact Fees, Exclusionary Zoning, and the Density of New Development. *Journal of Urban Economics* 30(2): 242–256.

Hamilton, B., and A. Roell. (1982). Wasteful Commuting. *Journal of Political Economy* 90(5): 1035–1053.

Heimlich, R. E., and W. D. Anderson. (2003). *Development at the Urban Fringe and Beyond: Impacts on Agriculture and Rural Land.* ERS Agricultural Economic Report no. 803. Washington, DC: U.S. Department of Agriculture.

Henderson, J. V. (1985). The Impact of Zoning Policies Which Regulate Housing Quality. *Journal of Urban Economics* 18: 302–312.

Hite, D., B. Sohngen, and J. Templeton. (2003). Zoning, Development Timing, and Agricultural Land Use at the Suburban Fringe: A Competing Risks Approach. *Agricultural and Resource Economics Review* 32(1): 145–157.

Kahn, M. (2000). The Environmental Impact of Suburbanization. *Journal of Policy Analysis and Management* 19(4): 569–586.

Kleinbaum, D. (1996). *Survival Analysis.* New York: Springer-Verlag.

Lawless, J. (1982). *Statistical Models and Methods for Lifetime Data*. New York: John C. Wiley and Sons.

Plantinga, A., and D. Miller. (2001). Agricultural Land Values and the Value of Rights to Future Land Development. *Land Economics* 77(1): 56–67.

Templeton, J. (2004). *Three Essays on Taxation and Land Use Change*. Unpublished dissertation. The Ohio State University, Columbus.

Turnbull, G. (1988). The Effects of Local Taxes and Public Services on Residential Development Patterns. *Journal of Regional Science* 28(4): 541–562.

5

Describing Land Use Change in Multidisciplinary Analyses

Jeffrey D. Kline

Economists increasingly face opportunities to collaborate with ecologists and other scientists in multidisciplinary research involving landscape-level analyses of socioeconomic and ecological processes. A common goal of such analyses is to describe potential changes in ecosystem processes and conditions resulting from forest policies and management actions addressing timber, wildlife, and wildfire objectives (e.g., Spies et al. 2002; Hayes et al. 2004). In particular, land use economists often are called upon to describe potential future land use changes that are likely to influence the effectiveness and outcomes of policies and management actions of interest. This typically involves developing statistical spatial empirical models describing land use changes and projecting future land use change scenarios for integration with other models describing socioeconomic and ecological processes.

Providing ecologists with the specific types of land use information they desire can present challenges regarding the availability of appropriate data, the need to adapt existing modeling methods to particular research issues of interest and data at hand, and unresolved econometric issues associated with spatial autocorrelation. Recent papers in economics literature have addressed spatial land use modeling issues and presented illustrative models (e.g., Bockstael 1996; Irwin and Geoghegan 2001). These papers are invaluable for their focus on the development of conceptually rigorous structural models and examination of econometric issues associated with spatial autocorrelation.

This chapter focuses on practical issues involved in providing land use information that is both conceptually rigorous and usable to researchers outside of economics, using spatial data that are often imperfect. It begins by describing the relatively recent adaptation of land use modeling methods of economists toward greater spatial specificity desired in integrated research with ecologists, focusing on data, conceptual modeling, and econometrics issues. This is followed by an example of a spatially explicit land use model developed as part of a multidisciplinary landscape-level analysis of socioeconomic and ecological processes in Oregon's Coast Range. The model characterizes the spatial dynamic distribution of humans on the forest landscape of western Oregon in terms of building densities, which serves as input into other models describing timber production and wildlife habitat.

The Challenges of Integration

Spatial land use models can be viewed as extensions of area-base models first developed by economists more than 20 years ago. Area-base models describe proportions (or shares) of land in forest, agriculture, urban, or other discrete use categories, within well-defined geographic areas, usually counties, as functions of socioeconomic and geophysical variables aggregated at the particular geographic unit of analysis. Published examples are numerous (Alig 1986; Alig and Healy 1987; Alig et al. 1988, 2004; Cropper et al. 1999; Hardie and Parks 1997; Hardie et al. 2000; Lichtenberg 1989; Parks and Murray 1994; Plantinga 1996; Plantinga et al. 1990, 1999; Stavins and Jaffe 1990; White and Fleming 1980). Future land use shares are computed using projected explanatory variable values and provide aggregate regional or national land use projections commonly reported in national resource assessments, such as the Resources Planning Act Assessment (Haynes 2002). Although the spatial detail of such projections is limited to the geographic unit of analysis, usually counties, this has sufficed for national resource assessments. Ecologists, however, often desire land use projections at finer spatial scales more relevant to the ecological processes they study. The desire to account for land use change in ecological analyses has led to the development of more spatially explicit models to project the rate and location of land use change at finer spatial scales.

What economists have come to call "spatial" land use models generally rely on discrete land use data sampled from satellite imagery, aerial photographs, or systematic land inventories, combined with other spatial data describing socioeconomic and geophysical variables. These data are used to estimate discrete choice (e.g., logit or probit) models describing the likelihood of a particular land use change occurring at a given location and point in time (Bockstael 1996; Bradshaw and Muller 1998; Chomitz and Gray 1996; Kline and Alig 1999; Kline et al. 2001; Nelson and Hellerstein 1997; Wear and Bolstad 1998; Wear et al. 1996). By focusing on general land use categories, these models differ from related research focused on describing changes in land cover, such as deforestation or cropping patterns, that may occur within the general categories (e.g., Lambin et al. 2003), although the empirical methods used in both types of models often are similar. In terms of information provided, the primary difference between spatial land use models and their area-base ancestors is the unit of analysis—typically a county with area-base models versus a pixel or point observation with spatial models. This refinement in spatial scale has led economists to focus on reconsidering the most appropriate combination of conceptual frameworks, data, and econometric methods for spatial land use modeling (Bockstael 1996; Irwin and Geoghegan 2001). Less attention has been given to whether land use models meet the informational needs of ecologists or others involved in the provision of policy guidance.

A weakness of many spatial land use models is their reliance on discrete data describing land use as a simple hierarchy of forestry, agricultural, and urban uses. Often defined by data sources, such as the National Resources Inventory (Nusser and Goebel 1997) and the USDA Forest Service's Forest Inventory and Analysis Program (Frayer and Furnival 1999), discrete land use classes imply a level of abstraction that may be inappropriate in multidisciplinary analyses. They tend to describe where humans are and are not present on landscapes, and may be inadequate to characterize the spatial and temporal interactions of humans as agents affecting landscape-level ecological processes. Also, discrete choice models estimated with land use data typically result in predicted probabilities—the probability of conversion, for example—which can be difficult to interpret in ecological or natural science models. Conversion probabilities may be good relative indicators of change, but more information may be needed to predict new development (Bockstael 1996, *1174*).

Another difficulty in spatial land use modeling is a frequent lack of appropriate data with which to construct conceptually rigorous explanatory variables. Empirical models typically are specified using proxy variables describing potential rents earned from different land uses in terms of socioeconomic and geophysical factors. Although spatial data describing geophysical factors such as slope, elevation, and soil quality increasingly are available from geographic data sources, socioeconomic data are less so. For example, models describing forest and farmland conversion to urban uses typically call for timber and agricultural commodity prices as proxies for forestry and farming land rents, which generally are unavailable at spatial scales finer than states or regions. Potential urban land rents can be described using proxies such as population densities (Bradshaw and Muller 1998; Wear and Bolstad 1998), but obtaining these in digitized form at census tract and block levels is often not possible for all but recent years. Land prices increasingly are available from digitized tax lot data, but these too can lack temporal coverage and can poorly represent actual land values if not kept current by local tax assessors. More generally, confidentiality problems related to spatial socioeconomic data often occur when data-gathering agencies restrict the uses of certain information to protect the privacy of surveyed individuals. Considering such factors, it is clear that the development of appropriate econometric specifications for any land use model necessarily requires trade-offs among conceptual rigor, data quality and availability, and the particular research needs at hand.

A final issue involves potential spatial dependence present in spatial land use data, which area-base models typically have not addressed. Spatial dependence can result from omitted spatial variables that influence the land use decisions of landowners, such as weather-related variables, and spatial behavioral relationships, such as common ownership of sampled plots of land. The first leads to inefficient but asymptotically unbiased estimated coefficients; the second can lead to inefficient and biased estimated coefficients (Nelson and Hellerstein 1997). Bockstael (1996) and Irwin and Geoghegan (2001), among others, review empirical issues involved in estimating spatial land use models. The development of standard protocols for addressing spatial dependence in statistical models is relatively recent (e.g., Sohngen and Alig 2001; Fleming 2004). Among the more popular methods in applied work at the time of the study described in this chapter were purposeful sampling (Fortin et al. 1989; Haining 1990; Helmer 2000) and the inclusion of spatial lag variables (e.g., Wear and Bolstad 1998).

A Spatial Land Use Model from Oregon

An example of how land use change can be characterized in multidisciplinary analyses is provided by a spatial land use model developed for the Coastal Landscape Analysis and Modeling Study (Spies et al. 2002). The study analyzes the aggregate socioeconomic and ecological effects of forest policies in western Oregon's Coast Range mountains by linking stand-alone models describing land use change, timber production, and wildlife habitat, among other factors. The study region is bordered by the Pacific Ocean on the west and the Willamette Valley, extending from Portland south to Eugene, on the east (Figure 5-1). Forest policies in the region attempt to achieve a mix of forest goods and services by spatially distributing different forest practices over watersheds, landscapes, and ownerships. Recent policy concerns have focused on maintaining habitat for northern spotted owls (*Strix occidentalis caurina*) and coho salmon (*Oncorhynchus kisutch*). The study integrates quantitative analyses of ecological and socioeconomic processes to test whether forest policy goals (restricting cutting near spotted owl nest sites, for example) are consistent with projected future outcomes (availability of spotted owl habitat).

Identifying Relevant Land Use Information

One socioeconomic factor expected to have a significant impact on forestry in western Oregon is land use change resulting from forestland conversion to

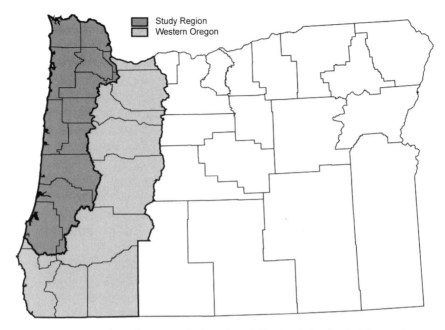

Figure 5-1. Coastal Landscape Analysis and Modeling Study Region in Western Oregon

residential, commercial, and industrial uses. Currently, 70 percent of Oregon's 3.4 million people live in the Willamette Valley, and the population there is expected to grow by 1.3 million new residents in the next 40 years (Franzen and Hunsberger 1998). Research in western Oregon and elsewhere suggests that as forest landscapes become more populated, the intensity with which remaining forest landowners manage their lands for timber production declines, resulting in variety of potential economic and ecological implications (Kline et al. 2004). In this study, land use modeling must account for such effects by describing the future distribution of humans throughout the study region.

Probit models initially developed for the study described land use change among discrete forest, agriculture, and urban categories (Kline and Alig 1999; Kline et al. 2001). Integrating projected conversion probabilities into timber production and ecology models proved difficult, however. Forestland area in western Oregon historically has been substantially greater than urban land area, causing projected forestland conversion probabilities to be very low over much of the study area and of little value in identifying likely locations of future conversion. Also, although forestland conversion to urban use categories has been a relatively slow process, significant land use change has occurred as dispersed, low-density development (Azuma et al. 2002). Such development has become a concern of forest managers and policymakers in recent years because of its potential adverse impacts on forestry productivity (Barlow et al. 1998; Wear et al. 1999), incompatibility with timber production (Egan and Luloff 2000), and increased wildfire risk near homes. Characterizing this form of development was of particular interest to the study.

An alternative to discrete land use data exists in spatial data depicting historical building counts in western Oregon developed by the Pacific Northwest Research Station's Forest Inventory and Analysis Program. The data consist of aerial photo-point observations of building counts (number of buildings of any size or type within 80-acre circles surrounding points on aerial photos) on nonfederal land. Aerial photos were taken in 1974, 1982, and 1994 (Azuma et al. 2002). With nearly 24,000 photo-points, the data provide almost 72,000 observations of building counts varying in space and time. Tracking building counts on individual photo-points at each of three points in time provides two observations of change in building counts (number of new buildings constructed) for each photo-point. When combined with other spatial data using a geographical information system (GIS), the entire data set comprises 44,928 observations.

Conceptual Framework

Spatial land use models based on discrete land use data generally assume that landowners choose the land use that maximizes the present value of future net returns derived from their land (Bockstael 1996; Irwin and Geoghegan 2001). For example, they might convert a forest or farmland parcel to an urban use once the present value of future returns generated by the parcel in urban use less conversion costs equals or exceeds returns generated by the parcel remaining as forest or farmland. Such assumptions are implied in the survival-time analyses found in Chapters 3 and 4 of this book, as well as in the assessment of use value taxation in Chapter 8.

Characterizing individual behavior in this way applies neatly to estimating discrete choice (logit or probit) models describing observed changes among discrete land use classes on individual parcels, or models of development timing seeking to forecast the future time at which individual farm or forest parcels will convert to alternative uses. The building-count data in this study, however, describe locally aggregated decisions of unknown numbers of individual landowners regarding construction of new buildings on land of all types. Hence, a conceptual framework characterizing development as numbers of new buildings within relatively local geographic areas is needed.

Within any local area, landowners face a range of development opportunities regarding new housing, businesses, and industry. Decisions regarding such opportunities are influenced by potential future rents to be earned from any one opportunity relative to rents earned from existing land uses. Within the 80-acre vicinity of sample points comprising building-count observations in this study, local landowners likely face similar types of development opportunities, subject to zoning and topographic differences that affect potential building sites. The extent to which we observe new buildings in any given local area is assumed to be a function of the potential returns to be earned from new development, as well as local zoning and topographic characteristics. The building counts identify newly constructed buildings and can be used to estimate Poisson and negative binomial models describing new development as a function of these factors.

Regionally disaggregated economic data describing potential land rents earned from new development relative to forestry and agriculture are not available, so proxy variables must be identified. Conceptually, the value of land in developed uses has been viewed as a function of the spatial proximity to city centers (Capozza and Helsley 1989; Fujita 1982; Mills 1980; Miyao 1981; Wheaton 1982). Von Thunen viewed spatial proximity in terms of costs associated with transporting forest and agricultural commodities to markets, influencing whether forestry and agriculture were profitable in any given location (Barlow 1978, *37*). Modern society, however, views spatial proximity in terms of the difference between quality-of-life factors, such as housing, neighborhood characteristics, and environmental amenities, and the costs associated with commuting to employment destinations. More consistent with central place theory, this view explains location choices based on the relative economic advantages of locating people, business, and industries in particular clusters and patterns (King 1984).

One of the most important factors affecting land's development potential in western Oregon is its commuting proximity to employment opportunities offered by major cities of the Willamette Valley. Land within short commuting distances likely will have greater development potential than land within relatively longer commuting distances. Also, land within commuting distance to a large city likely will have greater development potential than land within a comparable commuting distance to a smaller city. Cities beyond reasonable commuting distances likely will have very little, if any, influence on development potential. We describe the influence of city size and location using a gravity index (Haynes and Fotheringham 1984; Reilly 1929) to account for the combined influence of population and proximity as economic forces effecting land use change (Shi et al. 1997). The gravity index is combined with variables describing other factors, such as topography, existing development, and land use zoning mandated by Oregon's Land Use Planning Program, which also can influence development patterns. Land use zoning in Oregon, for example, requires cities and counties to focus new development inside urban-growth boundaries and restrict development outside of these boundaries by zoning those lands for exclusive farm or forest use.

Variable Selection

We describe the development potential of land using a gravity index computed as

$$GRAVITY\ INDEX_i = \sum_1^K POPULATION_k \left(\frac{60 - TIME_{ik}}{60} \right), \qquad (5\text{-}1)$$

where K represents the number of cities within a 60-minute drive (or commute) of each photo-point i, *POPULATION* is the population (U.S. Bureau of the Census 1992) of each city k, and *TIME* is the driving time in minutes between photo-point i and city k. The gravity index is the sum of populations of cities within a 60-minute commute of each photo-point, weighted by the estimated driving time to each city's edge. The index sets a 60-minute threshold on the "reasonable" commuting time, based on our assumption that most Oregonians probably commute no more than one hour to work. Varying this threshold to reflect somewhat shorter or longer maximum commuting times did not substantially affect the sign, magnitude, or statistical significance of the gravity index estimated coefficient. Incorporated into the gravity index computation are 45 western Oregon cities having 5,000 or more persons in 1990 (U.S. Bureau of the Census 1992). Adjacent cities are combined and treated as larger metropolitan areas, reducing the total number of cities and metropolitan areas included in the analysis to 30.

Driving times used to calculate the gravity index were estimated using a GIS map of roads existing in 2001 to create a friction surface based on average driving times assumed for different types of roads. We assume that drivers average speeds of 60 miles per hour on primary roads, 25 miles per hour on secondary roads, and 10 miles per hour where there are no roads. Driving times are based on road data from a single point in time, because data describing road improvements are unavailable. As a consequence, we ignore potential endogeneity between land use change and road building noted by Irwin and Geoghegan (2001) among others. Ignoring such endogeneity can lead to two potential problems. First, we fail to account for improved physical access to land provided by new roads in the future. Second, because driving times are based on the modern road network rather than a potentially less extensive network existing when new buildings were constructed in the past, gravity indices could be overestimated, and their model coefficient underestimated, in magnitude. Both problems could result in underestimating projected changes in building counts.

We combine the gravity index with other explanatory variables describing existing building counts, topographic features of slope and elevation, and dummy variables describing land use zoning adopted under Oregon's Land Use Planning Program (Abbott 1994). We assume that together the variables characterize the value of land in developed uses over its value in undeveloped forest and agriculture. We expect greater numbers of new buildings in areas with higher gravity index values, and fewer in areas with low values. We further expect that higher existing building counts have a positive but diminishing impact on new buildings, because factors attracting existing development likely attract new development before building-density limits mandated by zoning are achieved. We anticipate slope to be negatively correlated with new buildings, because steeper slopes can be more difficult to build on. High elevations also can be negatively correlated with new buildings if they impede construction with poor physical access. The correlation can be positive, however, if they provide desirable views (Wear and Bolstad 1998). Hence, the net effect of elevation is an empirical question. We expect that land located within urban-growth boundaries adopted under Oregon's Land Use Planning Program will gain greater numbers of new buildings than land in forest or farm zones.

Model Estimation

The dependent variable $\Delta BUILDINGS$ was constructed by computing changes in building counts observed within 80-acre circles surrounding sample points at 10-year intervals between 1974 and 1984, and between 1984 and 1994. To adjust the building-count observations to consistent 10-year intervals, building counts for 1984 were approximated by interpolating between 1982 and 1994 values, and rounding to the nearest whole number. The dependent variable $\Delta BUILDINGS$ is measured as a count and is not continuous. Assuming $\Delta BUILDINGS$ is distributed as a Poisson leads to the negative binomial model

$$pr(\Delta BUILDINGS = y_i | \gamma) = \frac{e^{-\lambda_i} \lambda_i^{y_i}}{y_i!} \qquad (5\text{-}2)$$

$$y_i = 0, 1, 2, \ldots; i = 1, 2, \ldots, n$$
$$\text{where } \ln(\lambda_i) = \ln(\hat{\lambda}_i) + \gamma = \beta' x_i + \gamma$$

where γ is a random variable and $\exp(\gamma)$ has a gamma distribution with mean 1 and variance α, x_i is a vector of independent variables, and β' is a vector of coefficients to be estimated (Greene 1997). The negative binomial model is a general form of the Poisson model relaxing the Poisson assumption that the dependent variable's mean equals its variance (Wear and Bolstad 1998).

The panel nature of the data—generally two observations of building-count change per photo-point—creates the potential for correlation among pairs of time-series observations for individual photo-points to deflate standard errors and bias estimated coefficients. We can account for these potential correlations using a random effects negative binomial model (Greene 1995, *570–71*). Because group effects are conditioned out (not computed), projected values cannot be computed using the random effects model (Greene 1995, *567*), but the estimated coefficients can be compared with those of the model estimated without random effects.

A final estimation issue is potential spatial autocorrelation among the building-count observations, which to our knowledge has not previously been addressed in count-data models. In this case, peculiarities in data reporting complicate remedies routinely used in discrete models. Although the building-count data are based on a systematic photo-point sampling spaced on roughly a 1,370-meter average grid, Forest Inventory and Analysis Program policy requires that the UTM x and y coordinates of sample points each be "fuzzed" by up to 1,000 meters to protect the precise point locations. This inhibits both purposeful sampling and the development of reliable spatial lags of $\Delta BUILDINGS$, because sample points neighboring each observation cannot be identified with certainty. Given these difficulties, we assume that the 1,370-meter average spacing of sample points likely minimizes any spatial behavioral relationships unaccounted for by the gravity index, zoning, and other spatial explanatory variables, and we estimate the final model leaving potential spatial autocorrelation untreated.

Recognizing the potential for spatial autocorrelation, however, we did test four alternative spatial autocorrelation remedies using the fuzzed UTM coordinates: two based on purposeful sampling and two on the inclusion of spatial lag variables. The four models yielded estimated coefficients that were similar in sign, magnitude, and statistical significance to those of the presented model. Estimated spatial lag coefficients in the two models that included them were positive and statistically significant (P<0.01), suggesting that building-count changes observed on individual sample points do seem to be accompanied by changes on neighboring sample points. Building-density projections made using the alternative models differed from those of the presented model by 0.3 to 0.7 percent for undeveloped land, and 0.3 to 0.5 percent for undeveloped and low-density developed land combined (the two categories of particular interest here). Based as they are on imperfect UTM coordinates and somewhat ad hoc remedies, the alternative model results are not shown, but they are available from the author upon request.

Fuzzy UTM coordinates do not affect the slope, elevation and land use zoning variables included in the analysis, because they were developed using unfuzzed coordinates. Because the fuzziness is limited to one kilometer and the data span a geographic area of roughly 78,000 square kilometers, impacts to the gravity index variable are negligible. The general regression equation describes changes in building counts on photo-points from one time point to the next, where the specific explanatory variables are described in Table 5-1.

Table 5-1. Descriptions of Explanatory Variables Tested in the Empirical Model

Variable	Description
GRAVITY INDEX	Equal to the average of the gravity index computed (using Equation 5-2) at the beginning of each time period and the gravity index computed at the end of each time period (times 1/100,000). City populations for noncensus years estimated by interpolating between populations reported for census years (U.S. Bureau of Census 1992).
BUILDING COUNT	Number of buildings within an 80-acre circle surrounding photo-point (Azuma et al. 2002) at the beginning of each time period (times 1/100).
SLOPE	Percent slope at the sample point (times 1/100).
ELEVATION	Elevation in meters.
URBAN GROWTH BOUNDARY	Variable equals 1 if plot is located in an urban-growth boundary or rural residential land use zone; 0 otherwise.
FARM ZONE	Variable equals 1 if plot is located in a farm zone; 0 otherwise.
FOREST ZONE	Variable equals 1 if plot is located in a forest zone; 0 otherwise.
1994	Variable equals 1 if observation describes building-density change from 1984 to 1994; 0 otherwise.

This equation is given as

$$\Delta BUILDINGS = f(GRAVITY\ INDEX,\ BUILDING\ COUNT,\ SLOPE,$$
$$ELEVATION, URBAN\text{-}GROWTH,\ BOUNDARY,$$
$$FARM\ ZONE,\ FOREST\ ZONE,\ 1994). \qquad (5\text{-}3)$$

The model is highly significant, based on log-likelihood ratio tests of the Poisson model ($\chi^2 = 39,597, df = 9, p < 0.0001$) and negative binomial model tested against the null of the Poisson ($\chi^2 = 25,134, df = 1, p < 0.0001$). Random effects model coefficients are reasonably consistent with negative binomial coefficients, although the statistical significance of the beta coefficient in the random effects regression suggests that statistically significant random effects may be present.

Estimated coefficients for the linear and quadratic GRAVITY INDEX variables are statistically significant (P<0.01) and together suggest that, over time, building counts rise at an increasing rate with greater proximity to cities within commuting distance and higher population sizes of those cities (Table 5-2). Estimated coefficients for the linear and quadratic BUILDING-COUNT variables are statistically significant (P<0.01) and together suggest that existing building numbers have a positive but diminishing impact on future building-count increases. Estimated coefficients for SLOPE and ELEVATION are negative and

Table 5-2. Estimated Coefficients of Negative Binomial Models Describing Changes in Building Counts in Western Oregon

| Variable | Negative binomial regression | | Negative binomial regression with random effects |
	Coefficient	Marginal effect	
GRAVITY INDEX	−0.308 (−13.66)	−0.410	−0.045 (−2.36)
GRAVITY INDEX^2	0.048 (12.48)	0.064	0.009 (3.52)
BUILDING COUNT	24.999 (46.63)	33.312	16.971 (63.22)
BUILDING COUNT^2	−26.572 (−45.88)	−35.408	−26.720 (−59.28)
SLOPE	−7.530 (−30.59)	−10.034	−5.851 (−20.28)
ELEVATION	−2.127 (−28.43)	−2.835	−1.714 (−20.44)
URBAN GROWTH BOUNDARY	1.076 (7.13)	1.433	0.716 (5.22)
FARM ZONE	0.162 (1.09)	0.215	0.547 (3.97)
FOREST ZONE	−0.363 (−2.39)	−0.484	0.062 (0.43)
1994	−1.088 (−8.09)	−1.450	−1.168 (−9.70)
Alpha	4.385 (50.73)	—	2.148 (30.88)
Beta	—	—	0.884 (23.67)
Summary statistics:	Poisson log-L $= -37,214$		Log-L $= 24,357$
	$\chi^2 = 39,597, = 9, P < 0.0001$		
	Negative binomial log-L $= 24,647$		
	$\chi^2 = 25,134, df = 1, P < 0.0001^a$		

Notes: $N = 44,928$. The t-statistics for each estimated coefficient are in parentheses.

[a] Tested against the null of the Poisson model.

statistically significant (P<0.01), suggesting that slope and elevation have a negative impact on building-count changes. Relative to FARM ZONE and FOREST ZONE, estimated coefficients for URBAN-GROWTH BOUNDARY are positive and statistically significant (P<0.01), suggesting that Oregon's Land Use Planning Program has tended to concentrate new building construction within urban-growth boundaries since it mandated the adoption of statewide zoning.

Model Validation

In multidisciplinary research, an important part of empirical modeling is validating models by examining the potential accuracy of projected values. We evaluated the forecasting performance of previous versions of the negative binomial land use model by looking at the percentage of correct projections within the sample, estimating auxiliary models after reserving validation data sets; and examining several information indices suggested by Hauser (1978) and Wear and Bolstad (1998). We briefly describe only the first of these here; details regarding the other validation procedures can be found in Kline et al. (2003). Their general results, however, were that estimated coefficients of five auxiliary models, each estimated by excluding 20 percent of the sample, were consistent in sign, magnitude, and statistical significance with those of the main model estimated using the full sample, and also fell within the 95 percent confidence bounds of the main model coefficients; and that information indices suggested that the empirical models were both statistically significant and accurate, but that the models were better at predicting coarser (less precise) rather than finer (more precise) ending building-density classes.

Regarding the percentage of correct projections within-sample, we used the estimated negative binomial model coefficients (Table 5-2) to compute projected changes in building counts, which were added to initial building counts to compute within-sample projections of ending building counts for each observation ($N = 44, 928$). Projected changes in building counts were estimated by using the empirical model to compute the expected value of y_i as

$$E[y_i] = \lambda_i \qquad (5\text{-}4)$$

(Greene 1995, *551*). We compared projected to actual ending building counts to compute the percentage of correct projections. This percentage decreases as ending building counts increase, from a high of 100.0 percent for observations having an ending building count of zero to a low of 19.3 percent for observations having an ending building count of eight (Table 5-3). The percentage of correct projections within one building is higher, ranging from 100.0 percent for observations having an ending building count of zero or one to a low of 48.8 percent for those with an ending building count of eight. Greater accuracy at the lower range of ending building counts likely is due in part to the relatively large proportion of observations with relatively low building counts.

The purpose of the model in the Coastal Landscape Analysis and Modeling Study is to locate forestland with building densities of greater than 64 buildings per square mile—the point at which timber management and production are assumed to end in the study's timber production models. This threshold is consistent with an average forest parcel size of 10 acres per building (house), which is the minimum forest parcel size eligible for preferential assessment as forestland for property tax purposes in Oregon (Oregon Department of Revenue 1998). Based on an average household size of 2.45 persons (Azuma et al. 2002), the 64-buildings-per-square-mile threshold also is equivalent to 157 people per square mile, which is relatively consistent with the population density found by Wear et al. (1999) to be the point at which commercial timber production ends on private forestlands. Using the 80-acre basis of our building-count data, the 64-buildings-per-square-mile density threshold is equivalent to 8 buildings per 80 acres. The percentage of correct projections falling above

Table 5-3. Percentage of Within-Sample Correct Base Model Projections of Ending Building Counts and Ending Broad Building-Count Class

Class	Percent in class	Percent of class correctly projected	Percent correctly projected within one building
Ending building count[a]			
0	68.7	100.0	100.0
1	8.9	80.0	100.0
2	5.5	63.0	88.9
3	3.9	48.2	82.2
4	2.6	40.2	74.4
5	1.8	33.2	65.8
6	1.5	27.8	56.3
7	1.0	20.2	52.4
8	0.9	19.3	48.8
>8	5.2	81.8	86.4
Ending broad building-count class			
≤8	94.8	99.6	99.8
>8	5.2	82.8	86.4

Note: N = 44,928

[a] Building count within an 80-acre circle surrounding sample photo-point.

and below the threshold is relatively high—99.6 percent for the ≤8 class and 82.8 percent for the >8 class—suggesting that the model is probably adequate for the immediate purposes for which it is used.

Integrating Land Use Projections with Timber Production and Ecology Models

The estimated negative binomial coefficients (Table 5-2) are combined with projected gravity index values to compute increases in building counts on forest and agricultural land in western Oregon, given existing land use zoning. Existing and projected 80-acre building counts are converted to building densities per square mile. Projected city populations are based on county population projections for western Oregon through 2040 (Office of Economic Analysis 1997) and on extrapolation for 2040 to 2054. Building-density projections are used to create GIS maps of future low-density and urban development of forestlands that are inputs to timber production and habitat viability models (Kline et al. 2003).

Forestlands were delineated from agricultural lands using a vegetation map of 1995 forest and nonforest cover, and these delineations remain constant throughout the modeling time horizon. A base-year map of building densities was developed from the 1994 building-count data by interpolating between photo-point building-count values and converting these to densities per square mile. Projected changes in building densities at each 10-year modeling interval were added to the beginning building-density map for that interval to obtain the ending building-density map. For example, projected changes between 1994 and 2004 were added to 1994 building densities to obtain a 2004 building-density map. These maps delineate the forestland area available for timber production and wildlife habitat at each 10-year modeling interval according to low-density and urban building-density thresholds (Spies et al. 2002).

Timber production is assumed to end on forestlands attaining a low-density threshold of 64 buildings per square mile, the point at which standing trees are assumed to be no longer available for harvest for the remainder of the modeling time horizon. Wildlife habitat is assumed to end on forestlands attaining an urban threshold of 640 buildings per square mile, which most likely could be achieved only on lands zoned within urban-growth boundaries. Additionally, once low-density and urban lands are delineated, quarter-acre open vegetation patches (building footprints) are created for each projected new building. The building footprints are intended to represent the indirect impact of buildings on timber production and wildlife habitat in terms of their direct impacts on vegetative cover. The quarter-acre footprints are consistent with the average vegetation patch sizes found among a sampling of buildings in the study area. The footprints also are roughly equivalent in size to the basic spatial simulation unit used in Coastal Landscape Analysis and Modeling Study timber production models. The specific locations of building footprints are selected randomly according to estimated building densities for each unit.

Projected Low-Density and Urban Development

As shown in Table 5-4, land use data for 1994 indicate that western Oregon comprised about 9.9 million acres of nonfederal forest (7.2 million, 73 percent), agricultural (1.9 million, 19 percent), and mixed forest–agricultural land (0.8 million, 8 percent). Building-density data indicate that 61,920 acres (0.9 percent) of forestland, 136,787 acres (7.0 percent) of agricultural land, and 35,573 acres (4.6 percent) of mixed forest–agricultural land fell in the low-density class (64 to 640 buildings per square mile). Land exceeding the urban threshold (>640 buildings per square mile) is assumed to have converted from forest and agricultural uses to predominantly urban uses. Building-density projections suggest that by 2024, 37,440 acres (0.5 percent) of forestland, 113,666 acres (5.8 percent) of agricultural land, and 23,405 acres (3.0 percent) of mixed forest–agricultural land that existed in 1994 will have been converted to urban uses. Also by 2024, 103,680 acres (1.4 percent) of remaining forestland, 268,328 acres (14.7 percent) of agricultural land, and 70,215 acres (9.3 percent) of mixed forest–agricultural land will fall in the low-density class. By 2054, 105,840 acres (1.5 percent) of forestland, 350,129 acres (18.0 percent) of agricultural land,

Table 5-4. Projected Low-Density and Urban Development on Nonfederal Forested and Agricultural Land in Western Oregon, 1994–2054

| Land cover | *Building-density class*[a] | | | |
	Undeveloped *($\leq$64)*[b]	*Low-density* *(65 to 640)*[b]	*Urban* *($>$640)*	*Total undeveloped and low-density*[b]
Existing in 1994[c]				
Forest	7,138,080	61,920	—	7,200,000
Agriculture	1,806,213	136,787	—	1,943,000
Mixed	739,427	35,573	—	775,000
Total	9,683,720	234,280	—	9,918,000
Projected in 2024				
Forest	7,058,880	103,680	37,440	7,162,560
Agriculture	1,561,006	268,328	113,666	1,829,334
Mixed	681,380	70,215	23,405	751,595
Total	9,301,266	442,223	174,511	9,743,489
Projected in 2054				
Forest	6,952,320	141,840	105,840	7,094,160
Agriculture	1,134,906	457,965	350,129	1,592,871
Mixed	600,315	105,400	69,285	705,715
Total	8,687,541	705,205	525,254	9,392,746

[a] Buildings per square mile computed from projected building counts.

[b] Coastal Landscape Analysis and Modeling Study assumptions allow only forestland in the undeveloped class to contribute to timber production, while forestland in both the undeveloped and low-density classes contributes to wildlife habitat. Agricultural land was included in land use modeling but is not included in the other study analyses.

[c] Reported in Azuma et al. (2002).

and 69,285 acres (8.9 percent) of mixed forest–agricultural land that existed in 1994 will have been converted to urban uses. Also by 2054, 141,840 acres (2.0 percent) of remaining forestland, 457,965 acres (28.8 percent) of agricultural land, and 105,400 acres (14.9 percent) of mixed forest–agricultural land will fall in the low-density class.

Along with forest and agricultural land lost to urban uses, building-density projections suggest that greater numbers of people will be living in closer proximity to remaining forestlands in the future. The projected building densities are based on population values that are outside the range of data used to estimate the empirical model. To evaluate how reasonable the building density projections are, we compared per capita increases in low-density and urban development indicated by our spatial projections with per capita development rates indicated by 1997 National Resources Inventory data for Oregon (NRCS 1999). Our projections suggest that low-density and urban development will increase an average of 0.44 acre per new resident from 1994 to 2054. This rate is quite close to the average 0.46-acre increase in "developed land" per new resident in Oregon from 1982 to 1997, and below the national average of 0.69 acre per new resident, based on National Resources Inventory data.

Conclusions

The building-count model and resulting building-density projections are one example of how useful, conceptually rigorous land use information can be provided in multidisciplinary settings when data are imperfect. In the absence of spatial economic data describing land rents, we used information about city populations and locations to proxy potential rents earned from land in developed uses. Combined with data describing topographic features and land use zoning, the empirical model describes potential future land development in terms of numbers and locations of new buildings. Model validation procedures suggest that the likelihood of correctly projecting future building densities improves with the increasing coarseness of building-density classes desired. The model is better at projecting close to actual future building density classes than it is at projecting exact ones. The validation illustrates the trade-offs inherent in choosing between precision and accuracy when building-density classes, or any land use classes, are projected using spatial models.

This particular modeling approach was made possible by obtaining building-count data, which are unavailable from national land inventories and other common data sources and are relatively expensive to collect independently. Where such data are available, however, they can enable analyses that more closely match the needs of ecologists and others seeking to forecast natural resource productivity. Here, the data enabled empirical modeling of new buildings, which provides more information relevant to timber production and ecological analyses than do discrete land use classes. The model enables analysts to account for ranges of human occupation of forestland that are relevant to timber production and wildlife habitat. Unconstrained by discrete forest and urban delineations, the model provides land use information that potentially can be applied to a broader range of research issues.

Spatial land use models often suffer from a weak link between their conceptual framework and empirical application because of poor availability of data with which to construct conceptually appropriate explanatory variables. In this case, better information regarding potential forestry rents would enable more accurate accounting of the opportunity costs of forestland development. Related to this is the need to consider heterogeneity across forest stands when describing landowners' decisions to convert forestland to developed uses. An ideal data set would include information describing both land and landowners. In this particular application, such factors as species, age class, and standing volume likely are important in landowners' timber harvest decisions, which often coincide with forestland conversion. Other potentially influential factors might include a landowner's age, education, and income level; how much forestland he or she owns; and the overall management objectives (Kline et al. 2000). Obtaining linked data describing both land and landowners often is not possible, however, because of concerns about protecting the privacy of survey respondents. In this application, land use information is treated as an exogenous input into timber production models. Greater integration of land use and timber production analyses would allow for land use change and forest production decisions to be modeled as the endogenous decisions they often are.

Developing spatial land use models calls for new types of data and relatively new empirical techniques to address econometric issues presented by spatial data. Integrating spatial land use information into multidisciplinary research necessarily involves identifying relevant research issues and specific information needs of cooperating analysts, obtaining conceptually relevant spatial data with which to estimate empirical models, and adapting existing spatial econometric methods to suit the particular modeling objectives and data at hand. Given the wide variety of potential multidisciplinary research topics, a lack of regular and consistent spatial data sources, and an absence of universally accepted protocols regarding spatial land use analysis, no universal approach is likely to emerge for some time. Analysts will need to consider conceptual and empirical trade-offs associated with different types of data and modeling methods as they determine how best to meet their research objectives in a cost-effective manner.

References

Abbott, C. (1994). *Planning the Oregon Way.* Corvallis: Oregon State University Press.

Alig, R. J. (1986). Econometric Analysis of the Factors Influencing Forest Acreage Trends in the Southeast. *Forest Science* 32(1): 119–134.

Alig, R. J., and R. G. Healy. (1987). Urban and Built-Up Land Area Changes in the United States: An Empirical Investigation of Determinants. *Land Economics* 63(3): 215–226.

Alig, R. J., J. D. Kline, and M. Lichtenstein. (2004). Urbanization on the U.S. Landscape: Looking Ahead in the 21st Century. *Landscape and Urban Planning* 69(2–3): 219–234.

Alig, R. J., F. C. White, and B. C. Murray. (1988). Economic Factors Influencing Land Use Changes in the South-Central United States. Research Paper SE-272. Asheville, NC: U.S. Department of Agriculture, Forest Service, Southeastern Forest Experiment Station.

Azuma, D. L., K. R. Birch, A. A. Herstrom, J. D. Kline, and G. Lettman. (2002). Land Use Change on Non-Federal Land in Western Oregon, 1973–2000. Salem: Oregon Department of Forestry.

Barlow, R. (1978). *Land Resource Economics: The Economics of Real Estate.* Englewood Cliffs, NJ: Prentice-Hall.

Barlow, S. A., I. A. Munn, D. A. Cleaves, and D. L. Evans. (1998). The Effect of Urban Sprawl on Timber Harvesting. *Journal of Forestry* 96: 10–14.

Bockstael, N. E. (1996). Modeling Economics and Ecology: The Importance of a Spatial Perspective. *American Journal of Agricultural Economics* 78: 1168–1180.

Bradshaw, T. K., and B. Muller. (1998). Impacts of Rapid Urban Growth on Farmland Conversion: Application of New Regional Land Use Policy Models and Geographical Information Systems. *Rural Sociology* 63: 1–25.

Capozza, D. R., and R. W. Helsley. (1989). The Fundamentals of Land Prices and Urban Growth. *Journal of Urban Economics* 26: 295–306.

Chomitz, K. M., and D. A. Gray. (1996). Roads, Land Use, and Deforestation: A Spatial Model Applied to Belize. *World Bank Economic Review* 10: 487–512.

Cropper, M., C. Griffiths, and M. Muthukumara. (1999). Roads, Population Pressures, and Deforestation in Thailand, 1976–89. *Land Economics* 75(1): 58–73.

Egan, A. F., and A. E. Luloff. (2000). The Exurbanization of America's Forests: Research in Rural Social Science. *Journal of Forestry* 98(3): 26–30.

Fleming, M. (2004). Techniques for Estimating Spatially Dependent Discrete Choice Models. In *Advances in Spatial Econometrics: Methodology, Tools, and Applications*, edited by L. Anselin and R. J. G. M. Florax. New York: Springer-Verlag, 145–168.

Fortin, M., P. Drapeau, and P. Legendre. (1989). Spatial Autocorrelation and Sampling Design in Plant Ecology. *Vegetatio* 83: 209–222.

Franzen, R., and B. Hunsberger. (1998). Have We Outgrown Our Approach to Growth? *Sunday Oregonian*, December 13.

Frayer, W. E., and G. M. Furnival. (1999). Forest Survey Sampling Designs: A History. *Journal of Forestry* 97(12): 4–10.

Fujita, M. (1982). Spatial Patterns of Residential Development. *Journal of Urban Economics* 12: 22–52.

Greene, W. H. (1995). *LIMDEP Version 7.0: User's Manual.* Bellport, NY: Econometric Software.

———. (1997). *Econometric Analysis.* Upper Saddle River, NJ: Prentice Hall.

Haining, R. (1990). *Spatial Data Analysis in the Social and Environmental Sciences.* New York: Cambridge University Press.

Hardie, I. W. and P. J. Parks. (1997). Land Use with Heterogeneous Land Quality: An Application of an Area-Base Model. *American Journal of Agricultural Economics* 79(2): 299.

Hardie, I., P. Parks, P. Gottleib, and D. Wear. (2000). Responsiveness of Rural and Urban Land Uses to Land Rent Determinants in the U.S. South. *Land Economics* 76(4): 659–673.

Hauser, J. R. (1978). Testing the Accuracy, Usefulness, and Significance of Probabilistic Choice Models: An Information-Theoretic Approach. *Operations Research* 26: 406–421.

Hayes, J. L., A. A. Agar, and R. J. Barbour (eds). (2004). Methods for Integrated Modeling of Landscape Change: Interior Northwest Landscape Analysis System. General Technical Report PNW-GTR-610. Portland, Oregon: U.S. Department of Agriculture, Forest Service, Pacific Northwest Research Station.

Haynes, K. E., and A. S. Fotheringham. (1984). *Gravity and Spatial Interaction Models.* Beverly Hills, CA: Sage Publications.

Haynes, R. W. (2002). An Analysis of the Timber Situation in the United States, 1952 to 2050: A Technical Document Supporting the 2000 USDA Forest Service RPA Assessment. General Technical Report PNW-GTR-XXX. Portland, Oregon: U.S. Department of Agriculture, Forest Service, Pacific Northwest Research Station.

Helmer, E. H. (2000). The Landscape Ecology of Tropical Secondary Forest in Montane Costa Rica. *Ecosystem* 3: 98–114.

Irwin, E. G., and J. Geoghegan. (2001). Theory, Data, Methods: Developing Spatially Explicit Economic Models of Land Use Change. *Agriculture, Ecosystems and Environment* 85(1–3): 7–23.

King, L. J. (1984). *Central Place Theory.* Beverly Hills, CA: Sage Publications.

Kline, J. D., and R. J. Alig. (1999). Does Land Use Planning Slow the Conversion of Forest and Farmlands? *Growth and Change* 30: 3–22.

Kline, J. D., R. J. Alig, and R. L. Johnson. (2000). Fostering the Production of Nontimber Services among Forest Owners with Heterogeneous Objectives. *Forest Science* 46(2): 302–311.

Kline, J. D., D. L. Azuma, and R. J. Alig. (2004). Population Growth, Urban Expansion, and Private Forestry in Western Oregon. *Forest Science* 50(1): 33–43.

Kline, J. D., D. L. Azuma, and A. Moses. (2003). Modeling the Spatially Dynamic Distribution of Humans in the Oregon (USA) Coast Range. *Landscape Ecology* 18(4): 347–361.

Kline, J. D., A. Moses, and R. J. Alig. (2001). Integrating Urbanization into Landscape-Level Ecological Assessments. *Ecosystems* 4(1): 3–18.

Lambin, E. F., H. J. Geist, and E. Lepers. (2003). Dynamics of Land-Use and Land-Cover Change in Tropical Regions. *Annual Review of Environmental Resources* 28: 205–241.

Lichtenberg, E. (1989). Land Quality, Irrigation Development, and Cropping Patterns in the Northern High Plains. *American Journal of Agricultural Economics* 71(February): 187–194.

Mills, E. S. (1980). *Urban Economics.* Glenview, IL: Scott, Foresman and Co.

Miyao, T. (1981). *Dynamic Analysis of the Urban Economy.* New York: Academic Press.

NRCS (Natural Resources Conservation Service). (1999). Summary Report 1997 National Resources Inventory (revised December 2000). Washington, DC: U.S. Department of Agriculture.

Nusser, S. M., and J. J. Goebel. (1997). The National Resources Inventory: A Long-Term Multi-Resource Monitoring Programme. *Environmental and Ecological Statistics* 4: 181–204.

Nelson, G. C., and D. Hellerstein. (1997). Do Roads Cause Deforestation? Using Satellite Images in Econometric Analysis of Land Use. *American Journal of Agricultural Economics* 79: 80–88.

Office of Economic Analysis. (1997). Long-Term Population and Employment Forecasts for Oregon: State and Total Populations. Salem: Oregon Department of Administrative Services.

Oregon Department of Revenue. (1998). Specially Assessed Forestland. Salem: Property Tax Division, Valuation Section, Oregon Department of Revenue.

Parks, P. J., and B. C. Murray. (1994). Land Attributes and Land Allocation: Nonindustrial Forest Use in the Pacific Northwest. *Forest Science* 40(3): 558–575.

Plantinga, A. J. (1996). The Effect of Agricultural Policies on Land Use and Environmental Quality. *American Journal of Agricultural Economics* 78(November): 1082–1091.

Plantinga, A. J., J. Buongiorno, and R. J. Alig. (1990). Determinants of Changes in Non-Industrial Private Timberland Ownership in the United States. *Journal of World Forest Resource Management* 5: 29–46.

Plantinga, A. J., T. Mauldin, and R. Alig. (1999). Land Use in Maine: Determinants of Past Trends and Projections of Future Changes. Research Paper PNW-RP-511. Portland, OR: U.S. Department of Agriculture, Forest Service, Pacific Northwest Research Station.

Reilly, W. J. (1929). Methods for the Study of Retail Relationships. University of Texas Bulletin no. 2944. Austin.

Shi, Y. J., T. T. Phipps, and D. Colyer. (1997). Agricultural Land Values under Urbanizing Influences. *Land Economics* 73: 90–100.

Sohngen, B., and R. Alig. (2001). Spatial Econometrics: Potential Application to Land Use Change and Forestry. Working paper. Ohio State University, Columbus.

Spies, T. A., G. H. Reeves, K. M. Burnett, W. C. McComb, K. N. Johnson, G. Grant, J. L. Ohmann, S. L. Garman, and P. Bettinger. (2002). Assessing the Ecological Consequences of Forest Policies in a Multi-Ownership Province in Oregon. In *Integrating Landscape Ecology into Natural Resource Management*, edited by J. Liu and W. W. Taylor. New York: Cambridge University Press, 179–207.

Stavins, R. N., and A. B. Jaffe. (1990). Unintended Impacts of Public Investments on Private Decisions: The Depletion of Forested Wetlands. *American Economic Review* 80 (June): 337–352.

U.S. Bureau of the Census. (1992). *1990 Census of Population and Housing*. Washington, DC: U.S. Department of Commerce.

Wear, D. N., and P. Bolstad. (1998). Land-Use Changes in Southern Appalachian Landscapes: Spatial Analysis and Forecast Evaluation. *Ecosystems* 1: 575–594.

Wear, D. N., R. Lui, J. M. Foreman, and R. Sheffield. (1999). The Effects of Population Growth on Timber Management and Inventories in Virginia. *Forest Ecology and Management* 118(1–3): 107–115.

Wear, D. N., M. G. Turner, and R. O. Flamm. (1996). Ecosystem Management with Multiple Owners: Landscape Dynamics in a Southern Appalachian Watershed. *Ecological Applications* 6: 1173–1188.

Wheaton, W. C. (1982). Urban Residential Growth under Perfect Foresight. *Journal of Urban Economics* 12: 1–12.

White, F. C., and F. N. Fleming. (1980). An Analysis of Competing Agricultural Land Uses. *Southern Journal of Agricultural Economics* 12(4): 99–103.

6

Critical Mass

Does the Number of Productive Farmland Acres or Farms Affect Farmland Loss?

Lori Lynch

As farmland and the number of farms has decreased over the last 50 years, some have questioned whether there is a "critical mass" of agricultural land needed to sustain a viable agricultural sector. The total amount of farmland decreased by 20 percent in the United States between 1949 and 1997. In the Mid-Atlantic region, 50 percent of the farmland left the industry during this same period. The number of farms in the United States as a whole declined by 65 percent between 1949 and 1997, while the Mid-Atlantic lost farms at a rate of 71 percent. In metropolitan areas, agricultural land has been converted to alternative uses even faster than these averages (Lockeretz 1989; Gardner 1994). Given these patterns, one might question whether the continuing conversion of farmland to other uses will result in too few acres or too little farm activity to sustain an agricultural economy in certain areas.[1]

Many reasons exist for retaining farmland. Metropolitan residents have expressed concern about the loss of the amenities that farmland provides. Rural economies that are highly dependent on agricultural industries may suffer negative consequences when agricultural land is converted. Society as a whole may wish to retain an agricultural sector in order to maximize its welfare or economic well-being. Given such motives, many counties are trying to determine how much agricultural land must be retained to ensure a viable agricultural economy and the long-term preservation of amenities associated with farms and farmland. Government officials need to determine how much agricultural land is enough to ensure this retention. Therefore, it is important to establish whether the rate of farmland loss is affected by the level of agricultural activity within an area.

The idea that a critical mass of agricultural activity must be sustained in order for an area's agricultural economy to remain viable has a certain logic. The critical mass concept is based on the idea that economies of scale exist in both input and output businesses and services that are essential to agriculture. As production levels decline below a given threshold, costs will rise and support businesses will close or relocate. If input and output firms exit the county, the closest input supplier not only may be farther away for a farmer, but also may charge higher prices for inputs, veterinarian services, and equipment repairs because of reduced competition and the need to cover fixed costs. Similarly, if the nearest processor goes out of business because it cannot cover its fixed costs with a shrinking farm production, the nearest outlet for the product might involve additional transportation costs or a lower purchase price, either raising farmers' production costs or decreasing their revenue.[2] Changes in farmers' comparative advantage and their net revenues alter the relative returns of exiting farming. A decline in agriculture profits and thus a higher relative return for conversion to residential, recreational, or forestry uses may increase the rate of loss of farms and farmland in the area.

One may view research regarding a critical mass in agriculture as extending the urban economics literature on agglomeration externalities. In this vein of literature, people investigate whether synergies, innovativeness, and cost savings exist for like industries when they locate close to one another (localization economies such as Silicon Valley, California) and for different industries when they are located in a large city, despite higher rent and usually higher wage labor (urbanization economies). Agriculture might experience similar impacts on innovativeness and cost savings when operating in areas with other nearby agricultural enterprises. Most urban economics work in this area has focused on the location decisions of firms, but the related critical mass argument investigates decisions of farms to exit the agricultural economy and, often, to sell land to those who would convert it to residential, commercial, or other developed use.

Researchers and policymakers articulated the concept of critical mass and recognized its complexities as early as the 1970s. Lapping (1979) hypothesized that the critical mass level would vary from crop to crop, and that local growing conditions, traditions, and existing infrastructure would affect the profitability and sustainability of agriculture and thus the level of a critical mass threshold in any particular geographic area. Further, technological changes may change the threshold level over time. For example, the transition of suppliers from traditional farm-supply stores to Internet sales using delivery services might overcome some of the negative consequences of a local input supplier leaving the area.

Despite the recognition that a critical mass might exist, extensive research has not been conducted to prove the existence, or exact level, of such a threshold. A few studies have attempted to determine a critical mass. For example,

Dhillon and Derr (1974) estimated the critical size necessary to operate at or close to the minimum per-unit production cost. Focusing on agricultural commodities grown in the Philadelphia–New York–Boston corridor, they determined critical production levels for dairy, poultry, and fresh market vegetable production. In 2001, Daniels and Lapping used an either-or formulation, hypothesizing that at least 100,000 acres, $50 million in agricultural sales, or 20,000 acres of preserved farmland were needed to ensure a critical mass. Some programs have set goals for minimum continuous acres of preserved farmland (e.g., blocks of 1,000 contiguous acres) to slow the incursion of development (Anonymous 2001), and some counties have set a minimum level of aggregate farmland acres they wish to retain. The methodologies for defining these levels, in all except the Dhillon and Derr study, appear somewhat ad hoc.

Defining a critical mass would provide information for policymakers engaged in activities that impact land use decisions and the preservation of farms and farmland. To increase efficiency, farmland preservation programs may need to target areas where a critical mass of agricultural activity exists (Daniels and Lapping 2001), rather than spread their resources to those areas where agriculture is less likely to survive because they have already dipped below the critical mass. Given the limited funds available, prioritizing where and how to protect farmland ensures the highest level of open-space preservation and agricultural activity. Programs that target contiguous agricultural areas rather than random, noncontiguous farms may also achieve more success by reducing conflicts between farmers and residential or commercial neighbors.

Economic theory suggests that agricultural landowners will farm the land until the value in an alternative use exceeds the agricultural value. The net market value in many developed uses (commercial, residential, and industrial) is often greater than in agricultural use. Thus, at least in theory, the market will allocate the land to this privately optimal developed use. This use may not always be socially optimal, however, as the loss of farmland affects the general public and the value of remaining agricultural land, not just the individuals engaged in land purchases or sales. Maintaining land in agriculture can provide open space, improved quality of rural life, landscape vistas, and groundwater recharge areas, and it contributes to the local economy, all of which impact society as a whole. Agricultural land is also associated with less positive attributes that affect its neighbors, such as odors from livestock operations, drift from chemical pesticide, water-quality concerns from fertilizer use, insects, dust, noise, and slow-moving equipment on the roads. If the negative externalities outweighed the positive, the private market would retain too much land in agriculture.

The conversion of farmland can impact the value of the land remaining in agricultural use. Adjacent land use can affect agricultural land use in several ways. Population growth or suburbanization near farming areas can create problems for farmers. Nonfarm neighbors may object to nuisances related to traditional farming practices, such as those listed above, and may advocate limitations to these practices. Even in rural areas, incompatible activities in the surrounding landscape may affect the profitability of farms. For example, farmers may earn more profit operating within a thriving agricultural community than in a locale dominated by other land uses, be it a city, forest, or recreational area.

This chapter describes research conducted to establish whether a critical mass threshold exists for agricultural land. We analyze whether counties lose farmland at a faster rate if the number of acres or farms falls below a threshold level of acres. The study area includes six Mid-Atlantic states from 1949 to 1997. Because farmland loss can be affected by a variety of factors besides a critical mass, we also examine the effects of factors such as agricultural net returns and development pressure on the rate of farmland loss. The model both estimates the impacts of these factors and conducts an associated sensitivity analysis. Finally, we explore whether the effects of critical mass and other variables on agricultural land conversion appear to have changed over time.

Economic and Econometric Models

To investigate whether a critical mass threshold exists in the Mid-Atlantic agricultural sector, we analyze the difference in the rate of farmland loss for counties with varying levels of farmland acreage over time, holding constant all other variables.[3] The county's rate of farmland loss is modeled as a function of the number of productive agricultural acres, the net return in an agricultural use, the net value in a residential use, the existence of agricultural preservation policies, and the availability of off-farm income opportunities. When a county has a high number of productive acres, the farm sector can sustain a viable support sector, and local agriculture may remain competitive. Thus farmland and farm loss rates are hypothesized to be a function of the number of productive farmland acres, again holding all other variables constant.

Farmland might be converted for various reasons unrelated to the concept of critical mass. For example, theory states that it will be converted to nonfarm uses when the net value of an alternative use is higher than an agricultural use. This would increase the rate of farmland loss. If agricultural land is converted to housing because returns for agricultural use are lower than in a residential use, this is not evidence of critical mass. If, however, a county's farmland decreases below a certain critical level—only after which returns in agriculture fall below those of residential development—then this would provide some evidence of a critical mass. The farmland loss rate may also be high if the area has low or negative agricultural net return, even if residential, commercial, and industrial uses have low net values. In such cases, the farmland would be idled or possibly converted to forestland. It is important to recognize that this analysis does not assume that farmland is converted to housing rather than another nonagricultural land use; farms can also leave agriculture to become businesses or forests. Rather, the model attempts to isolate the effect of a critical mass from other reasons that farmland or farms might be lost.

Among factors hypothesized to influence farmland conversion, agricultural preservation programs purchase development rights on agricultural parcels, and preferential taxation programs decrease a farmer's property tax. Thus these programs can increase the relative return of retaining land in an agricultural use. Consequently, they can contribute to the retention of farmland acres and slow the rate of farmland and farm loss.

Off-farm employment may also increase or decrease the rate of farmland and farm loss. When off-farm income opportunities are high, farmers might choose to leave farming and enter other professions. This will tend to increase the rate of farmland and farm loss, unless this land is sold to another farmer. Alternatively, off-farm employment opportunities may decrease the farmland and farm loss rate if farmers supplement their farm income with off-farm income. Off-farm income may also be an important diversification strategy for farmers.

In addition to potentially confounding effects related to such factors as farmland preservation policies and off-farm income, the critical mass threshold itself may evolve over time. Improved communications and transportation infrastructure may reduce the costs of purchasing inputs and facilitate marketing. Growers may adapt when suppliers and processors exit the area. Adaptations could include switching to crops or animal products that are less reliant on these support industries. Farmers could shift to direct marketing rather than wholesaling. In addition, farming has experienced technological and structural changes over the last 50 years. The United States lost almost half of its farms between 1950 and 1970, partly because of mechanization and the consolidation of farms (Gardner 2002). U.S. average farm size and output per farm grew rapidly through the 1970s but have grown more slowly since then. Labor costs have decreased as a portion of total input costs beginning in the 1980s.

To account for such changes, a general model (Model 1) using farmland loss as the dependent variable is estimated for the entire time period 1949–1997, and then the sample is split into two periods with two additional models: 1949–1978 (Model 2a) and 1978–1997 (Model 2b). This allows the determination of a critical mass threshold and importance of other factors to vary by time period. We repeat the exercise using farm loss (number of farms rather than farm acres) as the dependent variable. Details of the econometric model are provided in the Appendix to this chapter.

Data and Study Area

Data were compiled from the agricultural and the population and housing censuses at the county level for the years 1949 through 1997, including the Mid-Atlantic states of Delaware, Maryland, New Jersey, New York, Pennsylvania, and Virginia (U.S. Department of Agriculture, 1999, 2001; U.S. Department of Commerce). In 1997, these six Mid-Atlantic states accounted for more than 26 million acres of farmland, representing 3 percent of U.S. total farmland and $12 billion (6 percent) of U.S. total sales. The analysis incorporates data on 269 counties[4] and 10 time periods of 4 to 5 years each. These time periods correspond to the years the agricultural censuses were taken. The data set was constructed as a panel by crop reporting district and by time period. A county's data were included in the crop reporting district to which it belonged. The USDA National Agricultural Statistics Service defines these crop reporting districts to reflect similar geography, soil types, and cropping patterns (Figure 6-1).

Because the two censuses were conducted on different schedules, we adjusted the population and housing census data to coincide with the years of the agricultural census data. The population and housing census is collected every 10 years, and the agricultural census every 4 to 5 years. We interpolated the population and housing census data by calculating a constant change in the

Figure 6-1. Distribution of Counties among Crop-Reporting Districts

variables between the census years and then used this change to adjust the population and housing census data to the year the agricultural census was collected. Thus, for example, if the population change were 25 percent for the 10-year period, it was assumed that the population grew 2.5 percent each year. Data from the 2000 census were not yet available. Therefore, extrapolations of the 1990 population and housing census data were conducted for 1992 and 1997, with the values calculated based on the change in the variables between 1980 and 1990. The rates of change were assumed to remain constant during the 1990s.

Counties with limited agricultural activity (fewer than five farms) in 1949 were excluded from the analysis: Bronx, Queens, Richmond, Kings, and New York, in New York State, and Arlington in Virginia. If the sales-per-acre data were not available for a county for confidentiality reasons, the county was deleted for that particular time period, but not from the entire analysis.

Table 6-1 provides the names, definitions, and descriptive statistics for the variables included in the analysis. The dependent variable is the rate of farmland

Table 6-1. Descriptive Statistics for the Entire Sample

Variable name	*Variable definition*	*Entire sample*	
		Mean	*Std. dev.*
PCFLAND	Percent reduction in farmland	7.58%	0.1256
HCLAND	Harvested cropland (1,000 acres)	54.372	47.097
HCLAND-SQUARED	Harvested cropland squared (1,000,000,000)	5.1724	9.710
PAGFFM	Percent of adults employed in agriculture, forestry, fisheries, and mining	9.99%	0.1056
SALESPER	Sales per acre ($/acre)	$549.07	2394.1100
EXPPERA	Expenses per acre ($/acre)	$331.51	2227.9300
POPPERA	Population per acre	0.5773	1.8430
MADUMMY	= 1 if county in metropolitan area	33.72%	0.4728
PCTOTHU	Percent change in total housing units	8.09%	0.0689
PCMFINC	Percent change in median family income	11.92%	0.0838
PCMHVAL	Percent change in median housing value	11.66%	0.1017
PHIGHSCH	Percent of adults with at least a high school education	48.41%	0.0185
PUNEMP	Unemployment rate	5.49%	0.0223
STAX	= 1 if state has preferential taxation program for agricultural land	56.63%	0.4957
PRESPROG	= 1 if state or county has purchase or transfer of agricultural conservation easement program	8.47%	0.2785

and farm loss for time period t. It is calculated as $\frac{A_{t+1}-A_t}{A_t}$, where A_t is the number of acres in the initial period. Farmland is defined by the agricultural census as consisting of land used for crops, pasture, or grazing. Woodland and wasteland acres are included if they are part of the farm operator's total operation. Conservation Reserve and Wetlands Reserve Program acreage is also included in this count. The rate of farmland loss averaged 7.58 percent and of farm loss 11.76 percent over the study period. Changes for individual counties can be much higher or lower than these averages, however. For example, some counties lost 100 percent of their farmland in a time period. One county gained 77.65 percent more farmland in t (many counties gained in the period between the 1974 and 1978 censuses).

Independent model variables illustrating the percentage change in specific factors use the initial year of the time period as the ending year of the calculation. For example, the percent change in housing units for time period t was calculated as $\frac{HU_t-HU_{t-1}}{HU_{t-1}}$, where HU_t is the total housing units at time t.

County-level harvested cropland acres in t proxy the acres that contribute to the critical mass threshold. Harvested cropland includes land from which crops were harvested or hay was cut, as well as that in orchards, citrus groves, Christmas trees, vineyards, nurseries, and greenhouses. These acres are better indicators of the level of agricultural activity. Idled farmland or acreage that is enrolled in the Conservation Reserve Program, for example, requires the purchase of few inputs, produces no output, and may not contribute in the same manner to maintaining a viable agricultural sector. We hypothesized that the county's rate of farmland and farm loss will increase if the level of harvested cropland falls below the threshold needed to sustain a viable agricultural support sector. Harvested cropland acreage is also included as a squared term. By including it in this manner, we can compute an acreage threshold required to ensure a critical mass. Harvested cropland averaged 54,372 acres per county, and the highest acreage in any one county was 334,294.

Because farmland and farm loss are affected by changes in agricultural returns per acre, demand for land for nonagricultural purposes, farmers' alternative employment opportunities, and preservation policies, we include variables to control for these factors. The percentage of the county population in agricultural, forestry, fishing, or mining activities in t is also included to indicate the dominance of these resource-based activities in the county. Employment in this type of work varied among counties from almost none to 70 percent, with an average of 9.99 percent.

Agricultural net returns are proxied by county-level agricultural sales per acre and expenses per acre in t. Farmers are more likely to remain in agriculture if sales increase more than expenses. Sales per acre averaged $549.07 in 1997 dollars, and expenses per acre averaged $331.51. Despite the almost 50 percent

Income Categories

☐ Same source of income

■ Changed largest income source

Figure 6-2. Counties That Changed Crop or Livestock Commodity from Which They Received Their Largest Share of Gross Income between 1949 and 1997

decrease in land devoted to agriculture in the Mid-Atlantic, total revenue decreased by only 1 percent in real terms between 1949 and 1997. Per-acre sales nearly doubled during this period. Price and technology changes are reflected in these expense and sales numbers. In addition, these numbers reflect shifts to alternative crops. By 1997, 42 percent of the study's counties derived the largest share of their income from a different commodity or animal source than they had in 1949 (Figure 6-2).

Decreases in agricultural net returns may also help explain the farmland loss that occurred in areas where the population decreased. Figure 6-3 depicts the areas where farmland decreased when the population decreased, and vice versa, for one decade of the study period—between 1987 and 1997.

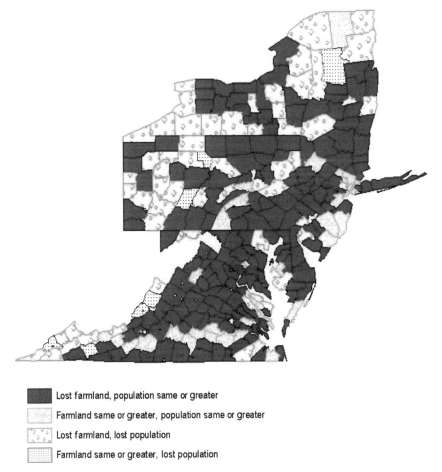

Lost farmland, population same or greater

Farmland same or greater, population same or greater

Lost farmland, lost population

Farmland same or greater, lost population

Figure 6-3. Changes in Farmland and Population between 1987 and 1997

Several variables represent demand for land for nonfarm uses: the population level scaled by the number of acres in the county, whether the county is in a metropolitan area, the percent change in total housing units, the percent change in median family income, and the percent change in median housing value. As population increases, demand for land in residential and commercial uses also increases. Thus population growth is hypothesized to increase the rate of farmland and farm loss. Total population in the six states has increased by 43 percent since 1950, climbing from 35 million to 50 million people. Given that the number of individuals per housing unit has decreased, we also include a direct indicator of the rate of growth in the housing stock. As the growth rate of housing units increases, the rate of farmland and farm loss is expected to increase. The percent change in total housing units averaged 8.09 percent, with some counties losing housing units at a rate of as much as 19 percent while others had a growth rate of 60 percent. As family income increases, people may demand larger homes, which usually sit on larger parcels. Thus we expect that an increase in income could increase the demand for farmland and accelerate the farmland and farm loss rate. Similarly, an increase in the median housing value may indicate an increase in the demand for land (Hardie et al. 2001) and accelerate the rate of farmland and farm loss.

An increasing proportion of farmers supplement their farm income with off-farm employment. Only 33 percent of Mid-Atlantic farmers reported working more than 100 days off the farm in 1949, but 44 percent did so in 1997. Their off-farm income opportunities will be greater if they are better educated and the unemployment rate in the county is low. An increase in off-farm opportunities, however, will increase the relative benefit of selling the land and shifting full-time to alternative employment. Off-farm opportunities are proxied by both the percentage of the county population that has at least a high school education and the percentage of unemployment. These opportunities could have either a positive or negative effect on the rate of farmland and farm loss. Education attainment increased over the time period, with an average of 48.41 percent of residents having a high school education. The unemployment rate averaged 5.49 percent, with a range of 0.07 to 14.5 percent. Increases in median family income might also signal a strong local economy and possibly more off-farm employment opportunities.

Policy variables are included to indicate whether the county has a preferential property tax program for agricultural land or some type of farmland preservation program. Preservation and taxation programs are hypothesized to slow the rate of farmland and farm loss. We consider four different types—state preferential property tax programs, state purchase of agricultural conservation easement programs, local purchase of agricultural conservation easement programs, and local transfer of development rights programs—and collected information on the existence of these programs by county (American Farmland Trust 1997, 2001a, 2001b, 2001c). A binary (has/has not) variable indicates whether the state had established a preferential property tax program by t. Another binary (has/has not) variable indicates whether the county had one or more local- or state-level preservation programs in place by t. Counties were credited with having a program if any locality within the county had a program that had preserved at least 1 acre. By 1982, all the states had established preferential property tax programs. By 1997, 44 percent of the counties had a local or state preservation program in place.

Results

Results of Farmland Loss Model 1

As the number of harvested cropland acres increased in a county, the rate of farmland loss decreased in the period 1949 to 1997 (Table 6-2). Counties with fewer acres of harvested cropland had higher rates of farmland loss. In terms of a critical mass, we found that counties below 189,240 harvested cropland acres had a higher rate of farmland loss. The identified threshold, however, is nearly out of the data range. Only 2 to 7 out of 269 counties exceeded 189,240 acres of harvested cropland in any time period. Therefore, the interpretation of this number as a threshold should be made cautiously.

The rate of farmland loss is also explained by sales per acre, expenses per acre, population per acre, unemployment rate, percent change in median family income, and percent change in housing units. The rate of farmland loss decreases as harvested cropland acres, sales, and percent change in income increase. The rate of farmland loss increases, however, as expenses, population, percent change in total housing units, and percentage of unemployment increase. As expected, counties with preferential taxation programs had a lower rate of farmland loss than counties without such a program. Holding all else constant, metropolitan counties lost farmland at a higher rate than nonmetropolitan ones.

We compute the predicted rate of farmland loss at the average value for the continuous variables and at zero (has not) for the binary variables. The predicted rate of farmland loss is 7.9 percent. We then estimate how much the predicted rate will change for a 10 percent increase in each variable we found to affect farmland loss. For binary variables, we compute the rate of farmland loss if they were equal to one (has a program). Table 6-3 contains the predicted rate and the new rate given the 10 percent increase.

The model predicts a baseline average rate of farmland loss of 7.9 percent. The rate decreases to 7.67 percent if the harvested cropland acres are increased 10 percent (Table 6-3). Sales and expenses per acre also affect the farmland loss rate. A 10 percent change in sales per acre has a greater effect than an equal percentage change in expenses. A 10 percent increase in sales per acre would decrease the rate of farmland loss to 7.83 percent (a change of –0.07), whereas a 10 percent increase in expenses per acre would increase the rate of farmland loss to 7.92 percent (a change of 0.02).

Development pressure also impacts the rate of farmland loss in Model 1. A 10 percent increase in population per acre increases the rate of farmland loss to 8.01 percent. Similarly, if the growth of housing stock increases 10 percent, the rate of farmland loss increases to 8.02 percent. Metropolitan counties lost farmland at a rate of 8.94 percent, and nonmetropolitan counties at a rate of 7.9 percent. Higher income growth levels and employment opportunities decrease the

Table 6-2. Results of Models 1, 2a, and 2b for Farmland Loss, Including All Observations Using Harvested Cropland as the Critical Mass Indicator

	Model 1 (1949–1997)	Model 2a (1949–1978)	Model 2b (1978–1997)
	Coefficient (Std. err.)	Coefficient (Std. err.)	Coefficient (Std. err.)
HCLANDD	−0.00058994***	−0.00969508***	−0.00004426
Harvested cropland	(0.0001)	(0.0002)	(0.0002)
HCLAND-SQUARED	0.0015587***	0.00268124***	−0.00015372
	(0.0006)	(0.0007)	(0.0010)
PAGFFM	0.0415	0.0477	0.0500
% resource employment	(0.0334)	(0.0381)	(0.0972)
SALESPER	−0.00001***	−0.00002***	0.00002***
Sales per acre	(0.0000)	(0.000002)	(0.000005)
EXPPERA	0.000005***	0.00001***	−0.00003***
Costs per acre	(0.0000)	(0.000002)	(0.00001)
POPPERA	0.0187***	0.0175***	0.0148***
People per acre	(0.0017)	(0.0019)	(0.0053)
MADUMMY	0.0103*	0.0193**	0.0078
Metropolitan area	(0.0059)	(0.0082)	(0.0088)
PCTOTHU	0.1587***	0.1780***	0.0823
%Δ housing units	(0.0401)	(0.0498)	(0.0861)
PCMFINC	−0.1321**	−0.1416**	−0.0588
%Δ income	(0.0540)	(0.0608)	(0.1311)
PCMHVAL	0.0236	−0.0025	0.0462
%Δ housing value	(0.0307)	(0.0448)	(0.0651)
PHIGHSCH	0.0141	0.0251	−0.0032
% high school	(0.0318)	(0.0462)	(0.0584)
PUNEMP	0.3207*	0.3313**	0.2931
% unemployment	(0.1255)	(0.1643)	(0.2201)
STAX	−0.0404***	−0.0358***	
Preferential tax	(0.0105)	(0.0112)	
PRESPROG	−0.0047		−0.0082
Preservation program	(0.0095)		(0.0111)
CONSTANT	0.0875**	0.1162***	0.0172
	(0.0387)	(0.0415)	(0.0514)
R^2	.1647	.2344	.0623
N	2604	1574	1030

Notes: *** indicates that based on an asymptotic t-test, the H_0: $\beta = 0$ is rejected using a 0.001 criterion; ** indicates rejection using a 0.05 criterion; and * indicates rejection using a 0.10 criterion. Std. err. is Standard Error. The number of observations in each model is indicated in the row labeled N. R^2 is a statistical measure of how well the overall variables explain farm and farmland loss; a higher number indicates a better fitting model.

Table 6-3. Effects of a 10% Increase in Significant Continuous Variables and Binary Variables Equaling 1 on the Rate of Farmland Loss for Each of the Estimated Models

	Model 1 1949–1997	Model 2a 1949–1978	Model 2b 1978–1997
Predicted probability	7.90%	10.12%	5.01%
Probability after 10% increase in continuous variables			
HCLAND	7.67%	9.82%	
Harvested cropland			
PCMFINC	7.73%	9.99%	
% Δ income			
SALESPER	7.83%	10.08%	5.10%
Sales per acre			
EXPPERA	7.92%	10.25%	4.91%
Costs per acre			
POPPERA	8.01%	10.30%	5.08%
People per acre			
PCTOTHU	8.02%	10.36%	
%Δ housing units			
PUNEMP	8.09%	10.37%	
% unemployment			
Binary variables			
STAX	4.06%	6.62%	
Preferential tax			
MADUMMY	8.94%	12.13%	
Metropolitan area			

rates of farmland loss. A 10 percent increase in median family income growth lowers the rate of farmland loss to 7.73 percent. If the unemployment rate increases by 10 percent, the rate of farmland loss increases to 8.09 percent. Education has no impact on the rate of farmland loss.[5]

Preferential taxation programs were found to have a significant effect on the rate of farmland loss. Counties with preferential taxation programs had a farmland loss rate of 4.06 percent; counties without one had a rate of 7.9 percent. The presence of other agricultural preservation programs (purchase of development rights, transfer of development rights, or purchase of agricultural conservation easements) did not impact the rate of farmland loss.

Results of Farmland Loss Models 2a and 2b

Models 2a and 2b demonstrate that the effect of independent variables on farmland loss changed over time. Moreover, the rate of farmland loss slowed about halfway through the study period. The actual average 5-year rate of farmland loss in 1949–1978 was 9.2 percent, and for 1978–1997, 5.1 percent.

Both agriculture and the pattern of city and housing development changed during this time. We found that the variables' impacts were not consistent over the two time periods, 1949–1978 (Model 2a, early) and 1978–1997 (Model 2b, late).[6] The early model's results were similar to those reported above for Model 1, but those of the late model differed. Estimated coefficients are reported in Table 6-2.

Counties with more harvested cropland have a lower rate of farmland loss in the early model, but the number of cropland acres in the late model had no effect on the farmland loss. The critical mass level in the early model was estimated to be 180,795 harvested cropland acres—similar to the threshold of 189,240 harvested acres in Model 1. But as before, few counties actually had more than 180,000 acres of harvested cropland acres. The early period appears to drive the threshold result of Model 1.

The predicted rate of farmland loss in the early model was 10.12 percent, and in the late model 5.01 percent. In the early model, a 10 percent increase in harvested cropland acreage resulted in a lower farmland loss rate of 9.82 percent, a change of 0.30 (Table 6-3); in the late model, the harvested cropland had no effect.

Similar to the results of Model 1, a higher net revenue decreased the rate of farmland loss in the early model. Expenses per acre had a bigger impact than sales per acre, however. A 10 percent increase in sales per acre decreased the rate of farmland loss to 10.08 percent (a change of –0.04). If expenses increased by 10 percent, the rate of farmland loss increased to 10.25 percent (a change of 0.13). In the late model, surprisingly, the opposite relationship is observed. A 10 percent increase in sales per acre increased the rate of farmland loss from the predicted 5.01 percent to 5.10 percent. A 10 percent increase in per-acre expenses decreased the rate of farmland loss to 4.91 percent.

Effects of other variables in the early model were similar to those reported above for Model 1. The resulting farmland loss rate following a 10 percent increase in these variables for the early model can be found in Table 6-3 and graphically in Figure 6-4. In the late model, except for population per acre, none of the other variables had an impact on the rate of farmland loss. A 10 percent increase in population per acre increased the rate of farmland loss from 5.01 to 5.08 percent. The overall explanatory power of the early model, though not high, was greater than that of the late model. The R^2 for the early model equaled 0.23; in other words, 23 percent of the variation of the rate of farmland loss was explained by the included variables. The R^2 for the late model was only 0.06; thus the late model did not explain 94 percent of the variation in farmland loss rates for these counties between 1978 and 1997. Obviously, many other variables are affecting the rate of farmland loss during this later period, but they are not well captured by the county-level census data and the proposed model. County-level variables may mask spatial changes that have

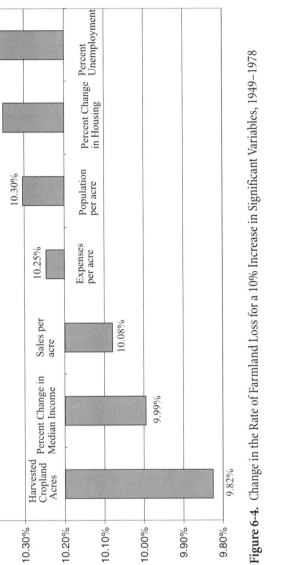

Figure 6-4. Change in the Rate of Farmland Loss for a 10% Increase in Significant Variables, 1949–1978

occurred in the farmland as well as other organizational adjustments. For example, many counties altered the crop and livestock mix, and the aggregate variables in the model may not capture these changes. Further research on individual sectors such as dairy or cattle may provide additional insights into the concept of a critical mass that a county-level analysis could not.

Results of Farm Loss Model 1

We find many of the same results for the rate of farm loss as for farmland loss, but differences in the effect of certain variables do exist. The rate of decrease in the number of farms shows no critical mass of harvested cropland acres (Table 6-4). Although no threshold exists, the higher the number of farmland acres, the lower the loss of farm numbers will be. During the time period, average farm size throughout the region increased from 106 to 185 acres. Therefore, the rate of farm loss was greater than the rate of farmland loss.

Factors that explain the rate of farm loss include harvested cropland, resource-based employment, sales per acre, expenses per acre, population per acre, percentage of unemployment, percentage of the county population with a high school education, percent change in median family income, and percent change in housing units. As harvested cropland, sales, resource-based employment, education, and income increase, the rate of farm loss falls. Similarly, as expenses, population density, total housing, and percentage of unemployment increase, the rate of farmland loss accelerates. A county with a preferential taxation program has a lower farm loss, as does one with a preservation program. Metropolitan counties, in contrast, had a higher farm loss rate.

The predicted 5-year farm loss rate from the model was 12.07 percent. We use this to determine the effects on the farm loss rate of a 10 percent change in the significant variables (Figure 6-5) or a change in the binary variables from has not to has (Figure 6-6). For example, if a county has 10 percent more harvested cropland acres, the 5-year rate of farm loss decreases from the predicted rate of 12.07 percent to 11.89 percent. If the average resource-based employment increased by 10 percent, the rate of farm loss decreased from the predicted 12.07 percent to 12.00 percent.

As with farmland, we found that as sales per acre increase, the rate of farm loss will decrease, and as the expenses per acre increase, the rate of farm loss will increase. Thus as the net returns to agriculture decrease in a county, it will lose farms at a quicker rate. If sales increased by 10 percent, the rate of farm loss decreased from the predicted rate of 12.07 percent to 12.04 percent. If expenses increased by 10 percent, the rate of farm loss increased from 12.07 to 12.09 percent. The effect of sales and expenses on farm numbers is smaller than on farmland loss. Also unlike patterns found in the farmland loss model, a change in sales per acre appears to have the same impact on farm numbers as expenses per acre. One may view this from two distinct perspectives: lower net returns

Table 6-4. Results of Models 1, 2a, and 2b for Farm Loss, Including All Observations Using Harvested Cropland as the Critical Mass Indicator

	Model 1 (1949–1997)	Model 2a (1949–1978)	Model 2b (1978–1997)
	Coefficient (Std. err.)	Coefficient (Std. err.)	Coefficient (Std. err.)
HCLANDD	−0.0002*	−0.0006***	0.0004***
Harvested cropland	(0.0001)	(0.0002)	(0.0002)
HCLAND-SQUARED	0.0001	0.0011	−0.0014**
	(0.0005)	(0.0007)	(0.0007)
PAGFFM	−0.0660**	−0.0797**	0.0826
% resource employment	(0.0294)	(0.0375)	(0.0673)
SALESPER	−0.000007***	−0.00001***	0.000004
Sales per acre	(0.000002)	(0.000002)	(0.000004)
EXPPERA	0.000007***	0.00001***	−0.000004
Costs per acre	(0.000002)	(0.000002)	(0.000007)
POPPERA	0.0108***	0.0090***	0.0204***
People per acre	(0.0015)	(0.0019)	(0.0037)
MADUMMY	0.0089*	0.0207***	0.0058
Metropolitan area	(0.0052)	(0.0083)	(0.0061)
PCTOTHU	0.1229***	0.1387***	0.0668
%Δ housing units	(0.0361)	(0.0506)	(0.0643)
PCMFINC	−0.1740***	−0.1538***	−0.0484
%Δ income	(0.0474)	(0.0593)	(0.0929)
PCMHVAL	0.0432	0.0692	−0.0258
%Δ housing value	(0.0269)	(0.0440)	(0.0516)
PHIGHSCH	−0.1328***	−0.1388***	−0.1105**
% high school	(0.0307)	(0.0499)	(0.0479)
PUNEMP	0.3000***	0.4618***	0.0349
% unemployment	(0.1151)	(0.1717)	(0.1620)
STAX	−0.0265***	−0.0086	
Preferential tax	(0.0095)	(0.0116)	
PRESPROG	−0.0173**		−0.0380***
Preservation program	(0.0086)	(0.0089)	
CONSTANT	0.1990***	0.2241***	0.1079*
	(0.0533)	(0.0276)	(0.0585)
R^2	0.3458	0.4772	0.0841
N	2604	1574	1030

Notes: *** indicates that based on an asymptotic t-test, the $H_0 : \beta = 0$ is rejected using a 0.001 criterion; ** indicates rejection using a 0.05 criterion; and * indicates rejection using a 0.10 criterion. Std. err. is Standard Error. The number of observations in each model is indicated in the row labeled N. R^2 is a statistical measure of how well the overall variables explain farm and farmland loss; a higher number indicates a better fitting model.

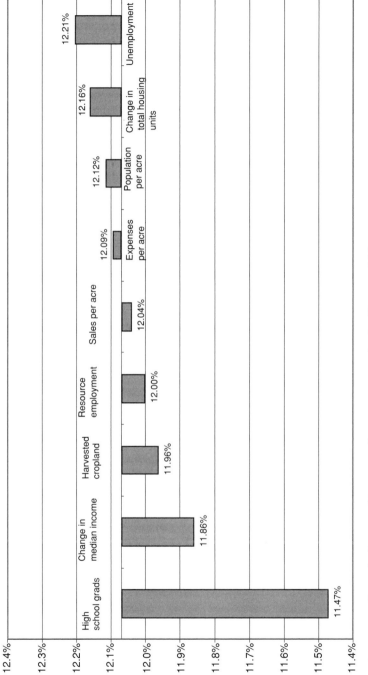

Figure 6-5. Change in the Rate of Farm Loss for a 10% Increase in Significant Variables, 1949–1997

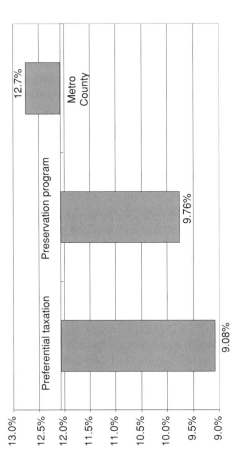

Figure 6-6. Change in the Rate of Farm Loss because of Preferential Taxation or Preservation Programs or Being a Metro County, 1949–1997

will not accelerate farm loss dramatically, or alternatively, even if net returns increase, the impact on the rate of farm loss will be small.

An increase in population per acre also increases the rate of farm loss, just as it increases farmland loss. If population per acre increases by 10 percent, the rate of farm loss increases from 12.07 to 12.12 percent. Similarly, the percent change in housing units in the county impacts the farm loss rate. As the percentage of housing units increases by 10 percent, the rate of farm loss increases from 12.07 to 12.16 percent. We found that being in a metropolitan area also increased the rate of change, but with a slightly lower impact on farm loss than on farmland loss. The rate of farm loss was 12.76 percent in metropolitan areas, compared with the predicted rate of 12.07 percent for nonmetropolitan counties.

Similar to the farmland loss model, here an increase in median family income is found to decrease farm loss. The effect of income is even larger on farm loss than on farmland loss. This could be a function of better off-farm employment opportunities or households with higher incomes choosing to purchase farms and keep them in production. A 10 percent increase in the median family income decreases the rate of farm loss from 12.07 to 11.86 percent. In contrast, farms were lost at a higher rate if the unemployment rate in the county was high. If the unemployment rate increases by 10 percent, the rate of farm loss increases from 12.07 to 12.21 percent. In such cases, farmers may have had fewer off-farm opportunities to supplement farm income and hence were more likely to sell their farms. Unlike in the farmland loss models, education affected the rate of farm loss. If the percentage of the county's population with a high school education increases by 10 percent, the rate of farm loss decreases from 12.07 to 11.47 percent.

The model also shows that having a preferential property tax assessment for agricultural landowners reduces the rate of farm loss—the same result as was found for farmland. Counties where preferential taxation existed had a farm loss rate of 9.08 percent, compared with the predicted rate of 12.07 percent. Similarly, having a preservation program (purchase of development rights, transfer of development rights, or purchase of agricultural conservation easements) resulted in a lower percentage of farms lost. Counties with these programs had a rate of farm loss of 9.76 percent. Thus we find that preservation programs are saving farms, although the results for farmland acres are mixed.

Results of Farm Loss Models 2a and 2b

We also estimated the models for the two time periods—1949–1978 (Model 2a, early) and 1978–1997 (Model 2b, late)—to determine if the impacts of variables were consistent over time. We found that although the results were remarkably similar to those reported above for Model 1, for the earlier time period, they diverged in the later years like those for farmland loss (Table 6-4). In the early period, no critical mass threshold for farm numbers was found, although a decrease in the number of harvested crop acres did increase the rate of farm loss. A decrease in the percentage of the county population that worked in resource-based sectors also increased farm loss. Sales and expenses per acre had slightly larger impacts in the early model. If sales increased by 10 percent, the rate of farm loss decreased from the predicted rate in the early model of 16.23 to 16.18 percent. If expenses increased by 10 percent, the rate of farm loss increased from 16.23 to 16.27 percent. In the early model, being in a metropolitan area had a bigger impact than in Model 1, increasing the rate of farm loss from 16.23 to 18.30 percent. Similarly, as the percentage of unemployment increased by 10 percent, the percentage of farms lost increased to 16.47 percent, a higher loss rate than in the more general Model 1. Interestingly, the existence of a preferential tax program had no effect on the farm loss rate in this early period, although many of the programs had begun by the end of this period. Many of the other variables estimated in this early period had the same magnitude of impact as in Model 1.

We do not find a critical mass threshold in the late model. In fact, contrary to expectations, the late model finds that as harvested cropland decreases, the rate of farm loss decreases as well. Changes in agriculture and development patterns may have altered the impact of many variables on the number of farms lost. As a whole, the late model did not explain a particularly large proportion of the observed loss of farms—the same result as was found in the farmland model. We do find that in this late period, an increase in population density per acre continues to increase the rate of farm loss. We also find that counties with agricultural preservation programs lose farms at a slower pace. The predicted farm loss rate during this late period was 6.13 percent. Counties with preservation programs lost farms at a rate of 2.32 percent. Given that all counties had a preferential taxation program by this time, we could not assess the existence of a differential rate for this type of program in the later years.

The Impact of Changes over Time on Farm and Farmland Loss

Model results suggest that patterns influencing farm and farmland loss are complex and likely have changed over time. Some evidence of a critical mass existed for the study area during the early period for farmland loss, although not for farm loss. The scale of agricultural activity in the latter half of the study period did not impact the rate of farmland loss, however, and actually had the reverse effect on farm loss. This raises some interesting questions with implications for the retention of agriculture.

First, to what extent have farmers adapted to the difficulties associated with shrinking input and output markets by shifting to alternative crops or marketing mechanisms? The data show that for 42 percent of the counties, the agricultural activity earning the highest gross income in 1997 was different from the activity that had generated the most income in 1949 (Figure 6-2). The implications of a county-level change from dairy to vegetables or from row crops to livestock require further investigation. Second, had the major technological changes in agriculture, in terms of improved mechanization and per-acre yields, occurred by the mid-1970s? Moreover, did these changes impact farm and farmland loss rate differently? Third, how did land development patterns change as a result of changes either in housing consumers' preferences or in land use or development policies? How did these changes impact the rate of farmland and farm loss? Fourth, how have counties responded to the high rate of farmland loss between 1949 and the early 1970s? Counties implemented preferential taxation programs and agricultural preservation programs, which we consider. Other responses, however, not incorporated in the model, might have been equally or more important.

The impact of sales and expenses per acre changed for the latter part of the study period. In the early period, the expected result was found: increased sales or decreased expenses resulted in a lower rate of farmland loss. But from 1978 to 1997, an opposite—and somewhat puzzling—result was found. The reason for this shift is unclear. It may be, however, that farmers with the most marginal agricultural land were the first to exit agriculture, leaving only the most productive land under cultivation. County average per-acre sales therefore would increase. Also, farmers could have switched crops. If they shifted to higher-value, smaller-acreage crops, such as berries or vegetables, farmland loss would occur simultaneously with higher per-acre sales. This begs the question of why they had not shifted to higher-value crops at an earlier time period.

The health of the local economy also was found to impact the rate of farmland conversion. Counties with higher median family incomes and lower unemployment had lower rates of farmland loss. This could be a function of better off-farm employment opportunities or people with higher incomes choosing to purchase farms and keeping them in production. Farmers in counties with high unemployment may have had fewer off-farm opportunities for themselves or family members and may have chosen to sell their farms and relocate. Policies that focus attention on local or regional economic performance could promote farmland retention. Examining farmland prices, Hardie et al. (2001, *131*) conclude that "policies developed for broader purposes may have as much or more effect on farmland prices as policies targeted directly at improving agricultural returns."

Population growth also resulted in higher rates of farm and farmland loss in every model. In the early period, the growth rate of the total number of housing units was positively related to the rate of farmland and farm loss as well. This is expected, as population growth and housing development tend to cause the conversion of agricultural land. Local communities can exercise control over the extent and pattern of new development through thoughtful planning. Given the Chesapeake Bay Foundation's (2000a, 2000b) finding that the rate at which land is being consumed exceeds the population growth rate by almost 2.5 times, policies could focus on reducing land consumption per house or per person to limit the impacts of both population growth and housing development on agriculture.

As expected, metropolitan counties had higher rates of farmland and farm loss over and above losses related to population and changes in housing stock. This implies that metropolitan counties that wish to maintain agriculture may need to be even more active in implementing policies and programs that encourage farmland retention and strengthen the agricultural economy. Alternatively, states might decide to target regions far from metropolitan areas for preservation and retention programs, while deemphasizing farmland preservation in metropolitan areas. This approach could retain agriculture on a statewide basis and allow states to use their limited resources efficiently.

Preferential property taxation programs were found to slow the rate of farmland and farm loss. All six states in this study had enacted such programs by 1982. Additional evaluation of these programs may be warranted, as well as an examination of who participates and who does not. A further property tax reduction might slow the rate of farmland loss even more. Such a reduction potentially could be financed through a higher conversion tax rate. The state or counties thus could recapture some of the benefits the farmers accrue from the preferential tax program. This conversion tax could be collected when landowners choose to convert the land from agriculture to a nonfarm use. Chapter 8 in this book highlights the various aspects of differential taxation programs that may lead to greater landowner participation and perhaps a higher rate of farmland retention.

Other agricultural preservation programs—purchase of development rights, transfer of development rights, or purchase of agricultural conservation easements—did not impact the rate of farmland loss, but did slow the loss of farms. Apparently, when some farmers are offered an option other than selling out, they are willing to take it. Few of these programs existed before the 1980s. Moreover, some programs have not had sufficient resources to preserve large numbers of acres. Farmland preservation programs may have more impact in the future if they are able to obtain increased resources and hence can enroll a greater number of acres.

Conclusions

The results do not provide clear evidence of a critical mass in agricultural economies in the Mid-Atlantic. They suggest that counties with fewer farmland acres lost farmland and farms at higher rates. An acreage threshold level was computed for farmland loss. Yet these calculated critical mass levels (189,240 acres per county in Model 1 and 180,795 per county in Model 2a) exceed the harvested cropland acres of most counties (97 percent) in the Mid-Atlantic region. Hence, even if a critical mass is applicable to farmland loss, our models suggest that it may entail a greater acreage of farmland than exists in the vast majority of the Mid-Atlantic counties. In addition, a critical mass of agricultural acreage was not found in the analysis of the 1978 to 1997 period. Counties with fewer harvested cropland acres did not have a higher rate of farmland loss but did have a lower rate of farm loss in the later period. Thus even if the computed levels were convincingly strong, the critical mass may have altered in the latter part of the study period, given the many changes over time.

Additional research is needed to more fully identify factors that affect the rate of farmland and farm loss and determine whether a critical mass exists. Farmers may have adapted to more limited support sectors in their regions by shifting to alternative crops or products that are less reliant on nearby suppliers or buyers. Specific sectors or commodities might be doomed once an area loses a certain number of acres, when the farmers cannot continue to produce these commodities profitably. Adaptation, however, could ensure the viability of the farm sector as a whole. A model incorporating all U.S. agricultural economies might further demonstrate whether and how much the level of a critical mass depends on cropping patterns and geography. In contrast, a more micro-level analysis could reveal information obscured by the present county-level analysis. A case study approach could provide insights about specific industries or agricultural sectors in specific regions during specific time periods. Alternatively, further analysis might consider individual farming sectors in different areas and how they have evolved over time.

Although this analysis does not provide a clear prognosis for the economic viability of the Mid-Atlantic's agricultural sector, it does suggest that the farm community has been resilient to large losses of farmland over time; that the health of the local economy in the county matters; and that controlling population growth and housing development is very important to slowing farmland and farm loss. The analysis also suggests that the recent emphasis on preserving a critical mass of agricultural land may be insufficient to ensure the long-term viability of an agricultural sector. As a result, decisionmakers may need to examine other policy objectives to sustain the sector.

Endnotes

1. This is a different question than that posed in the 1970s, when citizens advocated farmland preservation for food security reasons. Several research studies, including those by Fischel (1982) and Dunford (1983), analyzed whether the rate of farmland conversion would affect the national agricultural production capacity. They found that although farmland was disappearing from certain regions, sufficient national land resources were still available to ensure the nation's food security.

2. Alternatively, if smaller, locally based input and output firms are consolidated, permitting larger, more regionally focused businesses, they may achieve greater economies of scale. Then the major factor would be the effect of increased transportation costs on farmers' costs.

3. Another possible method to study this issue would be to examine the cost structures of input suppliers and processing firms. Even if businesses would permit us to do so, however, many of those we would want to study have exited the region over the past 50 years.

4. Independent cities of Virginia are also included in the analysis. In several cases, because of either aggregation in data or actual boundary changes during the study period, counties or independent cities have been combined for this analysis.

5. A correlation existed among these three variables: percent change in median household income, percent of the county with high school education, and percent of the county that is unemployed. The percent of high school education and percent change of income variables have a correlation coefficient of -0.52, and percent of unemployment and percent change in income variables have one of -0.32. This may explain in part the insignificant parameter estimates on percent of high school education in this and the ensuing models.

6. A likelihood ratio test indicated that estimating the two models separately for these time periods is statistically different from pooling the data ($\chi_{(13)}^2 = 77.78$).

References

American Farmland Trust. (1997). *Saving American Farmland: What Works.* Northampton, MA: American Farmland Trust Publications Division.

———. (2001a). Fact Sheet: Status of Selected Local PACE Programs. Northampton, MA: American Farmland Trust Technical Assistance.

———. (2001b). Fact Sheet: Transfer of Development Rights. Northampton, MA: American Farmland Trust Technical Assistance.

———. (2001c). Fact Sheet: Status of State PACE Programs. Northampton, MA: American Farmland Trust Technical Assistance.

Anonymous. (2001). Using Resources Wisely: How Much is Enough? *Landworks* 4(1): 3–5.

Chesapeake Bay Foundation. (2000a). *Future Growth in the Washington, D.C. Metropolitan Area.* Annapolis, MD. http://www.savethebay.org/land/landuse/maps/future_growth.html.

―――. (2000b). *Land and the Chesapeake Bay.* Annapolis, MD.

Daniels, T., and M. Lapping. (2001). Farmland Preservation in America and the Issue of Critical Mass. Paper presented at the American Farmland Trust National Conference, November 13, Chicago.

Dhillon, P. S., and D. A. Derr. (1974). Critical Mass of Agriculture and the Maintenance of Productive Open Space. *Journal of Northeastern Agricultural Economics Council* 3(1): 23–34.

Dunford, R. W. (1983). Further Evidence on the Conversion of U.S. Farmland to Urban or Transportation Uses. Washington, DC: Congressional Research Service.

Fischel, W. A. (1982). The Urbanization of Agricultural Land: A Review of the National Agricultural Lands Study. *Land Economics* 58: 236–259.

Gardner, B. L. (1994). Commercial Agriculture in Metropolitan Areas: Economics and Regulatory Issues. *Agricultural and Resource Economics Review* 23(1): 100–109.

―――. (2002). *American Agriculture in the 20th Century: How It Flourished and What It Cost.* Cambridge, MA: Harvard University Press.

Greene, W. (1995). Limdep, Version 7.0. Plainview, NY: Econometric Software.

Hardie, I. W., T. A. Narayan, and B. L. Gardner. (2001). The Joint Influence of Agricultural and Nonfarm Factors on Real Estate Values: An Application to the Mid-Atlantic Region. *American Journal of Agricultural Economics* 83(1): 120–132.

Lapping, M. B. (1979). Agricultural Land Retention Strategies: Some Underpinnings. *Journal of Soil and Water Conservation* 34(3): 124–126.

Lockeretz, W. (1989). Secondary Effects on Midwestern Agriculture of Metropolitan Development and Decreases in Farmland. *Land Economics* 65(3): 205–216.

U.S. Department of Agriculture, National Agricultural Statistics Service. (1999). *1997 Census of Agriculture,* 1A, 1B, 1C, CD-ROM set. Washington, DC: USDA/ NASS.

―――. (2001). *Agricultural Statistics.* Washington, DC: USDA/NASS.

U.S. Department of Commerce, Bureau of the Census. *Census of Agriculture,* 1950 to 1982. Washington, DC: USDC.

―――. *Census of Population and Housing,* 1950 to 1990. Washington, DC: USDC.

Appendix

Econometric Model

Several models were estimated to determine which of the following was the most appropriate econometric technique to use for the panel data: pooling the data, pooling the data with fixed effects representing each 5-year time period or crop-reporting district, or estimating a random effects model. Lagrange multiplier (LM) and Hausman tests (HT) *($LM_{(2)} = 1581.33$; $HT_{(14)} = 17.53$)* indicate that a random effects estimation procedure is more efficient. Thus the unexplained variation in the rate of farmland loss or the residual for the estimated model is composed of three parts: ε_{it}, μ_i, and w_t. The means of the three disturbances are assumed to be zero, and each has a variance equal to σ_ε^2, σ_μ^2, and σ_w^2, respectively. The covariances between the error terms are also assumed to be zero. The model incorporates both the within and between random components.

The random effects model to be estimated is defined by the following equation:

$$y_{it} = \alpha + \beta' x_{it} + \varepsilon_{it} + \mu_i + w_t \qquad (6\text{-}1)$$

(Greene 1995), where y_{it} is the vector of the county-level rate of farmland loss (or farm loss) for counties in crop reporting district i in the 5-year time period t; α is the vector of constants; β is the vector of estimated coefficients; and x_{it} is the matrix of county-level characteristics that explain farmland loss for crop reporting district i in the 5-year time period t, such as sales per acre, percent change in housing units, and the unemployment rate. ε_{it}, μ_i, and w_t are the error terms. They are the effects of unobserved variables that vary over both crop reporting district i and 5-year time period t, and within each crop reporting district and time period.

PART III

Land Conservation: Implications for Value and Taxation

7

Are Agricultural Land Preservation Programs Self-Financing?

JACQUELINE GEOGHEGAN, LORI LYNCH,
AND SHAWN J. BUCHOLTZ

The preservation of open space has become an important policy issue in the United States, as the conversion of farm and forest into residential and commercial uses continues. Private organizations and government entities have introduced a variety of mechanisms to preserve open space or slow its conversion, including cluster and exclusive agricultural zoning, purchase of and transfer of development rights (PDR/PACEs and TDRs), and outright purchase of open space using tax dollars or private donations. The public has demonstrated its support for open-space preservation by passing more than three-quarters of the 801 ballot initiatives between 1997 and 2003, generating funds of more than $24 billion (Land Trust Alliance 2003).

But even with this additional revenue, funds may still be insufficient to preserve a socially optimal amount of open space.[1] Thus policymakers may desire further information on the potential benefits and costs of open-space preservation of different types. Moreover, though private purchases of open space do occur, governments are likely to remain involved with the purchase of open space. This often requires a determination of which tracts to preserve and which financing mechanisms to use for the purchase of land or development rights. Although many ballot initiatives providing funding for open-space acquisition have passed, alternative funding mechanisms may be needed if the passage of subsequent bond initiatives becomes more difficult.

The potential benefits of preserving open space accrue to both the general public living throughout a region and private landowners living near preserved parcels. Some of these benefits may be capitalized into the value of neighboring parcels. Previous research (Nickerson and Lynch 2001) has shown little statistical evidence that the easement restrictions imposed by agricultural land preservation programs are capitalized into the price of preserved agricultural parcels. Other studies have suggested, however, that preserved agricultural open spaces can increase residential values of nearby parcels (Geoghegan 2002; Irwin 2002; Irwin and Bockstael 2001), suggesting that values of neighboring parcels may increase as a result of land preservation policies.

This potential capitalization of the value of open spaces may provide an additional mechanism for the funding of their preservation. More specifically, if the value of nearby parcels increases as a result of land preservation, some of this value may in turn be recaptured through property taxes; this provides an additional source of financing for open-space preservation. As a result, though current policies for land preservation may not provide an optimal amount of open-space provision, they do offer a source of benefits as well as a potential funding base.

This chapter examines one portion of the benefit from agricultural preservation programs—that accruing to adjacent homeowners—to determine how much additional land such programs can finance through the increase in tax revenue generated from nearby residential properties. Specifically, if the open space provided by preservation programs increases nearby residential land values and consequently generates higher property tax revenues, how many more acres of open space might this increase in tax revenue provide? We address this question using a unique spatially explicit database for three counties in Maryland. We focus on agricultural land preservation programs as a method of preserving open space, specifically those that involve the sale or transfer of development rights.[2] As of 2003, more than 1.3 million acres of land had been preserved in the United States using such programs (American Farmland Trust 2004a).

To estimate the effect of an agricultural preservation program on nearby residential properties, a statistical model of housing sales is estimated that includes traditional explanatory variables, such as housing and locational characteristics, as well as neighborhood land use variables. The land use variables were calculated using a geographical information system (GIS) to measure 10 different types of land use around each residential parcel. Open-space land uses are aggregated to either permanent or developable open spaces. Permanent open space includes agricultural and forested lands enrolled in preservation programs, as well as state and local parks and golf courses. Agricultural or forested land that does not have an easement attached is also considered open space, but this land is subject to future development and hence is denoted as developable open space.

The hypotheses to be tested are, first, that open space increases neighboring residential values and, second, that permanent open space, such as agricultural land with an easement, has a larger effect on housing prices, because residential buyers know it will never be converted to a residential subdivision. Estimated coefficients on the permanent open-space variable from the housing-value model, if positive and statistically significant, are then used in a simulation to assess potential impacts on tax-revenue generation. We increase the current level of permanently preserved agricultural open space by 1 percent to determine the increase in residential property values to adjacent landowners. This is subsequently used to calculate the level of increased property tax revenue generated, given current tax rates. Next, the number of acres of preserved agricultural land that could be financed with this additional revenue is calculated and compared with the number of acres associated with the 1 percent increase from the simulation to determine the potential for further purchases of easements on agricultural land.

Review of the Literature

Questions concerning the value of open spaces have been addressed in economics using a number of methodologies, with a recent review covering more than 60 articles on this topic (McConnell and Walls 2005). The economic methodologies used in valuing open space may be categorized into stated preference and revealed preference approaches. Stated preference methods rely on survey methods to directly elicit from individuals their values for environmental resources. Depending on the design of the survey, a broad array of specific open-space attributes may be valued using this approach. For example, Breffle et al. (1998) developed a survey to estimate the scenic, recreational, and habitat protection values of preserving open space in an urban setting.

Revealed preference approaches assess economic values based on actual, observed economic choices of individuals. Although a number of revealed preference approaches exist, one, the hedonic pricing method, is employed almost exclusively in open-space studies. This method uses information on housing prices to infer the value that individuals place on housing attributes, including local public goods such as open space.

Hedonic pricing models assume that a parcel of land is a heterogeneous good composed of a bundle of characteristics or attributes. Parcel characteristics—including environmental attributes, such as the amount of open space in the neighborhood—influence the sales price of the property. Different types of open space, such as parks, greenbelts, wetlands, forest preserves, and agricultural land, have been valued by this method, with approximately two-thirds of the studies cited in McConnell and Walls (2005) using the approach.

The early hedonic literature typically focused on proximity to urban parks and greenbelts as a determinant of housing price. Results of these studies generally found that as distance from a greenbelt or park increased, residential values decreased significantly, controlling for all other attributes (Correll et al. 1978; Hammer et al. 1974; Kitchen and Hendon 1967; McMillan 1974; Peiser and Schwann 1993; Shultz and King 2001; Weicher and Zerbst 1973). Later research analyzed how forestland affected residential prices (Garrod and Willis 1992a, 1992b, 1992c; Thorsnes 2002; Tyrvainen and Meittinen 2000), using hedonic models that included as independent variables either the distance to forest preserves or the amounts of different types of forestland surrounding residential properties. Results from these studies are mixed, suggesting that different types of forests may have different effects on housing prices (Garrod and Willis 1992c), and that only residential lots directly contiguous to a forest reserve command higher prices (Thorsnes 2002).

Still other research has focused on the effect of wetlands on housing prices (Doss and Taff 1996; Mahan et al. 2000). Similar to the results of forestland studies, the results of these studies depend on the wetland type considered. In both studies, some types of wetlands, such as forested ones, decrease home values while other types increase home values in the same suburban area.

The simultaneous effects of different types and sizes of open space at different spatial scales have been the focus of a large number of recent studies, where open space consists of both parklands (as had been studied previously) and other types of open space, such as agricultural and forested lands (Acharya and Bennett 2001; Bell and Bockstael 2000; Cheshire and Sheppard 1995; Geoghegan 2002; Geoghegan et al. 1997; Irwin 2002; Leggett and Bockstael 2000; Loomis and Seidl 2004; Smith et al. 2002). As with previous hedonic studies, different types of nondeveloped land uses are shown to affect housing prices differently. For example, Irwin (2002) shows that whereas public open space and land with easements increase local housing prices, nearby forestland decreases house prices. The negative externalities associated with animal production, such as odor and noise, have been shown to decrease nearby residential housing values (Herriges et al. 2005; Palmquist et al. 1997; Ready and Abdalla 2005).

In an analysis most closely related to this study, Geoghegan (2002) reports that permanent open space in Howard County, Maryland, increases nearby residential land values over three times as much as an equivalent amount of developable open space. The current study advances this hedonic model by including two other counties in Maryland and testing for the simultaneous determination of land use and land values (Irwin and Bockstael 2001), and addresses further statistical issues involved with the use of spatial data (Anselin 1988).

Farmland Preservation Programs in Maryland

Three Maryland counties—Howard, Calvert, and Carroll—are among the top 13 in the United States for preserved farmland acreage (Bowers 2000). In 2003,

Howard County had preserved 18,431 acres, Calvert 19,917 acres, and Carroll 37,844 acres, with preserved acreage at one-half, one-third, and one-fifth of total county farmland, respectively (American Farmland Trust 2004b).

Maryland Agricultural Land Preservation Program

As described by Lynch and Lovell (2002), the Maryland Agricultural Land Preservation Foundation (MALPF) has a purchase of development rights (PDR) program through which permanent easements on farmland are purchased, which was established in 1977. These easements prohibit nonfarm uses for current and all future owners. Appraisals and an "auction" are used to establish easement value. MALPF uses the lower of either a calculated easement value equal to an appraisal value minus the agricultural value or a bid made by the landowner. Farms are accepted in order of highest value per dollar bid until the budget is expended. Minimum eligibility criteria for a farm to participate were recently changed to include having at least 50 contiguous acres, or contiguity to another preserved farm, and 50 percent or more of its soil classified as USDA Class I, II, or III, or Woodland Group I or II.

MALPF's funding is derived from real estate and agricultural transfer taxes. The program expended $23.1 million in fiscal year 1999, and matching funds from the counties provided an additional $6.7 million. By June 2000, the state program had purchased easements on more than 185,871 acres statewide (Chesapeake Bay Commission 2001). Landowners in the three counties studied here can participate in MALPF. Carroll County farms are preserved primarily through this program. The average price per acre for development rights under the program is $1,961 for Calvert County, $1,165 for Carroll County, and $1,603 for Howard County.

County Programs

Lynch and Lovell (2002) also examined several county programs. Calvert County began a transfer of development rights (TDR) program in 1978. Landowners receive approximately one TDR for every five acres of land in a parcel. Once a TDR has been sold, a conservation easement is attached to the parcel, restricting all current and future landowners from additional residential, commercial, or industrial uses. Landowners sell the TDRs directly to the development firms; thus the financing of the land preservation is done primarily by development firms rather than through tax dollars. These developers can then use the TDRs to increase the housing density above the current zoning in a growth area. Developers' demand for increased density and landowners' reservation prices determine the number and price of TDRs sold. Developers' demand is influenced by the area's development pressure (demand for new housing) and the availability of designated growth areas where TDRs may be used.

Calvert County has also instituted a PDR program, called the Purchase and Retirement (PAR) fund, to purchase TDRs. Thus if demand among developers is low, landowners may sell TDRs to the county government until PAR program funds are exhausted. Development rights purchased by the program are retired. The prices paid in the PAR program are based on the average TDR market price, which is $2,517 per acre. Three-quarters of the 5 percent agricultural transfer tax on the purchase price of all Calvert County farmland converted to another use goes into funding the PAR program.

Started in 1978, Howard County's Purchase of Development Rights (PDR) program initially used two market-based appraisals to determine the easement price per acre. In 1989, the program switched to a point system based on parcel characteristics to determine the easement value. Having certain characteristics, such as road frontage, increases the amount the county will offer the landowner in exchange for an easement on the property. Once the landowner has sold the development rights, a conservation easement is attached to the parcel, restricting all current and future landowners from converting it to residential, commercial, or industrial use.

Howard County leverages available funds using an installment plan, under which commitments of $55 million were made by 1997. A farmer participating in this plan receives a county bond that pays tax-exempt interest payments twice a year, with a balloon payment of the principal in year 30. These bonds can be liquidated at any time. The PDR program is funded with one-quarter of the 1 percent real estate transfer tax levied against all county real estate transactions and three-quarters of the 5 percent agricultural transfer tax on all county farmland converted to another use. The average price per acre in this program between 1978 and 1997 was $5,366. The average easement payment pre-1989 was $2,316 per acre, and from 1989 to 1997, $6,420 per acre.

The Hedonic Model

Hedonic pricing models assume that a property is a heterogeneous good composed of a group of characteristics, each of which may influence the selling price of a piece of property. Such a model was estimated to test the hypothesis that different types of open space around a residential parcel contribute (positively) to residential land values. Encoded data of land parcels and associated sales transactions from the Maryland Department of Planning (2002) provided the transaction prices and housing characteristics. These include descriptions of the properties and residential structures. The data consist of 10,135 arm's-length transactions that occurred between July 1993 and June 1996. Of these, 1,676 are from Calvert County, 3,133 are from Carroll County, and 5,326 are from Howard County.

To explain the variation in the natural log of parcel transaction price (LN_PRICE), three types of explanatory variables are used: parcel and house characteristics, locational and neighborhood characteristics, and land use characteristics. The first set, parcel and house characteristics, includes the lot size. As with many previous hedonic models, the price of a parcel is assumed to be non-linearly related to its lot size. Thus the natural log of this variable (LN_ACRE) is used as an explanatory variable. Variables related to house characteristics include the natural log of the age of the house (LN_AGE), the natural log of the square footage of the house (LN_SQFT), and the number of stories (NUSTORY). Binary variables are included to control for the assessor's perceived quality of the house (AVERAGE, GOOD_VGOOD, with the omitted category of FAIR), to indicate if the house has a basement (BASEMENT), and to describe the construction type (FRAME, ALUM, with all other types excluded).

A second set of explanatory variables relates to the locations and neighborhood attributes of the parcels. The natural log of the Euclidean distance from each parcel to the nearer of Washington, D.C., or Baltimore—the two principal employment centers in the region—is included (LN_CITYDIST), as well as the natural log of the distance to the nearest town (LN_TOWNDIST). To account for neighborhood characteristics, variables were extracted from the *1990 Census of the Population* at the block group level for each parcel (U.S. Department of Commerce 1993). These include the natural log of population density (LN_POPDEN), percent of population with a college education or higher (%EDUCB), and median household income (MEDHSINC).

Data for other neighborhood characteristics, such as tax rates, public services, school quality, and crime rates, were not available at the parcel level. These characteristics vary, or are perceived to vary, more among than within counties in Maryland, however, and because the agricultural preservation programs also differ by county, we estimate the models separately for each county.

Finally, we created indices to measure the amount of preserved and developable agricultural, forested, and recreational open space surrounding each parcel. Preserved open space included the agricultural easement lands as well as private conservation land, which includes Maryland Environmental Trust lands, golf courses and cemeteries, and county and federal park land. The "other open space" category consisted of agricultural and forested lands that do not have easements.

Two indices were calculated for each type of open space. Land use was extracted for a 100-meter and a 1,600-meter buffer around each parcel, using the state of Maryland's 1997 GIS land use maps. As tax and assessment data are given for the centroid of each parcel rather than its boundaries, these indices include the land use of the actual parcels as well as that of neighboring lands. Heuristically, these two indices can be thought of as the "view" (100-meter-radius buffer, represented by SMPERMOPEN and SMAGFOREST) and the "20-minute walk" (1,600-meter-radius buffer, represented by LGPERMOPEN and LGAGFOREST) from the front door of each house. These variables were scaled to measure the percentage of total buffer area dedicated to each of the two types of open spaces. Summary statistics for the three Maryland counties can be found in Table 7-1.

These land use variables may be determined simultaneously with residential prices, as the parcels employed to calculate land use variables are usually part of the same real estate market as those used to estimate the hedonic model. Therefore, the same economic factors that affect the value of a parcel in a residential use also will affect the price of the adjacent parcel whose land use is being used to explain the first parcel's value. The probability that any individual parcel is developed or is in an open-space use may be, in part, a function of whether its neighboring parcel has been developed (Irwin and Bockstael 2001). If this simultaneity is ignored in the estimation procedure, the estimated coefficients on the land use variables would be biased, and incorrect policy conclusions could be drawn.

To address this issue, we follow Irwin and Bockstael (2001) and first estimate a model to explain these open-space variables. In identifying explanatory variables for this model, we selected variables that are correlated with these open-space variables but uncorrelated with the error term in the hedonic equation. These variables are (a) hypothesized to affect the relative costs and benefits of converting the land or maintaining it in an agricultural or forest use; (b) not factors that explain housing prices; and (c) not highly correlated with the observed explanatory variables that influence housing prices.

In addition to the soil attribute and slope variables used in Irwin and Bockstael (2001), we also include the distance to the nearest transportation node and a dummy variable for the presence of a current or planned sewer connection. The physical attributes measuring soil quality are clearly exogenous to land values and the other variables, as they are predetermined and do not change with a change in land use. Transportation node and city distance variables were tested for correlation, which was found to be small (ρ ranged from 0.02 to 0.23). Sewer service is expected to influence decisions in the future for these currently undeveloped land uses. If a statistical test indicated the presence of simultaneity in the price equation with the land use variables, then predicted values for the open-space measures (P_SMPERMOPEN, P_SMAGFOREST, P_LGPERMOPEN, and P_LGAGFOREST) from this regression were used, rather than the actual value for the land use buffers, in the housing-price model for each county.

Table 7-1. Descriptive Statistics and Variable Definitions by County

Variable name	Variable description	Calvert County		Carroll County		Howard County	
		Mean	Std. dev.	Mean	Std. dev.	Mean	Std. dev.
LN_PRICE	Natural logarithm of full transaction price, measured in dollars	11.9423	0.4143	11.9098	0.3471	12.3072	0.3457
(P_)LGPERMOPEN[a]	Percent of permanent open space within large radius	0.0502	0.0404	0.1214	0.0777	0.1245	0.0549
(P_)SMPERMOPEN[a]	Percent of permanent open space within small radius	0.0110	0.0797	0.0419	0.1650	0.0269	0.1130
(P_)LGAGFOREST[a]	Percent of agricultural and forested lands within large radius	0.5054	0.1653	0.5303	0.0838	0.3594	0.0932
(P_)SMAGFOREST[a]	Percent of agricultural and forested lands within small radius	0.2017	0.2724	0.1993	0.2727	0.1375	0.0780
LN_ACRE	Natural logarithm of parcel size, measured in acres	-0.3632	1.0826	-0.4869	1.0801	-0.8688	0.9082
LN_AGE	Natural logarithm of age of structure, measured in years	1.6401	1.5266	2.2654	1.5149	1.7306	1.3778
LN_SQFT	Natural logarithm of size of structure, measured in square feet	7.2793	0.4341	7.3892	0.3869	7.6759	0.4302
AVERAGE	Dummy variable for a structure of average quality	0.5752	0.4945	0.2831	0.4506	0.5807	0.4935
GOOD_VGOOD	Dummy variable for a structure of good or very good quality	0.0227	0.1489	0.0220	0.1468	0.3894	0.4877
NUSTORY	Number of stories of structure	1.4657	0.4733	1.6088	0.4712	1.8098	0.3862
BASEMENT	Dummy variable for presence of a basement with the structure	0.5931	0.4914	0.9524	0.2129	0.9326	0.2507
FRAME	Dummy variable for framed structures	0.4612	0.4986	0.0875	0.2825	0.6842	0.4649
ALUM	Dummy variable for aluminum structures	0.4755	0.4996	0.7038	0.4567	0.2186	0.4133
LN_POPDEN	Natural logarithm of population density for block group, measured in households per square mile	4.7608	0.8077	5.1915	0.9585	5.8756	1.1733
%EDUCB	Percent of bachelor's degree education attainment block group	0.0697	0.0247	0.0920	0.0361	0.1753	0.0543
MEDHSINC	Median household income of block group, measured in dollars	47,665	9,533	43,645	7,256	62,181	13,623
LN_CITYDIST	Natural logarithm of distance to Washington, D.C., or Baltimore, measured in 100 kilometers	11.1133	0.2367	10.6711	0.2233	10.1559	0.2362
LN_TOWNDIST	Natural logarithm of distance to nearest town, measured in 100 kilometers	7.6665	0.7375	7.8654	0.7486	8.4256	0.8121

[a] Either actual value or predicted value; see regression results in Tables 7-2, 7-3, and 7-4.

In addition to the simultaneity issue involved with estimating the hedonic model, the use of spatial data leads to the potential for bias and inefficiency if spatial effects are not taken into account. One of the most relevant of these effects is spatial autocorrelation in the residuals, which likely occurs when important variables common to all observations in a neighborhood are not observable by the researcher and thus are not included in the model. This type of spatial autocorrelation, if left uncorrected, can result in inefficient parameter estimates and biased standard errors, which can lead to incorrect conclusions concerning statistical significance of estimated parameters. Using standard spatial econometric techniques, adjustments were made to each of the hedonic models if statistical tests indicated the presence of spatial autocorrelation in the residuals.

Estimation Results

Test statistics demonstrated the need to modify the hedonic models to correct for spatial autocorrelation. The estimated parameter results for the corrected hedonic pricing models for Calvert, Carroll, and Howard counties are reported

Table 7-2. Regression Results for Calvert County

Variable name	Coefficient	Asymp. t-stat
CONSTANT	10.7624*	15.78
P_LGPERMOPEN	0.7118*	2.83
SMPERMOPEN	−0.1117	−1.67
P_LGAGFOREST	−0.3907*	−6.03
SMAGFOREST	−0.0496	−2.42
LN_ACRE	0.1002*	12.87
LN_AGE	−0.0287*	−6.28
LN_SQFT	0.3765*	19.49
AVERAGE	0.2020*	12.94
GOOD_VGOOD	0.4699*	11.56
NUSTORY	0.0655*	5.14
BASEMENT	−0.0008	−0.07
FRAME	−0.0311	−1.36
ALUM	−0.0464	−2.07
LN_POPDEN	−0.0393*	−2.85
%EDUCB	1.0015*	2.83
MEDHSINC	0.0000	−0.18
LN_CITYDIST	−0.1432*	−2.59
LN_TOWN	0.0265	2.02
Lambda	0.4067*	12.15
Adjusted R^2	0.7785	

*Statistical significance at the 5 percent level.

Table 7-3. Regression Results for Carroll County

Variable name	Coefficient	Asymp. t-stat
CONSTANT	11.6311*	32.47
P_LGPERMOPEN	−0.1171	−1.57
SMPERMOPEN	0.0317	1.33
P_LGAGFOREST	−0.2074*	−3.26
SMAGFOREST	0.0027	0.20
LN_ACRE	0.1338*	31.06
LN_AGE	−0.0610*	−20.15
LN_SQFT	0.2629*	24.00
AVERAGE	0.1551*	16.76
GOOD_VGOOD	0.3973*	16.69
NUSTORY	−0.0155	−1.83
BASEMENT	0.1330*	8.87
FRAME	−0.0488*	−3.79
ALUM	−0.0007	−0.08
LN_POPDEN	0.0274*	4.02
%EDUCB	0.0083	0.06
MEDHSINC	0.0000*	23.02
LN_CITYDIST	−0.1687*	−5.80
LN_TOWNDIST	−0.0048	−0.75
Lambda	0.2149	21.15
Adjusted R^2	0.7458	

*Statistical significance at the 5 percent level.

in Tables 7-2, 7-3, and 7-4. All three models included semiannual time dummy variables to control for inflation and other temporal effects, and all were found to be statistically significant. As these tables show, the estimated coefficients on the lot size and structural characteristics all meet a priori expectations and are statistically significant for the three counties, except for insignificant coefficients on NUSTORY for Carroll County and BASEMENT for Calvert County. Estimated coefficients for other characteristics varied both qualitatively and quantitatively by county. For example, the coefficient on LN_CITYDIST is negative and statistically significant in the Calvert and Carroll county regressions; the closer a parcel in these counties is to either Washington or Baltimore, the higher the sales price, as would be predicted by urban economic theory. LN_CITYDIST is not, however, statistically significant in Howard County. To explain this lack of significance, we argue that because Howard County is situated between Washington and Baltimore, it is possible that Howard residents value a location affording a dual-commute opportunity, as opposed to a location that affords a shorter commute to only one city.

We originally hypothesized that the closer a parcel is to a town, the higher the price. Our findings show, however, that the distance to the nearest

Table 7-4. Regression Results for Howard County

Variable name	Coefficient	Asymp. t-stat
CONSTANT	10.1107*	1661.01
P_LGPERMOPEN	0.5869*	3.91
SMPERMOPEN	0.0489*	2.02
P_LGAGFOREST	−0.2035	−2.31
P_SMAGFOREST	0.1482	1.75
LN_ACRE	0.1114*	23.79
LN_AGE	−0.0566*	−18.56
LN_SQFT	0.2031*	29.46
AVERAGE	0.2300*	14.07
GOOD_VGOOD	0.4120*	23.06
NUSTORY	0.0734*	8.97
BASEMENT	0.0731*	7.15
FRAME	−0.0538*	−6.00
ALUM	−0.0601*	−5.65
LN_POPDEN	0.0041	0.74
%EDUCB	0.1601	1.62
MEDHSINC	0.0021*	5.70
LN_CITYDIST	0.0154	1.68
LN_TOWNDIST	0.0004	0.05
Lambda	0.6339	167.09
Adjusted R^2	0.7741	

*Statistical significance at the 5 percent level.

town (LN_TOWNDIST) is not statistically significant in Carroll and Howard counties, but it is positive and significant in Calvert County. Calvert residents pay more to be farther away from towns, possibly because not all of the county's towns provide desirable amenities or employment opportunities. Towns between and within these counties vary enormously. For both Carroll and Howard, we find a high degree of correlation between distance to towns and distance to city, but dropping this variable from the estimation did not change any of the results appreciably.

Hypothesis tests on the estimated coefficients for the block-group census variables resulted in some unexpected outcomes. In Howard County, the estimated coefficient on LN_POPDEN is not statistically significant; in Carroll, it is positive and statistically significant; and in Calvert, it is negative and statistically significant. Population density could have two opposite effects on housing prices. Our a priori hypothesis was that population density is a measure of congestion. Nevertheless, it is conceivable that population density acts as a proxy for the density of other goods and services that might attract people and bid up the housing prices, although we hope to have captured these locational amenities that are capitalized in the value of the home through inclusion of other right-hand-side variables. MEDHSINC has the expected positive coefficient in Carroll and Howard counties, but it is not statistically significant in Calvert County. The coefficient on %EDUCB is positive and statistically significant only in Calvert County. These census variables are averages over the block group rather than for the microneighborhoods surrounding the transaction parcels that make up the data set. Unfortunately, these are the most disaggregated estimates available for these neighborhood attributes.

The policy-relevant coefficients on the four open-space land use variables in each of the counties also revealed mixed results. The statistical test for simultaneity of land value and surrounding land uses indicated that the predicted values for the large-buffer P_LGPERMOPEN and P_LGAGFOREST measures should be used for both Calvert and Carroll counties, whereas in Howard County, predicted values should be used for these two variables as well as the small-buffer P_SMAGFOREST measure. Given the functional form used for the hedonic estimation, the estimated coefficients on these variables can be interpreted as elasticities. In Calvert County, the estimated coefficient on the large permanent open space (P_LGPERMOPEN) is positive and statistically significant, with an estimated elasticity of 0.71, so that for a 10 percent increase in permanent open space in the large buffer, housing values on average increase by 7 percent. In Howard County, the estimated coefficients for both the large (P_LGPERMOPEN) and small (SMPERMOPEN) permanent open-space variables are positive and statistically significant, with estimated coefficients of 0.59 and 0.05, respectively. In Carroll County, these two estimates are not statistically significant.

A variety of hypotheses may explain these results. Carroll County residents could value open forested and agricultural lands less than do residents of Calvert and Howard because this county has a greater amount of these lands. In the large buffer, however, Carroll had a mean of 12 percent permanently preserved open space and 53 percent unpreserved agricultural and forested lands around the parcels examined. Howard had a mean of 13 percent permanently preserved open space and 36 percent unpreserved agricultural and forested lands. Calvert had only 5 percent permanently preserved open space but 51 percent unpreserved agricultural and forested lands. Similarly, in the small buffer, Carroll had a mean of 4 percent permanently preserved open space and 20 percent agricultural and forested lands, Howard had a mean of 3 percent permanently preserved and 14 percent agricultural and forested lands, and Calvert had a mean of 1 percent permanently preserved and 20 percent agricultural and forested lands. Thus, although Carroll has more open space around each parcel (65 percent, compared with 56 percent in Calvert and 49 percent in Howard), it seems unlikely that the differences in open space immediately surrounding the parcels alone explain the results.

If we consider open space beyond those surrounding individual houses, we find that more agricultural land is available in Carroll County. In 1997, Carroll had 178,000 acres of agricultural land, compared with 40,000 in Howard and 45,000 in Calvert. In addition, while the rate of housing development is increasing in Carroll, the county has not experienced the conversion rates seen in Howard and Calvert in the last 25 years. Thus Carroll County residents may have a lower willingness to pay for open space because of a perception that a sufficient quantity of open space exists and that it is not disappearing quickly.

Another possibility is that Carroll farmers use different production practices than Howard or Calvert farmers. For example, they might start farming earlier in the morning; have a higher density of animals, with the accompanying odors and insects; spray insecticides more frequently; or employ some other practice that neighboring residents find objectionable. Carroll County has many more animals than the other two counties, with 260 million chickens and almost 31,000 cattle and calves, whereas Howard has 987 chickens and 4,266 cattle and calves, and Calvert has 869 chickens and 1,570 cattle and calves. Therefore, although residents receive some positive externalities from the presence of nearby open space, they also receive negative externalities—negating the positive effects.

Additionally, we hypothesize that open space is a luxury good and will have more value in counties where incomes are higher. Howard County's median income is much higher on average than those of the two other counties, but Carroll's average median income of $44,000 is not much lower than Calvert's $48,000. In conclusion, further analysis is needed to explain the lack of significance in Carroll County. Although the results for Howard County were robust, we find that for the models in Carroll and Calvert, the estimated coefficients were sensitive to changes in the variables and specification.

Interestingly, the agricultural and forested land measures (AGFOREST) were either negative and statistically significant or not statistically significant in all three counties, suggesting that individuals either do not wish to live near these lands or are not willing to pay a premium to do so. We remain perplexed by this result. Whereas permanent open space did have an impact in two counties, open space in agricultural or forest use that may be developed in the future was not important or decreased the value of the property. Perhaps these farms use production practices that generate negative externalities to the neighbors. Or maybe the insecurity of not knowing what changes might occur next to a parcel at some time in the future fosters a lack of willingness to pay to be in close proximity to open space. Other possible explanations are that the forests abutting these properties might be considered unsightly or that people might prefer to have a view, which trees might block. Deer have become an issue in these counties, as they eat homeowners' landscape plants, cause car accidents, and increase the incidence of Lyme disease—all of which make forestland less desirable. These explanations notwithstanding, we still find it surprising that homeowners are not willing to pay a premium to be near agricultural or forested land.

Here, the central policy focus relates to the effect of permanent open space on housing values. Based on regression results, Carroll County will have no additional property tax revenues from increases in preserved agricultural land, as this land use variable had no effect on housing value. Consequently, we now focus exclusively on Calvert and Howard counties to conduct the simulations.

Simulations

How much additional land can agricultural easement programs finance through the resulting increase in property tax revenues? To answer this question, we use the estimated elasticities from the regression models for Howard and Calvert counties to simulate the increase in property taxes associated only with houses located near current agricultural easements, for a 1 percent increase in neighboring agricultural easements. Both the large and small permanent open-space measures were statistically significant for Howard County, so the larger measure is used for the simulations. (As the small buffer is part of the larger buffer, the use of both would result in double counting.)

We increase permanent open space by 1 percent and calculate the increase in tax revenue associated with the resulting increase in housing values. Taking information on land use around preserved agricultural parcels in Howard and Calvert counties, the area of low-density (0.4 units per acre) and medium- to high-density (8 units per acre) residential land for a one-mile (approximately 1,600-meter) radius buffer was calculated. This area was multiplied by the relevant housing density to compute the expected number of houses within this one-mile distance from each preserved parcel.

With the average value of houses being $134,245 for Calvert and $227,963 for Howard, the total value of expected housing in each buffer was calculated. The increase in property values was then calculated using the estimated elasticity, assuming that current preserved agricultural land has increased by 1 percent. Next, this increase in parcel value was multiplied by the county property tax rate ($0.89 per $100 for Calvert, $1.04 per $100 for Howard) to determine how much tax revenue would be generated each year by the simulated increase in preserved agricultural land. Finally, using the average county easement payment over the period 1993–1997 ($2,855 for Calvert, $5,274 for Howard), the total number of new acres of agricultural easement that could be purchased with the increased tax revenues from just one year of property tax revenue was computed. Simulation results are presented in Table 7-5.

Table 7-5. Simulation Results for the One-Mile Buffer of Each Agricultural Easement

	Howard County	Calvert County
[1] Sum of total housing within one mile of each easement	41,631	29,526
[2] Average housing price	$227,963	$134,245
[3] Expected housing value (= [1]*[2])	$9,490,251,998	$3,963,690,359
[4] 1% increase in acres of open space	181	148
[5] Estimated elasticity from estimated model	0.5869	0.7118
[6] Expected housing value increase for a 1% increase in open space (= [3]*[5])	$55,695,442	$28,214,618
[7] Additional property tax collected on increased value	$579,233	$251,674
[8] Average easement price per acre	$5,274	$2,855
[9] Additional acres of easement that could be acquired (= [7]/[8])	110	88

For a 1 percent increase in preserved agricultural land (148 acres) in Calvert County, the increase in housing values within a one-mile radius of preserved parcels generated sufficient tax revenue to purchase an additional 88 acres in the first year. Assuming no real change in housing prices and no change in the property tax rate, the county could preserve an additional 2,640 acres in 30 years. For a 1 percent increase in preserved agricultural land (181 acres) in Howard County, the increase in housing values within a one-mile radius of preserved parcels generated sufficient tax revenue to purchase an additional 110 acres in one year, or increase the preserved acreage by 3,300 acres in 30 years. If real housing prices and assessments were to increase over this period, and if the increase in tax revenues grows at a faster rate than any potential increase in easement costs, even more acres could be purchased.

Conclusions

Many agricultural land preservation programs have inadequate resources to preserve all the parcels that the general public may wish to see protected and that agricultural landowners would be willing to enroll. Programs are looking for innovative funding mechanisms or new sources of funds. Beyond the social benefits that permanently preserved agricultural land can provide to the region's residents as a whole, positive impacts may accrue directly to the owners of parcels neighboring the preserved land. These benefits usually are recaptured partially through increased property taxes yet are not explicitly realized.

The increased tax revenue could be used for additional easement acquisitions rather than entering the county's general fund. This is especially important in states where the agricultural land preservation programs are funded at least in part by the continued conversion of agricultural land to other uses. In Maryland, for example, the agricultural transfer tax is generated when farmland leaves an agricultural use for a residential, commercial, or industrial use, and this tax revenue is used to finance farmland preservation.

Lynch and Lovell (2002) determined that preserving 1 acre of land at the average easement price per county, with the agricultural transfer tax as the sole funding mechanism, would require converting $64,080 worth of farmland in Calvert County and $124,933 in Howard County. Using the 1997 value of land and buildings per acre of $3,584 in Calvert and $5,518 in Howard County (USDA/NASS 1997), it would take the conversion of almost 17.9 farmland acres in Calvert and 22.6 acres in Howard to finance the preservation of 1 acre.

We find that preserved open space does increase property values on adjacent residential parcels in two of the three examined counties in Maryland. Assuming that the existing open space increases by 1 percent, using simulations based on the spatial econometric model, we find that the increased property tax revenue from these agricultural easements could generate enough revenue to purchase a significant portion of these open-space acres, especially if one considers that the tax revenue increases continue in perpetuity. In both Howard and Calvert counties, the revenue generated from an increase in permanent open space could purchase approximately 60 percent of the increase of the newly preserved lands in the first year alone.

Conversely, in Carroll County, property values are not affected by proximity to open space. Residents here may value open forest and agricultural lands less because the county as a whole has more of them. Because of these results for Carroll County, we do not demonstrate our first hypothesis that open space itself universally increases property values. In fact, unpreserved agricultural and forested lands decreased the values in both Carroll and Calvert counties. Thus further research may be needed to determine the attributes of open space for which residents are willing to pay.

This research has the potential to contribute to the analysis of other government conservation and infrastructure programs. For example, if the government intervenes and changes land use in ways that generate positive externalities, such as implementing dune and beach grass restoration programs that decrease beach erosion and thus improve the quality of the beach for nearby homeowners and other beach visitors, then the financing of these programs could be partially funded from some diversion of the increased housing values' impact on property tax (Parsons and Noailly 2004). Conversely, similar findings might be used to assess the implications of negative land use externalities (e.g., from development or congestion) on the capacity of communities to generate tax revenues, perhaps as a guide for establishing impact fees or permit costs for activities that generate negative impacts on property values.

Endnotes

1. It is well known that markets will underprovide open-space lands because of the public-goods nature of many of the amenities generated by such lands. As the argument for the underprovision of open space by markets is covered in various other chapters in this book, it is omitted here.

2. Sale or transfer of development rights typically results in the attachment of an easement to the title of the land, restricting current and all future owners from converting the parcel to a residential, commercial, or industrial use (Lynch 2005).

References

Acharya, G., and L. L. Bennett. (2001). Valuing Open Space and Land-Use Patterns in Urban Watersheds. *Journal of Real Estate Finance and Economics* 22(2/3): 221–238.

American Farmland Trust. (2004a). Fact Sheet: Status of State PACE Programs. Washington, DC: American Farmland Trust.

———. (2004b). *Conserving the Washington-Baltimore Regions Green Network: The Time To Act Is Now.* Washington DC: American Farmland Trust.

Anselin, L. (1988). *Spatial Econometrics: Methods and Models.* Dordrecht, The Netherlands: Kluwer Academic Publishers.

Bell, K. P., and N. E. Bockstael. (2000). Applying the Generalized Method of Moments Estimation Approach to Spatial Problems Involving Microlevel Data. *Review of Economics and Statistics* 82(1): 72–82.

Bowers, D. (2000). Sixth Annual Survey. *Farmland Preservation Report* 10(9): 1–7.

Breffle, W. S., E. R. Morey, and T. S. Lodder. (1998). Using Contingent Valuation to Estimate a Neighborhood's Willingness to Pay to Preserve Undeveloped Urban Land. *Urban Studies* 35(4): 715–727.

Bromley, D. W., and I. Hodge. (1990). Private Property Rights and Presumptive Policy Entitlements: Reconsidering the Premises of Rural Policy. *European Review of Agricultural Economics* 17(2): 197–214.

Chesapeake Bay Commission and the Trust for Public Land. (2001). *Keeping Our Commitment: Preserving Land in the Chesapeake Watershed.* Annapolis, MD.

Chesapeake Bay Foundation. (2002). Future Growth in the Washington, D.C. Metropolitan Area. Annapolis, MD. http://www.savethebay.org/land/landuse/maps/future_growth.html.

Cheshire, P., and S. Sheppard. (1995). On the Prices of Land and the Value of Amenities. *Economica* 62(May): 247–67.

Correll, M. R., J. H. Lillydahl, and L. D. Singell. (1978). The Effects of Greenbelts on Residential Property Values: Some Findings on the Political Economy of Open Space. *Land Economics* 54(May): 207–17.

Doss, C. R., and S. J. Taff. (1996). The Influence of Wetland Type and Wetland Proximity on Residential Property Values. *Journal of Agricultural and Resource Economics* 21(1): 120–129.

Fischel, W. M. (1985). *The Economics of Zoning Laws: A Property Rights Approach to American Land Use Controls.* Baltimore, MD: Johns Hopkins University Press.

Gardner, B. D. (1977). The Economics of Agricultural Land Preservation. *American Journal of Agricultural Economics* 59(December): 1027–1036.

Garrod, G., and K. Willis. (1992a). The Amenity Value of Woodland in Great Britain: A Comparison of Economic Estimates. *Environmental and Resource Economics* 2: 415–34.

———. (1992b). The Environmental Economic Impact of Woodland: A Two Stage Hedonic Price Model of the Amenity Value of Forestry in Britain. *Applied Economics* 24(7): 715–28.

———. (1992c). Valuing Goods' Characteristics: An Application of the Hedonic Price Method to Environmental Attributes. *Journal of Environmental Management* 34: 59–76.

Geoghegan, J. (2002). The Value of Open Spaces in Residential Land Use. *Land Use Policy* 19(1): 91–98.

Geoghegan, J., L. Wainger, and N. E. Bockstael. (1997). Spatial Landscape Indices in a Hedonic Framework: An Ecological Economics Analysis Using GIS. *Ecological Economics* 23(3): 251–64.

Hammer, T. R., R. E. Coughlin, and E. T. Horn IV. (1974). The Effect of a Large Urban Park on Real Estate Values. *American Institute of Planners Journal* 40(4): 274–77.

Herriges, J. A., S. Secchi, and B. A. Babcock. (2005). Living with Hogs in Iowa: The Impact of Livestock Facilities on Rural Residential Property Values. *Land Economics.*

Irwin, E. G. (2002). The Effects of Open Space on Residential Property Values. *Land Economics* 78(4): 464–480.

Irwin, E. G., and N. E. Bockstael. (2001). The Problem of Identifying Land Use Spillovers: Measuring the Effects of Open Space on Residential Property Values. *American Journal of Agricultural Economics* 83(3): 698–704.

Kitchen, J. W., and W. S. Hendon. (1967). Land Values Adjacent to An Urban Neighborhood Park. *Land Economics* 43(August): 357–61.

Land Trust Alliance. (2003). *Americans Invest in Parks and Open Space: LandVote 2003.* Washington, DC: Land Trust Alliance.

Leggett, C. G., and N. E. Bockstael. (2000). Evidence of the Effects of Water Quality on Residential Land Prices. *Journal of Environmental Economics and Management* 39(2): 121–144.

Loomis, J., and V. R. Seidl. (2004). A Hedonic Model of Public Market Transactions for Open Space Protection. *Journal of Environmental Planning and Management* 47(1): 83–96.

Lynch, L. (2005). Protecting Farmland: Why Do We Do It? How Do We Do It? Can We Do It Better? In *Land Use Problems and Conflicts: Causes, Consequences, and Solutions,* edited by Stephan J. Goetz, James S. Shortle and John C. Bergstrom. New York: Routledge, 279–300.

Lynch, L., and S. J. Lovell. (2002). Hedonic Price Analysis of Easement Payments in Maryland Agricultural Land Preservation Programs. Department of Agricultural and Resource Economics Working Paper 02-13. University of Maryland, College Park.

———. (2003). Combining Spatial and Survey Data to Explain Participation in Agricultural Land Preservation Programs. *Land Economics* 79(2): 259–276.

Mahan, B. L., S. Polasky, and R. M. Adams. (2000). Valuing Urban Wetlands: A Property Price Approach. *Land Economics* 76(1): 100–113.

Maryland Department of Planning. (2002). *MdProperty View.* Statewide Property Map and Parcel Database. Baltimore, MD. http://www.mdp.state.md.ud/data.mdview.htm.

McConnell, K. E. (1989). The Optimal Quantity of Land in Agriculture. *Northeastern Journal of Agricultural and Resource Economics* 18(October): 63–72.

McConnell, V., and M. Walls. (2005). The Value of Open Space: Evidence from Studies of Non-Market Benefits. Report. Washington, DC: Resources for the Future.

McMillan, M. (1974). Open Space Preservation in Developing Areas: An Alternative Policy. *Land Economics* 50(November): 410–17.

Nickerson, C., and L. Lynch. (2001). The Effect of Farmland Preservation Programs on Farmland Prices. *American Journal of Agricultural Economics* 83(2): 341–351.

Palmquist, R. B., F. M. Roka, and R. Vukina. (1997). Hog Operations, Environmental Effects, and Residential Property Values. *Land Economics* 73(1): 114–124.

Parsons, G. R., and J. Noailly. (2004). A Value Capture Property Tax for Financing Beach Nourishment Projects: An Application to Delaware's Ocean Beaches. *Ocean and Coastal Management* 47: 49–61.

Peiser, R. B., and G. M. Schwann. (1993). The Private Value of Public Open Space within Subdivisions. *Journal of Architectural and Planning Research* 10(Summer): 91–104.

Ready, R. C., and C. W. Abdalla. (2005). The Amenity and Disamenity Impacts of Agriculture: Estimates from a Hedonic Pricing Model. *American Journal of Agricultural Economics.*

Shultz, S. D., and D. A. King. (2001). The Use of Census Data for Hedonic Price Estimates of Open Space Amenities and Land Use. *Journal of Real Estate Finance and Economics* 22(2/3): 239–252.

Smith, V. K., C. Poulos, and H. Kim. (2002). Treating Open Space as an Urban Amenity. *Resource and Energy Economics* 24: 107–129.

Thorsnes, P. (2002). The Value of a Suburban Forest Preserve: Estimates from Sales of Vacant Residential Building Lots. *Land Economics* 78(3): 426–441.

Tyrvainen, L., and A. Meittinen. (2000). Property Prices and Urban Forest Amenities. *Journal of Environmental Economics and Management* 39(2): 205–223.

USDA/NASS (U.S. Department of Agriculture, National Agricultural Statistic Service). (1993–1997). *Agricultural Statistics.* Washington, DC: USDA/NASS. Various annual issues.

U.S. Department of Commerce, Bureau of the Census. (1993). *1990 Census of the Population: General Population Characteristics, U.S. Summary.* Washington, DC: Government Printing Office.

Vesterby, M., A. Daugherty, R. Heimlich, and R. Claassen. (1997). Major Land Use Changes in the Contiguous 48 States. AREI Updates No. 3. USDA/ERS/NRED, June.

Weicher, J. C., and R. H. Zerbst. (1973). The Externalities of Neighborhood Parks: An Empirical Investigation. *Land Economics* 49(February): 99–105.

Wolfram, G. (1981). The Sale of Development Rights and Zoning in the Preservation of Open Space: Lindahl Equilibrium and a Case Study. *Land Economics* 57(3): 398–413.

8

Land Development and Current Use Assessment

RICHARD W. ENGLAND AND ROBERT D. MOHR

During the twentieth century, state and municipal governments in the United States witnessed an ongoing conversion of agricultural land and other forms of open space to metropolitan uses. As Morris (1998) notes, "Since 1957, every state has responded to development pressures by allowing or requiring preferential property tax treatment of farmland, and in some states other open space land. . . . [T]he most common policy assesses the land at its value in its current agricultural or open space use." Such policies are known as current use (or use–value) assessment. With the sole exception of Michigan, every state employs some form of a current use assessment program (American Farmland Trust 1997). The literature is replete with works that assess the potential impacts of such programs on landowners and land conservation (e.g., Anderson 1986, 1993; Bentick 1979; Bentick and Pogue 1988; Lopez et al. 1988).

The use of these programs remains controversial. Many researchers in this area argue that current use assessment has been largely ineffective at preserving open space (Ferguson 1988; Malme 1993). Others suggest that differential taxation may indeed influence the extent and rate of development (Lopez et al. 1994). Still others feel that uncertainty still surrounds differential taxation policies, and the optimality of differential taxation may vary according to the specific types of incentives offered to landowners (Johnston 2003). These different perspectives notwithstanding, it remains clear that for the individual landowner, the potential profits of development typically dwarf the tax incentives favoring rural uses. At the same time, current use programs are expensive, with tax expenditures that might exceed $1 billion per year (Anderson and Griffing 2000; Heimlich and Anderson 2001).

170

In spite of these critiques, current use assessment continues to benefit from popular support, and removal or replacement of these programs likely would face significant political obstacles (Beattie and Ransom 1979). Furthermore, theoretical research does support the conclusion that current use programs might postpone development (Anderson 1993; Tavernier and Li 1995), and Chapter 4 of this volume illustrates that taxes, in general, can affect development patterns. Additionally, Marshall (1995), Johnston (2003), and others argue that current use programs might be more effective if they were designed more carefully to account for incentive effects.

This chapter is based on the premise that current use programs can be improved by accounting for the specific incentives they offer landowners, thereby providing a more effective use of the tax revenues forgone through such programs. More specifically, it focuses on the tax treatment of properties that are first enrolled in and then later withdrawn from current use assessment, and explores how different features of a current use program might affect the timing of the decision to develop a parcel of land. The results presented here also provide an interesting parallel to Chapter 4, which creates an empirical model of development timing. Although that chapter addresses—using empirical data from an Ohio county—the role of various taxation attributes on development timing, it explicitly omits consideration of differential or use value taxation. This chapter, in contrast, provides a theoretical perspective specifically designed to assess the potential impacts of policies not considered in the earlier chapter.

We begin by providing an empirical survey of development penalties, documenting that parcels withdrawn from current use assessment programs are taxed differently in different states. Policies range from no penalty for withdrawal to penalties based on market value or previous tax savings. This interstate variation indicates the need to consider how the structure of current use programs might affect the timing of development. Next, we use an intertemporal model to analyze a landowner's decision to develop a parcel of land already enrolled in a current use assessment program. We then consider the original decision to enroll a parcel. Altogether, the analysis highlights factors that might affect the degree to which current use assessment preserves undeveloped land. The results also underscore the difficulty a local government might have in influencing the behavior of landowners.

An Empirical Survey of Development Penalties

Except for potential changes in eligibility rules, current use assessment typically allows for variation in only two policy elements: the penalty for development and the property tax rate. Different types of development penalties have been enacted by various states, as revealed by data from state government websites,

Table 8-1. Current Use Assessment States with No Development Penalty (2002)

Arizona	Iowa	Montana	South Dakota
Arkansas	Kansas	New Mexico	West Virginia
Florida	Louisiana	North Dakota	Wyoming
Idaho	Missouri	Oklahoma	

a search of states' revised annotated statutes for relevant passages, and phone interviews with state tax officials (e.g., to help with the interpretation of statutory language).[1] We find that the states fall into three categories: those that impose no penalty at all when a parcel is removed from current use property classification (no-penalty states); those that collect several years of tax savings, plus interest, for the period immediately prior to development (rollback states); and those that collect a penalty based on the market value of the property at the time of its development (percent-payback states).

Fifteen states do not collect a penalty when a landowner withdraws agricultural and sometimes other rural properties from current use classification (Table 8-1). What is striking about these states is that, with the exceptions of Arizona and Florida, they are relatively rural and have few rapidly growing metropolitan regions. In such instances, enactment of current use assessment might have been originally motivated more by a desire to grant tax relief to farmers and ranchers than by a desire to deter metropolitan sprawl.

Another seven states fall into the percent-payback category, meaning that they collect a penalty based on the market value of a parcel during the year it no longer qualifies for current use assessment because of a land use conversion. As

Table 8-2. Current Use Assessment States with Percent-Payback Penalties (2002)

State	Percent-payback penalty
California	12.5 percent of market value, with local option for higher percentage
Connecticut	10 percent of market value during first year of classification, with percentage falling to 0 after 10 years of classification
Maine	Open space: 6 percent of market value if 10 or fewer years, falling to 4 percent if 20 or more years of classification
	Forest: 30 percent of difference between market and current use values if 10 years or less, falling to 20 percent of difference if 20 years or more
Maryland	5 percent of market value if parcel size $\geq$ 20 acres
	4 percent of market value if parcel size $<$ 20 acres
New Hampshire	10 percent of market value
Rhode Island	10 percent of market value if six or fewer years, falling to 0 percent if 15 or more years of classification
Vermont	20 percent of market value

summarized in Table 8-2, California, Maryland, New Hampshire, and Vermont simply collect a fixed percentage of market value during the year of property reclassification. Three other states, Connecticut, Maine, and Rhode Island, employ a sliding-scale version of this type of penalty: The percentage of market value collected as a penalty declines with the number of years that a parcel has been enrolled in current use.

More common than the percent-payback penalty is the rollback penalty, a development deterrent used by 26 states. In these jurisdictions, a landowner must pay the difference between taxes actually paid during recent years of current use assessment and those that would have been paid with market-value assessment, plus accrued interest. As shown in Table 8-3, the maximum number of years of tax reimbursement for which a landowner is liable during the year of property reclassification varies greatly among these states. In Indiana, for example, a farmer who decides to convert his land into a residential subdivision might owe the tax collector 10 years of tax savings, plus interest. In nearby Illinois, on the other hand, a farmer in a similar situation would owe only 3 years of tax savings, plus accrued interest.

Because of the significant variation among states, one would expect to observe interstate differences in the impact of current use on the development decisions of private landowners. In the 15 states without development penalties, the incentive to enroll properties with market values greater than their rural use values is very strong. At the same time, property owners will be relatively less likely to leave parcels enrolled once their communities face metropolitan

Table 8-3. Current Use Assessment States with Rollback Penalties (2002)

Maximum years of tax savings recaptured	States	
10	Delaware; Hawaii (Honolulu County)	Indiana; Oregon (exclusive farm use zone)
7	Alaska; Colorado	Washington (tax savings + accrued interest + 20%)
6	Nevada	Pennsylvania
5	Maine (farmland); Massachusetts (forest); Nebraska; New York (5 × tax savings of most recent year)	Oregon (not exclusive farm use zone); South Carolina; Tennessee (open space); Texas; Utah; Virginia
4	Massachusetts (farmland)	
3	Alabama; Georgia; Illinois; Minnesota	North Carolina; Ohio; Tennessee (farms and forest)
2	New Jersey	Wisconsin

growth pressures and opportunities to benefit from land conversion arise. Different incentives will apply in states with more imposing conversion penalties. The various penalty structures in other states indicate the need for a model that offers some hypotheses about how different program structures affect land use change and incentives to enroll.

An Intertemporal Model of Development

To analyze the impact of current use assessment on local land use patterns, we apply England and Mohr's (2003) model of a representative landowner who owns a single parcel of undeveloped land on a metropolitan fringe. The structure of this model closely follows Anderson (1993) but extends his work by adding several features critical to program design.

First, the model adds specific functional forms to the trajectory of rents for developed and undeveloped land, which allow the derivation of intuitive comparative statics with unambiguous signs. In addition, it explicitly allows for the possibility that landowners value the nonpecuniary benefits of their land. This feature is central to the policy discussion on current use assessment and should be included in the model, particularly given pervasive anecdotal evidence that many agricultural landowners retain these lands not for pecuniary reasons, but because of a desire to maintain nonpecuniary benefits, such as keeping the family farm or preserving the character of a rural community.

Lawmakers justify tax benefits for agriculture and land preservation in terms of preserving family farms, the rural landscape, and areas of historic value; market prices may not reflect these benefits. To the extent that such nonpecuniary values accrue to individual landowners, we wish to investigate how they affect the operation of a current use program.[2]

Most important, this model extends Anderson (1993) by explicitly accounting for the penalty that a landowner might face for removing a parcel from a current use assessment program. This inclusion gives additional policy relevance to the model, as the penalty is the policy variable that a state government could most easily change. We add depth to this policy discussion by explicitly considering a landowner's option to enroll in a current use program and the optimal construction of penalties under such a scenario.

In the model that follows, a landowner must decide at what point in time, D, to develop a parcel enrolled in current use assessment. While undeveloped, the parcel generates a stream of pecuniary benefits, $c(t)$, and a stream of nonpecuniary benefits, $n(t)$. We initially assume that the parcel is enrolled in a current use program, so the landowner must pay a penalty, $P(D)$, at the time of development. Once land is developed, it generates only pecuniary benefits,

$u(t)$. Both before and after development, the landowner must pay a property tax, at a constant rate, τ, on the assessed value of land, $A(t)$. Thus the owner chooses the time of development, D, to maximize the present value of a stream of payments described by

$$\underbrace{\int_{t=0}^{t=D} [c(t) + n(t) - \tau A(t)]e^{-rt}dt}_{\substack{\text{Present value of returns} \\ \text{to undeveloped land,} \\ \text{net of taxes}}} - \underbrace{P(D)e^{-rD}}_{\substack{\text{Present value} \\ \text{of development} \\ \text{penalty}}} + \underbrace{\int_{t=D}^{t\to\infty} [u(t) - \tau A(t)]e^{-rt}dt}_{\substack{\text{Present value of} \\ \text{returns to developed} \\ \text{land, net of taxes}}},$$

(8-1)

where r represents the owner's discount rate and t denotes time.

The method for determining assessed value, $A(t)$, differs for undeveloped and developed parcels. For undeveloped parcels, the local tax authority assesses land by capitalizing pecuniary income, $c(t)$. In other words, the assessor values the land as if the land were to remain forever undeveloped:

$$\text{for } 0 < t < D,\ A(t) = \int_{t'=t}^{t'\to\infty} c(t')e^{-r(t'-t)}dt', \tag{8-2}$$

where t' tracks time.[3] Developed properties are assessed according to the present value of the stream of pecuniary benefits:

$$\text{for } t \geq D,\ A(t) = \int_{t'=t}^{t'\to\infty} u(t')e^{-r(t'-t)}dt'. \tag{8-3}$$

Until now, we have presented the model in full generality. In order to ensure tractable solutions, we now assume that the pecuniary and nonpecuniary benefits of undeveloped land remain constant at values $\bar{c}$ and $\bar{n}$, respectively. We capture the impact of metropolitan population growth by assuming that the rent on developed land initially equals $\bar{u} < \bar{c}$ and then increases according to a growth rate of g. To ensure closed-form solutions, we further consider the case where taxes are positive but never confiscatory, so that the tax burden never exceeds the instantaneous return to land. Finally, we assume that the return on land is less than the interest rate, so no arbitrage profits exist.[4]

The model's basic features are captured in Figure 8-1, which represents the trajectory of urban and rural land rents ($\bar{c}$, $\bar{n}$, and $u(t)$) on the vertical axis and time (t) on the horizontal axis. At time zero, developed land earns a rent of $\bar{u}$. Developed land rents rise, however, and at $t = M$, the rents on developed land equal the pecuniary benefit to undeveloped land. If the landowner's

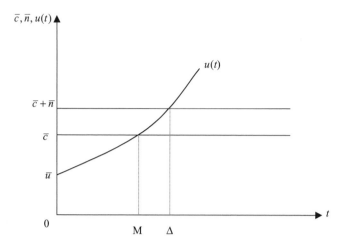

Figure 8-1. Trajectory of Urban and Rural Land Rentals

development decision is undistorted by taxes, then development occurs at time Δ, where $\bar{c} + \bar{n} \equiv \bar{u}e^{g\Delta}$.

To consider factors that influence the effectiveness of a current use program, we solve the optimization problem for a participating landowner. We then use this solution to identify how changes in model parameters affect the time of development, D. This analysis therefore indicates conditions under which a current use program might be particularly effective (or ineffective) at preserving land. Having solved the landowner's problem, we complete the model by allowing the landowner to choose whether to enroll. In order to make this choice, the landowner must calculate the net present value of benefits from enrollment. This last piece of the model allows assessment of the full impact of policy variables on land use patterns. In particular, we can show how changing the development penalty affects both the likelihood of enrollment in a current use program and also the timing of development.

To determine the point in time at which a parcelholder chooses to develop, we substitute Equations 8-2 and 8-3 into Equation 8-1, and then solve the landowner's problem:

$$\underbrace{\left(\left(1 - \frac{\tau}{r}\right)\bar{c} + \bar{n}\right)}_{\substack{\text{Instantaneous} \\ \text{return from} \\ \text{undeveloped land}}} - \underbrace{P'(D)}_{\substack{\text{Effect of} \\ \text{penalty} \\ \text{changing}}} + \underbrace{r\,P(D)}_{\substack{\text{Value of} \\ \text{delaying} \\ \text{penalty}}} = \underbrace{\left(1 - \frac{\tau}{(r-g)}\right)\bar{u}e^{gD}}_{\substack{\text{Instantaneous return} \\ \text{from developed land}}} \qquad (8\text{-}4)$$

The landowner develops when the returns to developed land have risen to a level just equal to the returns on undeveloped land. Because the undeveloped land is enrolled in a current use program, this calculation of relative returns also accounts for the penalty for withdrawal, which has two effects. First, the landowner knows that the penalty might change over time. If withdrawal penalties are based on market value or a repayment of tax savings, then the penalty rises as market land prices rise. The term $P'(D)$ reflects the degree to which the penalty changes over time. Second, even if the penalty does not change, the landowner's calculation of return recognizes the benefits of delaying a penalty payment by developing later. The term $r\,P(D)$ reflects the value of such delay.

Equation 8-4 also shows that current use programs generally delay development. Recall that Δ identified the point in time when the landowner would have developed a parcel if that decision had been influenced by taxes. From this equation, it is now possible to verify that $D > \Delta$ when $P'(D) \leq r\,P(D)$, even if $\bar{n} = 0$. That is, even those landowners who gain no utility from preservation will develop later.

Equation 8-4 is particularly useful for analyzing the penalties for withdrawing from current use assessment. The equilibrium condition shows that the penalty has two effects. First, by delaying development, the landowner obtains an instantaneous gain of $r\,P(D)$. The larger $P(D)$ is, the more important this factor. On the other hand, delaying means that penalties might either rise or fall, so the landowner also considers $P'(D)$. If the penalty declines over time, so that $P(D) > 0$ and $P'(D) < 0$, then both the penalty and the change in penalty work toward influencing landowners to delay development. In this context, it is interesting to note that penalties in many states *rise* over time. In the 7 states where the penalty is a percentage of property values and the 26 where the penalty equals property tax savings plus interest, postponing development leads to rising penalties in our model. Hence, the model clearly demonstrates that the penalty structure in many states is designed in ways that actually encourage landowners to develop their land more quickly, compared with the development timing that would occur given a declining penalty structure.

To understand how other factors affect the development decision, we differentiate Equation 8-4 with respect to $\bar{n}$, $\bar{c}$, $\bar{u}$, g, τ, and r. The partial derivatives reveal how development time, D, is related to changes in model parameters. Table 8-4 summarizes these results.

The first two rows of the table show the impact of changing the relative returns on land. Increasing the relative returns to undeveloped land delays development, whereas increasing the rents of developed land hastens development. Both the level and the growth rate of urban rents affect the development decision. Also, although an increase in either $\bar{n}$ or $\bar{c}$ delays development, development decisions are more responsive to changes in nonpecuniary values. The reason for this surprising result is that an increase in the pecuniary benefit is partially offset by an increase in assessed value. An increase in the nonpecuniary benefit, on the other hand, accrues entirely to the landowner without a change in tax burden.

Table 8-4. Influences on Development Date of Parcels Already Enrolled in a Current Use Assessment Program

Influence on decision	Impact on date
Higher rents from rural use $(\bar{n}, \bar{c})$	Later
Higher rents from urban use $(\bar{u}, g)$	Sooner
Higher property tax rate (τ)	Later
Higher discount rate (r)	Sooner
Higher penalty level	Later
Escalating penalty over time	Sooner

The effects of changes in the tax and discount rates are also interesting. Since current use programs allow participants to avoid the full burden of property taxes, the programs are more effective in the presence of high tax rates. Analogously, the programs are less effective under high discount rates. Current use benefits the landowner because it assesses land as if it were to be kept undeveloped forever. The landowner gains because the assessor does not account for the fact that the land could earn significant rents in a perhaps distant future. This benefit decreases if these potential future rents are discounted at a higher rate.

Although they provide insight, the results in Table 8-4 can give only a partial analysis of a landowner's behavior, because they assume participation in a current use program. In order to understand the exact impact of a current use program, we compare these results to the comparative statics for a landowner who does not participate in current use assessment. If a landowner chooses not to participate, then land is assessed at market value, the landowner develops at $D = \Delta$, and taxes do not distort the development decision. In order to distinguish the development times of the enrolled landowner and the nonenrolled landowner, we use D to denote the former and Δ to denote the latter. Table 8-5 summarizes how Δ changes as parameter values change.

Comparing the two tables reveals some interesting differences between the landowners who do and do not participate in a current use program. The first two rows of the tables are identical. Changing the relative returns from

Table 8-5. Influences on Development Date of Parcels Not Enrolled in a Current Use Assessment

Influence on decision	Impact on date
Higher rents from rural use $(\bar{n}, \bar{c})$	Later
Higher rents from urban use $(\bar{u}, g)$	Sooner
Higher property tax rate (τ)	No change
Higher discount rate (r)	No change

developed and undeveloped land affects both enrolled and nonenrolled parcels in similar ways. If a parcel is not enrolled, however, then the landowner reacts equally to changes in either the pecuniary or nonpecuniary value. This contrasts with enrolled parcels, whose owners delay development disproportionately in response to a change in the nonpecuniary value. This follows because, at Δ (where $\Delta \geq M$), the assessed value depends only on the developed value of land. Neither $\bar{n}$ nor $\bar{c}$ affects the landowner's tax burden at the margin. Finally, τ and r affect only enrolled parcels. Variations in these parameters therefore change the relative effectiveness of a current use program in preserving undeveloped land.

Choosing to Enroll in a Current Use Program

The net benefit, $B(D)$, to the landowner who participates in a current use program and develops at time D consists of the present value of tax savings, $S(D)$, minus the present value of the penalty, minus the present value of net forgone rents, $R(D)$, from Δ to D. Thus

$$B(D) = S(D) - P(D)e^{-rt} - R(D). \tag{8-5}$$

Comparing Equation 8-5 to the last two rows of Table 8-4 gives insight into the issues a tax authority faces in structuring a penalty. The right-hand side of the equation indicates that as penalties increase, the benefits to the landowner decline. Therefore, participation in current use programs also declines. Table 8-4 shows, however, that increased penalties on enrolled parcels delay development. In constructing a penalty, a tax authority must trade off preserving enrolled parcels against lower participation.

This trade-off becomes more evident as we compare the two most common types of policies. We first consider no penalty, as is the policy in 15 states, and then compare this to a rollback penalty equal to the property tax savings plus interest charges, as in another 26 states. If a state charges no penalty for development, then $B(D) = S(D) - R(D)$, and it is straightforward to verify that $B(D) > 0$. If the tax authority charges no penalty, then all eligible landowners would enroll. On the other hand, if the penalty requires a repayment of tax savings plus interest, then $P(D)e^{-rt} = S(D)$, meaning that $B(D) < 0$. With this penalty, no parcels would enter current use classification. At the time of development, the landowner must forfeit all the tax benefits of the program but is not reimbursed forgone rents.

Clearly, the modeling of both of these penalty structures is stylized. With no penalty, the model predicts that participation in current use programs would become universal. With a penalty equal to tax savings plus interest, the model predicts that the program would generate no enrollment. In reality, some states with no penalties nonetheless have low enrollment rates, and states that recapture tax savings still have enrolled parcels. The former might be explained by informational and transaction costs associated with enrollment. Overlapping policies for agricultural assistance might also mean that landowners already get a similar tax benefit without needing to enroll their parcels. The latter might occur because many states charge only the tax savings during the years immediately before withdrawal from the program, which would make actual penalties smaller than those in our model. By abstracting from these features, however, the model shows that even simple penalty structures create drawbacks for a tax authority that tries to influence development decisions. With no penalty, the taxing jurisdiction offers reductions even to those owners who delay development very little. By attempting to recapture all of the tax savings, on the other hand, the tax authority would leave no incentives for landowners to enroll.

Conclusions

This chapter uses a simple model of land use to produce several interesting hypotheses about the impacts of current use property assessment. Although theoretical results alone fall short of providing a simple quantitative recipe that communities might use to determine optimal use value taxation policies, they nonetheless provide insight into the implications of different types of tax and penalty structures. For example, if landowners enjoy nonpecuniary benefits from occupancy of undeveloped land, then they will delay development for a time, even though land conversion is implied by the "highest and best use" criterion. Although current use programs postpone development even without nonpecuniary benefits, development decisions are most responsive to changes in nonpecuniary benefits. Furthermore, our analytical results show current use programs to be especially effective when property tax rates are high or when landowners' intertemporal discount rates are low.

A particularly interesting feature of our modeling exercise comes from considering the effects of land conversion penalties. For enrolled parcels, a current use assessment program most effectively postpones development by featuring penalties that decline over time. Many state programs, however, include penalties that rise. A deeper understanding of the role of penalties comes from considering a landowner's decision to enroll in a current use program. With the two most common types of penalties, one could induce universal enrollment, whereas the other could lead to no participation in the current use program.

Our analysis has a number of important public-policy implications. First, current use assessment cannot permanently protect rural lands from conversion to urban uses. At best, this preferential assessment of rural lands will simply defer land development. Second, the absence of development penalties in some states strips current use assessment of a primary incentive to defer development at all. Legislatures in those states should consider whether introducing penalties is warranted in order to justify the significant property tax savings enjoyed by many rural landowners. Finally, even in those states with current use programs that are relatively well designed, public officials need to seize the opportunity to permanently protect rural lands with high conservation values through public acquisition or purchase of development rights.

Endnotes

1. See England (2002) for additional details. For another related survey, see Skjaerlund and Sinischo (1998).

2. Lawmakers justify tax policies based on nonpecuniary benefits accruing to the public at large, not simply those accruing to the landowner. Development decisions depend, however, on the degree to which those benefits are internalized.

3. Although conceptually accurate, Equation 8-2 simplifies the situation. In reality, assessors do not have the perfect foresight needed to evaluate an infinite stream of payments. In fact, they use rules of thumb to assess properties, and substantial lags often occur between changes in market values and assessed values.

4. See England and Mohr (2003) for the mathematical expression of these restrictions.

References

American Farmland Trust. (1997). *Saving American Farmland: What Works.* Northampton, MA: American Farmland Trust Publications Division.

Anderson, J. E. (1986). Property Taxes and the Timing of Urban Land Development. *Regional Science and Urban Economics* 16(4): 483–92.

———. (1993). Use-Value Property Tax Assessment: Effects on Land Development. *Land Economics* 69(3): 263–69.

Anderson, J. E., and M. F. Griffing. (2000). Measuring Use-Value Assessment Tax Expenditures. *Assessment Journal* 7(1): 35–48.

Beattie, G., and R. Ransom (1979). *Use Value Assessment: Its Causes, Its Characteristics, Its Effects.* Land Policy Roundtable, Case Studies Series no. 302. Cambridge, MA: Lincoln Institute of Land Policy.

Bentick, B. L. (1979). The Impact of Taxation and Valuation Practices on the Timing and Efficiency of Land Use. *Journal of Political Economy* 87(4): 859–68.

Bentick, B. L., and T. F. Pogue. (1988). The Impact on Development Timing of Property and Profit Taxation. *Land Economics* 64(4): 317–24.

England, R. W. (2002). Current Use Property Assessment and Land Development: A Review of Development Penalties. *State Tax Notes* 26(11): 793–96.

England, R. W., and R. D. Mohr. (2003). Land Development and Current Use Assessment: A Theoretical Note. *Agricultural and Resource Economics Review* 32(1): 46–52.

Ferguson, J. T. (1988). Evaluating the Effectiveness of Use-Value Programs. *Property Tax Journal* 7: 157–64.

Heimlich, R. E. and W. D. Anderson. (2001). *Development at the Urban Fringe and Beyond: Impacts on Agricultural and Rural Land.* Agricultural Report no. 803, Economic Research Service, U.S. Department of Agriculture.

Johnston, R. J. (2003). Farmland Preservation and Differential Taxation: Evaluating Optimal Policy under Conditions of Uncertainty. *Agricultural and Resource Economics Review* 32(2): 198–208.

Lopez, R. A., A. O. Adelaja, and M. S. Andrews. (1988). The Effects of Suburbanization on Agriculture. *American Journal of Agricultural Economics* 70(2): 346–58.

Lopez, R., F. Shah, and M. Altobello. (1994). Amenity Benefits and the Optimal Allocation of Land. *Land Economics* 70(1): 53–62.

Malme, J. (1993). *Preferential Property Tax Treatment of Land.* Working paper wp93jm1. Cambridge, MA: Lincoln Institute of Land Policy.

Marshall, P. (1995). Achieving Mutual Goals by Adjusting Use-Value Taxation. *Land: Issues and Problems* 82 (December).

Morris, A. C. (1998). Property Tax Treatment of Farmland: Does Tax Relief Delay Land Development? In *Local Government Tax and Land Use Policies in the United States,* edited by H. F. Ladd. Cheltenham, UK: Edward Elgar, 144–67.

Skjaerlund, D., and A. Sinischo. (1998). Use Value Farmland Assessment: A Comparison Study of 50 States. *Planning and Zoning News* 16(12): 5–12.

Tavernier, E. M., and F. Li. (1995). Effectiveness of Use-Value Assessment in Preserving Farmland: A Search-Theoretic Approach. *Journal of Agricultural and Applied Economics* 27(2): 626–35.

9

Alternative Valuation Strategies for Public Open-Space Purchases

Stated versus Market Evidence

John Loomis, Andrew F. Seidl, Kerri L. Rollins, and Vicki Rameker

Land is a complex natural resource that has diverse values for different people. Understanding what those values are and how they change over time is important in order to obtain the greatest benefit from our finite land resources. Early economic perspectives emphasized the value of land for food and fiber production, viewing land solely as capital in the production of private goods, whose commodity values were reflected through market transactions. As many countries have developed from agrarian to urban, however, and as food scarcity has been replaced by food abundance, the economic view of land has broadened.

Agricultural landscapes and forests near cities and towns now are recognized as providing more than just food and fiber commodities. These lands can also provide beneficial services to society, such as wildlife habitat, recreational opportunities, scenic views, and buffers from the noise and congestion of developed areas. The value of these beneficial spillovers or local public goods from farm- and forestlands are not fully reflected in market transactions, however. Conversely, intensively cultivated or grazed lands may be a nonpoint source of water pollution; such adverse spillovers are not reflected in the market price of food. The total value of farm- and forestlands to society is the sum of the private market values of the food, fiber, and other commodities, corrected for positive and negative spillovers or externalities.

Whether agricultural land preservation has a positive net benefit depends on the alternative uses of the land in the absence of public policies for agricultural preservation, such as agricultural subsidies or conservation easements. If the alternative use of agricultural land is residential or commercial, land conversions frequently result in the loss of beneficial agricultural externalities, and a new set of negative externalities associated with residential or commercial land arises. Often the negative externalities of development, such as the loss of water infiltration or wildlife habitat, are worse than the negative externalities associated with agriculture. If the lack of policies to preserve agricultural land result in a return of land to a climax forested condition, however, farmland conservation may have net environmental costs. In some areas where farmland has been abandoned, these lands have reverted to second-growth forests, which frequently provide greater environmental benefits than the agricultural land that preceded it. The empirical determination of the net effect is based on spatial attributes, such as the location of farmland relative to existing development and roads, as well as natural characteristics, such as soils, slope, and climate.

Determining the most socially beneficial land use policies, then, requires information regarding the nonmarket values associated with various types of developed and undeveloped lands. Although some might question the role of welfare analysis—including nonmarket valuation—in public policy development (e.g., see Chapter 2 of this book), such information increasingly is incorporated into public policy assessments, including those associated with land use and preservation (Freeman 2003). The challenge for public policy analysts is quantifying the monetary values of nonmarket benefits and costs associated with different types of land preservation.

Measurement of Public Goods Associated with Forest and Farmland

Local public-good uses of undeveloped lands include flood absorption to maintain a more natural hydrograph and prevent flooding, groundwater recharge, and aesthetic (scenic) benefits for traveling residents and visitors. Quasi-public goods include the provision of privacy and scenic vistas exclusively enjoyed by private properties near open spaces such as forests and farmland. It is well known that markets undersupply such public goods. This occurs because the benefits of public goods are nonexcludable, thus making it nearly impossible for farmers or private forest landowners to charge the public for the full range of open-space benefits provided by their land. Open space also can provide resources or services that are owned in common, rather than privately, by defined groups. For example, agricultural land often provides grazing habitat for migratory waterfowl, a resource collectively owned and managed by state and federal wildlife agencies.

Although market prices of farm- and forestland do not reflect public-good values, the willingness to pay principle on which market prices are based still applies. That is, price reflects willingness (and ability) to pay for an additional unit of the good. To reach an economically optimum amount of agricultural land preservation, we need to know the public's marginal willingness to pay for the public-good attributes, which, when added to private-market benefits, can be compared with the costs (both private and external). As is well known, estimating these public-good benefits without a market is difficult. This lack of explicit market values for open space is also a challenge to cities and counties, which often are limited to paying fair market value for lands. The approaches discussed in this chapter can be useful alternatives when directly comparable sales are not available to determine the value of open space.

Techniques Used to Quantify Benefits of Open Space

Traditionally, techniques for valuation of public goods such as open space or its attributes can be grouped into two major types: revealed preference and survey-based, or stated preference, methods. Revealed preference methods, such as the hedonic property value method, use related market transactions such as land or house price differentials of properties located close to open space to reveal the value of open space to nearby residents. Hedonic property models relate land attributes to the price of land. Traditional hedonic property models allow inferences of the effects of adjacent open space, wildlife, and other environmental amenities on land or housing prices. House price differentials therefore will reflect the benefits of open space to nearby residents. Survey-based methods include contingent valuation and conjoint analysis, which directly elicit households' values for open space. The contingent valuation method (CVM) estimates value by constructing a hypothetical market or voter referendum for the environmental amenity, and then asks people what they would pay for the amenity rather than go without it. More recently, hybrid approaches have combined actual market behavior and survey methods (e.g., Rosenberger and Walsh 1997). For a more complete discussion of CVM, see Loomis and Walsh (1997).

New Markets in Open Space and a Public Hedonic Model

Beginning in the late 1960s, and increasing quickly in number through the 1990s, there are now hundreds of government programs and land trusts in the United States have been dedicated to preserving agricultural land and other open space through fee-simple purchase, purchase of development rights, and conservation easements (Albers and Ando 2003). Conservation easements are voluntary legal agreements between a property owner and a government agency or qualified conservation organization such as a land trust. Once established, the easement permanently limits a property's uses in order to protect its conservation values. Collectively, government programs and land trusts have carried out thousands of purchases and conservation easements in nearly every state in the U.S.

Government and land trust transactions for open space provide an opportunity to value the public attributes of open space using a novel application of the hedonic property value method. This application is somewhat different than traditional hedonic approaches. Rather than attempt to arrive at the value of amenity attributes to private residential landowners by analyzing house price differentials, we evaluate government purchases of open space to reveal the public values of open-space attributes. Thus the variable of interest is the price paid by the government or land trust for purchase or conservation easement. The attributes are the public-good attributes of open space (e.g., presence of groundwater protection). In order to infer public values from these government transactions for open space, we must assume that the government agencies involved efficiently translate their constituents' preferences for and benefits of open space into purchases of appropriate land parcels. Conceptually, this approach might be viewed as similar to that used in Chapter 11 of this book, in that it infers public preferences through the actions of a representative government.

Although public-choice theory may cast some doubt on the general assumption that government actions appropriately reflect constituents' preferences (Stroup and Baden 1983), we believe that in the case of open-space provision in Colorado, the assumption is tenable, because city and county agencies must regularly obtain voter approval for sales taxes to purchase open space, and many cities and counties have citizen advisory boards to provide input on purchases. Thus both direct and indirect feedback mechanisms from citizens to the city and county open-space agencies may keep these agencies' actions consistent with citizen preferences. The advent of these public-market transactions for open space also provides a new avenue for external validation checks on survey-based values of open space.

In this chapter, we compare a commonly used dichotomous choice contingent valuation survey question with a more conservative trichotomous choice contingent valuation survey question for valuation of open space in a city in Colorado. We then compare these survey values to values estimated from real transaction data on public open-space purchases. Specifically, we use public market transactions data to estimate a public hedonic equation relating the public agency's purchase price to attributes of open space. Using this regression equation, we can calculate what a public agency would pay for a particular parcel of open space, based on actual transactions that have taken place. We then compare this calculated transaction value with results from the contingent valuation survey to determine if the two estimates have construct validity (i.e., appear to reflect the same underlying value or point at the same target). We acknowledge this is not a direct, controlled experiment comparison, but we nonetheless believe that it sheds light on the value of open space derived from the two methods. These techniques also may provide city and county open-space

Table 9-1a. Logit Equations Used to Calculate WTP: Standard Dichotomous Choice

Variable	Recreation lands		Nature lands		Both land types	
	Coefficient	*P-value*	*Coefficient*	*P-value*	*Coefficient*	*P-value*
Constant	−1.56	0.009	−0.501	0.461	−1.64	0.009
Cost	−0.011	0.020	−0.010	0.022	−0.013	0.001
RecImp	0.735	0.000	—	—	0.853	0.000
NatImp	—	—	0.352	0.036	—	—
N	139		141		140	
Log likelihood	−81.98		−88.14		−76.82	
Model χ^2	24.2***		14.41***		34.82***	

Notes: * = significant at the 0.10, ** = significant at the 0.05, *** = significant at the 0.01.

Differences in Mean WTP

Table 9-1a presents logit coefficients for the standard dichotomous choice question format that are used to calculate mean WTP using the formula in Equation 9-1. The cost coefficient is negative and significant, whereas the variables for ratings of recreational importance of open space (RecImp) and nature importance (NatImp) are positive and significant. Table 9-1b presents the results of the multiple bounded logit estimation using the trichotomous choice responses. The added statistical efficiency of this approach is evident by the greater number of coefficients that are significant at the 0.01 level.

Table 9-2 presents the means and 95 percent confidence intervals calculated from the logit equations in Tables 9-1a and 9-1b. In all three cases, mean WTP is significantly lower when using the trichotomous choice question format. In fact, the dichotomous choice WTP is about three times larger than the trichotomous choice. These results indicate that offering the third alternative

Table 9-1b. Multiple Bounded Logit Equations Used to Calculate WTP: Trichotomous Choice

Variable	Recreation lands		Nature lands		Both land types	
	Coefficient	*P-value*	*Coefficient*	*P-value*	*Coefficient*	*P-value*
Constant	−0.643	0.167	−1.763	0.002	−.565	0.190
Cost	−0.044	0.000	−0.048	0.000	−0.036	0.000
RecImp	0.728	0.000	—	—	0.458	0.001
NatImp	—	—	0.775	0.000	—	—
N	155		155		155	
Log likelihood	−160.0		−165.96		−208.285	
Wald statistic	71.00***		71.82***		75.62***	

Notes: * = significant at the 0.10, ** = significant at the 0.05, *** = significant at the 0.01.

Table 9-2. Comparison of Mean WTP and 95% Confidence Intervals

	Dichotomous choice		*Trichotomous choice*	
	Mean	*95% CI*	*Mean*	*95% CI*
Recreation land	$108	66–510	$42	34–52
Nature land	$116	71–490	$30	25–40
Both land types	$106	73–221	$34	27–44

in the trichotomous choice format reduces the proportion of yes responses and significantly lowers mean WTP. It is of course difficult to determine the true value of WTP for open space. To shed some light on this value, we turn to an analysis of actual market transactions for open space.

Analysis of Actual Open-Space Transactions in Colorado

Our CVM results of $40 to $100 WTP per household per year, and results of other CVM studies, are often met with skepticism regarding whether individuals actually would pay the amounts implied by survey responses. Besides our study, there have been several CVM studies of households' annual WTP for open space. Converting the annual values per household into a present value per acre using a 10 percent interest rate yields a low estimate of $530 per acre for the southern United States (Bergstrom et al. 1985), $540 per acre for a mountain county in Colorado (Rosenberger and Walsh 1997), and $140,727 per acre for 5.5 acres of land adjacent to the city limits of Boulder, Colorado (Breffle et al. 1998).

One way to assess the general validity of the CVM responses is to compare results with actual market transactions. The state of Colorado provides a good opportunity for such a comparison, because the residents of more than 25 Colorado counties and municipalities have voted to tax themselves to preserve public attributes of undeveloped or agricultural lands, often in partnership with land trusts. The votes to increase their sales taxes by $2.50 for every $100 of purchases suggest that the expressions of WTP obtained in our CVM survey are real. These voting results, however, do not directly shed light on whether the magnitude of WTP estimates reflects actual public WTP for open-space lands.

To assess WTP magnitudes, we compare stated-preference (CVM) WTP estimates to values estimated based on public purchases of open-space lands. In cooperation with some 37 local, state, regional, and national land trusts, approximately 660,000 acres of Colorado private lands have been permanently preserved from residential or commercial development by purchase of conservation easements or outright fee-simple purchase of the land. These purchases

are not identical to those described in our survey, however. In order to calculate the public value of the type of land parcels described in our survey,
we estimate what we have denoted a "public hedonic regression equation" of
available transactions. Like other hedonic analyses, ours is a reduced form of
the underlying demand and supply for the land parcels. We first examine the
demand side, followed by an assessment of the supply side.

Factors Influencing Public Demand for Open Space

We identified the potential attributes influencing the demand for open space
by reviewing traditional hedonic property method studies, as well as conducting discussions with open-space acquisition specialists for public agencies and
nonprofit land conservancies. Based on this preliminary research, we hypothesized that the following variables (which include the usual demand shifters
of income and area population) would influence only the public demand for
open space:

- Air quality or groundwater quality. If protecting the parcel aids in maintaining air quality or groundwater quality, it is expected to increase the price
  per acre as open space to a public buyer, for public-health reasons.
- Wildlife corridor. If the parcel of land is used as an existing wildlife migration
  corridor, it is expected to increase the price per acre as open space, to a public
  buyer whose citizens value wildlife.
- Income. Open space is expected to be a normal good, the benefits of which
  would increase with income. Further, higher-income counties are expected
  to have greater spending per capita, holding all else constant. Hence, higher
  income will generate higher sales and property tax revenue, on average.
  Since open-space purchases by cities and counties are either fully or partially
  paid for with sales taxes or mill levies, higher-income communities may be
  expected to have greater payment capacity for open-space land.
- Population. Larger county populations are expected to increase the price
  per acre of open space to a public buyer, reflecting the larger number of
  individuals who would benefit from the nonrival public good. In addition,
  from a purely financial perspective, more people would be paying taxes for
  the land, thereby increasing payment capacity for the land.

Factors Influencing the Supply and Cost of Open Space

The land desired for open space includes farm-, ranch-, and forestland. To
calculate the supply price, ideally one would obtain data on returns per acre
in the current use of the land. Unfortunately, these data were not available

for the specific open-space parcels purchased by cities and counties. Hence, following Plantinga and Miller (2001), we used proxy variables to represent the opportunity cost of the land, and in the spirit of that study, we tested several county average agricultural land values:

- CntyAverageAgLandValue. Average agricultural land value for the county from the USDA Economic Research Service.
- FloodIrrigatedAgLandValue. Average county agricultural land values for flood irrigated lands.
- DrylandAgLandValue. Average county dryland agricultural land values.
- GrazingAgLandValue. Average county grazing-land values.

The last three variables were obtained from the Colorado Department of Local Affairs (2000). As these variables are correlated (especially dryland and grazing-land values, with an r = 0.95), each one of the four will be tested and the best predictor retained in the model. In the stylized model, this set of variables will be labeled as AgLandValue. We expect that the higher the value of agricultural land, the higher the dollar amount the seller of open space will demand and the buyer will have to pay.

An indicator variable reported by the public open-space purchasers that reflects whether there was active farming should also be a useful measure of the land's agricultural returns:

- Workfarm: If the land is being used for agricultural purposes, it is expected to be associated with higher mean cost per acre, as the opportunity cost would be higher for land actively farmed than for land not in cultivation.

Variables Affecting both Demand and Supply of Open Space

The following variables are hypothesized to affect both the public-demand and private-supply price of an open-space parcel:

- Access to water. If the parcel contains or provides access to water bodies, such as a lake or river, it is expected to increase the value per acre as open space to a public buyer and increase its value to the current landowner, thereby increasing the amount the seller would require and the buyer must pay.
- Wetland. If the land parcel contains wetlands, this would be a desirable characteristic to public entities, because wetlands provide wildlife habitat, floodwater buffers, nutrient capture, and water purification, among other valued services. This would imply a higher positive value to the buyer. On the supply side, however, if the land has a preexisting wetland, it is expected to decrease the cost per acre of open space. This is due to lower opportunity

costs of wetlands, as these lands often cannot be developed or can be used intensively only after an elaborate permitting process, including mitigating any adverse effects on wetlands. The sign on this variable is ambiguous, as the demand and supply effects work in opposite directions. The variable could, for example, have an insignificant net effect on open-space purchase price if one factor effectively offsets the other.

- Acres. The size of the parcel influences the price per acre (Nickerson and Lynch 2001), with larger parcels associated with a lower cost per acre, holding all else constant. This would be expected on the demand side, as a result of diminishing marginal value to buyers of large parcels. On the supply side, the landowner may accept a lower price per acre if the public buys a large tract in its entirety, as this will reduce the transaction cost to the seller. Moreover, few buyers are able to afford very large land parcels. Hence, less competition may exist for large parcels, further reducing the price per acre.

- Easement. The type of rights being purchased influences the price that a landowner will seek and a buyer is willing to pay. If the land is being purchased outright (fee simple), the landowner typically will require a higher price per acre than if the transaction involves only the purchase of development rights (e.g., a conservation easement). The variable easement is expected to have a negative sign, as a permanent easement will reduce the price a landowner will require (compared with the complete sale of the land) as well as the amount a public entity would be willing to pay, because only the development rights are being acquired.

Reduced-Form Regression Equation and Net Effect of Each Variable

As is typical in traditional hedonic analysis, a reduced-form first stage or rent gradient is estimated that combines the demand and supply effects. Equation 9-2 presents the reduced-form model specification, along with the expected signs on each coefficient. (Assuming that the beta coefficients indicate the absolute value of the effect, the signs preceding each coefficient indicate the expected sign of the effect.)

$$
\begin{aligned}
\text{price per acre} = {} & \beta_0 - \beta_1(\text{Acres}) + \beta_2(\text{AccessWater}) + \beta_3(\text{AirQuality}) \\
& + \beta_4(\text{Groundwater}) + \beta_5(\text{WildlifeCorridor}) + \beta_6(\text{Income}) \\
& + \beta_7(\text{Population}) - \beta_8(\text{Easement}) +/- \beta_9(\text{Wetland}) \\
& + \beta_{10}(\text{Working Farm}) + \beta_{11}(\text{AgLandValue}) \qquad (9\text{-}2)
\end{aligned}
$$

Data Sources for Open-Space Transactions

The Denver metropolitan area or Front Range urban counties experienced an average growth rate of 28.7 percent from 1990 to 1998. The Front Range accounts for some 75 percent of Colorado's current population and 82 percent of its income. The city of Loveland lies within this area. For the purposes of illustrating the application of the public hedonic method and comparing these values to the Loveland CVM values, we acquired data on open-space transactions along the Front Range. To collect data on purchases and easements, we contacted agencies or groups known to purchase open-space land or conservation easements, including state agencies that fund or acquire land for open space or wildlife habitat, county and city open-space departments, and land trusts. We then contacted these agencies and groups for transaction data. All transactions were cross-referenced and duplicate transactions were eliminated. From purchase documentation provided on each transaction, we coded the demand and supply variables in the model. If the documentation was inadequate on any variable, we obtained the necessary information through personal or telephone interviews, emails, or faxes. Despite these efforts, the data are limited; we simply coded most of the characteristic variables as equal to one if the property had this particular feature and zero if it did not, rather than providing a more quantitative measure, such as area of wetland on the property.

Results of Open-Space Market Transactions Regression

The data comprise multiple land sale observations on 8 of the 11 counties along the Front Range. To test for potential fixed effects of sales within a county, a fixed-effects regression model was estimated. Unlike Nickerson and Lynch (2001), our county constants were not statistically significant (p values for each county constant were 0.22 or higher), indicating that once one accounts for the effects of the independent variables in Equation 9-2, there is no additional systematic difference in sales prices across counties. Table 9-3 presents the results of the regression model, as well as the means of the untransformed variables. The average price per acre was $13,800, with an average size parcel of 2,878 acres. About 10 percent of the properties had or provided access to surface waters such as rivers or lakes, 25 percent contained wetlands, and 30 percent were working farms at the time of purchase. About 73 percent of the transactions were fee-simple purchases, and 27 percent were conservation easements or purchases of development rights.

The regression model is estimated in a double log form, with logs of price per acre and all the continuous variables such as acres, income, and population.

Table 9-3. Public Hedonic Equation Regression Results

Variable	Coefficient	t–Stats	Probability	Mean[a]
Dependent variable: log of cost per acre				
Constant	6.115	1.04	0.299	n/a
Log of acres	−0.512	−9.27	0.0000	2,878
Access to water	0.561	1.56	0.1208	0.11
Air quality	0.255	0.29	0.382	0.17
Groundwater	0.656	1.07	0.284	0.04
Wetlands	−0.7637	−2.88	0.004	0.25
Wildlife corridor	0.0520	0.227	0.821	0.52
Easement	−0.454	−1.87	0.064	0.27
Working farm	0.392	1.56	0.127	0.30
DrylandAgValue	0.0118	1.80	0.074	25.29
Log income	0.0749	0.121	0.903	25,992
Log population	0.335	2.32	0.021	285,820
R^2	0.5768	Adjusted R^2		0.538
Sample size	134	S.E. of regression		1.177
F-statistic	15.117	Prob(F-statistic)		0.0000

[a] Means are of the untransformed variables for continuous variables.

The remaining variables are dummy (binary) variables, with a value of one indicating the presence of the characteristic on the land and zero indicating absence of the characteristic. Other than the different measures of agricultural returns, multicollinearity is not apparent (the highest pairwise correlations are 0.27 to 0.29, and most are less than 0.1). The overall explanatory power of the cross-sectional model is quite good, with over half the variation in price per acre explained by model variables (adjusted $R^2 = 0.54$). Signs of most variables are in accordance with our prior hypotheses, with Log of acres having a negative and significant influence on the price per acre, Easement being negative and significant (as compared with fee-simple purchase), and Population being positive and significant. The significant negative sign on Wetlands indicates that the price per acre of lands containing wetlands is lower than average, suggesting that the low opportunity cost to landowners appears to offset the increased value to open-space buyers. The supply-side measure of agricultural opportunity cost to the private landowner, county average value per acre in dryland farming (DrylandAgValue), is positive and significant at the 10 percent level (p $= 0.07$).

Results in Table 9-3 suggest that presence of a wildlife corridor, protection of groundwater, and protection of air quality do not have a systematic influence on the price paid by public buyers in our sample. This lack of significance of these open-space characteristics may be due to the measurement of these variables as dummy variables, rather than as continuous (quantitative) metrics. It also may be due to slight differences in the definitions of these terms among the various sampled land-purchasing agencies. To the extent that these variables are truly insignificant determinants of the price of open space, however, this insignificance may provide useful information to real estate appraisers and public open-space acquisition officials.

Implicit Prices of the Significant Characteristics

Table 9-4 presents the implicit prices of the more significant characteristics, calculated at the means of other variables, such as acres and income. The presence of water adds $9,767 per acre to the price. A parcel having wetlands reduces the price by $8,945 per acre. A conservation easement reduces the price per acre by $5,707, or alternatively, purchasing the open space instead of a conservation easement would increase the price per acre by $5,707 per acre. Each additional 1,000 people in a county or city increases the implicit price via demand shift effect by $16 per acre.

We can also illustrate the open-space appraisal or benefit transfer potential of our public hedonic model by providing estimated market prices per acre for specific types of open lands that may not have actually been available as paired sale properties. For example, an acre of unfarmed prairie with no water or wetlands would be estimated to have a price of $10,675 along the Front Range of Colorado. Alternatively, purchase of an acre of working farmland with no water or wetlands in that same region would have an estimated price of $21,297 per acre along the Front Range of Colorado.

Comparison of Loveland's CVM Estimates with Inferred Colorado Market Transaction Value

There have been no sales identical in size and location to the natural area lands described in the CVM survey. Nonetheless, the public hedonic equation allows out-of-sample estimation of the market value of parcels not present in the sample, as long as these parcels may be appropriately characterized using

Table 9-4. Implicit Price per Acre of Significant Attribute and Demand Shift Variables

Variable	Implicit price per acre
Access to water	+$9,767
Wetland	−$8,945
Easement	−$5,707
+1,000 population	+$16

the variables present in the model (and drawn from existing land parcels in the sample). Thus, using the coefficients in Table 9-3, we set the independent variables at values appropriate for Loveland, Colorado, using that city's population, income, and value of agricultural land. We also use the size of the land area as described in the CVM survey (500 acres). We code the characteristic dummy variables as purchase of working farmland that has no access to water or wetlands, protects air quality but not groundwater quality, and is a wildlife corridor (because it is a natural area). The resulting value is $28,983 per acre. We use this value as an estimate of the market transaction value for the land described in the CVM survey.

The trichotomous choice CVM estimated an annual value per household of $30 for land type most similar to the open-space land acquired in our study. This value per household must be expanded from the sample to the number of households in Loveland. Given the low response rate, we assume that nonresponding households would have a zero WTP. Expanding estimated WTP to the percentage of responding households in the sample area results in $11,337 per acre, using a 10 percent interest rate. Thus this trichotomous choice CVM estimate is about half the $28,983 per acre that the public hedonic equation predicts using the area's population, income, and characteristics of the open space described in the survey. Using the same procedures but with the $116 per household from the dichotomous choice CVM, the resulting value per acre is $43,836, substantially above the prices that are estimated would be paid based on similar sales. Hence, the two CVM question formats appear to bracket the amount that public agencies actually pay for open space in Colorado.

This type of convergent validity gives credence to the use of CVM for providing at least a rough estimate of what the public would pay for open space. These results are somewhat sensitive to the assumptions used to compare values, however. For example, aggregate values derived from the CVM survey may be higher if nonresponding households are assumed to have something other than a zero value for open-space conservation.

Conclusions

This chapter compares two approaches to estimating the value of open-space preservation to the public, based on stated (CVM survey) and revealed (public open-space purchase) evidence. Stated preference values are estimated using both trichotomous and dichotomous choice CVM survey instruments. The trichotomous choice CVM survey question format is designed to provide a more conservative estimate of WTP for open space than with more commonly used dichotomous approaches. As expected, the trichotomous approach yields a substantially lower WTP than the dichotomous choice question format. This estimate is also approximately half of that which public agencies would be expected to pay for open space in Colorado based on similar market transactions. In contrast, the dichotomous choice CVM question format yields an overestimate of the price agencies would be expected to pay for similar open space.

We emphasize that the above comparisons are not exact external validity tests, such as might be obtained from experiments comparing households' cash willingness to pay with stated willingness to pay (e.g., Champ et al. 1997) or intended votes with results from an actual binding referendum (e.g., Vossler and Kerkvliet 2003). Nonetheless, the comparisons in this study indicate that willingness-to-pay values estimated through trichotomous choice and dichotomous choice CVM responses bracket the values that public agencies would be expected pay for open space in Colorado, based on prior market transactions. Given this evidence, we conclude that the CVM estimates can provide a reasonable estimate of the values the public actually would pay for open space, based on the actions of public agencies and land trusts presumably making open-space purchases in the public interest.

Using either CVM estimates or the public hedonic regression estimates, it is clear that open space is quite valuable to Colorado residents. The overall mean price per acre for open-space purchases was $13,800; the presence of or access to water increases the price per acre by $9,767. Reliance on a conservation easement (rather than fee-simple purchase), however, significantly reduces the cost per acre of open-space preservation (−$5,707 per acre). The public hedonic equation also may be used to forecast the price per acre of open-space parcels that contain unique combinations of attributes not present in the original sample. Thus the method can serve as an alternative to traditional real estate appraisal techniques when agencies must determine fair market values of open-space lands but lack identical transactions from which to estimate values. The public hedonic analysis also provides a simple external validity check on the CVM estimates of WTP for open space found in the literature.

These methods have applicability to value open space in other states with active public open-space programs. Public agencies interested in understanding the values of open space to citizens might find the contingent valuation method survey approach informative. In contrast, states with extensive open-space transactions might find systematic analysis of such transactions using the public hedonic approach a helpful alternative appraisal technique for determining fair market value of unique open space when directly comparable sales are not available. Both the survey approach and the public hedonic analysis provide useful information for prioritizing open-space parcel decisions and can offer significant information to better inform the land use policy process.

References

Albers, H. J., and A. W. Ando. (2003). Could State-Level Variation in the Number of Land Trusts Make Sense? *Land Economics* 79(3): 311–27.

Bergstrom, J., B. Dillman, and J. Stoll. (1985). Public Environmental Amenity Benefits of Private Land: The Case of Prime Agricultural Land. *Southern Journal of Agricultural Economics* 17: 139–49.

Breffle, W., E. Morey, and T. Lodder. (1998). Using Contingent Valuation to Estimate a Neighborhood's Willingness to Pay to Preserve Undeveloped Urban Land. *Urban Studies* 35(4): 715–27.

Brown, T., P. Champ, R. Bishop, and D. McCollum. (1996). Which Response Format Reveals the Truth about Donations to a Public Good? *Land Economics* 72(2): 152–66.

Carson, R., N. Flores, K. Martin, and J. Wright. (1996). Contingent Valuation and Revealed Preference Methodologies. *Land Economics* 72(1): 80–99.

Carson, R., T. Groves, and M. Machina. (1999). Incentive and Information Properties of Preference Questions. Plenary address, European Association of Resource and Environmental Economists. Oslo, Norway.

Champ, P., R. Bishop, T. Brown, and D. McCollum. (1997). Using Donation Mechanisms to Value Nonuse Benefits from Public Goods. *Journal of Environmental Economics and Management* 33(2): 151–62.

Colorado Department of Local Affairs. (2000). *13th Annual Report to the Governor and the General Assembly. Division of Property Taxation.* Denver: Colorado Department of Local Affairs.

Cummings, R., D. Brookshire, and W. Schulze. (1986). *Valuing Environmental Goods.* Totowa, NJ: Rowman and Allanheld Publishers.

Cummings, R., and L. Taylor. (1999). Unbiased Value Estimates for Environmental Goods: A Cheap Talk Design for the Contingent Valuation Method. *American Economic Review* 89: 649–65.

Freeman, A. M. III. (2003). *The Measurement of Environmental and Resource Values: Theory and Methods.* Washington, DC: Resources for the Future.

Hanemann, M. (1989). Welfare Evaluations in Contingent Valuation Experiments with Discrete Response Data: Reply. *American Journal of Agricultural Economics* 71(4): 1057–61.

Hoehn, J., and A. Randall. (1987). Satisfactory Benefit–Cost Indicator. *Journal of Environmental Economics and Management* 14: 226–47.

Loomis, J., T. Brown, B. Lucero, and G. Peterson. (1996). Improving Validity Experiments of Contingent Valuation Methods: Results of Efforts to Reduce the Disparity of Hypothetical and Actual Willingness to Pay. *Land Economics* 72(4): 450–61.

———. (1997). Evaluating the Validity of the Dichotomous Choice Question Format in Contingent Valuation. *Environmental and Resource Economics* 10: 109–23.

Loomis, J., and R. Walsh. (1997). *Recreation Economic Decisions.* 2nd ed. State College, PA: Venture Publishing.

Neil, H., R. Cummings, P. Ganderton, G. Harrison, and T. McGuckin. (1994). Hypothetical Surveys and Real Economic Commitments. *Land Economics* 70(2): 145–54.

Nickerson, C., and L. Lynch. (2001). The Effect of Farmland Preservation Programs on Farmland Prices. *American Journal of Agricultural Economics* 83(2): 341–50.

Park, T., J. Loomis, and M. Creel. (1991). Confidence Intervals for Evaluating Benefit Estimates from Dichotomous Choice Contingent Valuation Studies. *Land Economics* 67(1): 64–73.

Plantinga, A., and D. Miller. (2001). Agricultural Land Values and the Value of Rights to Future Land Development. *Land Economics* 77(1): 56–67.

Rosenberger, Randy, and Richard Walsh. (1997). Nonmarket Value of Western Valley Ranchland Using Contingent Valuation. *Journal of Agricultural and Resource Economics* 22(2): 296–309.

Stroup, R., and J. Baden. (1983). *Natural Resources: Bureaucratic Myths and Environmental Management.* San Francisco: Pacific Institute.

Vossler, Christian, and Joe Kerkvliet. (2003). A Criterion Validity Test of the Contingent Valuation Method: Comparing Hypothetical and Actual Voting Behavior for a Public Referendum. *Journal of Environmental Economics and Management* 45(3): 631–49.

Welsh, M., and R. Bishop. (1993). Multiple-Bounded Discrete Choice Models. In *Benefits and Costs Transfers in Natural Resources Planning,* edited by J. Bergstrom. Sixth Interim Report, W-133. Athens: Department of Agricultural Economics, University of Georgia, 331–352.

PART IV

Rural Amenities and Landscape Conservation

10

A Multifunctional Approach to Northeastern Agriculture

SANDRA S. BATIE

Europe has a multifunctional paradigm that challenges the market-oriented viewpoint of agriculture in the modern economy. The European term "multifunctional agriculture" refers to the mostly nonmarket benefits from agriculture, in contrast to the market benefits from the provision of raw materials for the food and fiber industries. This concept of agriculture draws on a more holistic view of systems and sustainability (Josling 2002). Supporters of multifunctional agriculture argue that it "is rich in diversity and traditions, intent on preserving the countryside, a living rural world that offers rural employment" (Barthélemy 2001).

In Europe, agricultural policy frequently garners more public support when it is tied to broader social objectives. Because the market does not reward farmers for the production of most nonmarket benefits, supporters of multifunctional agriculture advocate providing assistance to farmers for such benefits through various agricultural policies (Potter 1998). An example of such an incentive is public compensation of farmers for the loss of market revenues because they provide wildlife habitat (Dobbs and Pretty 2001a). Some markets, however, do reflect these public preferences. For example, people often are willing to pay a premium for food that is "sustainably grown" (Moon et al. 2002) or has a particular regional identity, such as some cheeses.

As the Northeast United States becomes increasingly urban and affluent, it is showing an attendant interest in the multifunctional attributes of agriculture. This interest is predictable. The value of nonmarket benefits is tied to rising incomes (i.e., the income elasticity for multifunctional attributes is higher than that for traditional food and fiber). Furthermore, the more populated regions of the country are the most concerned with protecting multifunctional rural amenity attributes (Hellerstein et al. 2002). Where rising incomes are combined with more urban values, the demand for the multifunctional attributes of agriculture increases (Schweikhardt and Browne 2001).

Much of the economics literature and debate with respect to multifunctional agriculture is related to trade issues. A key concern is whether European attempts to protect multifunctional attributes are merely disguised barriers to trade (Blandford and Boisvert 2002; Orden et al. 1999). The focus of this chapter, however, is on the concept of multifunctionality and how it relates to the changing nature of northeastern U.S. agriculture, as well as implications for policy-relevant research.

The Concept of Multifunctionality in the United States

The concept of multifunctional agriculture appears to be gaining acceptance in the United States in general, and the Northeast region in particular, although the use of the term is still quite limited. At least three major types of evidence (albeit circumstantial) support this assertion: the growth in related public policies, research, and market and nonmarket demands. This evidence is fragmentary, but taken together, it appears to reflect a growing interest of society in a different relationship with agriculture and farming systems than has historically been the case.

Public Policies

In the United States, recent years have seen a greater number of public policies that focus on the connection of farmland with other valued attributes. Local, state, and federal policy attention to agrienvironmental "harms" has been significant and is growing, and the number and funding of programs to compensate farmers for agrienvironmental improvements are increasing. The 2002 Farm Bill, for example, contains the Wetlands Reserve Program, Conservation Security Program, and Environmental Quality Incentives Program. Furthermore, public agencies and private conservation organizations are cooperating to purchase conservation easements from agricultural landowners, frequently aided by favorable federal and state income and property tax laws (Mullarkey et al. 2001).

The considerable interest in the contribution of agriculture to the provision of open space and attendant benefits is also evidenced by support of policies to protect these benefits from urban-development forces. A recent study of state and local open-space protection policies by the Brookings Institution (Hollis and Fulton 2002) notes a "dramatic surge in both the creation and the enhancement of open space programs in the last 10 years. Thirty-two of the

50 states have created new programs or have significantly enhanced existing ones since 1999; of these, 21, or 66 percent, are among the most rapidly urbanizing states in the nation."

Because of their more urban nature, it is not surprising that all of the northeastern states have open-space or agricultural conservation programs. Maine, Rhode Island, New Jersey, New York, and Delaware have experienced major funding increases in these programs since 1999. All but one of the top eight states in self-funded farmland protection programs in 2001 were in the Northeast, with the exception of Colorado, and 8 of the 10 most active counties in farmland protection were in northeastern states (Hollis and Fulton 2002). It also appears that the programs in these states are more focused on attributes stemming uniquely from agriculture (Hellerstein et al. 2002).

Research

The enhanced interest of university researchers also suggests an increased demand for multifunctional attributes of agriculture. Lyson et al. (2001) investigated the relationships between the type of local agriculture and the attendant welfare implications for rural communities. Lyson (2000) delineated the characteristics that suggest a more "civic agriculture," including concerns about high-quality, value-added products that are oriented to local markets, are smaller in scale, and rely on site-specific knowledge to protect the environment. "Civic agriculture" bears a strong resemblance to the European "multifunctional agriculture."

The University of California's Sustainable Agricultural Research and Educational Program provides another research example. They are investigating community food systems, which include not only access to adequate, affordable and nutritious diets, but also local and sustainable food production, processing, and consumption. The university also contributes to the Northeast Research Project (University of California 2005), one component of which identifies many indicators of "foodshed sustainability," including environmental issues and protection of the agricultural resource base, as well as food security and access.

Market and Nonmarket Demands

Other evidence of societal interest in multifunctional attributes of agriculture comes from emerging and expanding market and nonmarket institutions throughout the country. These arrangements include the growth in market demand for organic food of more than 20 to 25 percent per year (Dimitri and Greene 2002); the success of retail stores that promote the connection of retail food between producers and communities (e.g., Wegman's); the increase in farmers' markets near population centers, which allows some farmers to grow new crops and market them in new ways (Heimlich and Anderson 2001); the growth of regional labels, such as those provided by the Food Alliance in the Northwest; the growth of ecolabels, such as California Clean; the rapid growth of agritourism or agrientertainment opportunities; and emerging markets for sustainable agricultural and forestry products (Batie 2001). Even the New York Catskills Watershed Agricultural Program, designed to ensure a potable water supply for New York City while protecting the livelihoods of farmers in the watershed, appears to point to a renewed relationship between society and agriculture and the associated multifunctional benefits (National Research Council 2000).

Societal interest also is reflected in the increasing attention given by various nongovernmental organizations (NGOs) and foundations to the relationship of agriculture to multifuctional attributes. NGOs include those that focus on farmland protection (e.g., American Farmland Trust); provide consumer information (e.g., the Organic Alliance and the Slow Food Movement); promote sustainable agriculture (e.g., the Land Institute); focus on community (e.g., Community Alliance with Family Farmers); promote ecolabels (e.g., Salmon Safe); and focus on food safety and security (e.g., Growing Gardens). The Joyce Foundation and the W.K. Kellogg Foundation show considerable interest in the relationship of society to food and to agriculture. Both recently supported projects linking farming systems with various environmental and community benefits.

Northeastern Agriculture and Multifunctional Attributes

Over time, northeastern agriculture has undergone many transitions, and three basic types of rural land uses have emerged (Carpenter and Lynch 2002; Dunn 2002). The first type is characterized as lower-quality land that is in a poorer location and tends to be forested. Although this land is scenic and, as such, tends to be a good location for recreational and summer homes, it generally is not of high enough land quality nor situated in a location with the potential to offer significant profits for agricultural purposes.

The second type is high-quality land that is well located and holds livestock enterprises that currently are consolidating. Two-thirds of the Mid-Atlantic region's total agricultural sales are from livestock (Carpenter and Lynch 2002). This land is most likely to be used for large-scale dairy, poultry, or hog production. Such farms tend to be under considerable pressure from encroaching development. Not only do land prices rise with development pressures in these situations, but conflicts abound as neighbors complain about "factory farms," odor, flies, degraded water quality, and animal welfare.

The third type is high-quality, well-located land that is either transitioning into a higher-valued agricultural enterprise or moving away from production agriculture to "consumer-responsive" agricultural enterprises (those that offer higher-valued products and services produced and designed with end consumers in mind). Lapping and Pfeffer (1997) state that the shift to higher-valued products in northeastern agriculture is occurring particularly near cities. Most of the land in the Northeast is rural, with continued agricultural production. But in contrast to those in much of the rest of the nation, northeastern farms, especially those in the rural-urban fringe, are more specialized in the production of higher-valued products, are smaller, make more intensive use of their resources, and sell more products directly to consumers (Carpenter and Lynch 2002).

A trend toward higher-valued products is particularly noticeable in those Mid-Atlantic states where livestock sales are declining. These states have seen the largest increase in sales per acre in the region. Delaware has had the highest average per-acre sales in the region since 1974, with sales averaging $1,192 per acre in 1997. New Jersey is second highest, with an average of $838 per acre, and Maryland is third, at $609 per acre. All three of these states have experienced substantial declines in their dairy industries since the 1950s (Carpenter and Lynch 2002).

Consumer-responsive enterprises include such food crops as mushrooms, greens, herbs, maple syrup, wine, and organic vegetables, and animals such as horses, goats, llamas, free-range organic chickens and their eggs, venison, and even fish. Other products include wood chip bedding or alfalfa hay for horses, cut flowers, bedding plants, jellies, and pies. Services might include horse boarding and training, farm vacation tours, wine tasting, and school field trips (Lapping and Pfeffer 1997). With respect to northeastern farms in rural-urban fringe areas, Lapping and Pfeffer note that "the largest declines are in dairy and poultry production, and the greatest increases are in farms that sold mostly other animal products, mainly horse farms" (1997, 97).

Some believe that this third type of agriculture is most likely to be the focus of demand for multifunctional attributes. Many of these types of farms are near urban centers and hence subject to rising opportunity cost of land. They also tend to be found in areas undergoing serious transitions in the main source of farm income. Within the Northeast, large parts of the metropolitan agricultural community are actively developing alternative models of farm organization that depart from the highly specialized, government-supported and regulated agricultural system that for so long has dominated the national food system. The diversification of farm operations and production is geared toward specific market niches offering premium price opportunities in rural-urban fringe areas (Lapping and Pfeffer 1997). These farms also are undergoing significant challenges with respect to profitability. Yet for the most part, they appear to represent a form of agriculture that people have been willing to tax themselves to preserve (Myers 1999, 2001; Nickerson and Hellerstein 2003).

Many of these urban-fringe farms also appear to involve high risks, perhaps requiring high product prices to justify the investments placed in them. The economics of such transitions, including the conditions of long-term profitability for various enterprises, have not been well studied, however. The policy challenge is to find an effective way to reflect public demands for multifunctional attributes so that this type of agriculture can become more profitable. Such a challenge suggests a research agenda.

Implications for Policy-Relevant Research

To better understand the demands for multifunctional agriculture and draw appropriate policy implications, important policy-relevant research needs to be addressed.

Consumer Demand

The need exists to assess and understand the trends in consumer demands—both market and nonmarket—for multifunctional attributes stemming from agriculture. Aldington (1998) distinguishes among three major types of "multiple functions" of agriculture: food security, environmental, and socioeconomic. Socioeconomic functions involve the provision of income and employment, particularly to assure the viability of rural communities. Aldington notes that these functions can be complements (or even joint products) to one another, such as when the provision of a rural landscape has both environmental and socioeconomic attributes. Multifunctional attributes also can be competitive, as when food production leads to the degradation of the environment.

Which of these functions are being demanded by the public when they support multifunctional agriculture? It would appear that many demands for various functions actually are nested together. The overarching goal is to preserve the countryside, but this preservation is desired for many reasons, which can include the desire to sustain a more pleasing landscape, preserve the environment, maintain local foods and traditions, protect small-scale agriculture, or protest industrialized commercial agriculture and attendant land use patterns (Libby 2002).

A recent survey of Kent County, Michigan, by Norris and Deaton (2002), demonstrates some of these points. The county is home to Grand Rapids, the state's second-largest city. It is experiencing significant growth in development and attendant loss in agricultural lands. When survey participants were asked what values they associated with agriculture, responses included "farmland provides a sense of local heritage" (92 percent), "farmland provides open space" (91 percent), and "farmland protects water quality" (49 percent). When asked which farmlands should be included in a Kent County farmland protection program, the respondents answered "protect farmland with high environmental values" (89 percent),[1] "protect productive farmland" (87 percent), and "protect farmland next to highways" (45 percent). Other studies had similar results. For example, Kline and Wichelns (1996), using factor analysis, identified the prime reasons for concern about Rhode Island farmland preservation as related to the environment, local food, rural communities, aesthetics, growth, and access to land. These reasons are not discrete, but are nested together; they are perceived to be joint products stemming from certain types of farm enterprises.

The nesting of these concerns complicates policy design, because finding an effective solution to the demand for one attribute will not necessarily result in satisfaction of the demand for another. It may well be that the character of the rural economy is an important element in these nested demands, and therefore a program that subsidizes a farmer to reduce environmental harms from a confined animal feeding operation may do little to satisfy other demands. Or if the public supports a farmland protection program because they believe it will meet their set of nested demands for open space and small-scale, pastoral agriculture, they are likely to feel duped if large-scale confined animal feeding operations begin to dot the landscape in the protected areas.

Demand analysis is complicated further by the spatial uniqueness of the demands. The provision of multifunctional attributes is unique to location and the propinquity of other activities. For example, a farm protected for a "viewscape" is more valuable if neighboring farms also are so protected. Furthermore, the costs and benefits associated with the provision of multifunctional attributes will be spatially varied, as will the link with agricultural production. Some areas will be better suited to the provision of ecological services, for instance, while the demand for rural amenities will probably be stronger around metropolitan areas (OECD 2001). Moreover, some areas closer to urban centers may be valued more highly than others for certain multifunctional attributes.

All of these things raise some important research questions: What regional differences exist with respect to demands for multifunctional attributes? How important are site-specific differences in the "joint production" of multifunctional attributes? What is the spatial dimension of the various multifunctional attributes? And how do spatial factors influence the cost of supplying multifunctional attributes? (OECD 2001).

Important scale differences also can exist between the provision of the multifunctional attributes and the resulting benefits or costs. That is, some attributes are more local in their impacts, whereas others are more regional or even global. The scale that is relevant for surface pollution can be different from the scale for groundwater; similarly, the relevant scale will be different for landscape amenities versus rural employment (OECD 2001).

The link of multifunctional attributes to agriculture also is in need of more careful investigation (Hellerstein et al. 2002). The political debate frequently assumes that the provision of multifunctional attributes is directly proportional to the provision of commodity outputs, but such a relationship is not usually true (Blandford and Boisvert 2002; Claassen et al. 2001; Mullarkey et al. 2001). To what extent and at what comparative price can some multifunctional attributes (such as open space) be provided by nonagriculturally linked activities? Is agriculture merely an instrument to achieve many multifunctional attributes, or is the protection of agriculture integrally embedded with these other demands?

Further, there appear to be trade-offs between protecting flat, fertile lands, which are most likely to remain in farming, and those with a more desirable set of multifunctional attributes, such as hilly land, pastures, or unique landscapes (Hellerstein et al. 2002). What is the nature of these trade-offs, and how can a proper balance be achieved?

A need exists for empirical research focused on estimating the demand for multifunctional, noncommodity attributes. Much of the existing research addresses farmland protection. Although research has been conducted on the willingness to pay for farmland protection (e.g., Bowker and Didychuck 1994), as well as public perceptions with respect to farmland protection (e.g., Kline and Wichelns 1996, 1998), few studies have differentiated which farmland the public was interested in saving (Deaton et al. 2003).

Long-Run Viability

Another important area of research is to estimate the long-run returns to production systems that provide these multifunctional attributes and use this information to identify where needs exist for public programs and policies that reflect consumer demands for multifunctional attributes.

Researchers should investigate the long-run viability of agricultural producers supplying multifunctional attributes, such as wildlife hunting, ecotourism, agritourism, or more direct marketing (e.g., alfalfa hay to horse owners). A better understanding of the potential and emerging opportunities, and the threats to farm survival in various regions and by types of farm, would help identify "missing markets" for multifunctional attributes. This analysis, in turn, can be used to determine the existence of public support for public-sector or NGO programs and policies to better reflect consumer demands for multifunctional attributes. Such an analysis also would clarify the financial requirements of farmers to fulfill these nonmarket demands.

Nongovernmental Efforts

Research also is needed to analyze the applicability and limitations of efforts led by private parties, NGOs, the public sector, and public-private partnerships to supply multifunctional attributes. The current set of government policies influencing agriculture for the most part is not well designed for the provision of multifunctional attributes. The Farm Bill policy, for example, reflects these demands in only a minor way. The bill's main purpose is to influence the behavior of an increasingly smaller set of commercial crop farmers, not to provide multifunctional attributes. The conservation and environment programs historically have been quite small in comparison with the commodity title, and they tend to have multiple, nontargeted objectives (Batie 2001). In addition, federal environmental policies addressing agrienvironmental problems have attended mostly to the environmental harms that come from either habitat destruction or large-scale animal feeding operations.

Local and state programs have had spotty records and rarely seek to integrate land use and community economic policy in a manner that recognizes agriculture as an important activity (Lapping and Pfeffer 1997). Still, it has been the state, local, and NGO programs (e.g., private land trusts) for farmland protection, differential farmland tax assessments, agricultural districts and zoning, and community-supported agriculture that have attempted to solve the "missing markets" problem. There is certainly room for more analysis of existing programs as well as new ones, including a significant reorientation of the national agricultural policy to ensure capture of multifunctional benefits. In this regard, it might be useful to examine European experiences of such policies (e.g., Dobbs and Pretty 2001a and b; Johnson and Hanrahan 2004; Kleijn and Sutherland 2003; Potter and Goodwin 1998).

Thus, policy analysis should include investigations into how various programs have performed with respect to their desired final objectives. For example, no consensus appears to have emerged, in either the United States or Europe, to suggest that the pursuit of multifunctional agriculture is adequate environmental policy (Josling 2002). Is environmental diversity actually enhanced by wildlife habitat programs directed at farmers? Do rural communities really gain when local agricultural enterprises are assured of financial viability? What changes would need to be made in the design of existing or new programs to better achieve these objectives? When are various multifunctional attributes in conflict?

Conclusions

Although considerable evidence indicates the existence of unmet public demands for multifunctional attributes, the demand for and supply of these attributes have not been well investigated. Neither the traditional government-supported nor deregulated agricultural markets can be relied on to provide most multifunctional attributes. Furthermore, the appropriate institutions to supply these "missing market" functions are still evolving. More research addressing the cost-effectiveness of these existing institutions, as well as the design of alternative institutions, would provide useful guidance to policymakers and NGOs interested in obtaining more benefits from agriculture.

Endnotes

1. High environmental values were defined in the study as those associated with soil erosion, wildlife habitat, and surface and groundwater quality.

References

Aldington, T. J. (1998). *Multifunctional Agriculture: A Brief Review from Developed and Developing Country Perspectives.* Internal Document 29. November. Rome, Italy: Food and Agriculture Organization of the United Nations, Agriculture Department.

Barthélemy, D. (2001). Multi-functionality of Agriculture: A European and French Point of View. Seminar paper presented at Michigan State University, Department of Agricultural Economics. November, East Lansing, MI.

Batie, S. S. (2001). *Public Programs and Conservation on Private Lands.* Paper prepared for Private Lands, Public Benefits: A Policy Summit on Working Lands Conservation, National Governors' Association. March, Washington, DC.

———. (2003). The Multifunctional Attributes of Northeastern Agriculture: A Research Agenda. *Agricultural and Resource Economics Review* 32(1): 1–8.

Blandford, D., and R. N. Boisvert. (2002). Multi-functional Agriculture and Domestic/International Policy Choice. *Estey Centre Journal of International Law and Trade Policy* 3(1): 106–18.

Bowker, J. M., and D. D. Didychuk. (1994). Estimations of Nonmarket Benefits of Agricultural Land Retention in Eastern Canada. *Agricultural and Resource Economics Review* 23(2): 218–25.

Carpenter, J., and L. Lynch. (2002). Is There a Critical Mass of Agricultural Lands Needed to Sustain an Agricultural Economy? Evidence from Six Mid-Atlantic States. Report to the Maryland Center for Agro-Ecology. March. College Park: Department of Agricultural and Resource Economics, University of Maryland.

Claassen, R., L. Hansen, M. Peters, V. Breneman, M. Weinberg, A. Cattaneo, P. Feather, D. Gadsby, D. Hellerstein, J. Hopkins, P. Johnston, M. Morehart, and M. Smith. (2001). *Agri-environment Policy at the Crossroads: Guidepost on Changing Landscape.* Agricultural Economic Report no. 794. Washington, DC: U.S. Department of Agriculture, Economic Research Service.

Deaton, B. J., E. N. Patricia, and J. P. Hoehn. (2003). Setting the Standard for Farmland Preservation: Do Preservation Criteria Motivate Citizen Support for Farmland Preservation? *Agriculture and Resource Economics Review* October, 272–281.

Dimitri, C., and C. Greene. (2002). *Recent Growth Patterns in the U.S. Organic Foods Market.* Bulletin no. 777. Washington, DC: USDA Economic Research Service.

Dobbs, T. L., and J. N. Pretty. (2001a). *The United Kingdom's Experience with Agri-environmental Stewardship Schemes: Lessons and Issues for the United States and Europe.* Joint Paper 2001-1. March. Brookings: Department of Economics, South Dakota State University; Colchester, England: University of Essex Centre for Environment and Society.

———. (2001b). *Future Directions for Joint Agricultural-Environmental Policies: Implications of the United Kingdom Experience for Europe and the United States.* Research Report 2001-1 and Occasional Paper 2001-5. August. Brookings: South Dakota State University Economic; Colchester, England: University of Essex Centre for Environment and Society.

Dunn, J. W. (2002). Personal communication with the author on rural land uses. Department of Agricultural Economics, Pennsylvania State University, June 4.

Heimlich, R., and W. D. Anderson. (2001). *Development at the Urban Fringe and Beyond: Impacts on Agriculture and Rural Land.* Report no. 803. Washington, DC: USDA Economic Research Service.

Hellerstein, D., C. Nickerson, J. Cooper, P. Feather, D. Gadsby, D. Mullarkey, A. Tegene, and C. Barnard. (2002). *Farmland Protection: The Role of Public Preferences for Rural Amenities.* Agricultural Economic Report no. 815. Washington, DC: USDA Economic Research Service.

Hollis, L., and W. Fulton. (2002). Open Space Protection: Conservation Meets Growth Management. Discussion paper. April. Washington, DC: Brookings Institution Center on Urban and Metropolitan Policy.

Johnson, B. A., and C. E. Hanrahan. (2004). *Green Payments in U.S. and European Union Agricultural Policy.* Washington, DC: Congressional Research Service.

Josling, T. (2002). Competing Paradigms in the OECD and Their Impact on the WTO Agriculture Talks. In *Agricultural Policy for the 21st Century*, edited by L. Tweeten and S. R. Thompson. Ames: Iowa State University Press, 245–64.

Kleijn, D., and W. J. Sutherland. (2003). How Effective Are European Agri-environment Schemes in Conserving and Promoting Biodiversity? *Journal of Applied Ecology* 40: 947–69.

Kline, J., and D. Wichelns. (1996). Public Preferences and Farmland Preservation Programs. *Land Economics* 72(4): 538–49.

———. (1998). Measuring Heterogeneous Preferences for Preserving Farmland and Open Space. *Ecological Economics* 26(1998): 211–24.

Lapping, M. B., and M. J. Pfeffer. (1997). City and Country: Forging New Connections through Agriculture. In *Visions of American Agriculture*, edited by W. Lockerentz. Ames: Iowa State University Press, 91–104.

Libby, L. (2002). Farmland Is Not Just for Farming Anymore: The Policy Trends. In *Agricultural Policy for the 21st Century*, edited by L. Tweeten and S. R. Thompson. Ames: Iowa State University Press, 184–203.

Lyson, T. (2000). Moving toward Civic Agriculture. *Choices* 15(3): 45.

Lyson, T. A., R. J. Torres, and R. Welsh. (2001). Scale of Agricultural Production: Civic Engagement and Community Welfare. *Social Forces* 80(1): 311–27.

Moon, W., W. J. Florkowski, B. Brückner, and I. Schonhof. (2002). Willingness to Pay for Environmental Practices: Implications for Eco-Labeling. *Land Economics* 78(1) 88–102.

Myers, P. (1999). *Livability at the Ballot Box: State and Local Referenda on Parks, Con-
    servation, and Smarter Growth, Election Day 1998*. Washington, DC: Brookings In-
    stitution Center on Urban and Metropolitan Policy.

————. (2001). *Growth at the Ballot Box: Electing the Shape of Communities in November
    2000*. Washington, DC: Brookings Institution Center on Urban and Metropolitan
    Policy.

Mullarkey, D., J. Cooper, and D. Skully. (2001). Do Mixed Goals Distort Trade? *Choices*
    16(1): 31–34.

National Research Council. (2000). *Watershed Management for Potable Water Supply:
    Assessing the New York City Strategy*. Washington, DC: National Academy Press.

Nickerson, C. J., and D. Hellerstein. (2003). Protecting Rural Amenities through Farm-
    land Preservation Programs. *Agricultural and Resource Economics Review* 32(1):
    129–44.

Norris, P. E., and B. J. Deaton. (2002). Public Opinions about Farmland and Farmland
    Preservation: Results from a Survey in Kent County, Michigan. Staff Paper 2002-10.
    East Lansing: Michigan State University, Department of Agricultural Economics.

OECD (Organisation for Economic Co-operation and Development). (2001). *Multi-
    functionality towards an Analytical Framework*. Paris: OECD Publications.

Orden, D., R. Paarlberg, and T. Roe. (1999). *Policy Reform in American Agriculture*.
    Chicago: University of Chicago Press.

Peterson, J. M., R. N. Boisvert, H. de Gorter. (1999). Multi-functionality and Opti-
    mal Environmental Policies for Agriculture in an Open Economy. Working paper
    99-29. Ithaca, NY: Department of Agricultural, Resource and Managerial Eco-
    nomics, Cornell University.

Potter, C. (1998). *Against the Grain: Agri-environmental Reform in the United States and
    European Union*. New York: CAB International.

Potter, C., and P. Goodwin. (1998). Agricultural Liberalization in the European Union:
    An Analysis of the Implications for Nature Conservation. *Journal of Rural Studies*
    14: 287–98.

Schweikhardt, D. B., and W. P. Browne. (2001). Politics by Other Means: The Emergence
    of a New Politics of Food in the United States. *Review of Agricultural Economics* 23(2):
    302–18.

University of California. (2005). *Consumers, Commodities, and Communities: Local
    Food Systems in a Globalizing Environment*. Northeast Research Project NE-185.
    http://sarep.ucdavis.edu/cdpp/foodsystems/countystudies.htm.

11

Farmland Preservation Programs and the Importance of Rural Amenities

Cynthia J. Nickerson and Daniel M. Hellerstein

Despite the relatively small fraction of the American landscape dedicated to urban uses and being converted to those uses each year, concern is growing about the disappearance of farmland in some parts of the country. Although not every region is experiencing the same rate of farmland conversion— e.g., the Northeast lost 54 percent (18.9 million acres) of its cropland and grassland pasture and range between 1945 and 1997, while the corn belt lost 7 percent (8.4 million acres)—all states have enacted programs to preserve farmland. Some now spend millions of dollars annually for this purpose, through such mechanisms as use value assessments and purchase of development rights programs. Concerns at the federal level have increased as well. Over the last decade, funding for the Federal Farmland Preservation Program has increased more than tenfold, from about $53 million total for 1996–2001 to nearly $600 million total over the six years beginning in 2002.

A motivation for preserving farmland may arise from public desires to maintain agricultural activity. But the existence of federal conservation programs that limit agricultural production (e.g., the Conservation Reserve Program) suggests that other reasons may be important as well, such as the desire to maintain rural amenities associated with agricultural land uses. Indeed, for taxpayers, protection of rural amenities, which include such things as scenic views, wildlife habitat, agrarian cultural heritage, and open space, may be among the most important reasons for supporting farmland preservation programs. Yet few studies have provided a comprehensive assessment of the types of rural amenities that these programs are likely to target and protect.

217

In this chapter, we attempt to do so, by examining farmland preservation program legislation, focusing on the methods used by one particular type of program to prioritize parcels for preservation, and looking at how the provision of rural amenities varies across the country. Underlying this research is the desire to understand what positive benefits are sought by the public and provided through farmland preservation programs. In this sense, this chapter provides an empirical perspective on the arguments in the previous chapter in that it seeks to determine which of the many multifunctional attributes of agriculture are targeted by government programs in various states.

Most of the existing research on rural amenities provided by farmland has attempted to elicit information on values that people place on this land and its amenities. These studies have often found that people are willing to pay positive amounts to preserve farmland. The amounts vary significantly across locations, however. For example, residents of Greenville County, South Carolina, surveyed by Bergstrom et al. (1985) were willing to pay less than $1 annually to protect 1,000 acres of agricultural land from dense development. Surveyed residents in several places in Alaska indicated a willingness to pay more than $17 annually to preserve the same amount of land (Beasley et al. 1986). Sheridan County, Wyoming, residents were willing to pay about $60 annually (Rosenberger and Walsh 1997).[1]

Just as people's stated values for preserving farmland and its amenities vary, analyses of property sales reveal that preferences for living near farmland are not uniform across the country. In 1996, property values in Southold, New York, were higher for houses farthest from farms and lower for those adjacent to a farm (Johnston et al. 2001). During that same decade, property values in central Maryland increased for properties with pastureland or preserved open space nearby but were lower for those near cropland (Bockstael 1996). A separate study in that same region found that people also paid more to be close to permanently preserved land, favoring land preserved by easements over publicly owned parkland (Irwin 2002). Indeed, that study predicted that preserved farmland could generate benefits of at least $10,000 to $52,000 per acre, depending on how many residential properties would benefit (e.g., whether nearby residential properties were developed at 5 acre or 1 acre densities).[2]

Much less is understood about exactly what objectives people seek when they support farmland preservation programs. One study of Rhode Island residents found more support for protecting groundwater, wildlife habitat, and natural places than for agricultural objectives such as protecting local food supplies or maintaining a farming heritage (Kline and Wichelns 1996). Using the same data, Kline and Wichelns (1998) also found that residents' preferences for different types of land uses (e.g., fruit and vegetable farmland versus woodland) and for private or public access to the land varied depending on whether respondents had environmentally oriented or farming-oriented attitudes. In contrast, in a North Carolina county, support for farmland preservation programs arose as much from wanting to protect food supplies and farming heritage as from a desire to protect the environment by keeping land in open space (Furuseth 1987). Chicago-area focus groups reported that ensuring future food supplies, protecting family farms, and controlling development were most important (Krieger 1999). Delaware residents most valued maintaining the agricultural way of life, access to locally grown products, and protecting water quality (Duke and Hyde 2002).

Even though relatively few studies have addressed such issues, it appears that a wide range in values and preferences for farmland amenities may exist across the country. In interpreting these findings, however, it is important to bear in mind how context-specific circumstances can affect the outcomes of an analysis. For example, the extent of land that remains in agriculture at the time of a survey can influence stated preferences about goals or willingness to pay to preserve farmland. For example, in the Rhode Island survey where people reported preferences for protecting environmental amenities, only 7 percent of the land remained in a farming use at the time of the survey (Kline and Wichelns 1998). In contrast, agriculture was a predominant land use in the Chicago collar county study area, where respondents reported preferences for primarily agricultural related amenities (Krieger 1999). In the North Carolina study, where both environmental and agricultural amenities were important, one-third of the county was urbanized (Furuseth 1987). Also, in many areas, numerous complex programs exist to preserve rural lands, and they may have overlapping objectives. This array may contribute to difficulties survey respondents face when asked to choose which attributes they consider most important to protect through farmland preservation programs.

Rather than use surveys of individuals to estimate rural amenity values, this chapter seeks to investigate what farmland preservation programs themselves reveal about the importance of rural amenities. In doing so, we consider programs in place across the country. We begin by describing factors that are likely to influence decisions of farmland preservation agencies in theory, and how the presence of other rural land preservation programs affects these decisions. We then examine enabling legislation for a wide variety of programs in the Lower 48 states. This analysis reveals the extent of spatial variation in objectives and the array of rural amenities protected through these state-level programs. Next, we look at how program implementation and decision criteria used by agencies to select among competing offers can reveal the types of amenities most likely to be protected. Although we reach no definitive conclusions regarding the values individuals have for different amenities, we are able to offer some general findings on the types of amenities most likely to be protected by farmland preservation programs.

Rural Amenities, Public Goods, and Farmland Protection

Broadly defined, rural amenities encompass a variety of goods and services that provide utility to consumers, and whose provision requires a rural setting. Rural settings refer to lands that begin at the edges of cities, where the landscape is not dominated by human settlement.[3] Agriculture and forest are predominant land uses one would find in such a setting.

What distinguishes the goods and services referred to as rural amenities is that a rural landscape is involved in their production. They are analogous to the multifunctional attributes of farmland identified by Batie in the previous chapter. Generic commodities such as bushels of corn purchased at a store are not considered to have rural amenity value, even though they likely were produced in a rural setting, because the value of such commodities is derived from attributes like nutritional content and flavor. Corn that is identified as being locally grown, however, could have amenity value, which consumers may be willing to pay for through higher product prices.

Most rural amenities have the distinction of not being readily tradable in markets. Scenic farm views or the agrarian cultural heritage of an area, for example, are not tradable and have a public-goods nature. That is, it is difficult to exclude anyone from consuming these goods or services, and one person's consumption does not preclude or reduce others' ability to consume the same goods or services.

It is well known that public goods are underprovided by the free market. The potential underprovision of rural amenities from agricultural land arises because of their public-goods nature. When rural amenities are nonexcludable, rural landowners cannot extract compensation from consumers or profit from their production. Lower profits translate into lower land rents, rendering farmland less expensive for developers to purchase and convert to residential uses. If, however, rural landowners could capture the value of rural amenities, such as by requiring consumer payment, it would increase the profitability of farming. This would tend to postpone conversion of farmland to nonfarm uses, as developers would have to generate higher income streams in order to bid the land away from a farming use.

But even if rural landowners could sell rural amenities to individual consumers, they might still be underprovided. This could happen because individuals purchasing a rural amenity will consider only their own well-being when considering trade-offs between this rural amenity and other commodities— even though their purchase of a rural amenity would provide a good that can be enjoyed by all. The result is that each individual would choose to purchase too small an amount of the rural amenity relative to the social optimum (Samuelson 1954). These tendencies, related to the public-goods nature of most rural amenities, represent one of the primary reasons that markets fail to provide socially optimal levels of these amenities. This market failure is the principal justification, from a neoclassical economic perspective, for the existence of farmland protection programs.

Several mechanisms have evolved to help correct the market failure that arises when rural lands are developed too soon. These include private (non-governmental organization) initiatives, such as private rural land trusts, which have been formed to accept charitable donations of rural lands. Donations may incorporate the entire interest in the land or a partial interest, such as the development rights associated with the land. These mechanisms also include initiatives in which individuals join together to collectively preserve farmland. Under some circumstances, this tactic can result in the efficient provision of rural amenities. When amenities are highly localized, the flow of benefits could be retained by a limited group. An example of this would be the decision to subdivide a farmed parcel and situate house lots in a circular pattern around a core of open land that continues to be farmed. To the extent, however, that the rural amenities provided by the protected farm yield benefits (such as scenic views) to noncontributors, the problem of underprovision is likely to remain.

The most common approach to the preservation of farmland is through government programs. Government actions take the form of both regulatory and voluntary approaches. Many jurisdictions use zoning regulations, both voluntary (e.g., agricultural districts) and involuntary (e.g., agricultural zoning). Zoning often is associated with differential assessment, which sets property taxes based on current land uses rather than "best and highest use" values. History has shown that zoning and differential assessment rules have been modified when development pressures become sufficiently strong. Thus they have not proven to be a dependable means of maintaining rural land uses over the long run. Outright government ownership is another means of preserving land uses and is a common strategy for providing amenities for which public access is essential, such as the establishment of parks to provide outdoor recreational opportunities. Outright government purchase of farmland that is maintained in that use is rare, however.

Government programs that purchase partial interests in the land leave the land in private ownership and generally do not allow public access. These programs include purchase of development rights (PDR) programs, which involve a voluntary agreement by the landowner to forgo development of the land. In a PDR program, a government agency typically pays the landowner a lump sum for all of the development rights, which are then retired. The landowner retains all other rights to the land, including the right to continue farming. The government thereby achieves the objective of maintaining a rural land use without having to take on the responsibility of managing the land.

Farmland Protection Legislation

The creation of farmland preservation programs involves familiar processes of government: passing enabling legislation, securing funding from general revenues or a dedicated stream, and allocating these funds through a bureaucracy. This process can offer evidence as to a program's objectives, and each step in the creation and implementation of a program reveals something about which amenities are considered to be the most important to protect, even though the steps are not motivated exclusively by public preferences for amenities.

The use of legislation or government action as evidence of the importance of certain rural amenities has several limitations. For one, the enactment of legislation is sensitive to both the demand for rural amenities and the supply of rural lands. Regions where farmland is abundant have less need for farmland protection legislation, even if the population of these regions has a high demand for farming-related amenities. Another limitation is that this approach presumes that the actions of government appropriately reflect the values of the general public, though this may not necessarily be the case. These limitations notwithstanding, analysis of public programs can provide some insight into variation in the importance of certain types of rural amenities across regions, particularly if viewed within an appropriate conceptual model.

The reasons for enacting farmland legislation can be numerous. Nickerson and Hellerstein (2003) developed a conceptual model that can motivate the reasons for differences across farmland preservation programs. The model highlights a number of points. First, there is no such thing as a single rural amenity; rather, there are a number of rural amenities, with different types of rural lands providing them to different extents. For example, any rural lands can provide open space and wildlife habitat, but pastoral scenic beauty and the cultural heritage associated with farming as a way of life are uniquely provided by farmland.[4] A subset of rural amenities that are uniquely provided by farmland can be defined as "farm" amenities, and those that may be provided by *any* rural lands as "generic" amenities.

Second, the value of protecting an additional unit of an amenity, referred to as the marginal value, is not static, even if it could be measured in the same location over time. This is because the marginal value depends on those amenities that are currently available and the extent to which they substitute for each other. For example, when farm and generic amenities are not close substitutes, and if other preserved rural lands provide an ample quantity of generic amenities, welfare-maximizing farmland preservation programs can be expected to focus on protecting farm amenities. Conversely, if little other rural land is preserved, then such programs can be expected to protect both farm and generic amenities. Third, the relative values of many types of rural amenities are a function of land use patterns and the geographic distribution of the population.

The enabling legislation of farmland preservation programs often contains statements relating to purpose. Hellerstein et al. (2002) analyzes these purpose statements for a broad set of programs related to agricultural land preservation. These programs include laws that establish agricultural districts, agricultural protection zoning, comprehensive growth management, conservation easements (such as PDRs), differential assessment, and right to farm. Using the online links of American Farmland Trust (AFT 2002a, 2002b, 2002c) or state sources for codes, Hellerstein et al. analyzed the purpose and findings clauses embedded in these sets of state code and identified the occurrence of key phrases referring to specific rural amenities and objectives. The initial step was to review the state-level laws pertaining to farmland preservation in the 48 contiguous states. This process yielded a large number of catchphrases relating to an underlying core set of objectives.

To synthesize this information, each phrase was categorized on the basis of an identified objective. Based on a literature review and our reading of the enabling legislation, we developed a list of five broad categories of objectives: orderly development, food security, local economy, environmental services, and protection of rural amenities (Table 11-1a). Since we are specifically

Table 11-1a. Legislative Language of Farmland Preservation Programs: Description of Objectives[a]

Objective	Description	Number of states mentioning category[b]
Orderly development	Orderly development of rural land, low density, physical space, lower public utility provision costs, prevention of sprawl	18
Food security	Local or national food security: quantity or quality	30
Local economy	Preserving local agricultural or timber economy, agricultural or timber jobs, other natural resource economies and jobs	24
Environmental services	Pollution reduction, groundwater recharge, flood control, water quality or quantity, air quality	29
Protection of Rural amenities	Protection of amenities including those described in Table 11-1b	36

[a] Hellerstein et al. 2002.

[b] Total number of states' legislation reviewed = 48.

Table 11-1b. Legislative Language of Farmland Preservation Programs: Description of Amenities Sought for Protection[a]

Amenity	Description	Number of states mentioning category[b]
Open space	Usually visual, including prevention or slowing of development	31
Rural/agrarian character	Agrarian cultural heritage; historic, nostalgic, or unique terrain; preserve farming, active agriculture, or agricultural viability; live rural way of life; have a sense of community or place	31
Wildlife habitat	Includes wildlife habitat and natural areas	24
Scenic beauty	Aesthetics, usually visual, including scenic beauty, viewing wildlife or farm activities	30

[a] Hellerstein et al. 2002.

[b] Total number of states' legislation reviewed = 48.

interested in information about which amenities are sought for protection, we also consider the four underlying components that constitute the amenities category: open space, rural/agrarian character, wildlife habitat, and scenic beauty. Table 11-1b summarizes these variables.[5]

Figure 11-1 graphically displays the states that identified each of the objectives in their farmland preservation enabling legislation. This map overlays the objectives on two base layers. The first base layer (solid) is the location of cropland and grassland pasture and range, from the 1990 National Land Cover Database. The second base layer (crosshatched) identifies areas of the country subject to urban influence, the extent of which was determined using a gravity model and *1990 Census of Population* data by block group.[6] Although land uses and population pressures change over time, these base maps at least provide a snapshot in time of the areas where agriculture may be most subject to urbanization and thus provide context.

Our review of the enabling legislation of farmland preservation programs suggests that program objectives are nonuniform across the country. Most of the variation appears to exist across rather than within regions. The Northeast, Lake, and Pacific regions place emphasis on almost all of the objectives. With one exception, all three states in the Pacific region mention all five categories. States in these regions also tended to have enacted the broadest portfolio of farmland protection programs.

Protection of rural amenities is mentioned most often—by 36 states, including all of those in the Northeast, Lake, Appalachian, and Pacific regions. Three states—Florida, Nevada, and Utah—give this as the sole reason for their farmland preservation programs. In sparsely populated states, the continued

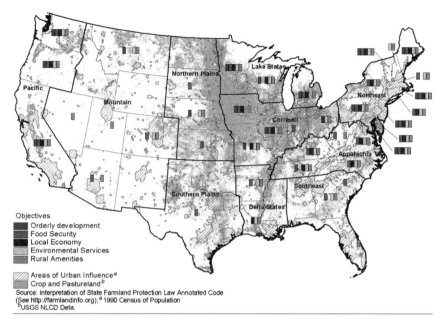

Figure 11-1. Objectives of State-Level Farmland Preservation Legislation

Source: Nickerson and Hellerstein (2003).

relative abundance of rural amenities may make protective legislation seem unnecessary, whereas those with more dense populations often have less remaining farmland, leading them to enact a broad portfolio of programs to protect many types of rural amenities. Orderly development and local economy are goals of farmland protection laws primarily in the same four regions and are mentioned by a total of 18 and 24 states, respectively. Food security has broad appeal and is emphasized in 30 state codes in all regions, but it is least represented in the Mountain region as a goal. These 30 states primarily seek to protect local food supplies; only 3 of them—Michigan, California, and Oregon—also mention national food security in state legislation. Food security is the sole program goal for five states: Indiana, Kansas, South Dakota, South Carolina, and Texas. In heavily agricultural states with an abundance of farmland and limited development pressures, food security objectives may be evidence of the influence of farmer interests, which may favor farmland preservation programs because the programs support the incomes of agricultural producers.

Figure 11-2 displays those states that identified specific rural amenities as program protection priorities. Of the states seeking to protect amenities, nearly all want to protect more than one type. The exception is Nevada, which identified scenic beauty as important to protect through its farmland preservation

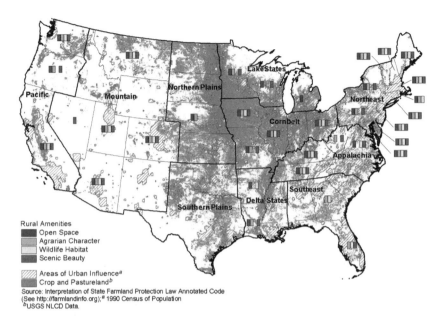

Figure 11-2. Rural Amenities Objectives of State-Level Farmland Preservation
Legislation

Source: Nickerson and Hellerstein (2003).

programs. The protection of open space and agrarian character are sought by
31 states, with nearly as many wishing to maintain scenic beauty. Those that
did not mention these amenities as goals tend to be clustered in the Northern
and Southern Plains regions. Protecting wildlife habitat does not appear to be
important in the Lake, Northern and Southern Plains, and most of the Delta
regions.

We used frequency counts to analyze the hypothesis of independence of
the categories described in Tables 11-1a and 11-1b, in order to gain insight
into which objectives states attempt to achieve simultaneously when enacting
farmland preservation programs. An exact Pearson chi-square was used as a
measure of the null hypothesis of independence (low probability values support
the alternative of dependence) (Agresti 1996). Table 11-2 displays these results.

In all cases where states seek to promote orderly development, protect the
local economy, or protect environmental services via farmland preservation
programs, those states also seek to protect rural amenities. Orderly development and local economy goals do not appear to be significantly related
to objectives for protecting wildlife habitat and natural areas, however. Concerns over protecting environmental services seem to be significantly related
to all the amenity subcategories. The results also suggest that concerns about

Table 11-2. Independence of Amenity and Other Objectives: Results of Chi-Square Tests

		Reference category			
			Types of amenities		
Objective	*Amenity objective*	*Open space*	*Agrarian character*	*Wildlife habitat*	*Scenic beauty*
Orderly development	**9.6** **(.0019)** (+)	**15.79** **(.0001)**	**7.43** **(.0064)**	1.42 (.2330)	**5.33** **(.0209)**
Food security	2.35 (.1251) (+)	1.96 (.1611) (+)	1.96 (.1611) (+)	2.17 (.1400) (+)	.285 (.5937) (+)
Local economy	**16.0** **(.0001)** (+)	**20.49** **(.0001)** (+)	**11.02** **(.0009)** (+)	3.00 (.0833)	**12.80** **(.0004)** (+)
Environmental services	**24.4** **(.001)** (+)	**26.05** **(.0001)** (+)	**20.13** **(.0001)** (+)	**10.54** **(.0012)** (+)	**12.82** **(.0003)** (+)

Notes: Test statistic is an exact Pearson $\chi^2(1)$, with the probability value in parentheses. Boldface values are significant (at 95% CI). A (+) indicates that more states have both objectives than have just one or none.

protecting local food supplies are independent of concerns for protecting rural amenities.

Protection of Amenities through Purchase of Development Rights Programs

Increasingly, farmland protection agencies are adopting PDR programs to preserve farmland permanently. PDR program managers also must make choices about which parcels of farmland best accomplish program goals. Although PDR programs are voluntary, and participation depends in part on idiosyncratic differences among landowners, the programs typically are oversubscribed, which allows the program manager to choose which parcels to preserve from a pool of applicants.

In practice, voluntary programs such as PDR are implemented using a set of ranking criteria to choose among land parcels with varying characteristics. These criteria reflect the agency's best efforts to achieve program goals, which may, directly or indirectly, include the protection of rural amenities. The program manager's problem is one of choosing parcels for preservation from a set of J applicants $(j = 1...J)$, based on the parcels that are ranked highest according to a given ranking scheme. Adapting a simple, linear ranking mechanism used to model other conservation programs (Cattaneo et al. 2002), the decision can be characterized as

$$\underset{B_j}{Max} \quad \sum_{j \in J} B_j \left[\sum_{k=1}^{K} \alpha_k x_{ij} \right] \tag{11-1a}$$

$$\text{subject to} \sum_{j=1}^{J} B_j \cdot E_j \le M, \tag{11-1b}$$

where $B_j = 1$ if a parcel is chosen for preservation, α_i is the weight assigned to the kth objective ($k = 1 \ldots K$), and x_{ij} is the jth parcel's (or landowner's) characteristic being weighted. The program manager chooses parcels subject to a budget constraint, where E_j is the cost of purchasing the easement (development rights) on the jth parcel, and M is the amount of government funding available for easement purchases.

Essentially, the weights (α_k) capture the contributions to social welfare from the various land characteristics. They are expressions of relative preferences for different characteristics and amenities associated with agricultural land; they also may capture the relative scarcity of particular farmland attributes. To the extent that Equations 11-1a and 11-1b are an accurate "reduced form" for the conceptual model developed by Nickerson and Hellerstein (2003), optimizing these equations (given a set of offered parcels) will optimize social welfare. (For more information regarding the optimal selection of a land conservation portfolio for particular objectives, see Chapter 13, which addresses such issues in greater detail.)

Just as farmland preservation program objectives are likely to vary spatially across the country, we can expect the α_k values to vary across preservation programs. To discern how the priorities for protecting parcel characteristics, and weights assigned to those priorities, vary across programs, we conduct a comparative analysis of ranking criteria used in several state and local PDR programs. The weights can be interpreted as indirect measures of the relative importance of protecting the targeted parcel characteristics and the underlying rural amenities that are likely to be associated with them. We also investigate the factors that contribute to variation in these weights and the implications for the protection of amenities and the design of farmland preservation programs.

We analyze the ranking criteria adopted by 27 separate state and county PDR program agencies. We include PDR programs that currently use point systems to objectively rank parcels; are established, with a significant history of easement purchases; and are oversubscribed, so that the rankings actually were used to select or reject parcels for preservation (AFT 2002a, 2002b). Several, such as the Delaware state program, are not included because they currently prioritize parcels for preservation on the basis of least cost. Others, including the Massachusetts and Vermont state programs as well as the Sonoma County, California, program, identify preservation priorities but are excluded from the analysis because the criteria for prioritizing purchases is not clearly designated with a point system.

Because state and local governments in the Northeast were the first to adopt PDR programs and tend to have the most active programs, observations from programs in this region represent about 88 percent of our sample. Our analysis thus will be most representative of the Northeast. We recognize that the states here may have priorities for rural land preservation that are systematically different from those of the rest of the nation, because they are the most developed, may have different settlement patterns and population demographics, and have the broadest and oldest set of farmland preservation programs. In many ways, however, the Northeast may be a bellwether for other rapidly growing regions, a point emphasized by Batie in Chapter 10.

The ranking criteria for all the programs taken together considered 36 different characteristics, which were related to several broad factors: soil productivity, farm importance, development pressure, road access or frontage, environmental significance, parcel size and contiguity, and other considerations. Table 11-3 summarizes these data.[7] To facilitate comparison of the ranking systems, the descriptive statistics are reported in terms of percentage of total points allocated to the various priorities.

Our analysis of the 27 PDR programs suggests that although similarities exist in the types of considerations given priority, the weights that different programs assign to different groups of characteristics vary substantially. On average, PDR programs assign 36 percent of points to lands that have the most productive soils for agricultural uses: those that have prime soils for row cropping or are currently using the land for cropping or pasture for livestock. All but one program grants higher priority to parcels with better soil quality or a greater amount of land in traditional agricultural uses.

The second most important priority is preserving large or contiguous blocks of land, with programs assigning an average of 26 percent of points to this category. Twenty-four of 27 programs assign at least 10 percent of points to preserving large blocks of land. The third most important priority for the average program is protecting farmland that has the highest probability of being converted but is located in agricultural or rural areas defined by local land use plans. Of the 24 programs that assign weight to this priority, the percentage of points ranges from 0 to 40 (average of 12 percent). Less than 10 percent of points are allocated to categories of priorities that protect family- and owner-operated farms, farmland along roads and highways, and farmland with particular environmental, historic, or scenic significance.

The priority given to preserving productive soils and row cropping and pasture uses has implications for the protection of rural amenities. First, it suggests preferences for preserving agrarian character or farm amenities. Although it is true that these farming operations jointly provide certain generic amenities, farming uses of land are necessary conditions for providing farm amenities. It is also possible that this priority is simply a result of PDR agency desires to make programs most attractive to commercial farm interests. Because these farms

Table 11-3. Factors Considered in PDR Program Ranking Criteria and Descriptive Statistics

Factor for which points are awarded	Description	Mean	Std. dev.	Min.	Max.
Soil productivity	Soil productivity or capability, percent tillable, use of land for crops and pasture	36.296	19.207	0	75.000
Farm importance	Owner-operated, history of family farming, important to agricultural community, farm capital improvements, specialty farm, unique production	9.519	11.369	0	50.000
Development pressure	Significant nonagricultural use nearby, near or in water and sewer service areas, minimal septic limitations	12.444	9.394	0	40.000
Road access/ frontage	Public road frontage	3.611	5.565	0	19.000
Environmental significance	Environmental, historic, or scenic importance; water and soil conservation plans	5.685	9.225	0	45.000
Parcel size and contiguity	Parcel size; adjacent or near easements, districts, agricultural security areas, or permanent open space; in agriculturally zoned area	25.630	15.719	0	60.000
Other	Local government support, relative best buy, special conditions	6.815	9.684	0	35.000

Notes: N = 27. Descriptive statistics are based on the percentage of points allocated to the identified factor.

are the most likely to remain profitable, the likelihood that farm amenities will be provided in the longer run may be greater.

A potential drawback of favoring cropland is that, relative to other rural land uses, such as woodland operations, such land may exacerbate environmental problems as a result of higher runoff from fertilizers and topsoil. This priority given to cropland thus might be interpreted as simultaneously expressing limited preferences for environmental service-related amenities. We note, however, that many programs tend to require farmers to adopt water quality and soil conservation plans as a condition for easement sale, rather than include such environmental service preferences in the ranking criteria. Thus even though the programs assign minimal points to environmental criteria in their ranking schemes, the design of PDR programs generally is not inconsistent with protecting environmental quality amenities.

The second-highest priority given, on average, to the preservation of larger farms and blocks of farms suggests a preference for preserving parcels in clusters. This spatial arrangement of preserved lands arguably could contribute to a number of farm and generic amenities: agrarian character, open space, wildlife habitat, and scenic beauty. Also, fewer borders with nonfarm neighbors may minimize nuisance complaints arising from normal farming activities (e.g., smell of recently spread manure), further contributing to maintaining agrarian character.

The third-highest priority given to farmland facing development pressure suggests a preference for rural lands closer to population concentrations. This priority may favor the provision of generic open-space amenities.

Underlying factors, related to the demand and supply for farmland characteristics, may help explain the observed weights assigned to the different priorities. Given the small size of the dataset, Nickerson and Hellerstein (2003) used correlation coefficients to investigate relationships and found that several weights were correlated with population and supply of farmland and prime lands (see Table 11-4). For example, the weight assigned to road access seems to be related to several explanatory factors. Jurisdictions with greater population densities and more changes over time appear to assign higher weights to the road access factor, as do those with larger losses of prime lands. The ranking criteria reveal that most PDR programs that include road frontage or access as a factor do so because of a desire to provide scenic views. The

Table 11-4. Correlations between PDR Ranking Weights and Explanatory Variables

Factor	Popden	%prime	%farm	Popdenchg	%primechg	%farmchg
Soil productivity	−0.01945 (0.9233)	0.09822 (0.6331)	0.08305 (0.6805)	0.17677 (0.3778)	−0.00852 (0.9671)	−0.04384 (0.8281)
Farm importance	−0.13479 (0.5027)	**−0.32251** **(0.1081)**	−0.07748 (0.7009)	−0.00381 (0.9850)	0.16866 (0.4102)	0.08670 (0.6672)
Development pressure	0.04704 (0.8158)	0.05875 (0.7756)	−0.17337 (0.3871)	0.04144 (0.8374)	−0.02644 (0.8980)	0.15074 (0.4530)
Road access/ frontage	**0.53381** **(0.0041)**	−0.26702 (0.1873)	**−0.46785** **(0.0139)**	**0.29806** **(0.1310)**	**−0.48263** **(0.0125)**	**−0.42815** **(0.0223)**
Environmental significance	−0.03384 (0.8669)	−0.26383 (0.1928)	−0.08176 (0.6852)	−0.15364 (0.4442)	0.15750 (0.4422)	0.09338 (0.6432)
Parcel size and contiguity	−0.19951 (0.3184)	**0.37637** **(0.0581)**	**0.37634** **(0.0530)**	−0.16779 (0.4028)	0.10404 (0.6130)	0.07898 (0.6954)

Notes: Bold values are significant at the 10% one-sided confidence interval. Numbers in parentheses are probability values.

correlations tentatively suggest that PDR programs rank road frontage higher when population density is high and increasing, and when less farmland remains and is declining. All of these factors limit the ability to provide scenic view amenities. Also, our analysis indicates that jurisdictions with smaller percentages of prime farmland are those most likely to weigh farm importance factors higher, which may contribute to providing agrarian heritage amenities.

The analysis also implies that jurisdictions assign higher weights to preserving larger farms or contiguous blocks of farms in PDR programs when levels of prime land and farmland are higher. Priority given to this criterion might be indicative of desires to protect generic open space, wildlife habitat, and scenic beauty amenities. A chi-square analysis suggests that the largest (negative) changes in the percentage of prime farmland are somewhat associated with less weight given to environmental attributes, which may imply that other concerns take precedence in periods of significant farmland losses.

Conclusions

A review of legislation enabling a wide range of farmland preservation programs, as well as the selection criteria used in 27 PDR programs with point-based ranking systems, offers insight on how such programs operate to protect rural amenities.

State and local governments use farmland preservation programs to accomplish multiple objectives and protect a large number of rural amenities. Legislation in the more densely populated regions is often concerned with protecting the widest variety of rural amenities, whereas it is less so in sparsely populated states and regions. The variation we noted across regions suggests that, from a national perspective, regionally or locally designed programs to protect amenities may be better targeted than a one-size-fits-all program.

It also appears that PDR programs, at least those that employ point-based systems for selecting among offers, favor protecting high-quality soils and actively farmed agricultural lands rather than passive open-space uses. This implies that farm amenities are more likely to be provided than generic environmental or rural amenities. Although land with good soil and farming uses can provide a variety of amenities, these are necessary conditions for the provision of farm amenities, such as agrarian heritage.

Other studies imply that in some areas, the public may be interested in preserving a broader mix of farmlands that includes orchards and other unique land types (e.g., Kline and Wichelns 1998), or less productive lands that may do a better job at providing generic amenities. Yet at present, too few studies exist on public preferences for amenities to allow researchers to draw general implications for the design of PDR programs. An increased understanding of public preferences for farm over generic amenities can have important policy implications, however. Such knowledge could directly improve the efficiency of PDR programs by determining how much—or whether any—targeting of particular farmland attributes is necessary. If residents of a particular jurisdiction prefer generic amenities, little or no targeting may be necessary, and PDR administrators could prioritize farm parcels on the basis of which cost the least to preserve. In cases where residents prefer specific farm amenities, it may be optimal to target those particular amenities.

Public preference is only one of several factors that are likely to influence selection priorities. Because PDR programs are voluntary, administrators also are faced with the task of designing programs that are attractive to potential participants. Thus the priority given to the best soils and active farm operations could represent a program feature designed to garner the support of farm interests. Also, program managers may need to make a trade-off between the long-term provision of farm amenities, from farms deemed most likely to survive, and the optimal set of rural amenities that the public desires today, which could be obtained if farm survival were not an issue. That is, by selecting the best agricultural lands today, the probability that the land will end up being idle, and therefore not provide farm amenities at any point in the future, is diminished. Many jurisdictions also have other programs that protect a variety of rural lands, such as parks and forestland, and thus certain types of amenities already may be well protected in some regions. Finally, some land preservation programs may be more responsive to those representing active farm interests than to the general public, leading them to favor the preservation of attributes associated with active farming in contrast to the generic amenities that may be desired by the general public (Swallow 1997).

Even though PDR programs tend to assign little explicit priority to protecting environmental services in their parcel selection criteria, they often require that water quality and soil conservation practices be adopted as a condition for eligibility to sell development rights. This implies that protecting at least some environmental services is given high priority. One also could argue that PDR programs prioritize the protection of these and other environmental services simply by removing the potential for the land being converted to a more intensive use that is likely to be more environmentally detrimental. An example is the protection of groundwater recharge areas provided by farmland enrolled in PDR programs, but not by land in developed uses.

PDR rankings have implications for the spatial distribution of preserved lands and the rural amenities they provide, favoring amenities that are best produced by larger blocks of farmland and on lands facing development pressure. A preference for larger blocks appears to be correlated with areas that have a higher base of existing farmland and prime land, whereas the priority given to farms facing development pressure does not appear to be correlated with population or farmland quantity measures.

Not all PDR programs use point systems to prioritize the purchase of easements on agricultural lands; those that do not either tend to consider the same factors but use more subjective ranking systems or consider other factors altogether. For example, we noted that some other PDR programs that do not use point systems intentionally distribute preservation funds across the jurisdiction; one reason could be to create a broad base of support for program continuation. In others, the desire to preserve as much farmland as possible at least cost leads to prioritizing applications based on the lowest per-acre cost or on the largest discount at which landowners offer to sell development rights. These strategies can result in significantly different outcomes from point-based systems, such as a more scattered pattern of preserved farms or the preservation of lands distant from where significant numbers of residents live.

Our analyses provide a broader and different perspective in exploring the relationship of farmland protection programs and rural amenities than those of previously published research. They supplement existing studies in the literature that use survey data from a limited geographic area to assess public preferences over goals or willingness to pay to protect farmland. Our findings imply that farmland preservation programs may protect a wide variety of amenities. Variation in the design of PDR programs is not easily explained by factors that are likely to characterize areas with farmland losses, however, which suggests that different amenities may be provided or favored in areas facing similar threats to their farmland bases.

Endnotes

1. These are average per-household values, converted to year 2000 constant dollars.

2. This is well above the $2,000 per acre average cost the state of Maryland's farmland preservation program pays for easements (http://www.mda.state.md.us/agland/main.htm).

3. It is useful, especially in the United States, to add another boundary: where the wildlands begin. Since "city's edge" and "start of the wildlands" rarely are sharply delineated, this is meant to be suggestive of landscapes defined, but not dominated, by a human presence.

4. Note that this bifurcation is a simplification of a continuum, with different rural amenities being more or less dependent on the presence of active agriculture.

5. We evaluated the legislation by using a yes-no indicator if at least one of a state's farmland protection laws mentioned that particular output. We also evaluated the legislation using a weighted classification, which assigned higher scores when the legislation contained more language about a given output. The conclusions we drew were not significantly different from those reported here.

6. An urban influence index, essentially a measure of urban proximity, was derived for the entire United States using census block population data and GIS-based statistical smoothing techniques. This measure is derived from a "gravity" model of urban development and increases as nearby population increases and/or as distance from the parcel to population decreases. The index used population within a 50-mile radius of each parcel and a linear (rather then squared) inverse distance weighting. See Barnard (2000) for details.

7. Points assigned to use of land for specialty crops arguably could be allocated to the soil productivity rather than farmland management category, as we have done. Either way these points are allocated, the general conclusions remain the same.

References

AFT (American Farmland Trust). 2002a. Fact Sheet: Status of State PACE Programs. http://www.farmlandinfo.org (accessed January 2002).

———. 2002b. Fact Sheet: Status of Local PACE Programs. http://www.farmlandinfo. org (accessed January 2002).

———. 2002c. State Farmland Protection Statutes by State. http:// www.farmlandinfo. org/fic/laws.html (accessed January 2002).

Agresti, A. 1996. *An Introduction to Categorical Data Analysis.* New York: John Wiley and Sons.

Barnard, C. H. 2000. Urbanization Affects a Large Share of Farmland. *Rural Conditions and Trends* 10(2): 57–63.

Beasley, S. D., W. G. Workman, and N. A. Williams. 1986. Estimating Amenity Values for Urban Fringe Farmland: A Contingent Valuation Approach: Note. *Growth and Change* 17(4): 70–78.

Bergstrom, J., B. Dillman, and J. Stoll. 1985. Public Environmental Amenity Benefits of Private Land: The Case of Prime Agricultural Land. *Southern Journal of Agricultural Economics* 17(1): 139–49.

Bockstael, N. E. 1996. Modeling Economics and Ecology: The Importance of a Spatial Perspective. *American Journal of Agricultural Economics* 78: 1168–80.

Cattaneo, A., S. Bucholtz, J. Dewbre, and C. Nickerson. 2002. The CRP Balancing Act: Trading Off Costs and Multiple Environmental Benefits. Selected paper presented at the American Agricultural Economics Association meetings. July, Long Beach, CA.

Duke, J. M., and R. A. Hyde. 2002. Identifying Public Preferences for Land Preservation Using the Analytic Hierarchy Process. *Ecological Economics* 42(1–2): 131–45.

Furuseth, O. 1987. Public Attitudes toward Local Farmland Protection Programs. *Growth and Change* 18(3): 49–61.

Hellerstein, D., C. Nickerson, J. Cooper, P. Feather, D. Gadsby, D. Mullarkey, A. Tegene, and C. Barnard. 2002. *Farmland Protection: The Role of Public Preference for Rural Amenities.* Agricultural Economics Report no. 815. Washington, DC: U.S. Department of Agriculture, Economic Research Service.

Irwin, E. G. 2002. The Effects of Open Space on Residential Property Values. *Land Economics* 78(4): 464–80.

Kline, J., and D. Wichelns. 1996. Public Preferences Regarding the Goals of Farmland Preservation Programs. *Land Economics* 72(4): 538–49.

———. 1998. Measuring Heterogeneous Preferences for Preserving Farmland and Open Space. *Ecological Economics* 26(2): 211–24.

Krieger, D. 1999. Saving Open Spaces: Public Support for Farmland Protection. Working Paper Series wp99-1. April. Chicago: Center for Agriculture in the Environment.

Nickerson, C. J., and D. Hellerstein. 2003. Protecting Rural Amenities through Farmland Preservation Programs. *Agricultural and Resource Economics Review* 32(1): 129–44.

Samuelson, P. 1954. The Pure Theory of Public Expenditure. *Review of Economics and Statistics* 36(4): 3817–3819.

Swallow, S. K. 1997. Modelling Public Preferences for Environmental Management Planning and Decisions. In Proceedings of the Biennial Meeting of the Scandinavian Society of Forest Economics, edited by O. Saastamoinen and S. Tikka. Mekrijärvi, Finland, March 1996. *Scandinavian Forest Economics* 36(1): 23–41.

12

Support for Conservation Policies and Values for Conservation

Are They Related?

ROBERT J. JOHNSTON, STEPHEN K. SWALLOW,
DANA MARIE BAUER, AND LISA D. PHILO

E conomists frequently assess stated preferences for land use outcomes as either independent of information regarding policy implementation mechanisms or a function of a vaguely specified management process. The rural public, however, not only may be concerned with the consequences of land management, but also may have systematic preferences for policy procedures applied to management goals. There is no guarantee that residents of rural or urban-fringe communities will support policies that are consistent with their preferences for land use outcomes. To the contrary, they may have preferences for certain outcomes, such as conservation of wildlife habitat, public access, or open space, but be unwilling to accept the management processes necessary for those outcomes (Philo and Johnston 2004).

Researchers are beginning to accept that causes of environmental outcomes—whether policy or otherwise—may influence people's willingness to pay to obtain or avoid those outcomes (Bulte et al. 2005). Moreover, evidence suggests that individuals may have distinct preferences for policy methods used to preserve environmental amenities or fund environmental programs (Johnston et al. 1999; Kask et al. 2002; Rosenberger et al. 1996). Despite such evidence, economics research has provided little information on whether preferences for particular land use outcomes are correlated with support for associated policies.

Consider the example of Charlestown, Rhode Island, where in October 2002, the town council voted against a proposed policy that would have imposed a $1,500 impact fee on each new house built in the community. The impact fee was proposed as a means to fund open-space and habitat conservation. The council rejected this policy measure despite substantial evidence that Rhode Island residents value farmland, forest, and open-space conservation (Philo and Johnston 2004). Such patterns suggest that though residents may hold significant value for the preservation of rural amenities, they may be unwilling in some cases to enact policies required to obtain these outcomes. Despite a positive value for a land use outcome, a lack of support for associated policy tools may preclude otherwise beneficial policy change.

This chapter examines relationships among the rural public's support for various land management policies and its goals for land use outcomes, considering preferences within the context of alternative proposals to manage residential growth and conserve landscape attributes in southern New England. We combine two distinct types of empirical data gathered from the Rhode Island Rural Land Use Survey (Johnston et al. 2000): responses collected from choice experiments addressing rural land use outcomes and data from a Likert-scale analysis of policy support.

Choice experiments ask respondents to choose between pairs of hypothetical policy scenarios that differ across a range of environmental, aesthetic, financial, or other dimensions. By analyzing respondents' choices in a variety of scenarios, it is possible to estimate relative values for environmental amenities and willingness to trade off different outcomes. The choice experiment section of the survey asked respondents in four Rhode Island towns to consider and choose between alternative land use (i.e., development and/or conservation) options for a hypothetical 400-acre tract of forested land located in their town of residence (just over 1 percent of each town's total land area). Analysis of these results provides insight into preferences and values for land use outcomes.

A subsequent section of the survey asked the same respondents to indicate their degree of support for or opposition to 21 different policy options that could be used to influence land use. Strength of support was indicated on a five-point Likert scale, ranging from "strongly oppose" to "strongly support." These data provide insight into respondents' support for land management mechanisms. Initial findings are drawn from a qualitative comparison of these Likert-scale policy support ratings and results of the choice experiment model of conservation and development (outcome) preferences. We explore these initial findings more formally through a model integrating principal-components factor analysis of Likert-scale responses with the discrete choice model of land use preferences.

Modeling Choices among Conservation and Development Plans

The Rhode Island Rural Land Use Survey was designed to assess rural residents' willingness to pay (WTP) for attributes of residential development and conservation, willingness to trade off different types of land use outcomes, and degree of support for associated policy tools. Survey development required more than 18 months. Besides conducting background research, we interviewed policymakers and residents and met with 14 focus groups to help design and test survey questions, determine the selection and levels of land use, and derive management plans for consideration in choice scenarios (Johnston et al. 2003). Pretests were conducted with individual respondents to ensure that the survey language and format could be easily understood, and that respondents shared interpretations of survey questions and instructions (cf. Johnston et al. 1995).

Respondents' choices among development and conservation plans are interpreted within a standard random utility model framework, which allows their willingness to pay for (or value of) land use outcomes to be estimated based on observed choices across pairs of development and conservation plans. Theoretical details of this approach are summarized in the technical appendix at the end of this chapter.

The survey began with background information and a reminder of trade-offs implicit in development choices, followed by choice instructions and questions. Information was presented on simplified maps of hypothetical development and conservation plans. Attributes to be considered included protected open space (acreage, location, access), residential development (housing density, acreage, location, dimension), unprotected undeveloped land (both adjacent to and isolated from developments), scenic views, wildlife habitat (for various species groups), recreational facilities, traffic, and taxes (Johnston et al. 2003). Table 12-1 summarizes the attributes distinguishing the plans considered by respondents.

For each question, respondents were given the choice to vote for a "current" or "alternate" development plan for the same 400-acre undeveloped parcel of forestland. They were told the approximate location of this parcel in their community. Each respondent considered three potential pairs of current and alternate development or conservation options that would alter the existing state of the site. Respondents were instructed to consider each pair independently, but assume that all applied to the same parcel.

Respondents were also told that if they did not vote for either plan, development would automatically occur according to the current plan (Adamowicz et al. 1998). This framework was chosen to mimic actual community considerations of development proposals, wherein a landowner possesses the property rights necessary to permit development and has proposed a specific development or conservation plan. Officials may seek to influence the configuration of the proposed plan, however, delaying required permits unless design changes are made. As a result, although some form of development or conservation is virtually certain, officials may exert some control over its ultimate form (Johnston et al. 2003).

Table 12-1. Variables Characterizing Development and Conservation Plans in the Rhode Island Rural Land Use Survey: Definitions and Summary Statistics

Variable name	Description	Units and measurement	Mean (std. dev.)
Adjacent open space	Difference between acres of open space adjacent to developments and roads in CDP and ADP	Acres in CDP minus acres in ADP (range: −200 to 200)	−3.41967 (95.091)
Isolated open space	Difference between acres of open space not adjacent to developments and roads in CDP and ADP	Acres in CDP minus acres in ADP (range: −200 to 200)	2.62028 (53.724)
Development size	Difference between acres of residential development in CDP and ADP	Acres in CDP minus acres in ADP (range: −200 to 200)	−1.77646 (90.806)
Development density	Difference between housing density in CDP and ADP	Houses/acre in CDP minus houses/acre in ADP (range: −2 to 2)	−0.00666 (0.9759)
Large mammal	Difference between habitat quality for large mammals in CDP and ADP	Difference in wildlife habitat quality scale (1 = worst; 5 = best)	0.00370 (1.2193)
Small mammal	Difference between habitat quality for small mammals in CDP and ADP	Difference in wildlife habitat quality scale (1=worst; 5=best)	−0.01628 (1.2194)
Common bird	Difference between habitat quality for common birds in CDP and ADP	Difference in wildlife habitat quality scale (1=worst; 5=best)	0.05107 (1.7511)
Uncommon bird	Difference between habitat quality for uncommon birds in CDP and ADP	Difference in wildlife habitat quality scale (1=worst; 5=best)	0.00370 (1.7038)
Wetland species	Difference between habitat quality for wetland species in CDP and ADP	Difference in wildlife habitat quality scale (1=worst; 5=best)	−0.04663 (1.7359)
Traffic light	Difference between dummy variables indicating the presence of a traffic light on the main road in CDP and ADP	Difference between dummy variables for CDP and ADP	−0.00518 (0.7018)

Table 12-1. (*Continued*)

Variable name	Description	Units and measurement	Mean (std. dev.)
Tax change	Difference in additional annual taxes and fees between CDP and ADP (resulting from management plan)	Dollars in CDP minus dollars in ADP (Range: −$325 to $325)	−1.22132 (154.33)
Low-visibility development	Difference between dummy variables indicating presence of development either highly screened or not visible from main road in CDP and ADP. Survey versions included eight photographs characterizing different development visibility levels; four of them are characterized as low-visibility development.	Difference between dummy variables for CDP and ADP	−0.00740 (0.6928)
Edge-area ratio	Difference between the edge-area ratio of residential development shown in CDP and ADP. All ratios calculated as the sum of the perimeter(s) divided by the sum of the area(s) of land highlighted for residential development in a development plan.	Calculated at a scale of 1 unit = 933.37 ft. (e.g., a 1 unit × 1 unit square block is equivalent to 20 acres or ∼871,180 square feet, with an edge-area ratio of 4) (range: −14.85 to 8.5)	0.01904 (3.6702)
Two-part cluster	Difference between dummy variables indicating presence of a two-section, fragmented development in CDP and ADP. In all cases, development sections are rectangular.	Difference between dummy variables for CDP and ADP	0.00962 (0.4241)
Four-part cluster	Difference between dummy variables indicating presence of a four- or five-section, fragmented development in CDP and ADP. In all cases, development sections are rectangular.	Difference between dummy variables for CDP and ADP	−0.02072 (0.5947)

Continued

Table 12-1. (*Continued*)

Variable name	Description	Units and measurement	Mean (std. dev.)
On-road development	Difference between dummy variables indicating presence of developments located adjacent to main roads in CDP and ADP	Difference between dummy variables for CDP and ADP	0.00962 (0.7133)

Notes: CDP = current development plan; ADP = alternate development plan.

Fractional factorial design was used to construct survey questions with an orthogonal array of attribute levels.[1] This resulted in 128 unique choice questions divided among 43 different survey booklets. The survey design has the added advantage of reducing the potential for yea-saying (Blamey et al. 1999; Boyle et al. 1998), as most plans incorporated both positive and negative elements. Hence, in most questions, neither the current nor alternate plan offered a clearly superior choice for a respondent wishing to express environmental motivations.

Surveys were mailed to 4,000 randomly selected residents of four Rhode Island rural communities—Burrillville, Coventry, Exeter, and West Greenwich—following the total survey design method (Dillman 2000). Of 3,702 deliverable surveys, 2,157 were returned, for a response rate of 58.2 percent. Response rates ranged from 50.4 percent (Coventry) to 58.7 percent (West Greenwich). Individual choice models are estimated for Burrillville and Exeter. Results for Coventry and West Greenwich, which offer little additional insight, are suppressed for the sake of brevity and to allow sufficient discussion of the Burrillville and Exeter results. The Burrillville model incorporates 1,351 responses to choice questions from 528 surveys received from this community; the Exeter model incorporates 1,338 responses from 538 surveys.

Choice Model Results: Initial Findings

Model results are presented in Table 12-2. Burrillville results are based on a random effects logit model (Greene 2003). A random effects model for Exeter would not converge given traditional maximum likelihood methods; hence, standard logit results are presented for this community. Both models are statistically significant at p < 0.0001. Of 16 model attributes, 11 are significant in the Burrillville model and 13 in the Exeter model. In the table, the sign and relative size of parameter estimates indicate whether the associated variable is perceived as a positive or negative aspect of land use, and show the relative importance placed on the variable when given choices between land use plans.

Table 12-2. Choice Model Results: Base Specification

	Burrillville model			Exeter model		
	Parameter estimate	*z statistic*		*Parameter estimate*	*z statistic*	
Intercept	−0.051686	−0.74		0.172756	−2.56	∗∗∗
Edge-area ratio	0.140387	5.08	∗∗∗	0.122696	4.42	∗∗∗
Two-part cluster	−0.187741	−1.00		−0.543437	−2.87	∗∗∗
Four-part cluster	−0.478766	−3.38	∗∗∗	−0.381821	−2.78	∗∗∗
Isolated open space	0.006478	4.62	∗∗∗	0.006776	4.64	∗∗∗
Adjacent open space	0.003523	4.67	∗∗∗	0.004272	5.71	∗∗∗
On-road development	−0.220212	−2.01	∗∗	−0.308200	−2.77	∗∗∗
Large mammal	0.149862	2.63	∗∗∗	0.121017	2.24	∗∗
Small mammal	−0.061103	−1.09		−0.065327	−1.21	
Common bird	0.119919	3.07	∗∗∗	0.129623	3.27	∗∗∗
Uncommon bird	−0.020583	−0.52		0.010469	0.28	
Wetland species	0.004121	0.10		0.074446	1.85	∗
Development density	−0.928414	−10.32	∗∗∗	−0.850958	−10.40	∗∗∗
Development size	−0.006295	−6.41	∗∗∗	−0.007224	−7.35	∗∗∗
Traffic light	0.208801	2.11	∗∗	0.088353	0.91	
Low-visibility development	0.118877	1.22		0.240758	2.56	∗∗∗
Tax change	−0.004833	−9.74	∗∗∗	−0.004946	−10.69	∗∗∗
$\ln(\sigma_v)$	−1.80	1.07		—	—	
σ_v	0.41	0.22		—	—	
ρ	0.14	0.13		—	—	
$-2\text{LnL }\chi^2$	441.52	∗∗∗		470.12	∗∗∗	

∗ $p < 0.10$

∗∗ $p < 0.05$

∗∗∗ $p < 0.01$

Signs of significant parameter estimates correspond with prior expectations derived from focus groups (Johnston et al. 2002). For example, respondents tended to prefer development plans with characteristics such as: larger areas of preserved open space, both isolated from and adjacent to roads and developments (Isolated open space; Adjacent open space); smaller areas of developed land (Development size); lower housing densities (Development density); improved habitat for large mammals (Large mammal), birds (Common bird; Uncommon bird), and wetland species (Wetland species); low-visibility development (Low-visibility development); and lower taxes (Tax change).

Results also shed light on the relative values that respondents place on particular development and conservation outcomes. For example, the marginal utility (or relative value) associated with changes in Isolated open space is greater than that associated with Adjacent open space (approximately 100 percent greater in Burrillville and 50 percent greater in Exeter).[2] Moreover, the marginal utility lost as a result of an additional acre of Development size is roughly the same magnitude as that gained through an additional acre of Isolated open space—suggesting that residents might be compensated for acres lost to development through the preservation of the same number of acres of Isolated open space. For open space adjacent to developments (Adjacent open space), however, additional offsetting acreage would be required, given its relatively lower value to residents. Although such findings alone may be of significant interest to policymakers, the question to be addressed here is whether these and other model results correspond with support for associated policy tools.

Characterizing Support for Land Use Policies

The survey also asked respondents to indicate their degree of support for 21 different land use management policy options on a five-point Likert scale ranging from "strongly oppose" (one) to "strongly support" (five). Policy options were selected with the assistance of local land use officials, and their nontechnical descriptions were refined through focus groups and pretests. These options included zoning changes, fee-based land preservation techniques, tax policies, housing caps, and various types of impact fees, among others.

All respondents considered the same set of 21 policy options. Table 12-3 lists the policy options rated by respondents and the mean support ratings associated with each. Mean scores above 3.0 indicate that the average respondent supports the policy option, with higher scores indicating greater support. Mean scores below 3.0 indicate that the average respondent opposes the policy option, with lower scores indicating greater opposition.

Results for Burrillville and Exeter reveal a high degree of consistency in policy support across the 21 management tools. As expected, respondents indicated general support for conservation policy options and opposition to those that encourage development. The specific characteristics of policy tools, however, are relevant to policy support. For example, tools that encourage conservation through explicit tax increases (e.g., options 5 and 9) are generally opposed by residents, whereas other conservation options tend to receive strong support. Results also illustrate that opposition to policies encouraging residential development (e.g., options 2 and 12) exceeds opposition to otherwise analogous policies encouraging commercial development (e.g., options 1 and 13). Such findings indicate that residents distinguish among the details of policy mechanisms that might be used to encourage similar land use outcomes.

Table 12-3. Likert-Scale Strength-of-Support Ratings for Land Use Policy Options

Option	Description (survey text)	Burrillville mean rating (n = 528)	Exeter mean rating (n = 538)
1	Attract new commercial development to your town by offering tax incentives	2.69 (1.29)	2.46 (1.28)
2	Attract new residential development to your town by offering tax incentives	2.03 (1.02)	1.74 (0.86)
3	Encourage preservation by reducing property taxes on undeveloped land	4.14 (0.83)	4.06 (0.94)
4	Encourage new development by expanding public water and sewer services	2.53 (1.07)	2.08 (1.04)
5	Discourage people from moving into your town by increasing the tax rate	2.00 (0.88)	1.91 (0.87)
6	Revitalize town or village centers using new public funds	3.77 (0.89)	3.17 (1.05)
7	Purchase and preserve undeveloped land with private funds (e.g., land trust donations)	4.06 (0.76)	4.11 (0.78)
8	Purchase and preserve undeveloped land with public funds (e.g., public bond issues)	3.63 (3.63)	3.51 (1.09)
9	Purchase and preserve undeveloped land through a new real estate sales tax	2.64 (1.14)	2.72 (1.14)
10	Collect fees from developers to offset costs of additional public services for new developments	4.10 (0.83)	4.18 (0.83)
11	Collect fees from developers to offset additional environmental damages from new developments	4.24 (0.78)	4.29 (0.81)
12	Encourage residential development by decreasing zoning restrictions	1.94 (0.94)	1.74 (0.95)
13	Encourage commercial development by decreasing zoning restrictions	2.11 (1.07)	2.00 (1.11)
14	Require new developments to preserve some undeveloped land	4.15 (0.78)	4.22 (0.78)
15	Require trees and shrubs between new houses and roads	3.96 (0.84)	4.16 (0.80)
16	Further protect water resources by increasing zoning restrictions	4.03 (0.78)	4.08 (0.85)
17	Further protect wildlife resources by increasing zoning restrictions	4.01 (0.83)	4.00 (0.87)
18	Require new commercial development to occur along major roadways	3.81 (0.94)	3.74 (1.02)
19	Require new commercial development to occur within town or village centers	2.85 (1.09)	3.12 (1.11)
20	Institute a cap on the total number of new homes allowed to be built each year	4.06 (0.90)	4.04 (0.96)
21	Tighten enforcement of existing zoning and subdivision regulations	3.92 (0.84)	4.01 (0.86)

Factor Analysis of Land Use Policy Support

Although visual analysis of Table 12-3 allows informal assessment of patterns in policy support, analysis of such patterns is complicated by the large number of tools that respondents were asked to assess and the associated variation in individual Likert-scale responses. In such instances, additional insight often can be gained through the use of data reduction techniques, which may reveal patterns unapparent from casual observation of data patterns. Here, factor analysis is used to estimate a small number of underlying constructs, or latent variables, that together account for a large percentage of observed variation in Likert-scale responses (Variyam et al. 1990). In nontechnical terms, one may think of factor analysis as identifying underlying themes that may assist researchers in understanding observed response patterns. Results of the factor analysis will be a critical component of a model (presented later) that seeks to quantify statistical relationships between preferences for land use outcomes and support for policy tools.

As results may differ across communities, we estimate results for Burrillville and Exeter separately, using principal-components factor analysis of the response correlation matrix (Reyment and Joreskog 1996) in an attempt to isolate latent factors that account for response heterogeneity (Bollen 1989). Strong and intuitive results for the two factor analyses suggest that variation in respondents' support for policy tools is systematic and may be explained using a reasonable number of factors.

Seven factors are retained in the Burrillville model based on a minimum eigenvalue of 1.0, accounting for 63.4 percent of the variation in Likert-scale responses.[3] These factors are rotated using the VARIMAX method (Reyment and Joreskog 1996). The rotated factor pattern for Burrillville is shown in Table 12-4. Based on the observed patterns of factor loadings, the seven factors are denoted as (1) Pro-zoning, (2) Pro-develop, (3) Anti-(impact) fee, (4) Pro-purchase, (5) Pro-tax, (6) Relocate commercial, and (7) Pro-commercial. These factors may be interpreted as underlying tendencies among respondents that account for a large percentage of the variation in their responses to the 21 different management tools.

For example, factor 1 (Pro-zoning) is so named based on its high factor loading (i.e., a loading greater than 0.5 in absolute magnitude) on policy tools 15, 16, 17, 20, and 21, indicating strong support for policy options related to stricter zoning or restrictions on new development. Factor 2 (Pro-develop) is characterized by high factor loadings for tools 2, 4, 12, and 13, indicating support for policy options that encourage new residential or commercial development. Factor 3 (Anti-fee) incorporates high negative loadings for options associated with the use of impact fees (tools 10 and 11). Factor 4 (Pro-purchase) is characterized by high loadings on tools 3, 7, and 8, representing different fee-simple methods of purchasing and preserving undeveloped land. Factor

Table 12-4. Rotated VARIMAX Factor Loadings: Strength of Support for Policy Options (Burrillville)

Policy tool		Factor 1 Pro-zoning	Factor 2 Pro-develop	Factor 3 Anti-fee	Factor 4 Pro-purchase	Factor 5 Pro-tax	Factor 6 Relocate commercial	Factor 7 Pro-commercial
1	Commercial tax incentives	−0.26340	0.22814	0.00610	−0.06867	−0.07978	0.07004	**0.73347**
2	Residential tax incentives	0.00416	**0.75585**	0.11073	−0.02229	0.00249	0.04416	0.02388
3	Reduce undeveloped land tax	0.07067	−0.12315	−0.08567	**0.62285**	−0.13503	−0.04884	−0.22588
4	Expand water & sewer	0.01641	**0.63368**	0.21774	−0.03302	−0.07953	0.00253	0.29827
5	Increase tax rate	0.11791	−0.16002	0.03549	0.07820	**0.66605**	0.02767	−0.12051
6	Revitalize town centers	0.24571	0.05107	0.20863	0.48418	−0.16735	0.02815	0.47503
7	Purchase & preserve w/ private funds	0.07854	−0.28818	−0.30906	**0.62868**	−0.01338	0.04956	−0.00280
8	Purchase & preserve w/ public funds	0.13052	−0.06863	−0.06289	**0.77369**	0.24399	0.07103	0.00184
9	Purchase & preserve w/ tax funds	0.21075	0.10222	−0.18525	0.41065	**0.56260**	0.10172	−0.11085
10	Impact fees for public services	0.08597	−0.09084	**−0.88037**	0.02616	−0.00762	−0.02894	−0.02475
11	Impact fees for environ. damages	0.23472	−0.12084	**−0.82635**	0.12042	0.06586	0.03234	0.01381
12	Relax residential zoning	−0.17714	**0.75434**	0.13312	−0.17671	−0.00872	0.03060	0.09478
13	Relax commercial zoning	−0.27533	**0.51506**	−0.08866	−0.22662	0.01525	0.00497	0.48879
14	Require developers to preserve land	0.33180	−0.12274	−0.47205	0.18617	−0.41888	0.24529	−0.06088
15	Require trees & shrubs	**0.68090**	0.04176	−0.09842	0.09806	−0.15135	−0.03259	0.07193
16	Zoning for water protection	**0.78354**	−0.06898	−0.16708	0.07676	0.01668	0.02535	−0.20924
17	Zoning for wildlife protection	**0.79233**	−0.01699	−0.14077	0.20304	0.07913	0.00364	−0.22218
18	Require commercial dev. on roads	0.04161	−0.18711	−0.15093	0.03275	−0.26901	**0.63081**	0.29361
19	Require commercial dev. in town	−0.01641	0.12491	0.04068	0.04196	0.11691	**0.85311**	−0.04644
20	Development cap	**0.56570**	−0.34274	−0.20391	−0.00910	0.25867	−0.06261	0.26897
21	Tighten zoning enforcement	**0.58661**	−0.34444	−0.15907	−0.02728	0.30294	0.06220	0.13636

Note: **Bold type** indicates loadings > 0.5.

five (Pro-tax) loads highly on tools 5 and 9, both of which involve an explicit increase in taxes to obtain conservation objectives. Finally, factors 6 and 7 (Relocate commercial, Pro-commercial) are associated with support for commercial development policies.

Seven factors are retained in the Exeter model, again based on a minimum eigenvalue of 1.0. These factors account for 64.5 percent of the variation in Likert-scale responses. Factors again are rotated using the VARIMAX method, with the rotated factor pattern shown in Table 12-5. Based on factor loadings, the seven factors are denoted as (1) Pro-zoning, (2) Restrict develop, (3) Pro-develop, (4) Anti-purchase, (5) Anti-fee, (6) Pro-tax, and (7) Anti-commercial center.

Factor scores for the Exeter sample reveal patterns similar to those found in the Burrillville model. Factor 1 (Pro-zoning) is characterized by high (> 0.5) loadings on tools 16, 17, and 21, with a loading of 0.45 on tool 15; this is similar to factor 1 in Burrillville. Factor 2 (Restrict-develop) loads highly on tools 14, 15, and 18, indicating support for tools that restrict residential development attributes but do not explicitly reduce acres or density. Factor 3 (Pro-develop) is characterized by high loadings on tools 1, 2, 4, 12, and 13, which provide incentives for development or relax restrictions on developers. This is analogous to factor 2 in Burrillville. Factor 4 (Anti-purchase) is characterized by high negative loadings on tools 7 and 8, and is the near converse of factor 4 in Burrillville. Factor 5 (Anti-fee), with high negative loadings on tools 10 and 11, is analogous to factor 3 in Burrillville. Factor 6 (Pro-tax) is associated with a loading greater than 0.5 on tool 5, with a loading of 0.44 on tool 9; this parallels factor 5 in Burrillville. Finally, factor 7 is associated with high negative loading on tool 19, which would require commercial development to occur in town centers.

An Initial Comparison: Land Use Preferences versus Policy Support

The two separate analyses of preferences for land use outcomes and support for policy tools need to be contrasted and statistically combined in order to assess relationships between land use preferences and policy support. To assess these relationships, we begin with a relatively informal, qualitative comparison of the results, followed by a more formal statistical model that combines choice model and Likert-scale data.

Initial comparison of contingent choice results (Table 12-2) with Likert-scale policy ratings (Table 12-3) points to numerous areas in which preferences for land use outcomes coincide with support for associated policy mechanisms. Findings here are largely qualitative and indicate that at a general, aggregate level, respondents appear to support policies (in the Likert-scale analysis) that

Table 12-5. Rotated VARIMAX Factor Loadings: Strength of Support for Policy Options (Exeter)

Policy tool		Factor 1 Pro-zoning	Factor 2 Restrict develop	Factor 3 Pro-develop	Factor 4 Anti-purchase	Factor 5 Anti-fee	Factor 6 Pro-tax	Factor 7 Anti-commercial center
1	Commercial tax incentives	−0.30503	0.19232	**0.67126**	0.20581	0.01898	0.08940	−0.02226
2	Residential tax incentives	0.10710	−0.41094	**0.62820**	0.07559	0.16889	−0.17565	0.00715
3	Reduce undeveloped land tax	0.15736	0.18420	−0.10717	−0.42748	−0.08749	0.14792	0.45592
4	Expand water & sewer	−0.07378	−0.19679	**0.65176**	0.00771	0.15226	−0.20069	−0.01770
5	Increase tax rate	0.09829	−0.11473	−0.01790	−0.09521	0.08516	**0.80518**	0.06820
6	Revitalize town centers	0.01154	−0.06202	0.43302	−0.49285	−0.04536	−0.01641	−0.30135
7	Purchas & preserve w/ private funds	0.14696	0.24484	−0.28622	**−0.64612**	−0.09335	−0.10966	−0.01437
8	Purchase & preserve w/ public funds	0.17296	−0.00664	−0.17489	**−0.75714**	−0.11638	0.18775	−0.01351
9	Purchase & preserve w/ tax funds	0.20877	−0.10992	−0.10268	−0.49531	−0.25985	0.43641	−0.09560
10	Impact fees for public services	0.05886	0.08247	−0.08934	−0.10273	**−0.90638**	0.00271	−0.00061
11	Impact fees for environ. damages	0.25540	0.05003	−0.10477	−0.05097	**−0.87954**	−0.01876	0.00098
12	Relax residential zoning	−0.18965	−0.20814	**0.63264**	0.09566	0.27619	−0.12891	0.06180
13	Relax commercial zoning	−0.35229	0.17448	**0.70645**	0.23240	0.06425	0.11908	0.00430
14	Require developers to preserve land	0.15254	**0.60511**	−0.18953	−0.30537	−0.07814	−0.17416	0.01682
15	Require trees & shrubs	0.45056	**0.54075**	−0.05144	−0.03745	−0.14110	−0.14022	0.06077
16	Zoning for water protection	**0.86128**	0.02835	−0.11717	−0.08808	−0.14221	0.05986	−0.02692
17	Zoning for wildlife protection	**0.86260**	0.00979	−0.10957	−0.12319	−0.17161	0.08126	−0.00774
18	Require commercial dev. on roads	−0.06999	**0.58768**	0.14089	0.12910	−0.16016	−0.07116	−0.41033
19	Require commercial dev. in town	0.04542	0.07335	−0.04331	−0.09416	0.00487	−0.01564	**0.83494**
20	Development cap	0.39394	0.32582	−0.26192	−0.00684	−0.21848	0.43169	−0.00489
21	Tighten zoning enforcement	**0.56813**	0.32051	−0.30869	−0.17694	−0.09004	0.16529	0.08047

Note: **Bold type** indicates loadings > 0.5.

generate outcomes for which marginal utility is positive (in the choice model).

For example, aversion to residential development found in the choice model coincides with support for development-constraining policy tools. Choice model results reveal negative marginal utility associated with the size and density of residential developments (Table 12-2; Development size, Development density). Similarly, Likert-scale results show strong support for policies that explicitly limit or cap development (e.g., Table 12-3, option 20). In contrast, policies that contribute to an increase in development (Table 12-3, options 1, 2, 4, 12, 13) received low Likert-scale preference scores—in all cases less than 2.75 on a 5-point scale. Options that contribute to an increase in residential development (Table 12-3, options 2, 12) are the lowest rated of all.

Negative marginal utility associated with the placement of new residential development alongside main roads (Table 12-2, On-road development) coincides with support for a requirement that trees and shrubs be placed between new houses and roads (Table 12-3, option 15). Similarly, respondents' support for policies that preserve undeveloped land (Table 12-3, options 3, 7, 8, 9, 14) coincides with positive marginal utility of preserved open space (Table 12-2, Isolated open space, Adjacent open space). The specific mechanism again is relevant, however. Policies preserving undeveloped land using public bonds and real estate transfer taxes (Table 12-3, options 8, 9) ranked lower than other conservation mechanisms, including preservation by land trusts and through reductions in taxes on undeveloped lands (options 3, 7). The real estate transfer tax was the only conservation option to receive a support rating less than 3.0 (the threshold between policy support and opposition). Hence, widespread value for open-space conservation does not guarantee support for the full range of associated policies.

Despite general agreement between aggregate policy support and choice model results, there is some evidence of discord between land use preferences and policy support. For example, we find strong support for a requirement that housing developers conserve open space as part of residential developments (Table 12-3, option 14). Choice model results, however, reveal a relatively lower preference for open space located adjacent to residential development than for otherwise identical open space isolated from developments (Table 12-2, Adjacent open space versus Isolated open space). Thus the most highly rated mechanism for open space conservation provides a type of open space less valued by existing residents. Were policymakers to preserve open space based solely on insights from the Likert-scale analysis, the resulting land use outcome—a preponderance of open space adjacent to developments—could be welfare-reducing compared to an alternative policy that preserved more highly valued open space isolated from roads and developments.

Other results that show less-than-universal correspondence between policy support and land use outcome preferences are found in the context of wildlife habitat conservation. Relatively strong support for protection of wildlife resources using increased zoning restrictions (Table 12-3, option 17) is associated with generally positive marginal utility associated with gains in wildlife habitat quality (Table 12-2, Large mammal, Common bird). The choice model does not reveal positive marginal utility for all types of habitat, however. For example, the parameter estimates associated with gains in small mammal and uncommon bird habitat are not statistically significant, suggesting that these variables did not influence most respondents' choices (Table 12-2, Small mammal, Uncommon bird). Moreover, parameter estimates for Small mammal are negative for both Burrillville and Exeter residents, suggesting that, if anything, residents may wish to see reduced habitat for such species. Hence, support for policies that preserve wildlife resources in general does not imply that residents support improvements in all types of wildlife habitat.

Combined Econometric Analysis

The above findings reflect broad comparisons of independent choice models and Likert-scale analyses. They do not formally indicate, however, whether support for particular types of policy tools is correlated with preferences for related land use outcomes. We address this question by incorporating the estimated factor scores, which characterize underlying patterns in respondents' policy support, as explanatory variables in a statistical model of conservation and development choices. The resulting model allows us to assess whether support for particular land use tools helps explain respondents' choices regarding specific land use outcomes. Formally, we estimate a model incorporating principal-components factor scores of Likert-scale responses as variables within the random effects choice model of land use outcomes (Johnston et al. 2001). This combined model is used to assess potential correlation between preferences for land use outcomes and support for policy tools.

The combined choice model incorporates interactions among factor scores associated with policy tools that influence residential development or land conservation. These include factors 1 through 5 in Burrillville and factors 1 through 6 in Exeter. Factors related primarily to commercial development are omitted from the discrete choice model, as this model addresses only residential development alternatives. As before, independent statistical analyses are conducted for Burrillville and Exeter.

Estimated factors are included in the random effects logit models as standardized factor scores, with a mean of zero and standard deviation of one. This simplifies interpretation of estimated logit parameters, as the scores indicate the extent to which a factor score for a particular respondent differs from that of the sample mean (Kline and Wichelns 1998). Factor scores are included both as linear terms and as quadratic interactions with other variables. This enables assessment of whether support for various management tools, as characterized by factor scores derived from principal-components factor analysis, is correlated with preferences for development or conservation outcomes.[4] Results for the combined choice model are given in Table 12-6.

Both the Burrillville and Exeter models are statistically significant at p < 0.0001. A log-likelihood ratio test of the unrestricted models versus restricted models in which all effects related to Likert-scale factors are constrained to zero rejects the null hypothesis of zero collective influence at p < 0.01 (Burrillville $-2\text{LnL } \chi^2 = 133.98$, df = 85; Exeter $-2\text{LnL } \chi^2 = 200.06$, df = 102). This indicates that the factor scores, considered jointly, have a statistically significant impact on the model.

The joint significance of factor score interactions does not indicate, however, whether these interactions represent intuitive or nonintuitive correlations between land use preferences and policy support. To assess the potential intuition underlying model results, we consider individual interactions associated with selected factor scores. Although statistically significant interactions are associated with all factor scores, we target discussion around factors with a relatively large or highly significant set of interactions.

Are Support for Conservation Policies and Values for Outcomes Related?

Although the combined factor analysis–choice experiment model suggests numerous intuitive correlations between support for land use management tools and marginal utility of attributes associated with those tools, model results also highlight the potential risk in presuming that such correlations exist on a wide scale or that all correlations match simple intuition. Statistically significant correlations do exist, but results do not indicate a particularly pervasive set of associations between policy support and outcome preferences. Indeed, statistically significant interactions appear to be the exception rather than the rule. Of 80 total interactions included in the combined model for Burrillville, only 15 are statistically significant at p < 0.10. In the Exeter model, 18 out of 96 interactions are significant. These results suggest substantial independence between indicators of policy support and the marginal utility of associated land use attributes. Although the reason for this is unknown, it may be related in part to poorly defined associations between certain management tools and outcomes among typical respondents.

Some of the more statistically significant correlations are those involving the marginal utility of housing density and tax changes. Both Burrillville and Exeter responses show a significant interaction (at p < 0.01 in both models) between the Pro-development factor and the marginal utility of housing density. Similarly, Tax change (the change in household taxes) has significant interactions with at least two factor scores in each model. Marginal utility for most model attributes, however, is correlated (at $p < 0.10$) with at least one factor score in at least one of the two estimated models. The following sections highlight principal areas in which policy support is associated with statistically significant changes in land use preferences and others in which expected relationships failed to materialize.

Support for Zoning

A greater score for factor 1 (in both Burrillville and Exeter) implies stronger support for zoning tools. Among statistically significant interactions for Burrillville respondents, those with higher scores for the Pro-zoning factor have a stronger aversion to housing density, as indicated by the negative and statistically significant parameter estimate associated with Pro-zoning × development density. Given common perceptions of zoning as a tool used to place constraints on housing density, the significance of this interaction is to be expected.

Among Exeter respondents, those with greater scores for the Pro-zoning factor reveal a higher marginal utility of open-space preservation (Adjacent open space, Isolated open space) and of developments less visible from main roads (Low-visibility development). Higher Pro-zoning factor scores are also correlated with lower marginal utility associated with the division of developments into multiple smaller clusters (Four-part cluster). Hence, while results suggest correlation between support for zoning tools and preferences for land use attributes that might be influenced by zoning, results differ across the two communities.

Support for Pro-Development Policies

Among Burrillville respondents, interactions involving factor 2 (Pro-develop) indicate intuitive correlations between support for policies favoring land development and a reduction in negative preference associated with increases in housing density (Development density), the size of residential developments (Development size), and the presence of developments adjacent to main roads (On-road development). Utility associated with these land use attributes may be positive for those with particularly high scores for Pro-develop, but negative for the average respondent. This indicates that support for development-promoting policies is correlated with more positive preferences for attributes of residential development.

Exeter results reveal significant and intuitive correlations between support for development-promoting policies and a reduction in negative marginal utility associated with housing density (Development density) and in the marginal utility of habitat improvements for large mammals (Large mammal) and uncommon birds (Uncommon bird). Other statistically significant correlations have less obvious intuition, however. For example, the positive sign of Pro-develop × low-visibility development indicates that higher Pro-develop factor scores are correlated with a stronger preference for reductions in development visibility. Simply put, those who more strongly favor policies that promote development are more averse to highly visible developments—a result that counters common intuition. Similarly, higher Pro-develop factor scores are correlated with an increased marginal utility of certain types of open-space preservation (Pro-develop × isolated open space > 0). Hence, among Exeter respondents, greater support for development-promoting policies is associated with higher values for certain types of open-space conservation—another counterintuitive result. Such findings highlight potential conflicts between policies supported by respondents and land use outcomes that may be desired.

Opposition to Impact Fees

Within the Burrillville sample, opposition to impact fees is correlated with lower marginal utility of open space adjacent to roads and developments. This result is intuitive, as funds from impact fees often are used to preserve community open space in the vicinity of new developments. Among Exeter respondents, higher Anti-fee factor scores are strongly correlated with a reduction in the negative marginal utility of housing density (i.e., a more positive reaction to housing density). This again is an expected result, suggesting that individuals with a more positive reaction to housing developments are more likely to oppose impact fees.

Support for or Opposition to Land Purchases for Conservation

A lack of statistical significance also may be of potential importance. For example, the model demonstrates no significant relationship between strength of support for the purchase and preservation of undeveloped land and the marginal utility of preserved open space. Among Burrillville respondents, factor 4 characterizes the extent to which respondents favor tools that result in the purchase and preservation of open space. The associated interactions Pro-purchase × isolated open space and Pro-purchase × adjacent open space are not statistically significant at $p < 0.10$ (for Pro-purchase × adjacent open space, $p < 0.12$). That is, from a statistical perspective, support for the purchase and preservation of open space is not correlated with the marginal utility of preserved open space.

Among Exeter respondents, factor 4 characterizes the extent to which respondents oppose tools that result in the purchase and preservation of open space. As in Burrillville, this factor has no significant correlation with respondents' preferences for open-space preservation: respondents who are less likely to support open-space conservation methods do not appear to have lesser preferences for open-space conservation itself. Exeter responses, however, do show a significant and intuitive correlation between opposition to purchase and preservation of open space and an increased marginal utility of income (i.e., tax changes), suggesting that residents who are more averse to tax increases are also less likely to support the purchase of open space. This is an expected result.

Support for Tax Policies

The Pro-tax factor score characterizes a respondent's willingness to support policies that include explicit tax increases. Among other statistically significant correlations, the significant parameter estimate associated with Pro-tax × isolated open space in Burrillville and Pro-tax × adjacent open space in Exeter indicates that the welfare gain associated with open-space preservation is greater for those with higher Pro-tax factor scores. Also in both samples, positive and significant parameter estimates associated with Pro-tax × tax change support the intuitive result that higher Pro-tax factor scores are associated with a lower marginal utility of income (or tax changes). That is, those respondents who tend to support policies associated with community-wide tax increases are less averse to conservation outcomes that are more costly to their households.

Unexplained Relationships

A variety of statistically significant results are neither clearly intuitive nor counterintuitive. For example, tax changes (Tax change) for Burrillville respondents are relatively less important for respondents with higher Pro-zoning scores, an effect that lacks obvious economic intuition. Similarly, opposition to impact fees (Anti-fee) among Exeter residents is associated with higher marginal utility for the preservation of common bird habitat. These results do not counter common intuition, but neither are they expected. Other statistically significant correlations lacking obvious intuitive explanations may be found throughout both models, suggesting that relationships between policy support and land use outcome preferences may be more complex—and less intuitive—than is commonly assumed.

Conclusions

The literature provides much insight into the preferences of rural residents for certain land management outcomes, but preferences for outcomes do not necessarily imply matching support for the underlying policy processes. Nonetheless, economists typically disassociate preferences for management outcomes from detailed analyses of policies that might generate those outcomes. This may result in misleading or, at best, partial guidance to policymakers. The analysis in this chapter indicates that preferences for management outcomes are sometimes, but not necessarily, correlated with support for associated policy tools. Although numerous intuitive and statistically significant correlations do exist, statistical significance does not guarantee an intuitive or easily interpretable relationship.

These findings highlight the potential limitations of preference elicitation methods used in isolation. Although typical choice models may reveal the marginal utility of management outcomes, they often fail to assess whether estimated preferences are linked with a corresponding support for management options able to deliver valued outcomes. Similarly, surveys that assess strength of support for management tools rarely assess the welfare implications of land use outcomes that would result from application of those policies. By overlooking the possibility of significant positive or negative correlations, researchers risk unanticipated public reactions to the policy process. This study highlights such potential complexities in the hope of stimulating further research to aid in rural policy development.

Model results indicate a number of key findings related to the potential correspondence between policy support and preferences for land use outcomes. First, the marginal utility for management outcomes often is independent of support for tools that might be used to achieve those outcomes. Second, significant correlation between support for management tools and marginal utility of management outcomes may be more prevalent for particular types of outcomes, such as housing density or tax changes. Third, relationships between support for policies and preferences for outcomes are sometimes less intuitive than is typically assumed.

These conclusions have potential implications for the policy process in rural or urban-fringe communities, particularly in cases where residents' support is required to enact policy. For example, one might speculate that if welfare gain resulting from open-space preservation is not correlated with support for tools designed to accomplish this goal (perhaps because residents have imperfect or inaccurate perceptions of management tools), then policymakers might face difficulty in obtaining a broad base of unequivocal resident support. In areas where policy support and welfare effects coincide, however, constituency building might be more effective.

This chapter provides case-study evidence that public support for land use policy may not always correspond with goals for land conservation and development. These results are limited in at least two important respects, however. First, model results indicate that correlations between policy support and outcome preferences may vary across communities, suggesting that broader-scale research is needed to assess the generality of the results presented here. Second, the analysis does not explicitly quantify the effect of alternative policy mechanisms on the marginal utility or willingness to pay for land conservation or development outcomes.

Table 12-6. Combined Choice Model Results

	Burrillville random effects logit model		Exeter random effects logit model	
	Parameter estimate	z statistic	Parameter estimate	z statistic
Linear attributes				
Intercept	0.07758	1.00	−0.22687	−2.77***
Edge-area ratio	0.19372	6.00***	0.15199	4.29***
Two-part cluster	−0.32325	−1.51	−0.51347	−2.22**
Four-part cluster	−0.62014	−3.86***	−0.50080	−2.98***
Isolated open space	0.00869	5.24***	0.00720	3.92***
Adjacent open space	0.00473	5.47***	0.00479	5.23***
On-road development	−0.32627	−2.60***	−0.36659	−2.72***
Large mammal	0.20133	3.12***	0.17991	2.76***
Small mammal	−0.07232	−1.15	−0.08848	−1.39
Common bird	0.12395	2.83***	0.09654	2.02**
Uncommon bird	−0.06152	−1.39	0.02437	0.56
Wetland species	0.02315	0.51	0.08757	1.80*
Development density	−1.10914	−10.34***	−1.05341	−9.75***
Development size	−0.00706	−6.36***	−0.00866	−7.18***
Traffic light	0.24119	2.17**	0.14324	1.26
Low-visibility development	0.16377	1.51	0.24504	2.17**
Tax change	−0.00525	−9.09***	−0.00631	−9.86***
Factor 1 interactions				
Pro-zoning × edge-area ratio	0.03617	1.11	0.02745	0.82
Pro-zoning × two-part cluster	−0.34357	−1.48	−0.09642	−0.39

Continued

Table 12-6. (*Continued*)

Burrillville random effects logit model

	Parameter estimate	z statistic
Factor 1 interactions		
Pro-zoning × four-part cluster	0.07518	0.44
Pro-zoning × isolated open space	0.00113	0.71
Pro-zoning × adjacent open space	-0.00003	-0.04
Pro-zoning × on-road development	-0.00938	-0.07
Pro-zoning × large mammal	0.00759	0.12
Pro-zoning × small mammal	0.01526	0.24
Pro-zoning × common bird	-0.01672	-0.36
Pro-zoning × uncommon bird	-0.09371	-2.03**
Pro-zoning × wetland species	0.03232	0.68
Pro-zoning × development density	-0.22294	-2.14**
Pro-zoning × development size	-0.00145	-1.29
Pro-zoning × traffic light	0.07196	0.66
Pro-zoning × low-visibility development	0.16377	1.38
Pro-zoning × tax change	0.00194	3.44***
Factor 2 interactions		
Pro-develop × edge-area ratio	-0.00051	-0.02
Pro-develop × two-part cluster	-0.04866	-0.21
Pro-develop × four-part cluster	0.25963	1.55
Pro-develop × isolated open space	-0.00118	-0.70
Pro-develop × adjacent open space	-0.00000	-0.00
Pro-develop × on-road development	0.21904	1.81*
Pro-develop × large mammal	0.03904	0.59
Pro-develop × small mammal	0.04285	0.68

Exeter random effects logit model

	Parameter estimate	z statistic
Factor 1 interactions		
Pro-zoning × four-part cluster	-0.37666	-2.12**
Pro-zoning × isolated open space	0.00511	2.44**
Pro-zoning × adjacent open space	0.00186	1.92*
Pro-zoning × on-road development	0.03739	0.27
Pro-zoning × large mammal	0.06156	0.90
Pro-zoning × small mammal	0.05665	0.87
Pro-zoning × common bird	-0.05187	-1.04
Pro-zoning × uncommon bird	0.00150	0.03
Pro-zoning × wetland species	0.02661	0.50
Pro-zoning × development density	-0.08365	-0.87
Pro-zoning × development size	-0.00047	-0.38
Pro-zoning × traffic light	-0.01987	-0.17
Pro-zoning × low-visibility development	0.19556	1.66*
Pro-zoning × tax change	-0.00004	-0.07
Factor 2 interactions		
Restrict develop × edge-area ratio	0.04612	1.34
Restrict develop × two-part cluster	-0.04645	-0.21
Restrict develop × four-part cluster	-0.21466	-1.18
Restrict develop × isolated open space	0.00100	0.53
Restrict develop × adjacent open space	-0.00039	-0.40
Restrict develop × on-road development	0.00713	0.05
Restrict develop × large mammal	0.02898	0.43
Restrict develop × small mammal	0.03271	0.49

Variable	Coefficient	t-value
Pro-develop × common bird	−0.03845	−0.89
Pro-develop × uncommon bird	0.00071	0.02
Pro-develop × wetland species	−0.05858	−1.24
Pro-develop × development density	0.25970	2.68***
Pro-develop × development size	0.00223	2.08**
Pro-develop × traffic light	0.17265	1.57
Pro-develop × low-visibility development	0.09646	0.88
Pro-develop × tax change	−0.00056	−1.09

Factor 3 interactions

Variable	Coefficient	t-value
Anti-fee × edge-area ratio	−0.00821	−0.27
Anti-fee × two-part cluster	−0.11404	−0.52
Anti-fee × four-part cluster	0.09276	0.58
Anti-fee × isolated open space	−0.00200	−1.18
Anti-fee × adjacent open space	−0.00155	−1.74*
Anti-fee × on-road development	−0.11520	−0.93
Anti-fee × large mammal	0.03776	0.58
Anti-fee × small mammal	−0.09316	−1.49
Anti-fee × common bird	0.10055	2.24**
Anti-fee × uncommon bird	−0.05620	−1.31
Anti-fee × wetland species	−0.03083	−0.67
Anti-fee × development density	0.09999	1.14
Anti-fee × development size	0.00094	0.81
Anti-fee × traffic light	−0.16560	−1.48
Anti-fee × low-visibility development	0.12544	1.13
Anti-fee × tax change	−0.00033	−0.63

Factor 4 interactions

Variable	Coefficient	t-value
Pro-purchase × edge-area ratio	0.03820	1.21
Pro-purchase × two-part cluster	−0.40161	−1.83*

Variable	Coefficient	t-value
Restrict develop × common bird	0.01197	0.25
Restrict develop × uncommon bird	−0.02369	−0.49
Restrict develop × wetland species	−0.02347	−0.47
Restrict develop × development density	−0.02512	−0.26
Restrict develop × development size	0.00240	1.98**
Restrict develop × traffic light	0.01346	0.11
Restrict develop × low-visibility development	0.10386	0.88
Restrict develop × tax change	0.00133	2.24**

Factor 3 interactions

Variable	Coefficient	t-value
Pro-develop × edge-area ratio	−0.04005	−1.18
Pro-develop × two-part cluster	−0.01097	−0.05
Pro-develop × four-part cluster	0.15616	0.90
Pro-develop × isolated open space	0.00342	1.83*
Pro-develop × adjacent open space	−0.00055	−0.60
Pro-develop × on-road development	0.08319	0.62
Pro-develop × large mammal	−0.12396	−1.82*
Pro-develop × small mammal	−0.06639	−1.05
Pro-develop × common bird	0.01158	0.23
Pro-develop × uncommon bird	−0.09249	−1.97**
Pro-develop × wetland species	0.04576	0.89
Pro-develop × development density	0.32707	3.29***
Pro-develop × development size	0.00062	0.51
Pro-develop × traffic light	0.10391	0.91
Pro-develop × low-visibility development	0.21997	1.84*
Pro-develop × tax change	−0.00011	−0.19

Factor 4 interactions

Variable	Coefficient	t-value
Anti-purchase × edge-area ratio	−0.01431	−0.41
Anti-purchase × two-part cluster	0.00413	0.02

Continued

Table 12-6. (*Continued*)

Burrillville random effects logit model	Parameter estimate	z statistic	Exeter random effects logit model	Parameter estimate	z statistic
Factor 4 interactions			**Factor 4 interactions**		
Pro-purchase × four-part cluster	0.00492	0.03	Anti-purchase × four-part cluster	−0.10306	−0.58
Pro-purchase × isolated open space	0.00200	1.22	Anti-purchase × isolated open space	−0.00213	−1.01
Pro-purchase × adjacent open space	0.00134	1.57	Anti-purchase × adjacent open space	−0.00147	−1.52
Pro-purchase × on-road development	−0.00009	−0.00	Anti-purchase × on-road development	−0.14861	−1.07
Pro-purchase × large mammal	−0.08574	−1.35	Anti-purchase × large mammal	−0.06191	−0.92
Pro-purchase × small mammal	0.11317	1.75*	Anti-purchase × small mammal	0.00138	0.02
Pro-purchase × common bird	−0.02193	−0.50	Anti-purchase × common bird	0.06176	1.19
Pro-purchase × uncommon bird	0.00068	0.01	Anti-purchase × uncommon bird	−0.03672	−0.81
Pro-purchase × wetland species	0.00214	0.05	Anti-purchase × wetland species	0.03901	0.76
Pro-purchase × development density	−0.13803	−1.39	Anti-purchase × development density	−0.05802	−0.56
Pro-purchase × development size	−0.00063	−0.57	Anti-purchase × development size	0.00137	1.09
Pro-purchase × traffic light	0.12755	1.14	Anti-purchase × traffic light	0.01084	0.09
Pro-purchase × low-visibility development	0.01603	0.14	Anti-purchase × low-visibility development	−0.00098	−0.01
Pro-purchase × tax change	0.00057	1.08	Anti-purchase × tax change	−0.00301	−4.72***
Factor 5 interactions			**Factor 5 interactions**		
Pro-tax × edge-area ratio	0.05578	1.65*	Anti-fee × edge-area ratio	−0.05868	−1.66*
Pro-tax × two-part cluster	−0.16358	−0.68	Anti-fee × two-part cluster	0.11907	0.48
Pro-tax × four-part cluster	−0.37328	−2.14**	Anti-fee × four-part cluster	0.11236	0.66
Pro-tax × isolated open space	0.00380	2.30**	Anti-fee × isolated open space	0.00013	0.06
Pro-tax × adjacent open space	0.00122	1.41	Anti-fee × adjacent open space	0.00007	0.07
Pro-tax × on-road development	−0.15582	−1.17	Anti-fee × on-road development	−0.00848	−0.06

Pro-tax × large mammal	0.00587	0.09
Pro-tax × small mammal	−0.04116	−0.65
Pro-tax × common bird	−0.00322	−0.07
Pro-tax × uncommon bird	−0.00981	−0.21
Pro-tax × wetland species	0.08994	1.85*
Pro-tax × development density	−0.02141	−0.22
Pro-tax × development size	0.00144	1.27
Pro-tax × traffic light	−0.03947	−0.36
Pro-tax × low-visibility development	−0.02486	−0.22
Pro-tax × tax change	0.00124	2.28**

Anti-fee × large mammal	−0.10928	−1.59
Anti-fee × small mammal	0.06736	1.03
Anti-fee × common bird	−0.01664	−0.34
Anti-fee × uncommon bird	0.03435	0.76
Anti-fee × wetland species	−0.09721	−1.91*
Anti-fee × development density	0.25776	2.87***
Anti-fee × development size	0.00145	1.21
Anti-fee × traffic light	−0.09829	−0.84
Anti-fee × low-visibility development	0.01059	0.09
Anti-fee × tax change	0.00067	1.29

Factor 6 interactions

Pro-tax × edge-area ratio	−0.02745	−0.81
Pro-tax × two-part cluster	0.13583	0.56
Pro-tax × four-part cluster	−0.07082	−0.42
Pro-tax × isolated open space	0.00043	0.23
Pro-tax × adjacent open space	0.00185	1.93*
Pro-tax × on-road development	0.08520	0.61
Pro-tax × large mammal	0.00645	0.10
Pro-tax × small mammal	0.00846	0.12
Pro-tax × common bird	−0.02302	−0.47
Pro-tax × uncommon bird	−0.04701	−0.97
Pro-tax × wetland species	0.01100	0.21
Pro-tax × development density	−0.07494	−0.80
Pro-tax × development size	−0.00319	−2.63***
Pro-tax × traffic light	0.08810	0.70
Pro-tax × low-visibility development	0.03707	0.31
Pro-tax × tax change	0.00347	5.24***

Continued

Table 12-6. (*Continued*)

	Burrillville random effects logit model		Exeter random effects logit model	
	Parameter estimate	z statistic	Parameter estimate	z statistic
Factor 6 interactions				
Factor main effects				
Factor main effects				
Pro-zoning	−0.05777	−0.73	0.12860	1.50
Pro-develop	−0.01081	−0.14		
Restrict develop			0.09911	1.12
Pro-develop			−0.06941	−0.83
Anti-fee	0.11629	1.46		
Anti-purchase			−0.08285	−0.95
Pro-purchase	−0.07608	−0.96		
Anti-fee			0.16370	2.02**
Pro-tax	−0.04493	−0.55	0.03015	0.35
−2LnLχ²	575.50***		670.18***	

* p < 0.10; ** p < 0.05; *** p < 0.01

Given these limitations, one promising direction for future research would be to incorporate detailed descriptions of policy options into choice questions evaluated by respondents. Analysts could then assess individuals' support for different policy mechanisms relative to the utility associated with land use outcomes. Such research, funded by the USDA National Research Initiative (Duke and Johnston 2002), is currently ongoing. More advanced analysis might also explore trade-offs among the attributes of the policy tools themselves, such as preferences for long-term flexibility, equity, and the distribution of benefits and costs. Qualitative research suggests that even subtle aspects of policy attributes and descriptions can have substantial implications for the reaction of voters. For example, Weigel et al. (2004) demonstrates that individuals make clear distinctions among policies based on issues such as whether programs involve voluntary or mandatory actions on the part of landowners, represent a "fair" return to taxpayers, or impose permanent restrictions on property rights. These and other details of policy implementation often are suppressed by economists when assessing values. Formal, quantitative research in this area could greatly facilitate academics' ability to extend the tools of preference assessment to aid in designing more successful land use policy programs.

Technical Appendix: A Choice Model of Preferences for Land Use Outcomes

Respondents' choices are assessed using a standard random utility (Hanemann 1984). To model a respondent's choice among policy plans, we define a utility function that includes attributes of a rural land use plan and the net cost of the plan to the respondent:

$$U(\cdot) = U(X_c, Y - F_c) = v(X_c, Y - F_c) + \varepsilon_c. \tag{12-1}$$

Here, X_c is a vector of variables describing attributes of policy plan c, Y is the disposable income of the respondent, F_c is the change in mandatory taxes and fees paid by the respondent under plan c, $v(\cdot)$ is a function representing the empirically measurable component of utility, and ε_c is econometric error.

The respondent compares a current development plan ($c = A$) and an alternate development plan ($c = B$) such that the change in utility (dU) is given by

$$dU = U(X_A, Y - F_A) - U(X_B, Y - F_B) = [v(X_A, Y - F_A)$$
$$-v(X_B, Y - F_B)] - [\varepsilon_B - \varepsilon_A] = dv - \theta. \tag{12-2}$$

The model assumes that a respondent assesses the difference in utility between the two plans and indicates the sign of dU by choosing either the current ($dU > 0$) or alternate ($dU < 0$) plan.

As the choice data comprise three choice experiment responses per survey, there is a possibility of correlated errors across responses (Alberini et al. 1997; Poe et al. 1997). We model this potential error correlation by splitting θ in Equation 12-2 into two components: $\tilde{\theta}$, which is iid across all respondents and for each individual respondent, and γ_h, representing systematic variation related to unobserved characteristics of respondent h. If the γ_h are assumed normally distributed across respondents, and we assume that $\tilde{\theta}$ has a logistic distribution, the model may be estimated as a random effects logit model (Greene 2003).

Endnotes

1. The statistical design was completed by Don Anderson of StatDesign.
2. The relative magnitude of marginal utility is indicated by the relative magnitudes of parameter estimates shown in Table 12-2.
3. An eigenvalue may be characterized as follows: if a nonzero vector $\mathbf{V}$ exists such that a matrix $\mathbf{A}$ multiplied by $\mathbf{V}$ is equal to $\mathbf{V}$ multiplied by a scalar λ, then λ may be referred to as the eigenvalue of matrix $\mathbf{A}$. Eigenvalues have many potential applications. Here, they are used to identify estimated factors that account for a relatively large portion of the observable variation in Likert-scale responses.
4. Preliminary models were estimated to assess whether the choice models should be amended to incorporate additional interactions with demographic attributes, such as age, education, and income. Likelihood ratio tests assessing the joint significance of appended interactions fail to reject the null hypothesis of zero joint influence at $p < 0.10$ for combined quadratic interactions, including a respondent's age, length of residency, and dummy variables indicating respondents with at least a four-year college education and those with income below \$40k (Burrillville $\chi^2 = 76.77$, df $= 68$; Exeter $-2LnL$ $\chi^2 = 81.60$, df $= 68$). Based on these results, we proceed with a final model that includes interactions with factor scores as detailed above but excludes interactions with demographic attributes.

References

Adamowicz, W., P. Boxall, M. Williams, and J. Louviere. (1998). Stated Preference Approaches for Measuring Passive Use Values: Choice Experiments and Contingent Valuation. *American Journal of Agricultural Economics* 80(1): 64–75.

Alberini, A., B. Kanninen, and R. T. Carson. (1997). Modeling Response Incentive Effects in Dichotomous Choice Contingent Valuation Data. *Land Economics* 73(3): 309–24.

Blamey, R. K., J. W. Bennett, and M. D. Morrison. (1999). Yea-Saying in Contingent Valuation Surveys. *Land Economics* 75(1): 126–41.

Bollen, K. (1989). *Structural Equations with Latent Variables*. New York: Wiley.

Boyle, K. J., H. F. MacDonald, H. Cheng, and D. W. McCollum. (1998). Bid Design and Yea Saying in Single-Bounded, Dichotomous Choice Questions. *Land Economics* 74(1): 49–64.

Bulte, E., S. Gerking, J. A. List, and A. de Zeeuw. (2005). The Effect of Varying the Causes of Environmental Problems on Stated WTP Values: Evidence from a Field Study. *Journal of Environmental Economics and Management* 49(2): 330–42.

Dillman. D. A. (2000). *Mail and Internet Surveys: The Tailored Design Method*. New York: John Wiley and Sons.

Duke, J., and R. J. Johnston. (2002). Land Conservation Techniques and Service Implementation: Assessing Context-Sensitive Priorities for the Policy Process. Proposal to USDA/CSREES/NRI. Newark: University of Delaware.

Greene, W. H. (2003). *Econometric Analysis*. 5th ed. Upper Saddle River, NJ: Prentice Hall.

Hanemann, W. M. (1984). Welfare Evaluations in Contingent Valuation Experiments with Discrete Responses. *American Journal of Agricultural Economics* 66(3): 332–41.

Johnston, R. J., D. M. Bauer, and S. K. Swallow. (2000). The Rhode Island Rural Land Use Survey. Kingston: Department of Environmental and Natural Resource Economics, University of Rhode Island.

Johnston, R. J., S. K. Swallow, and D. M. Bauer. (2002). Spatial Factors and Stated Preference Values for Public Goods: Considerations for Rural Land Development. *Land Economics* 78(4): 481–500.

Johnston, R. J., S. K. Swallow, D. M. Bauer, and C. M. Anderson. (2003). Preferences for Residential Development Attributes and Support for the Policy Process: Implications for Management and Conservation of Rural Landscapes. *Agricultural and Resource Economics Review* 32(1): 65–82.

Johnston, R. J., S. K. Swallow, and T. F. Weaver. (1999). Estimating Willingness to Pay and Resource Trade-Offs with Different Payment Mechanisms: An Evaluation of a Funding Guarantee for Watershed Management. *Journal of Environmental Economics and Management* 38(1): 97–120.

Johnston, R. J., T. F. Weaver, L. A. Smith, and S. K. Swallow. (1995). Contingent Valuation Focus Groups: Insights from Ethnographic Interview Techniques. *Agricultural and Resource Economics Review* 24(1): 56–69.

Johnston, R. J., C. R. Wessells, H. Donath, and F. Asche. (2001). Measuring Consumer Preferences for Ecolabeled Seafood: An International Comparison. *Journal of Agricultural and Resource Economics* 26(1): 20–39.

Kask, S. B., L. G. Mathews, S. Stewart, and L. Rotegard. (2002). Blue Ridge Parkway Scenic Experience Project Final Report. Report submitted in fulfillment of cooperative agreement CA5143990137. U.S. National Park Service.

Kline, J., and D. Wichelns. 1998. Measuring Heterogeneous Preferences for Preserving Farmland and Open Space. *Ecological Economics* 26(2): 211–24.

Philo, L. D., and R. J. Johnston. (2004). Land-Use Survey Examines Preferences for Conservation vs. Conservation Policy. *41° N: The Magazine of Rhode Island Land and Sea Grant* 2(2): 24–26.

Poe, G. L., M. P. Welsh, and P. A. Champ. (1997). Measuring the Difference in Mean Willingness to Pay When Dichotomous Choice Contingent Valuation Responses Are Not Independent. *Land Economics* 73(2): 255–67.

Reyment, R., and K. Joreskog. (1996). *Applied Factor Analysis in the Natural Sciences.* Cambridge: Cambridge University Press.

Rosenberger, R. S., R. G. Walsh, J. R. McKean, and C. J. Mucklow. (1996). Benefits of Ranch Open Space to Local Residents. Extension Bulletin XCM-201. Fort Collins: Cooperative Extension Agricultural Experiment Station, Colorado State University.

Variyam, J. N., J. L. Jorday, and J. E. Epperson. (1990). Preferences of Citizens for Agricultural Policies: Evidence from a National Survey. *American Journal of Agricultural Economics* 72(2): 257–67.

Weigel, L., J. Fairbank, and D. Metz. (2004). Lessons Learned Regarding the "Language of Conservation" from the National Research Program. Memorandum to the Nature Conservancy and Trust for Public Land. Public Opinion Strategies and Fairbank, Maslin, Maullin and Associates. http://northeast.fws.gov/stateplans/ Other% 20Resources_files/.

13

Integrating Biophysical and Economic Information to Guide Land Conservation Investments

PAUL J. FERRARO

Concerns over the effects of private land use on the supply of environmental amenities have led to an increasing global reliance on conservation contracting initiatives (Ferraro and Kiss 2002). The term "conservation contracting" describes the contractual transfer of payments from one party (e.g., government) to another (e.g., landowner) in exchange for land use practices that contribute to the supply of an environmental amenity. Such contracts include easements and short-term conservation leases. A key issue in the design of conservation contracting initiatives, as with any conservation policy, is how to integrate information about spatially variable biophysical and economic conditions into a cost-effective plan.

Much of the previous work on targeting scarce conservation funds has focused on the conservation of biological diversity. Targeting approaches favored by biological scientists and conservationists emphasize the environmental amenities that a given land unit produces, while often ignoring the costs of acquiring those amenities. For example, Dobson et al. (1997), based on their finding that endangered species in the United States were concentrated spatially, suggest that conservationists should focus their efforts on a small number of geographic areas. In response, Ando et al. (1998) assert that variability in economic factors is just as important as ecological variability in efficient species conservation, specifically noting that an approach that considers both economic and ecological variability could cost less than one-sixth the cost of an approach considering only ecological variability. A similar debate has developed over targeting ecosystem conservation investments at the global scale (Mittermeir et al. 1998; Balmford et al. 2000). Other studies by economists have demonstrated the importance of integrating biophysical and economic data, such as Polasky et al. (2001) in the case of species conservation in Oregon and Babcock et al. (1996, 1997) regarding the U.S. Conservation Reserve Program.

This chapter extends these previous analyses in several ways. First, the analysis presented here focuses on an increasingly common but little studied initiative: conservation contracting for water quality objectives. The results of the empirical analysis support previous empirical work suggesting that the failure to incorporate cost data in conservation investment decisions can lead to large efficiency losses. Moreover, studies of cost-efficient targeting (e.g., Ando et al. 1998; Polasky et al. 2001; Babcock et al. 1996, 1997) tend to focus on a single biophysical attribute, such as species absence or presence, erodibility of soil, or distance to water. Such a narrow focus, however, fails to consider the full range of biophysical attributes critical to the supply of an environmental amenity. Most conservation initiatives, such as the U.S. Conservation Reserve Program (USDA 1999) or World Wildlife Fund's Global 200 initiative (Olson et al. 2000), identify multiple biophysical attributes of interest.

In the context of habitat protection, Prendergast et al. (1999) point out that practitioners and policymakers rarely use the tools and results published in the academic literature, in large part because their development and application have not taken into account the objectives and approaches of practitioners and policymakers. To address this oversight, the empirical application of this chapter uses data available to decisionmakers and considers explicitly the actual approaches they use in the field. Additionally, the problem is approached at the geographic scale at which decisions are being made: individual parcels rather than large administrative districts or geographical information system (GIS) polygons on the landscape. We recognize that often little consensus exists about the appropriate way to estimate the environmental benefits provided by a single parcel and thus use multiple methods to guide the empirical analysis.

Scientific information increasingly suggests that biophysical thresholds are important when designing conservation initiatives. This chapter demonstrates the incorporation of such thresholds into the decisionmaking process, comparing the conservation contract portfolios selected with and without threshold constraints in the empirical analysis.

We begin by introducing the case study for the empirical analysis. Next, the data are characterized and the decision model developed, followed by the results of the empirical analysis. The model is then adapted to incorporate thresholds, and the effects of thresholds on the selection of optimal conservation contract portfolios are examined. Finally, we explore reasons why economic approaches to targeting land conservation investments are not often applied in practice.

Case Study: The Lake Skaneateles Watershed Program

The use of conservation contracts to achieve water quality objectives is becoming an increasingly popular policy tool (Johnson et al. 2001). The New York City Watershed Management Plan will spend $250 million on conservation contracting with private landowners in the Catskill–Delaware watershed over the next 10 years to protect the city's water supply and maintain its filtration waiver from the Environmental Protection Agency (EPA) (NRC 2000, *213–39*). Other initiatives include North Carolina's $400 million Clean Water Management Trust Fund (NCCWMTF 2003), Massachusetts's $60 million effort to acquire riparian land to protect Boston's Wachusett Reservoir (MDC 1999), and Costa Rica's $16 million-per-year attempt to secure conservation contracts in the watersheds of municipal water supplies and hydroelectric dams, among other areas (Snider et al. 2003).

In particular, scientists and policymakers have identified the establishment of vegetated riparian zones, which protect surface waters from inputs of nutrients, pesticides, eroded soil, and pathogens, as an important policy for improving water quality (Tilman et al. 2001). One such riparian buffer acquisition initiative is currently under way in upstate New York. The city of Syracuse (population 163,860) obtains its drinking water from Lake Skaneateles, which is located outside of the city's regulatory jurisdiction. The lake is 16 miles long and less than 1 mile wide on average, and its 60-square-mile watershed covers three counties, seven townships, and one village. The population of the watershed is about 5,000 residents, concentrated largely around the northern half of the lake, where the city's intake pipes are located. Land use is mainly a mix of forest (40 percent) and agriculture (48 percent), with cropping and dairy farming the most common.

The water from the lake is of exceptionally high quality, and the city, using only disinfection by chlorination, meets drinking water standards without coagulation or filtration.[1] In recent years, however, the city has come under increasing pressure to consider filtration in order to satisfy the provisions of the EPA's Surface Water Treatment Rule. In 1994, the city signed a memorandum of agreement (MOA) with the New York State Department of Health allowing it to avoid filtering water from the lake. The MOA requires that the city commit to a long-term watershed management program to reduce pathogen, chemical, nutrient, and sediment loading into the lake, an important part of which is a conservation easement acquisition program through which up to $5 million will be spent over a seven-year period (2001–2008) to secure easements on privately owned riparian parcels. By securing easements on riparian buffers in the watershed, the city hopes to avoid, or delay, the estimated $60 million to $70 million cost of a new filtration plant. The city wants to allocate its limited budget across the watershed in a way that will have the greatest effect on maintaining and improving water quality in the lake (Myers et al. 1998).

The focus of this analysis is on prioritizing the acquisition of easements from an available population of 202 riparian parcels in the upper watershed of Lake Skaneateles. Biophysical and economic data on these parcels were obtained from the geographical information system (GIS) database of Syracuse's Department of Water.[2] The southwestern end of the lake is protected public land and therefore is excluded from the analysis. Data on parcels at the southeastern end of the lake were not available at the time of analysis, but because they are far from the city's intake pipes, their exclusion is expected to have only minor effects on the final results.

Data and Conceptual Approach

Each riparian parcel in the watershed, when protected by an easement, is assumed to generate environmental benefits, e_i, to the city of Syracuse at a cost of $c_i + t_i$, where c_i represents the reservation price of the landowner for accepting an easement on his or her property and t_i is the transaction cost associated with creating and monitoring a contract. The unit of analysis is the parcel. Within each parcel, environmental benefits and costs are assumed to be uniformly distributed. In other words, acres on each parcel are considered homogeneous with regard to both environmental benefits and productive uses. These values may differ across different parcels, however. These are the same assumptions Syracuse used in its easement acquisition program.

Benefit Data. The city wishes to reduce sediment, chemical, pathogen, and nutrient loading into its water supply. Sophisticated hydrological models are not available for the Lake Skaneateles watershed, so to measure the contribution of each parcel to the city's water quality objectives, the Department of Water convened a scientific panel to help it develop a parcel-scoring system based on known land attributes in the watershed (Myers et al. 1998). The panel developed two potential systems: an interval-scale and a ratio-scale scoring equation. The equations, which are given in the appendix to this chapter, assign a score to each parcel; the higher the score, the higher the benefit from easement acquisition. Two other common parcel-scoring methods, the categorical scoring system (similar to that used by the U.S. Conservation Reserve Program) and the parcel-pollutant-weighting (PPW) model (Azzaino et al. 2002), are also used in the empirical analysis and are described in the appendix.

The interval-scale, ratio-scale, and categorical scoring equations use the same biophysical characteristics but weigh and normalize them differently (the characteristics have to be normalized so that parcel scores are not fundamentally altered by changes in measurement units). The PPW scoring equation differs from the other three in that it combines information on biophysical characteristics and results from pollution modeling in order to score each parcel.

Neither theory nor extant empirical evidence argues for the superiority of one scoring method over the others.

All four benefit-measuring methods generate parcel scores either from weighted linear functions of the attributes or by assignment of points to each parcel based on its biophysical attributes or land uses. Such scoring methods are quite common in the academic literature (e.g., Lemunyon and Gilbert 1993; Voogd 1983); federal agency guidelines (e.g., Allen 1983; Allen and Hoffman 1984; McMahon 1983; Terrell et al. 1982; USFWS 1981); water quality protection initiatives (e.g., FDEP 2000; Hruby et al. 2000; MDC 1999; Rowles and Sitlinger 1999; Smith et al. 1995); and the multibillion-dollar conservation efforts of the U.S. Conservation Reserve Program (Feather et al. 1998), land trusts (e.g., The Nature Conservancy; Master 1991), international habitat protection groups (e.g., World Wildlife Fund; see Olson et al. 2000), national wildlife protection initiatives (e.g., Partners in Flight, documented by Carter et al. 1999), and farmland protection initiatives (e.g., American Farmland Trust).[3]

In the absence of sophisticated hydrological models for the Skaneateles watershed, it is not possible to determine which of the four parcel-scoring methods is best.[4] If there is positive correlation among the different scoring methods (which would be expected if they are all attempting to measure the same amenity), a simple approach to prioritizing easement acquisition would be to identify the optimal buffer portfolios selected under several scoring methods and then identify a set of "high-priority" parcels that includes only those found in every portfolio (i.e., parcels in common within each optimal portfolio across the parcel-scoring methods). This approach is applied in the section on empirical results. As Table 13-1 demonstrates, the Spearman correlations among the parcel scores assigned by each scoring method are strongly positive.

Cost Data. It was not possible to estimate a hedonic equation of easement costs because of a lack of observations on sales of properties with easements in the region. A regional appraising company (Gardner 2000) estimated that the city would have to pay between 40 and 60 percent of a parcel's assessed land value to obtain an easement. An estimate of 50 percent is used in this analysis. A change in the percentage would affect only the number of parcels that can be

Table 13-1. Correlations among Parcel Scores by Scoring Method

Scoring method	Interval-scale	Ratio-scale	Categorical	PPW
Interval-scale	1			
Ratio-scale	0.96	1		
Categorical	0.94	0.92	1	
PPW	0.75	0.81	0.77	1

acquired for a given budget, not the order in which they are acquired. Based on transaction cost information from the Finger Lakes Land Trust, which operates in the region, a transaction cost of $5,000 per easement is also assumed. Varying the transaction cost from $2,500 to $12,500 did not generate dramatic changes in the parcel rankings.[5] Future analyses can incorporate new information on costs gathered by practitioners in the course of contacting landowners. The city also may want to consider using a procurement auction to solicit reservation prices from landowners (Cummings et al. 2003).

Optimal Easement Portfolio Selection Problem. An optimal easement acquisition program for the city of Syracuse can be viewed as one that maximizes the total benefit score subject to a budget constraint (see appendix for a more formal representation). This maximization problem is equivalent to ranking parcels from highest to lowest based on their $e_i/(c_i + t_i)$ ratio and accepting contracts until the budget is exhausted.

The city did not formulate its approach to easement acquisition in this manner, however. As with many conservation initiatives (e.g., Mittermeir et al. 1998), Syracuse planned to allocate its funds by ranking parcels from the highest score (e_i) to the lowest and acquiring easements until the budget was exhausted. In this approach, a critical level of environmental benefit, $\bar{e}$, exists for which all parcels with $e_i > \bar{e}$ are contracted.

The city's prioritization formulation ignores the opportunity costs of contracted parcels, and as suggested by previous empirical analyses, its portfolio for any given budget will generate lower benefit scores than the portfolio generated from the optimal portfolio. How much lower is an empirical question.

Empirical Results

Current city plans call for the expenditure of $1 million to $2.5 million on conservation easements, followed by an evaluation of whether further easement acquisitions are required. We therefore solve the optimal easement portfolio problem under each scoring method for budgets of $D = $1 million and $D = $2.5 million (maps of the corresponding optimal portfolios can be found in Ferraro 2002).

Table 13-2 presents, for each benefit-scoring method, the percentage of total environmental benefits available in the watershed that are secured by the optimal portfolio and by the portfolio that ignores opportunity costs (i.e., funds are allocated based on benefit scores alone). Consistent with previous research, large efficiency losses are associated with ignoring costs in the funding allocation decision. For a budget of $1 million, the benefit-only approach achieves 16 to 42 percent of that which the optimal approach achieves; for a budget of $2.5 million, it achieves 36 to 65 percent. The large efficiency gains from incorporating economic costs explicitly in the decisionmaking derive from the moderate

Table 13-2. Portfolio Performance When Opportunity Costs Are Ignored

Scoring method	Acquisition method	$D = \$1\ million$ % of total watershed benefits $\left(\sum\limits_{i=1}^{202} p_i\, e_i \middle/ \sum\limits_{i=1}^{202} e_i\right)$	$D = \$2.5\ million$ % of total watershed benefits $\left(\sum\limits_{i=1}^{202} p_i\, e_i \middle/ \sum\limits_{i=1}^{202} e_i\right)$
Interval-scale	*Optimal*	31%	62%
	Ignoring costs	8%	22%
Ratio-scale	*Optimal*	37%	72%
	Ignoring costs	15%	41%
Categorical	*Optimal*	31%	61%
	Ignoring costs	5%	26%
PPW	*Optimal*	39%	72%
	Ignoring costs	9%	47%

positive correlation between benefit (e_i) and cost (c_i) measures and the greater relative heterogeneity of costs compared with that of benefits (Ferraro 2003).

Although the formulation that integrates benefit and cost data is clearly beneficial, each scoring method generates a different "optimal" portfolio. One way to proceed would be to identify the parcels selected for acquisition under all four scoring methods. These parcels might be regarded as high-priority for an easement acquisition program because they are found in all four optimal buffers. Such an approach would fit well with Syracuse's approach to easement acquisition. Although the city has estimated that it might spend up to $5 million for easement acquisition, it plans to begin acquiring easements sequentially and evaluate periodically whether more will need to be acquired to meet water quality goals. Thus the city wants to know with which parcels it should begin its acquisition efforts. The set of high-priority parcels would be a reasonable place to start. For any given available budget, one can identify a set of priority parcels that exhausts the budget by changing the value of the budget under which the optimal buffers are derived.

Solving for the portfolios when the budget is $1 million, 11 parcels are found in each of the four optimal buffer solutions, and these easements can be acquired for $210,900. With a budget of $2.5 million, 46 parcels are found, at a cost of $1,445,150. Table 13-3 demonstrates how well the high-priority set of parcels performs compared with the optimal portfolios chosen under the four scoring equations when the budget is $210,900 and $1,445,150. For example, the high-priority portfolio, were its parcels to be scored according to the interval-scale scoring equation, achieves 92 percent of the benefits that are achieved by the optimal portfolio at a budget of $1,445,150. The data in the table suggest that even if one of the scoring equations were the true measure

Table 13-3. High-Priority Portfolio Performance under Four Parcel-Scoring Methods

	Percentage of total benefits achieved by high-priority portfolio			
Budget	*Interval-scale*	*Ratio-scale*	*Categorical*	*PPW*
$210,900	72%	82%	78%	82%
$1,445,150	92%	79%	82%	92%

of parcel benefits, the city of Syracuse would not lose a substantial amount of efficiency by selecting the high-priority portfolio of parcels.

Thus, as in previous analyses that looked at conservation investments in other contexts, we find that integrating both cost and benefit information explicitly into the decisionmaking in Lake Skaneateles can be vital to ensuring that scarce funds go as far as they can toward achieving policy objectives. The costs of acquiring and analyzing such information, however, can be substantial. Under which conditions is integrating cost and benefit information likely to be vital to effective decisionmaking, and under which conditions will the failure to use both cost and benefit data result in little, if any, loss in efficiency?

Assigning priority to land conservation investments on the basis of biophysical data alone would be appropriate only if benefits and costs were negatively correlated across sites *and* the relative spatial variability of benefits was greater than that of costs. If these two conditions do not hold, as they do not in Lake Skaneateles, an approach that ignores the heterogeneity of conservation costs across sites would perform poorly in ensuring that every dollar spent achieves the maximum environmental benefits possible.

Hence, in a habitat restoration program, for example, we would expect that the greater the positive spatial correlation between environmental benefits and restoration costs, and the greater the spatial variability of restoration costs compared with the variability of environmental benefits, the greater the efficiency losses if conservation agents ignore costs when making decisions on where to restore habitat. Even if costs and benefits were negatively correlated, but relative cost variability was much greater than relative benefit variability, large gains could result from integrating restoration costs into the prioritization process.

Ferraro 2003 demonstrates that the policy context in the case of investments in endangered-species recovery in the United States has attributes similar to those in the city of Syracuse case: benefits (reflected in the priority scores) and recovery costs are positively correlated, and recovery costs are more variable than priority scores across species. In such a situation, allocating funds based on priority scores alone would be quite inefficient in terms of obtaining the greatest benefit with available conservation funds. In fact, Ferraro shows that policy analysts examining expenditure decisions in this environment may find little or no positive relationship between the priority scores and the extent and likelihood of funding for species recovery when funds are being spent to maximize the environmental benefits of every dollar (because efficient expenditure decisions are determined mainly by cost variability).

Data from Balmford et al. (2003) suggest that at the global scale, the costs of habitat protection are spatially negatively correlated with the spatial benefits (using bird species density as a proxy for the benefits of habitat protection). High-biodiversity areas typically are found in low-income nations in which the opportunity costs of conservation are low. In such a context, focusing only on benefits may not yield a substantially inefficient conservation investment portfolio. The authors also note, however, that the habitat acquisition cost measures are much more variable than the benefit measures. Thus their analysis suggests that ignoring benefit data entirely and acquiring more detailed cost data with which to target global habitat conservation investments may be the most effective way of spending scarce conservation funds.

The same ideas can be applied to contexts in which benefits are ignored and only economic data are used to target conservation funds. For example, Ferraro 2003 examines Georgia's Environmental Protection Division (EPD) 2001 irrigation auction, in which the state compensated farmers who voluntarily agreed to stop irrigating their crops during the year. The budget was not sufficient to pay all farmers in the region, and thus the EPD asked economists at Georgia State University to design an auction to allocate the state's scarce procurement budget (Cummings et al. 2003).

Given that Georgia's irrigation water is not metered, and time and money for data collection were limited, a decision was made to allocate the "no-irrigation" contracts according to cost alone. Farmers bid the amount of money per acre they were willing to accept to forgo irrigation on their lands, the bids were ordered from lowest to highest, and the state procured contracts until the budget was spent. The decision to focus only on cost measures was justified based on agronomic expertise that suggested water use and contract costs are negatively correlated, and therefore the parcels that experience the greatest water use are also the lowest-cost parcels. Even with negative correlation between water use and contract costs, however, a high relative variability of water use compared with the relative variability of contract costs could have greatly decreased the cost-efficiency of the auction that assigned priority to contracts on the basis of cost alone. (No data exist on the spatial variability of anticipated water use among auction participants.)

In sum, results of this analysis and prior work show that conservation policies ignoring either costs or benefits in parcel selection are likely to result in a significant loss of total conservation benefits, compared with those that might be achieved under even a simplified system that considers both benefits and costs. Conditions under which nearly optimal conservation portfolios will result from prioritization strategies that ignore either benefits or costs are restrictive and unlikely to occur in a wide range of policy contexts.

Thresholds: Concepts and Problem Formulation

The emphasis on parcel-level attributes in the analysis above may be inappropriate if thresholds of riparian buffer area exist below which little, if any, water quality protection can be expected. The importance of biophysical thresholds in conservation policy design has been noted in a variety of contexts, including endangered species conservation (Lande 1987; Shaffer 1981; Wu et al. 2000) and water quality protection (Schueler 1994, 1995; Wang et al. 1997, 2000; Zoner and Limitz 1994), but only a few economic analyses have incorporated biophysical thresholds (e.g., Bulte and van Kooten 2001; Farzin 1996; Wu et al. 2000). Ignoring threshold effects, particularly when the available budget is small, may result in a substantial loss of environmental benefits. Interventions will be scattered over the landscape, and funding levels in any given target area may be inadequate to reach the threshold needed to maintain current water quality levels or achieve significant environmental improvements.

Evidence suggests that such threshold effects may indeed be relevant to land conservation for water quality or other ecological goals. In an empirical study, Wang et al. (1997) found that indicators of water quality were negatively correlated with the amount of agricultural land in the entire watershed and in a 100-meter-wide buffer along streams,[6] and that the relationship between agricultural land and water quality was nonlinear, with a substantial decline in water quality occurring after agricultural land use exceeded 50 percent. With more intensive agricultural use or urban uses, the threshold value decreased to between 10 and 20 percent.

A recent EPA (1999) report notes that "thresholds for a decline in water quality can take the form of size and amount of riparian buffer zones. Condition of riparian zones and changes in percent of buffer areas can indicate a decline in water quality due to soil erosion, sediment loading, and contaminant runoff." No general rules of thumb have been developed specifically for riparian areas, however. The empirical analysis below is intended to demonstrate one way in which biophysical thresholds can be incorporated into the targeting process, assuming that a certain threshold size is known. This is meant as an illustration only; we do not claim that such thresholds have been established in the Lake Skaneateles watershed.

The Lake Skaneateles upper watershed is made up of 16 subwatersheds, or catchments. The city has determined that each easement will be designed to secure a 100-foot-wide riparian buffer along the entire stream length of the property. The next section examines the effect of imposing a threshold requirement on the area of 100-foot-wide riparian buffer in a given catchment. Empirically, the threshold is examined at three levels: 50, 80, and 90 percent of the available riparian buffer in the catchment. With a 50 percent threshold, for example, no water quality benefits can be achieved in a catchment through conservation contracting unless at least 50 percent of the available 100-foot-wide riparian buffer is protected through easements. Thus a decisionmaker must now select not only the parcels, but also the catchments in which to establish conservation contracts.

Unlike the targeting approach used earlier, targeting conservation investments cost-efficiently in the presence of threshold effects is not as simple as ranking parcels by their benefit–cost ratio. One must have some basic understanding of constrained optimization and linear programming. The approach used below, and outlined in the appendix, can be implemented in Microsoft Excel's Solver algorithm, which allows a relatively straightforward way to program a constrained optimization problem.

Empirical Results

Again we solve for the optimal easement portfolio under each scoring method for budgets of $D = \$1$ million and $D = \$2.5$ million. As one would expect, threshold constraints result in spatial concentration of contracts on the landscape (spatial representation of the solutions can be found in Ferraro 2002). Table 13-4 presents the percentage of parcels in the optimal buffer portfolio incorporating thresholds that were also found in the optimal portfolio derived without threshold constraints.

For a given scoring method, the spatial concentration effect of thresholds on the optimal contract portfolio is generally greatest at low budget levels and high thresholds. For example, using the PPW scoring method with a budget of $1 million and a threshold of 50 percent, 85 percent of the parcels in the new threshold-constrained portfolio are also in the original optimal portfolio derived without threshold constraints. When the threshold is increased to 90 percent, only 44 percent of the parcels in the optimal portfolio also are found in the original one. At a threshold of 50 percent, a larger budget of $2.5 million increases the overlap to 92 percent. Anomalies exist, however, such as the greater overlap at a 90 percent threshold than at an 80 percent threshold under the interval-scoring method and a $1 million budget. Such anomalies can

Table 13-4. Percentage of Parcels in Optimal Portfolio under Threshold Constraints That Are Found in Original (No-Threshold) Portfolio

| *Threshold* | *D = $1 million* | | | | *D = $2.5 million* | | | |
	None	*50%*	*80%*	*90%*	*None*	*50%*	*80%*	*90%*
Interval-scale	100%	75%	65%	75%	100%	94%	89%	78%
Ratio-scale	100%	92%	71%	58%	100%	97%	87%	78%
Categorical	100%	80%	71%	68%	100%	93%	89%	85%
PPW	100%	85%	55%	44%	100%	92%	83%	77%

Table 13-5. Portfolio Performance When Thresholds Are Ignored

		$D = \$1\ million$			$D = \$2.5\ million$		
		% of total watershed benefits achieved under each threshold			% of total watershed benefits achieved under each threshold		
Scoring method	Acquisition method	50%	80%	90%	50%	80%	90%
Interval-scale	Optimal	28%	26%	25%	61%	56%	55%
	Ignoring thresholds	17%	0%	0%	49%	33%	8%
Ratio-scale	Optimal	36%	33%	31%	72%	68%	62%
	Ignoring thresholds	8%	0%	0%	67%	44%	31%
Categorical	Optimal	28%	26%	25%	60%	56%	54%
	Ignoring thresholds	16%	0%	0%	45%	38%	37%
PPW	Optimal	38%	33%	26%	72%	68%	60%
	Ignoring thresholds	11%	3%	0%	67%	9%	0%

result because, as the threshold increases, the number of acquired parcels, in comparison with the original no-threshold portfolio, may increase or decrease.

To examine the efficiency losses that arise when a conservation agency ignores threshold constraints when acquiring contracts, we compare the scores of the two portfolios. If the threshold constraint is not met in a catchment, contracts there yield no water quality benefits. The results are presented in Table 13-5. The efficiency losses associated with ignoring thresholds are substantial, particularly at low budget levels and high thresholds. For example, under a $1 million budget and an 80 percent threshold requirement, the portfolio derived without considering the threshold constraints achieves zero benefits under three of the four scoring methods. A lower threshold of 50 percent improves the portfolio's performance a little, but it still achieves only 24 to 59 percent of the benefits of the portfolio derived under explicit threshold constraints.

Thus the data from Lake Skaneateles suggest that the failure to recognize interdependent relationships among parcels that contribute to achieving conservation objectives can substantially lower the effectiveness of conservation investments per dollar expended. Ignoring threshold effects, particularly when available funds are few, can result in large forgone environmental benefits. Interventions tend to be scattered over the landscape, and funding levels in any given target area tend to be inadequate to reach the threshold needed to maintain current water quality levels or achieve significant environmental improvements.

The efficiency losses are even more substantial when one compares the scores of the portfolio that recognizes threshold constraints and opportunity costs with the scores of the portfolio that ignores them, targeting on the basis of benefit scores alone. The results of this comparison are presented in Table 13-6.

Table 13-6. Portfolio Performance When Opportunity Costs and Thresholds Are Ignored

		D = $1 million			D = $ 2.5 million		
		% of total watershed benefits achieved under each threshold			*% of total watershed benefits achieved under each threshold*		
Scoring method	*Acquisition method*	*50%*	*80%*	*90%*	*50%*	*80%*	*90%*
Interval-scale	*Optimal*	*28%*	*26%*	*25%*	*61%*	*56%*	*55%*
	Ignoring costs & thresholds	0%	0%	0%	15%	5%	0%
Ratio-scale	*Optimal*	*36%*	*33%*	*31%*	*72%*	*68%*	*62%*
	Ignoring costs & thresholds	0%	0%	0%	22%	6%	0%
Categorical	*Optimal*	*28%*	*26%*	*25%*	*60%*	*56%*	*54%*
	Ignoring costs & thresholds	0%	0%	0%	23%	3%	0%
PPW	*Optimal*	*38%*	*33%*	*26%*	*72%*	*68%*	*60%*
	Ignoring costs thresholds	6%	0%	0%	17%	9%	0%

With a budget of $1 million, the city of Syracuse likely would generate no environmental benefits if it were to acquire easements based on parcel scores alone.

The practitioner still faces the problem of choosing among the different optimal portfolios identified under each scoring rule. He or she could try the high-priority approach outlined earlier, focusing on parcels that are found in the solution of all four scoring methods, but the portfolios chosen this way will not necessarily achieve the thresholds in each catchment. In the Lake Skaneateles case, the high-priority portfolio of parcels selected from the optimal buffers when D = $2.5 million would come quite close to satisfying the threshold requirements. In the 50 percent threshold scenario, the high-priority portfolio (cost = $1.52 million) spans 10 catchments, of which 4 exceed the required buffer-area threshold, 3 are less than 7 percent below the threshold, 2 are less than 19 percent below, and 1 is less than 45 percent below. In the 80 percent threshold scenario, the high-priority portfolio (cost = $1.22 million) spans 5 catchments, of which 2 exceed the threshold and 3 are less than 8 percent below it. In the 90 percent threshold scenario, the high-priority portfolio (cost = $1.67 million) spans 4 catchments, of which 2 exceed the threshold and 2 are less than 3 percent below it. By increasing the budget or thresholds under which the contract portfolios are chosen, a practitioner is more likely to derive a high-priority set of parcels that comes close to meeting the required thresholds, although the degree to which this method is successful will be case specific.

If These Ideas Are So Great, Why Isn't Anyone Applying Them?

To many, the idea that integrating economic and biophysical data can produce better results than simply using biophysical data alone seems straightforward. So why is such an idea rarely applied in practice? Conditions exist under which acquiring and using economic data will not generate substantial improvements in efficiency, but the empirical studies cited in this chapter imply that such conditions are not widespread. Five obstacles to integrating economic and biophysical data are likely to be much more important factors in explaining why so few conservation initiatives attempt to incorporate biophysical and economic data explicitly in their decisionmaking.

The first and most obvious obstacle is the lack of awareness among conservation practitioners of the basic concepts outlined above. They are rarely trained in economic theory and tend to read natural science journals in which few or no economists publish. In conservation journals, such as *Biological Conservation*, articles on targeting conservation investments continue to be published without any reference to the opportunity costs of each investment. Academics often do not take into account the objectives and approaches of practitioners and policymakers. Furthermore, even with an awareness of the basic concepts, practitioners may be unaware of the methods through which biophysical and economic data can be integrated. Although the simple methods presented above do not require technical training, more complicated analyses that incorporate the interdependent nature of landscape-level processes, such as biophysical thresholds, require more sophisticated methods of analysis in which practitioners may lack training.

Second, despite many publications on sophisticated biophysical criteria-based conservation targeting, practitioners have not adopted this method. Prendergast et al. argue that practitioners often have a "general antipathy toward what is seen as a prescriptive approach to conservation" (1999, *484*). Incorporating economic data into sophisticated targeting approaches only exacerbates the sense that the practitioner's flexibility to make decisions has been reduced. Based on conversations with practitioners, it seems as if they often believe they are implicitly incorporating economic costs into the decisionmaking and thus do not need to formally enter these costs into the targeting algorithm.

Third, obtaining relevant economic data often can be more difficult than obtaining relevant biophysical data, because the latter is based on observable environmental characteristics whereas the former is based on unobservable landowner characteristics such as preferences. Practitioners often use one of two cost discovery methods: wait for a landowner to express interest in a conservation contract, and then negotiate over the contract price (often the approach used by land trusts); or estimate ex ante the likely willingness to accept of a small subset of landowners, typically through real estate appraisal methods, and then negotiate with landowners sequentially by parcel rank. An integrated targeting approach requires that practitioners have reasonably accurate cost data for all parcels on which they potentially could secure a contract. This chapter used coarse appraisal data to proxy for the actual willingness to accept of landowners, but it is uncertain how well such data represent the true underlying distribution of willingness to accept. Practitioners already stretched to define the biophysical characteristics of each parcel may find it too onerous to estimate the costs ex ante.

Fourth, conservation practitioners who make the decisions on the ground are often judged not on the efficiency with which they spend scarce conservation dollars, but on their ability to achieve given objectives. For example, in the Lake Skaneateles and the New York City watershed initiatives, local agents are evaluated largely on their ability to spend funds and meet acreage and farmer participation levels. Platt et al. report that New York City "is obligated to commit $250 million during the next 10 years to acquiring up to 335,000 acres" (2000, 15).[7] The land conservation portfolio that achieves these objectives may not be the one that meets an environmental quality objective at least cost.

The fifth obstacle, and the most difficult to tackle, lies in the quality of the data. Many conservation initiatives have budgets well below those of large cities such as Syracuse, New York City, and Boston, and they often lack adequate biophysical and economic data. When quantitative data are poor, it is unclear whether any gains can be achieved through formalization of the decisionmaking process. Indeed, such formalization might lead to egregious errors. The use of subjective expert opinion to guide decisionmaking might be more appropriate in such cases.

Conclusions

Policymakers and conservation practitioners worldwide seek flexible tools that permit the integration of biophysical and economic data into cost-effective conservation plans. This chapter demonstrates a way in which conservation agencies can integrate spatially variable biophysical and economic data in the absence of sophisticated biophysical modeling. Using common biophysical scoring methods in combination with economic data and simple optimization methods, a set of priority land parcels can be identified for contracting. In an empirical application, GIS data are used to identify a set of priority land parcels for a riparian buffer contracting initiative in upstate New York. To ensure that the results from this application were useful, the data selected for this application came from the decisionmakers themselves. Furthermore, the analysis explicitly considers the methods being used by decisionmakers and approaches the problem at the geographic scale at which decisions are being made.

This chapter also demonstrates a way in which conservation agencies can incorporate concerns about biophysical thresholds in their decisionmaking. The results corroborate previous empirical work suggesting that the failure to consider economic data in environmental investment decisions can lead to large losses in efficiency. Moreover, findings reveal that the potential efficiency losses associated with ignoring biological thresholds are also large. Reasons why practitioners may not desire or be able to integrate biophysical and economic data in decisionmaking are explored.

The actual decision process is emphasized in this chapter, rather than the underlying biophysical modeling, but clearly the results are only as good as the biophysical and economic information on which the analysis is based. We take as given the data available to the city of Syracuse and the way in which the city's practitioners express their preferences and objectives. If the reliability of the parcel-scoring functions or threshold estimates is poor, however, there is no guarantee the tools developed here improve on current practitioner methods.[8] The same caveat holds for the estimates of contracting costs. The use of high-priority portfolios such as those identified here may mitigate errors in benefit and cost estimation, but scholars and practitioners need to ensure that they have reliable information to feed into the decision analysis.

Integrating reliable biophysical and economic information is particularly important in the context of watershed conservation for three reasons. First, the level of environmental amenities and the costs of obtaining the amenities are likely to be positively correlated (e.g., conservation on large parcels with extensive waterfront and located near infrastructure are likely to be important for water quality objectives but also expensive). Second, in rapidly developing watersheds, the relative spatial variability of conservation contract costs is likely to be greater than the relative spatial variability of conservation benefits. And third, uncoordinated efforts to establish riparian buffers across the watershed are likely to lead to little or no water quality benefits. Collectively, these factors suggest that if practitioners fail to integrate the available biophysical and economic data, currently popular conservation contracting approaches for watershed protection may achieve far fewer environmental benefits than expected.

Technical Appendix: Scoring for Riparian Parcels and Optimization Methods

Interval-Scale Scoring Equation

The interval-scale scoring equation is as follows:

Environmental Benefit Score (EBS) = 0.20 Acreage + 0.20 Priority Zone

$+ 0.25$ (Distance to Intake)$^{-1} + 0.25$ Acres of Hydrologically Sensitive Land
$+ 0.10$ Stream Length.

Distance to Intake measures the planametric distance from the geometric center of the parcel to a point exactly midway between the city's two water intake pipes (closer parcels are more desirable). Priority Zone is a categorical variable, converted to a numeric scale, that captures the development potential and land use intensity of the zone in which a parcel is found. Stream Length is the length of the stream frontage in each parcel, and Acres of Hydrologically Sensitive Land includes hydric soils, steeply sloped soil, frequently flooded soils, and wetlands. The higher the parcel's EBS, the more desirable the parcel is for water quality protection. The standardized score of attribute i for parcel j, called an interval-scale score, derives from subtracting the minimum observed value for the attribute from the observed value and dividing this number by the difference between the maximum and minimum observed values for attribute i (see Ferraro 2001 for more details):

$$Interval - Scale\ Score_{ij} = \frac{OBS_{ij} - MIN_i}{MAX_i - MIN_i}.$$

Ratio-Scale Scoring Equation

The ratio-scale scoring equation uses the same attributes found in the interval-scale equation, but its form and normalization differ:

Environmental Benefit Score (EBS) $= 0.27$ Acreage $+ 0.27$ Priority Zone
$- 0.27$ Distance to Intake $+ 0.33$ Acres of Hydrologically Sensitive Land
$+ 0.13$ Stream Length.

Excluding the Distance to Intake weight, all the weights sum to 1. Each parcel is then penalized for its distance from the intake. All parcel scores are assumed to be greater than or equal to 0 (a parcel that generates a negative score from the ratio-scale scoring function is scored as 0). The ith attribute is scaled so that the most favorable observed value generates a score of 1, and every other parcel is compared to that parcel:

$$Ratio - Scale\ Score_{ij} = \frac{OBS_{ij}}{MAX_i}.$$

Categorical Scoring Equation

The categorical scoring equation is similar to what the U.S. Department of Agriculture uses in its Conservation Reserve Program (CRP). For each parcel, the CRP scoring system assigns points to a parcel's attributes. The total number of points achievable for each attribute is determined by relative weights (e.g., up to 10 points can be awarded for proximity to wetlands, and up to 15 points for endangered species habitat). The categorical scoring equation applied in this paper uses a similar point-scoring system for each land attribute listed in the interval-scale scoring equation. Each attribute is separated into three or four categories (e.g., 0–10 acres, 11–50 acres, 50+ acres), and up to 300 total points can be allocated to each parcel. The maximum number of points possible for each attribute is determined by the same weights used in the interval-scale scoring equation.

Parcel-Pollutant-Weighting Model

The parcel-pollutant-weighting (PPW) model is based on the approaches used by the New York State Department of Public Health (1999) and Hermans (1999) and is developed and explained in Azzaino et al. (2002). Briefly, each parcel is assigned a land-use classification. Based on this classification, the biophysical attributes of the land parcel (e.g., drainage area, distance to intake), and the results of a published water quality study (New York State Department of Health 1999), each parcel's potential loading of phosphorus and pathogens is assessed qualitatively. This qualitative assessment is then assigned an index number ranging from a high score of 10 to a low of 3.33. If a parcel is acquired for the riparian buffer easement, a percentage reduction in pollutant loading is assumed, based on the current qualitative assessment and data in Hermans 1999 (*136*). Equal weights are used on reductions in pathogens and phosphorous loadings.

Optimal Easement Portfolio Selection Problem

Syracuse's easement acquisition program can be viewed as a linear optimization problem:

$$\max_{p_i} \sum_i p_i \, e_i, \tag{13-1}$$

$$s.t.$$

$$\sum_i p_i \, (c_i + t_i) \leq D, \tag{13-2}$$

$$0 \leq p_i \leq 1, \tag{13-3}$$

where

p_i = Share of parcel i under conservation contract ($p_i = 1$ if parcel is fully contracted);

e_i = Environmental benefit score for parcel i (a scalar);
c_i = Contract cost for parcel i (the private opportunity cost of conservation);
t_i = Transaction costs for a contract on parcel i (e.g., legal fees, monitoring)[9]; and
D = Contracting agency's budget.

Other characteristics of this targeting formulation are detailed in Ferraro 2002.

Biophysical-Based Easement Portfolio Selection Problem

In this approach, a critical level of environmental benefit, $\bar{e}$, exists for which all parcels with $e_i > \bar{e}$ are contracted. If partial parcel contracting is permitted, a portion of a single parcel with $e_i = \bar{e}$ will be contracted until the budget is exhausted (the marginal parcel); i.e.,

$$p_i^B = 1 \ when \ e_i > \bar{e}, \tag{13-4}$$

$$p_i^B = 0 \ when \ e_i < \bar{e}, \tag{13-5}$$

$$p\bar{e}^B \in [0,1] \ when \ e_{\bar{e}} = \bar{e}$$

$$where \ p^{B_{\bar{e}}} = \frac{D - \sum p^B{}_i e_i}{c_{\bar{e}} + t_{\bar{e}}}. \tag{13-6}$$

Optimal Easement Portfolio Selection with Thresholds

A watershed is made up of $j = 1, \ldots, N$ subwatersheds, or catchments. A conservation agent has $\$D$ to spend on conservation contracts and wants to allocate these funds to maximize environmental benefits. Conservation contracts are used to secure easements on 100-foot-wide riparian buffers. The number of acres in a 100-foot-wide riparian buffer on the ith parcel in the jth catchment is designated as b_i^j. In order to receive any environmental benefits from contracts in the jth catchment, the conservation agent must contract for at least B^j acres of the available 100-foot-wide riparian buffer in the catchment. The optimal riparian buffer contract portfolio, in the presence of threshold constraints, is the solution to the following problem:

$$\max_{p_i^j, Y^j} \sum_{j=1}^{N} \sum_{i} p_i^j e_i^j, \tag{13-7}$$

$$s.t.$$

$$\sum_{j=1}^{N} \sum_{i} p_i^j c_i^j \le D, \tag{13-8}$$

$$\sum_i p_i{}^j b_i{}^j \le M Y^j \qquad j = 1, 2, \ldots, N, \qquad (13\text{-}9)$$

$$\sum_i p_i{}^j b_i{}^j \ge B^j Y^j \qquad j = 1, 2, \ldots, N, \qquad (13\text{-}10)$$

$$p^j \in [0, 1]; \; Y^j = \{0, 1\}, \qquad (13\text{-}11)$$

where

$p_i{}^j = $ Parcel i in catchment j; $p_i{}^j \in [0,1]$ ($p_i{}^j = 1$ if parcel is fully contracted);

$Y^j = $ Presence or absence of contracting in catchment j; $Y^j = \{0,1\}$ ($Y^j = 1$ if there is contracting in catchment j);

$e_i{}^j = $ Environmental benefit score of parcel i in catchment j;

$b_i{}^j = $ Acres of 100-foot-wide riparian buffer in parcel i in catchment j;

$c_i{}^j = $ Contract cost for parcel i in catchment j (includes transaction costs);

$B^j = $ Minimum acres of 100-foot-wide buffer that must be secured in catchment j for any benefits to be obtained from contracts in that catchment (i.e., the threshold); and

$M = $ A very large number (total riparian exposure of the Lake Skaneateles Watershed in feet).

Thus a decisionmaker must select not only the parcels on which to establish a conservation contract (p_i^j), but also the catchments in which to establish contracts (Y_j). Inequality 13-9 establishes the link between the values of the Y_j and p_i^j variables. This constraint indicates that if you are contracting on the ith parcel ($p_i^j = 1$), you must be working in the corresponding j^{th} catchment ($Y_j = 1$); otherwise the constraint would be violated. Inequality 13-10 indicates that if $Y_j = 1$, the acres of buffer in the catchment must exceed the threshold. The problem remains linear in the objective and constraints and hence is easily solved with standard linear programming packages, such as Microsoft Excel's Solver algorithm. The problem is not restricted to one threshold constraint; for example, one might want to add a threshold corresponding to a specific percentage of the drainage area in a catchment that must be buffered in order to obtain any benefits from easements in the catchment.

Endnotes

1. An estimated 20 million to 65 million Americans drink unfiltered surface water (DeZyane 1990), including citizens in the cities of New York, Boston, and San Francisco.

2. These data, stripped of owner information, can be downloaded at http://epp.gsu. edu/pferraro/research/workingpaper/workingpapers.htm.

3. Ferraro (2004) explores an alternative way to assign priority to conservation investments when the ecological benefits from investment cannot be collapsed into a single value.

4. Even if sophisticated models existed for estimating sediment, chemical, pathogen, and nutrient loading, one would have to somehow combine these measures to derive a measure of water quality benefits from an easement on a given parcel.

5. The exceptions were a few small, inexpensive parcels for which a change in transaction costs can have a large relative effect on easement cost.

6. Correlations were generally stronger, however, for the entire watershed than for the buffer.

7. Under its agreement with the EPA, New York City efforts also must entice at least 85 percent of the farmers in the watershed to join the pollution-reduction program.

8. Although the use of scoring functions like those used in this paper is widespread, evidence suggests that linear preference functions may be a poor proxy for decision-maker preferences (Keeney and Raiffa 1976) and that the identification of criteria weights is complicated even for experts (Borcherding et al. 1993). See Ferraro (2004) for an alternative.

9. Transaction costs may be fixed regardless of how much of the parcel is contracted, or they may be variable as in the formulation in inequality 13-2. Making transaction costs fixed would complicate the analysis, but it would have an inconsequential effect on the solution, because only the last parcel to enter the solution would be affected.

References

Allen, A. W. (1983). *Habitat Suitability Index Models: Beaver.* FWS/OBS-82/10.30. Revised. Washington, DC: U.S. Fish and Wildlife Service.

Allen, A. W., and R. D. Hoffman. (1984). *Habitat Suitability Index Models: Muskrat.* FWS/OBS-82/10.46. Washington, DC: U.S. Fish and Wildlife Service.

Ando, A., J. Camm, S. Polasky, and A. Solow. (1998). Species Distributions, Values, and Efficient Conservation. *Science* 279: 2126–28.

Azzaino, Z., J. M. Conrad, and P. J. Ferraro. (2002). Optimizing the Riparian Buffer: Harold Brook in the Skaneateles Lake Watershed, New York. *Land Economics* 78(4): 501–14.

Babcock, B. A., P. G. Lakshminarayan, J. Wu, and D. Zilberman. (1996). The Economics of a Public Fund for Environmental Amenities: A Study of CRP Contracts. *American Journal of Agricultural Economics* 78: 961–71.

———. (1997). Targeting Tools for the Purchase of Environmental Amenities. *Land Economics* 73(3): 325–39.

Balmford, A., K. J. Gaston, S. Blyth, A. James, and V. Kapos. (2003). Global Variation in Conservation Costs, Conservation Benefits, and Unmet Conservation Needs. *Proceedings of the National Academy of Sciences* 100: 1046–50.

Balmford, A., K. J. Gaston, and A. S. L. Rodrigues. (2000). Integrating Costs of Conservation into International Priority Setting. *Conservation Biology* 14(3): 597–604.

Borcherding, K., S. Schmeer, and M. Weber. (1993). Biases in Multiattribute Weight Elicitation. In *Contributions to Decision Research*, edited by J. P. Caverni,

M. Bar-Hillel, F. N. Barron, and H. Jungerman. Amsterdam: North Holland, 3–28.

Bulte, E. H., and G. C. van Kooten. (2001). Harvesting and Conserving a Species When Numbers Are Low: Population Viability and Gambler's Ruin in Bioeconomic Models. *Ecological Economics* 37(1): 87–100.

Carter, M. F., W. C. Hunter, D. N. Pashley, and K. V. Rosenberg. (1999). *Setting Priorities for Landbirds in the United States: The Partners in Flight Approach.* Ithaca, NY: Cornell Laboratory of Ornithology.

Cummings, R. G., S. K. Laury, and C. Holt. (2003). The Georgia Irrigation Reduction Auction: Experiments and Implementation. *Journal of Policy Analysis and Management* 23(2): 341–63.

DeZyane, J. (1990). *Handbook of Drinking Water Quality.* New York: John Wiley and Sons.

Dobson, A. P., J. P. Rodriguez, W. M. Roberts, D. S. Wilcove. (1997). Geographic Distribution of Endangered Species in the United States. *Science* 275:550–55.

EPA (Environmental Protection Agency). (1999). *Consideration of Cumulative Impacts in EPA Review of NEPA Documents.* May. Washington, DC: EPA, Office of Enforcement and Compliance Assurance (OECA), Office of Federal Activities. http://www.epa.gov/Compliance/resources/ policies/nepa/cumulative.pdf (accessed September 9, 2005).

Farzin, Y. H. (1996). Optimal Pricing of Environmental and Natural Resource Use with Stock Externalities. *Journal of Public Economics* 62(1–2): 31–57.

FDEP (Florida Department of Environmental Protection). (2000). *Current Biological Health and Water Quality of the Econlockhatchee River and Selected Tributaries, January and July 1999.* Orlando: FDEP, Surface Water Monitoring Section.

Feather, P., D. Hellerstein, and L. Hansen. (1998). Exploring Methods of Selecting Cropland for Conservation. *Agricultural Outlook* (September): 21–24.

Ferraro, P. J. (2001). Water Quality Protection and the Cost-Effective Targeting of Riparian Buffers in Georgia. Georgia State University Water Policy Working Paper no. 2001-004. Atlanta: Department of Economics, Andrew Young School of Policy Studies.

———. (2002). Conservation Contracting in Heterogeneous Landscapes: An Application to Watershed Protection with Threshold Constraints. Georgia State University Water Policy Working Paper no. 2002-010. Atlanta: Department of Economics, Andrew Young School of Policy Studies. http://epp.gsu.edu/pferraro/research/ workingpaper/workingpapers.htm (accessed September 9, 2005).

———. (2003). Assigning Priority to Environmental Policy Interventions in a Heterogeneous World. *Journal of Policy Analysis and Management* 22(1): 27–43.

———. (2004). Targeting Conservation Investments in Heterogeneous Landscapes: A Distance Function Approach and Application to Watershed Management. *American Journal of Agricultural Economics* 86(4): 905–18.

Ferraro, P. J., and A. Kiss. (2002). Direct Payments for Biodiversity Conservation. *Science* 298: 1718–19.

Gardner, K. V. (2000). Skaneateles Lake Watershed Land Protection Program: Methodology and Market Analysis for Conservation Easement Valuation. Ithaca, NY: North East Appraisals and Management Co.

Hermans, L. M. (1999). *Design of Phosphorus Management Strategies for the Cannonsville Basin.* Ithaca: New York State Water Resources Institute, Cornell University.

Hruby, T., S. Stanley, T. Granger, T. Duebendorfer, R. Friesz, B. Lang, B. Leonard, K. March, and A. Wald. (2000). *Methods for Assessing Wetland Functions.* Vol. 2. *Depressional Wetlands in the Columbia Basin of Eastern Washington.* Washington State Department Ecology Publication 00-06-47. Pullman: Washington State University.

Johnson, N., C. Revenga, and J. Echeverria. (2001). Managing Water for People and Nature. *Science* 292: 1071–72.

Keeney, R. L., and H. Raiffa. (1976). *Decisions with Multiple Objectives: Preferences and Value Tradeoffs.* New York: John Wiley.

Lande, R. (1987). Extinction Thresholds in Demographic Models of Territorial Populations. *American Naturalist* 13: 624–35.

Lemunyon, J. L., and R. G. Gilbert. (1993). The Concept and Need for a Phosphorus Assessment Tool. *Journal of Production Agriculture* 6: 483–86.

Master, L. (1991). Assessing Threats and Setting Priorities for Conservation. *Conservation Biology* 5: 559–63.

McMahon, T. E. (1983). *Habitat Suitability Index Models: Coho Salmon.* FWS/OBS-82/10.49. Fort Collins, CO: U.S. Fish and Wildlife Service, Habitat Evaluation Procedure Group.

MDC (Metropolitan District Commission). (1999). Land Acquisition Fact Sheet, FS98.01. July. Boston: MDC, Division of Watershed Management. http://www.state.ma.us/mdc/landacq.pdf (accessed September 9, 2005).

Mittermeir, R. A., N. Myers, J. B. Thompsen, G. A. B. Fonseca, and S. Olivieri. (1998). Global Biodiversity Hotspots and Major Tropical Wilderness Areas. *Conservation Biology* 12: 516–20.

Myers, S., L. Macbeth, and R. Nemecek. (1998). *Skaneateles Lake Watershed Management Plan.* Prepared for the U.S. Environmental Protection Agency and the New York State Department of Environmental Conservation. New York: City of Syracuse.

NCCWMTF (North Carolina Clean Water Management Trust Fund). (2003). *The North Carolina Clean Water Management Trust Fund 2003 Annual Report.* Raleigh: NCCWMTF.

New York State Department of Public Health. (1999). *New York State Source Water Assessment Program Plan.* Troy: New York State Department of Public Health, Bureau of Public Water Supply Protection.

NRC (National Research Council). (2000). *Watershed Management for Potable Water Supply: Assessing New York City's Approach.* Committee to Review the New York City Watershed Management Strategy. Washington, DC: National Academy Press.

Olson, D. M., E. Dinerstein, R. Abell, T. Allnutt, C. Carpenter, L. McClenachan, J. D'Amico, P. Hurley, K. Kassem, H. Strand, M. Taye, and M. Thieme. (2000). *The Global 200: A Representation Approach to Conserving the Earth's Distinctive Ecoregions.* Washington, DC: World Wildlife Fund, Conservation Science Program.

Platt, R. H., P. K. Barten, and M. J. Pfeffer. (2000). A Full, Clean Glass: Managing New York City's Watersheds. *Environment* 42(5): 8–20.

Polasky, S., J. D. Camm, and B. Garber-Yonts. (2001). Selecting Biological Reserves Cost-Effectively: An Application to Terrestrial Vertebrate Conservation in Oregon. *Land Economics* 77(1): 68–78.

Prendergast, J. R., R. M. Quinn, and J. H. Lawton. (1999). The Gaps between Theory and Practice in Selecting Nature Reserves. *Conservation Biology* 13(3): 484–92.

Rowles, J. L., and D. L. Sitlinger. (1999). *Assessment of Interstate Streams in the Susquehana River Basin.* Monitoring Report no. 12. July 1, 1997, to June 30, 1998. Publication no. 205. Harrisburg, PA: Water Quality and Monitoring Program Susquehanna River Basin Commission.

Schueler, T. (1994). The Importance of Imperviousness. *Watershed Protection Techniques* 1(Fall): 100.

———. (1995). The Peculiarities of Perviousness. *Watershed Protection Techniques* 2(Fall): 233.

Shaffer, M. L. (1981). Minimum Population Sizes for Species Conservation. *BioScience* 31: 131–34.

Smith, R. D., A. Ammann, C. Bartoldus, and M. M. Brinson. (1995). *An Approach for Assessing Wetland Functions Using Hydrogeomorphic Classification, Reference Wetlands, and Functional Indices.* Technical Report WRP-DE-10 and Operational Draft. Vicksburg, MS: U.S. Army Engineers Waterways Experiment Station.

Snider, A., S. K. Pattanayak, E. Sills, and J. Schuler. (2003). Policy Innovations for Private Forest Management and Conservation in Costa Rica. *Journal of Forestry* 101(4): 18–23.

Terrell, J. W., T. E. McMahon, P. D. Inskip, R. F. Raleigh, and K. L. Williamson. (1982). *Habitat Suitability Index Models.* Appendix A. *Guidelines for Riverine and Lacustrine Applications of Fish HSI Models with the Habitat Evaluation Procedures.* FWS/OBS-82/10.A. Washington, DC: U.S. Fish and Wildlife Service.

Tilman, D., J. Fargione, B. Wolff, C. D'Antonio, A. Dobson, W. Howarth, D. Schindler, W. H. Schlesinger, D. Simberloff, and S. Swackhamer. (2001). Forecasting Agriculturally Drive Global Environmental Change. *Science* 292: 281–84.

USDA (U.S. Department of Agriculture). (1999). Conservation Reserve Program Sign-Up 20: Environmental Benefits Index. Fact sheet. Washington, DC: Farm Service Agency.

USFWS (U.S. Fish and Wildlife Service). (1981). *Standards for the Development of Habitat Suitability Index Models.* 103 ESM. Washington, DC: USFWS.

Voogd, H. (1983). *Multicriteria Evaluation for Urban and Regional Planning.* London: Pion.

Wang, L., J. Lyons, P. Kanehl, R. Banneman, and E. Emmons. (2000). Watershed Urbanization and Changes in Fish Communities in Southeastern Wisconsin Streams. *Journal of the American Water Resources Association* 36(5): 1173–90.

Wang, L., J. Lyons, P. Kanehl, and R. Gatti. (1997). Influences of Watershed Land Use on Habitat Quality and Biotic Integrity in Wisconsin Streams. *Fisheries* 22(6): 6–12.

Wu, J., R. M. Adams, W. G. Boggess. (2000). Cumulative Effects and Optimal Targeting of Conservation Efforts: Steelhead Trout Habitat Enhancement in Oregon. *American Journal of Agricultural Economics* 82(2): 400–13.

Zoner, D., and N. M. Limitz. (1994). Should Numerical Imperviousness Be Used to Zone Watersheds? Center for Watershed Protection. *Watershed Protection Techniques* 1(Summer): 2.

PART V

Conclusion

14

Economics and Land Use Policy

Where Do We Go from Here?

Robert J. Johnston

Research addressing land use is increasingly driven by practical problems and questions emerging from the policy process. The trend toward direct involvement with those in management roles and practical policy issues represents an important strength of ongoing research. As this trend continues, economists are discovering the utility of nontraditional research methods and cooperative interdisciplinary work. Such efforts are exemplified by much of the research detailed in this book.

Despite these promising developments in land use policy research, significant challenges remain. Too often, policymakers do not use the information and data produced by economists' research. This is particularly common at the local level, where land use officials may lack the time, expertise, or incentives to consult academic journals or technical reports. Moreover, the findings reported in academic research may be viewed as overly abstract or poorly related to the place-based land use concerns facing local communities. Although many academic works claim to address the needs of local policymakers, decisions are often made without any consideration of this literature and based on criteria that academics might consider insufficient or oversimplified.

Reflecting such concerns in broader environmental policy, the 2004 Annual Meeting of the American Agricultural Economics Association featured an organized symposium called "Who Will Help the Social Planner?" which addressed many of the barriers to conducting research of optimal value to policymakers. Because academic research is driven by available funding, academic incentive structures, and the interests of researchers, research topics may appear esoteric to those responsible for policy development. In contrast, research conducted

293

directly for policy audiences may emphasize questions viewed as mundane by academic researchers or be hampered by institutional frameworks and bureaucracy often associated with government agencies. Somewhere between these extremes lies the target for many social scientists who seek to address issues of relevance to land use policy. It is not an unattainable goal. This book has been written with the conviction that research of academic merit need not be inaccessible, incomprehensible, or irrelevant to policy audiences.

Economics and Land Use Policy: The Promise of Future Research

This book presents research that addresses many questions relevant to land use policy. It does not attempt, however, to reflect all areas of inquiry associated with economics and land use. Rather, in keeping with its origin in the 2002 Northeastern Agricultural and Resource Economics Association (NAREA) Land Use Policy Workshop, it emphasizes issues of primary relevance to land use and policy on the rural-urban fringe. Such issues are particularly germane to the more highly developed rural and suburban areas of the Northeast, Southeast, and coastal West. Although some chapters (e.g., 1, 2, 10, and 11) are applicable to a wider range of policy issues and contexts, the book admittedly gives less attention to regions in which land development is viewed as less imminent. Similarly, it does not touch on issues related to land use and policy in high-density urban environments (cf. Banister et al. 1999).

Even within the research and policy contexts emphasized herein, broad areas exist in which significant uncertainty remains. Research in these areas may offer findings of significant value to the policy process. These issues involve complex but relevant problems, often characterized by conflicting results and arguments in the published literature. Many have been identified previously as research needs in a variety of land use policy contexts. Although this is far from an exhaustive list, important research areas reflected within this book—and for which additional research is needed—include the following:

- the spatial dynamics of land development, value, and market price;
- fiscal, financial, and equity aspects of conservation activities;
- the role of the policy process and institutions in conservation and development;
- the public's perception of and preferences for rural amenities; and
- structural shifts in land conversion and the changing role of land use policy.

The remainder of this chapter discusses each of these areas in turn, with an emphasis on key areas of uncertainty and questions of direct relevance for contemporary land use policy.

Spatial Dynamics of Land Development, Value, and Market Price

Empirical research often generates conflicting, unexpected, or otherwise uncertain results regarding the effects of conservation activities on nearby property values. As noted by Bockstael in the Foreword, such research is often beset by data limitations, omitted variables or missing information, and the complexity of spatial effects. The increasing availability of geographical information system (GIS) data and software ameliorates some of these difficulties, but it is only recently that researchers have begun to widely explore the promise of, and complexities associated with, the increasing use of such spatial data within economic models. Although commonly used by ecologists and community planners, explicitly spatial land use models represent a relatively new area of emphasis for many economists (Bockstael 1996).

The increasing availability of time-series data characterizing land use has also spawned greater interest in the forecasting of land use conversion, particularly in urban-fringe areas. Developing models to forecast the spatial patterns and dynamics of suburban sprawl and associated economic, social, and environmental change has proven to be far from a simple task, as many chapters in this book illustrate. Moreover, despite increased emphasis on forecasting land use change and the existence of a wide array of associated methodological approaches, there is still little consensus regarding the most appropriate methods or models for particular land use contexts (Verburg et al. 1999).

For example, large-scale, data-intensive urban land use and transportation simulation models have been developed for a small number of metropolitan areas, but these models maintain tractability through often unrealistic assumptions or by holding constant critical elements influencing growth (Harris 1985; Landis 1995). Moreover, up until recently, such models have been prohibitively expensive for development in all but the largest metropolitan areas. Although recent advances have rendered agent-based and other simulation models more readily tractable for rural or urban-fringe areas, many still disagree as to whether the insight provided by such endeavors justifies the cost (Coucelis 2002; Parker et al. 2002). There is also a lack of information regarding the relative performance of somewhat simpler approaches, such as hazard models and other methods used in this book, contrasted to those that are more complex and data-intensive.

Perhaps more fundamentally, the accuracy and validity of all land use simulations are constrained by the properties of underlying spatial models of growth and land use conversion. These and other limitations have led authors such as Klosterman (1994) to comment on the need for new generations of models that incorporate better-defined theoretical foundations. The question also has been raised as to whether the results of such models and findings of related research, though of clear interest to researchers, have been used by policymakers (Johnston 2002). Hence, while many research questions remain, and this area holds great promise for future inquiry, researchers face the challenge of ensuring that approaches are both theoretically and empirically valid, and also accessible to the broader policy audience.

Fiscal, Financial, and Equity Aspects of Conservation Activities

Chapter 7 asks whether conservation easements can pay for themselves. The analysis focuses on property value impacts of easements—a complex question in its own right. Conservation activities may influence a wide array of other factors, however, including the long-run demand for community services, property taxes levied on both conserved and nonconserved parcels, and the in- and outmigration of residents. Although the combined impact of conservation activities on communities' short- and long-term fiscal state is typically unknown, Anderson and King (2004) demonstrate that the net impact of conservation is not always positive. Common static approaches such as "cost of community service" and other fiscal impact analyses leave many questions unanswered and are generally unsuitable for predicting future impacts (Burchell et al. 1994; Heimlich and Anderson 2001). Although fiscal and financial aspects of land conservation ordinarily are given little attention by mainstream environmental and natural resource economists, the critical role of these issues in many communities points to the importance of such research.

Other issues that tend to be overlooked in the economics literature involve equity issues associated with conservation and development activities. Of the three main goals of land use planning—environment, economic development, and social equity (Banister et al. 1999, *xxii*)—resource economists studying land have paid arguably the least attention to social equity. This is perhaps surprising, given the substantial attention devoted to such issues in considerations of land use policy at the local, state, and federal levels. As stated by Zeckhauser, "[t]he distribution of costs and benefits of a regulatory policy is a major . . . concern of policymakers; indeed it is almost a preoccupation" (1981, *215*). To the extent that economic research fails to address or, at the very least, recognize such issues associated with land use, it risks the common charge of detachment from practical policy concerns.

The Role of the Policy Process and Institutions in Conservation and Development

Rural residents may not only be concerned with the consequences of land management, but may also have systematic preferences for the policy instruments applied to management goals. Preferences for outcomes do not necessarily imply matching support for the underlying policy process. Nonetheless, economists typically disassociate preferences for management outcomes from detailed analyses of policies that might generate those outcomes. These issues are addressed, at least in part, by Chapters 11, 12, and 13. Despite a naissance of research in this area, a clear need exists to better integrate research into public preferences for rural amenities with research regarding the policy process required to sustain those amenities.

The lack of contemporary economic research into the policy process through which land is managed is matched by a paucity of attention to the public and private institutions that influence land use policy. Although economists often view land use issues through the lens of individual preferences and behaviors, much conservation and development activity is influenced by institutions, both public and private. As noted by Albers and Ando (2003) and others, as well as Castle and Nickerson and Hellerstein in this book, economists have paid little attention to institutions that drive land conservation and conversion. Many facets of such issues are of direct relevance to policy. These include variants of the classic principal-agent problem: Do institutions responsible for land conservation and development respond appropriately to the desires of their constituents? It has been argued, for example, that the interplay among public and private conservation agents, landowners, and funding sources may not result in an optimal portfolio of conserved lands (Scott et al. 2001).

Similar charges may be levied at those representing development interests. For instance, the National Association of Home Builders frequently highlights the market demand for detached, single-family homes (NAHB 1999), presenting a free-market argument that rural "neighborhoods are being supplied by market-savvy builders attentive to the trade-offs that their customers are eager to make" (Gordon and Richardson 1998, 3). Some planners argue, however, that both builders and residents would benefit from an alternative approach to development, based on concepts of neotraditional cluster and flexible zoning (Arendt et al. 1994; Calthorpe 1993), were such development types made more widely available. While many economists cite excess development as a simple symptom of market failure associated with the external benefits and public goods provided by rural lands (or, conversely, the external costs of development), others argue that excess development is a direct result of institutions that encourage such activities (Fischel 1985). The mainstream economic preoccupation with individual choices often obscures the critical role of institutional behavior in both land use change and policy.

The need for research into the role of institutions in conservation and development is exacerbated by recent changes in the mechanisms through which land is conserved. Contemporary conservation activities are increasingly conducted by public-private partnerships, a form of land conservation virtually unknown prior to the 1970s but each decade comprising a larger share of conservation activity (Endicott 1993, 3). Similarly, the emergence of local land trusts as significant players in land conservation has led some researchers (e.g., Albers and Ando 2003; Anderson and King 2004) to begin to address the behavior of such organizations and implications for the optimality of land conservation. Although economists have begun to explore the implications of these and other institutions that affect land use in the United States, research regarding institutional aspects of land use policy still lags behind the substantial work addressing values, preferences, and behavior at the individual level.

Finally, incentives for particular types of activities, such as land conversion, among individuals or groups are contingent on the current state of legal institutions and income distribution. As noted by Bromley in Chapter 2, any assessment of land use benefits and costs is contingent upon the institutional and policy context in which it is conducted. Despite substantial work estimating the benefits and costs of land use policies and associated incentives for various types of land-affecting activities, little evidence exists regarding systematic relationships between such estimates and the institutional or policy contexts from which they are derived.

The Public's Perception of and Preferences for Rural Amenities

There is no shortage of research addressing nonmarket preferences for rural amenities associated with agricultural, forested, and other undeveloped lands. Despite this large and growing body of evidence, however, significant uncertainty remains regarding what the public values in farm, forest, and open-space land uses. Research clearly indicates that residents of many rural and urban-fringe areas are willing to pay to preserve valued rural amenities, but there is growing recognition—reflected in conferences and workshops addressing land use issues—that some areas of public preferences have been poorly elucidated by economic research (Abdalla 2001; Johnston 2002). Moreover, results of economic research are often poorly reflected in the policy process.

For example, state and local conservation agencies often emphasize conservation of prime soils and active agricultural land, although research suggests that the rural public places greater value on attributes such as scenic views and wildlife habitat—amenities that do not require active agriculture (Kline and Wichelns 1998). Similarly, land conservation policy often is based on the intuitively reasonable assumption that the highest marginal values are placed on those farm and forest amenities that are in the shortest supply. Anecdotal evidence suggests, however, that in some communities, residents may place greater marginal value on land uses in relatively greater supply (e.g., in an agricultural community, residents may favor the preservation of more common farmland over more scarce forested land), given the tendency of residents to define their surroundings in terms of the rural lands in greatest supply. A third example involves the common emphasis of valuation efforts on marginal parcel-level choices, ignoring the relationships between preferences on the margin and those for programmatic policies involving broader, nonmarginal changes in land conservation and development.

An additional limitation of existing work is a tendency to separate analysis of the positive and negative amenities (or externalities) of agricultural, forested, and open-space lands. Ready and Abdalla note that "[i]ncreasing attention is being paid to both positive and negative externalities from farmland and farming" (2005, *314*). Similarly, Johnston et al. comment that "residents neighboring active farmland may receive positive benefits from certain views or the lack of congestion, but receive negative benefits (harm) from other sounds, sights and smells associated with the day-to-day operation of a farm (American Farmland Trust 1997; Palmquist et al. 1997; Ready et al. 1997)" (2001, *319*). Despite evidence provided by these and other works that simultaneously address both positive and negative amenities of undeveloped lands, the preponderance of research on rural amenity values emphasizes either positive or negative amenities, but not both. As emphasized by Ready and Abdalla (2005), omitting consideration of either the positive or negative amenities of undeveloped lands can result in biased models or misleading policy conclusions.

These and other examples highlight a tendency among researchers to focus on easily measurable or assumed relationships and ignore underlying, more complex, or perhaps unexpected preference structures. Initial exploration of such issues frequently requires extensive use of qualitative research methods— e.g., focus groups and individual interviews—often given little emphasis by economists because of their cost, time intensiveness, or unfamiliarity. It also may necessitate a recognition of the validity and value of other disciplinary approaches to eliciting or understanding perceptions and preferences of rural or urban-fringe residents (e.g., Foster 2000; Johnston et al. 1995). Finally, researchers may need to relax or abandon common assumptions that simplify economic research. Although often unfamiliar to economists, alternative perspectives toward public preferences may have significant implications for economic research seeking to ascertain the underlying value of land use amenities, both positive and negative.

Structural Shifts in Land Conversion and the Changing Role of Land Use Policy

Recent shifts in land conversion behavior, patterns of land use change, and the influence of policy variables have required changes in the ways that social scientists view land (Irwin and Bockstael 2002). Researchers increasingly are grappling with complex spatial patterns of development unrecognized in classical approaches to land and with the necessity of interdisciplinary approaches to contemporary land use challenges. Moreover, the dynamic nature of relationships between land use policy and property rights, including rights to associated air, water, wildlife, and other resources, is increasingly being recognized. As noted by Bromley in Chapter 2, contemporary court rulings regarding property rights and land policy issues have redefined the landscape of allowable land use policies, while the growing threat of lawsuits at the local level influences the perceived practicality of policies that restrict private land uses for the public benefit. As a result, past assumptions and models of land use change may be inadequate to characterize contemporary patterns (Castle 2003; Irwin and Bockstael 2002).

Such changes offer both challenges and opportunities to economists who study land. Challenges relate to the ability of researchers to adapt both assumptions and methods to structural changes in the way society approaches land. Opportunities relate to the increasing recognition that private decisions related to land and conversion often fail to generate socially optimal outcomes, and that social science may assist in identifying policies and incentives to address such market failures. The ability of social scientists to adjust to the changing "landscape" of land use policy will have significant impacts on the relevance of future work.

Conclusions

Recent decades have seen an increased recognition of the importance of economics in policy development, including policies related to land use. Economists are contributing to policy development in many areas. Economic research regarding land use topics will continue; what is not known is the extent to which such work will influence policy, particularly at the state and local levels, where the majority of land use policy is administered (Press et al. 1996).

The recent emphasis of economics within policymaking affords economists with unprecedented opportunities to influence federal, state, and local decisions that will guide future land use. The burden lies on social scientists to provide information that is based on theoretically and empirically valid approaches, is relevant to issues at hand, integrates related work from other disciplines, recognizes the perspectives of others in the policy arena, and is useful to those not trained in the social sciences. The questions asked, however, need not be dictated by popular favor or the current political landscape. As stated by Bockstael in the Foreword, "[E]conomics has a long history of contributing framing and answering questions that, over the long haul, have changed the way society manages resources and the laws that protect these resources." Moreover, as noted by Castle, it is "unlikely that a single, grand economic model will ever permit an analysis of all land related economic events" (2003, *32*). Through diverse perspectives, however, economists have an opportunity to offer substantial insight into both land use change and the policies that guide it.

References

Abdalla, C. W. (2001). *Protecting Farmland at the Fringe: Do Regulations Work? Strengthening the Research Agenda*. Regional Center for Rural Development Paper no. 7. Northeast Regional Center for Rural Development, University Park, PA: Pennsylvania State University.

Albers, H. J., and A. W. Ando. (2003). Could State-Level Variation in the Number of Land Trusts Make Sense? *Land Economics* 79(3): 311–27.

Anderson, C. M., and J. R. King. (2004). Equilibrium Behavior in the Conservation Easement Game. *Land Economics* 80(3): 355–74.

Arendt, R., E. Brabec, H. Dodson, C. Reid, and R. Yaro. (1994). *Rural by Design: Maintaining Small Town Character*. Chicago: American Planning Association.

Banister, D., K. Button, and P. Nijkamp (eds.). (1999). *Environment, Land Use and Urban Policy*. Northampton, MA: Edward Elgar.

Bockstael, N. E. (1996). Modeling Economics and Ecology: The Importance of a Spatial Perspective. *American Journal of Agricultural Economics* 78(5): 1168–80.

Burchell, R. W., D. Listokin, W. R. Dolphin, L. Q. Newton, and S. J. Foxley. (1994). *Development Impact Assessment Handbook*. Washington, DC: Urban Land Institute.

Calthorpe, P. (1993). *The Next American Metropolis: Ecology, Community, and the American Dream*. New York: Princeton Architectural Press.

Castle, E. N. (2003). Land, Economic Change, and Agricultural Economics. *Agricultural and Resource Economics Review* 32(1): 18–32.

Coucelis, H. (2002). Why I No Longer Work with Agents: A Challenge for ABMs of Human-Environment Interactions. In *Agent Based Models of Land-Use and Land-Cover Change. Report and Review of an International Workshop, October 4–7, 2001*, edited by D. C. Parker, T. Berger, and S. M. Manson. LUCC Report Series no. 6. Bloomington: Anthropological Center for Training and Research on Global Environmental Change, Indiana University, 3–5.

Endicott, E. (ed.). (1993). *Land Conservation through Public/Private Partnerships*. Washington, DC: Island Press.

Fischel, W. A. (1985). *The Economics of Zoning Laws: A Property Rights Approach to American Land Use Controls*. Baltimore, MD: Johns Hopkins University Press.

Foster, C. (2000). Restoring Nature in American Culture: An Environmental Aesthetic Perspective. In *Restoring Nature: Perspectives from the Social Sciences and Humanities*, edited by P. H. Gobster and B. Hull. Washington, DC: Island Press, 71–96.

Gordon, P., and H. W. Richardson. (1998). Prove It: The Costs and Benefits of Sprawl. *Brookings Review* 16(4): 23.

Harris, B. (1985). Urban Simulation Models in Regional Science. *Journal of Regional Science* 25(4): 545–67.

Heimlich, R. E., and W. D. Anderson. (2001). *Development at the Urban Fringe and Beyond: Impacts on Agriculture and Rural Land*. Agricultural Economic Report no. 803. Washington, DC: U.S. Department of Agriculture, Economic Research Service.

Irwin, E. G., and N. E. Bockstael. (2002). Interacting Agents, Spatial Externalities, and the Evolution of Residential Land Use Patterns. *Journal of Economic Geography* 2(1): 31–54.

Johnston, R. J. (2002). Conserving Farm and Forest in a Changing Rural Landscape: Current and Potential Contributions of Economic Research. Regional Rural Development Paper no. 11. Northeast Regional Center for Rural Development. University Park PA: The Pennsylvania University.

Johnston, R. J., J. J. Opaluch, T. A. Grigalunas, and M. J. Mazzotta. (2001). Estimating Amenity Benefits of Coastal Farmland. *Growth and Change* 32(Summer): 305–25.

Johnston, R. J., T. F. Weaver, L. A. Smith, and S. K. Swallow. (1995). Contingent Valuation Focus Groups: Insights from Ethnographic Interview Techniques. *Agricultural and Resource Economics Review* 24(1): 56–69.

Kline, J., and D. Wichelns. (1998). Measuring Heterogeneous Preferences for Preserving Farmland and Open Space. *Ecological Economics* 26(2): 211–24.

Klosterman, R. E. (1994). An Introduction to the Literature on Large-Scale Models. *Journal of the American Planning Association* 60(1): 41–44.

Landis, J. D. (1995). Imagining Land Use Futures. Applying the California Urban Futures Model. *Journal of the American Planning Association* 61(4): 438–56.

NAHB (National Assocation of Home Builders). (1999). *Smart Growth: Building Better Places to Live, Work, and Play*. Washington, DC: NAHB Smart Growth Working Group.

NERCRD (Northeast Regional Center for Rural Development). (2002). Land Use Problems and Conflicts in the U.S.: A Comprehensive Research Agenda for the 21st Century. Rural Development Paper no. 10. University Park, PA: Northeast Regional Center for Rural Development, Pennsylvania State University.

Palmquist, R. B., F. M. Roka, and T. Vukina. (1997). Hog Operations, Environmental Effect, and Residential Property Values. *Land Economics* 73(1): 114–24.

Parker, D. C., T. Berger, and S. M. Manson (eds.). (2002). *Agent Based Models of Land-Use and Land-Cover Change. Report and Review of an International Workshop, October 4–7, 2001.* LUCC Report Series no. 6. Bloomington: Anthropological Center for Training and Research on Global Environmental Change, Indiana University.

Press, D., D. F. Doak, and P. Steinberg. (1996). The Role of Local Government in the Conservation of Rare Species. *Conservation Biology* 10(6): 1538–48.

Ready, R. C., and C. W. Abdalla. (2005). The Amenity and Disamenity Impacts of Agriculture: Estimates from a Hedonic Pricing Model. *American Journal of Agricultural Economics* 87(2): 314–26.

Ready, R. C., M. C. Berger, and G. C. Blomquist. (1997). Measuring Amenity Benefits from Farmland: Hedonic Pricing vs. Contingent Valuation. *Growth and Change* 28(Fall): 438–58.

Scott, J. M., R. J. F Abbitt, and C. R. Groves. (2001). What Are We Protecting? The United States Conservation Portfolio. *Conservation Biology in Practice* 2(1): 18–19.

Verburg, P. H., G. H. J. de Koning, K. Kok, A. Veldkamp, and J. Bouma. (1999). A Spatial Explicit Allocation Procedure for Modelling the Pattern of Land Use Change Based upon Actual Land Use. *Ecological Modelling* 116(1): 45–61.

Zeckhauser, R. (1981). Preferred Policies When There Is a Concern for Probability of Adoption. *Journal of Environmental Economics and Management* 8(3): 215–37.

Index